Israeli History, Politics and Society
*Series Editor*: Efraim Karsh, King's College London
ISSN 1368-4795

Providing a multidisciplinary examination in all aspects, this series serves as a means of communication between the various communities interested in Israel: academics, policy-makers, practitioners, journalists and the informed public.

Other books in the series:

Peace in the Middle East: The Challenge for Israel
*edited by Efraim Karsh*

The Shaping of Israeli Identity: Myth, Memory and Trauma
*edited by Robert Wistrich and David Ohana*

Between War and Peace: Dilemmas of Israeli Security
*edited by Efraim Karsh*

U.S.–Israeli Relations at the Crossroads
*edited by Gabriel Sheffer*

From Rabin to Netanyahu: Israel's Troubled Agenda
*edited by Efraim Karsh*

Israel at the Polls 1996
*edited by Daniel J. Elazar and Shmuel Sandler*

In Search of Identity: Jewish Aspects in Israeli Culture
*edited by Dan Urian and Efraim Karsh*

Israel: The Dynamics of Change and Continuity
*edited by David Levi-Faur, Gabriel Sheffer and David Vogel*

Revisiting the Yom Kippur War
*edited by P.R. Kumaraswamy*

Peacemaking in Israel after Rabin
*edited by Sasson Sofer*

Parties, Elections and Cleavages: Israel in Comparative and Theoretical Perspective
*edited by Reuven Y. Hazan and Moshe Maor*

ISRAEL: THE FIRST HUNDRED YEARS

# Israel:
# The First Hundred Years

*Volume II*
## From War to Peace?

Editor
# Efraim Karsh

**FRANK CASS**
LONDON • PORTLAND, OR

*First published in 2000 in Great Britain by*
FRANK CASS PUBLISHERS
Newbury House, 900 Eastern Avenue
London IG2 7HH

*and in the United States of America by*
FRANK CASS PUBLISHERS
c/o ISBS
5804 N.E. Hassalo Street
Portland, Oregon 97213-3644

*Website*: www.frankcass.com

British Library Cataloguing in Publication Data

Israel: the first hundred years
Vol. 2: From war to peace? – (Israeli history, politics and society)
1. Jews – Palestine – History – 20th century
2. Palestine – History – 20th century
I.Karsh, Efraim
956.9'4'05

ISBN 0 7146 4962 7 (cloth)
ISBN 0 7146 8023 0 (paper)
ISSN 1368-4795

Library of Congress Cataloging-in-Publication Data

A catalog record for this book is available from the Library of Congress

This group of papers first appeared in a Special Double Issue of
*Israel Affairs* 6/3–4 (Spring/Summer 2000), 'Israel: From War to Peace?'
ISSN 1353-7121 published by Frank Cass.

Printed in Great Britain by
Antony Rowe Ltd., Chippenham, Wilts.

# Contents

PART I: FROM WAR TO WAR

# The Forgotten War: Jewish–Palestinian Strife in Mandatory Palestine, December 1947–May 1948

## DAVID TAL

For quite some time the historiography of the 1948 Arab–Israeli war has been subjected to a vehement academic and public debate in Israel. The debate was triggered by a group of academics calling themselves the 'New Historians' who claimed to have uncovered new archival evidence relating to the creation of Israel and its first war with its Arab neighbours. Oddly enough, the actual state of research on the 1948 War lags far behind the debate on the subject, not least with regard to the initial stage of the war, namely the Jewish–Palestinian struggle preceding the Arab invasion of May 1948. There is no comprehensive study of that conflict and the literature on the subject can be divided into two schools of thought. Israeli historians tend to concentrate on the war's organizational aspects, depicting the period as a preparatory stage of the Jewish state's War of Independence.[1] Yet they have hardly touched the political thinking underlying the strategic planning and military actions of the Jewish armed forces in the struggle with the Palestinians.

The other historiographical school of thought, articulated by Palestinians and writers sympathetic to their cause, depicts Jewish actions as part of a deliberate and vicious attempt to take over the country and disinherit its indigenous population. Commenting on Walid Khalidi's writing in this vein, the American historian William Roger Louis expects that 'further detailed research will probably substantiate rather than alter' such conclusions and interpretation.[2]

What is glaringly missing from the latter narrative is the war itself. Nothing is said about the parties' war planning or their conduct and actions in the course of hostilities. The outcome of the Jewish–Palestinian strife is detached, according to this school of thought, from the historical process that produced it. Moreover, historians of both

David Tal is Lecturer in Military History at Tel Aviv University.

persuasions have downplayed, or ignored altogether, the Jewish–Palestinian war. Most importantly, they fail to explain how is it that the Palestine Arab community, which was twice the size of the Jewish community (about 1,200,000 Arabs compared to 600,000 Jews) and ostensibly enjoyed the support of the surrounding Arab states, still suffered such a devastating blow at the hands of the Jews.

This essay seeks to fill this lacuna and to shed new light on a conflict covered by layers of ideological polemic aimed at justifying one's own views and politics and negating contending approaches. By way of doing so, it will describe and analyse the sources, developments and turning points in the political and strategic thinking of both belligerents, and will offer an explanation for the Palestinian defeat.

More specifically, it will be shown that the Jewish acceptance of the United Nations Partition Resolution of 29 November 1947 was translated into the war strategy that was executed during the initial stages of the conflict. The Palestinians, for their part, determined to prevent such an eventuality, opted for a war for which they were unprepared and ill equipped. Riven by internal conflicts and in discord with the Arab governments, they were no match for the highly motivated, well-organized and unified Jews.

## JEWISH PREPARATIONS

Despite the violent nature of the Zionist–Palestinian conflict from its inception, the major battlefield for the Jews, at least until the second half of the 1940s, was the political arena. For a while, the British and international pledges of a 'National Home' for the Jews in Palestine, set forth in the Balfour Declaration and the League of Nations Mandatory charter, enabled the tiny Jewish community in Palestine (known as the Yishuv) to grow and flourish, despite the hostile attitude of the local Arab population. The Jews concentrated mainly on developing defensive capabilities against Arab harassment, co-operating as much as possible with the Mandatory government. Their aim was to claim the country through hard work and political activity. On the Jewish–Palestinian front, the Yishuv leadership had to cope with day-to-day security problems, mainly random raids and attacks by Palestinians against Jews. But the very existence of the Yishuv seemed secure, as long as British forces were in the country.[3]

Until the late 1940s, there was no serious consideration of the possibility that the confrontation with the local Arab community might become a full-scale intercommunal war. Military planning to secure the existence of the Jewish community underestimated the Palestinian–Arab threat. Such were Plan B of September 1945 and the May 1946 Plan. The latter plan was based on the assumption that any military confrontation between Palestine's Jewish and Arab communities would be similar to past hostilities, when the British were still in the country. It assumed that the Arabs would be better equipped and organized, yet suggested that they would confine themselves to local terror acts against industrial and economic targets. The Hagana reaction, according to the plan, should be to protect those targets and take measures to quell the terror campaign. Countermeasures would be restricted to retaliation attacks against political leaders ('personal terror'), public sites, vital Arab economic and industrial facilities, etc.[4] It was a defensive plan that set no offensive missions or goals for the Hagana. Nothing was said about the possibility of seizing territory held by the Arabs, for example, not to mention a full-scale assault against the Palestinian community or the take-over of the country.

It was British policy that predominated the Yishuv's post-war military thinking, as the Jews were disappointed by the continued adherence of the newly elected Labour government to the 1939 White Paper policy, contrary to promises given by Labour spokesmen before the July 1945 elections. The Mandatory authorities continued to restrict Jewish immigration to Palestine and prohibited the sale of land to Jews. The Yishuv leadership launched a political and military campaign to induce the British to revise this policy, and its struggle against the British policy lasted until the end of 1947.[5]

The turning point in the Hagana's strategic thinking occurred in December 1946, when David Ben-Gurion, Head of the Jewish Agency, assumed the defence portfolio. The act was meaningful in itself, as it signified the importance Ben-Gurion now attached to security matters – a subject he had hardly bothered with until then. In a speech delivered in December 1946 to the political committee of the 22nd Zionist Congress, Ben-Gurion outlined a new strategic direction for the Yishuv and the Hagana. The shift stemmed from the question: who was the enemy? Up to that moment, Hagana strategic thinking assumed that there were two enemies: the local Palestinians and the British authorities. The former were considered more of a hindrance than a real threat to the Yishuv; as to the latter, the Hagana supported and facilitated the political campaign organized by the Jewish leadership, which sought to put pressure on the British to abandon their anti-Zionist policy, manifested by the 1939 White Paper.[6]

Ben-Gurion now maintained that the struggle against the British, in which the Hagana had been engaged since 1945, was by and large over following the British surrender of the Palestine problem to the United Nations. Now, he claimed, the Arabs had become the enemy that posed the foremost threat to Jewish national aspirations: 'We should expect' an invasion by the armed forces of the neighbouring Arab states.[7] The shift in Ben-Gurion's threat perception concerned only the external danger posed by the armies of neighbouring Arab states. As to the local Palestinian threat, he held that 'an attack by the Palestinian Arabs will not jeopardize the Yishuv'.[8]

This view was shared by the Hagana Command; some of its foremost members believed that the possibility of war with the regular Arab armies should be seriously considered.[9] As to the Palestine Arabs, their capabilities were underestimated by the Hagana which viewed them as posing no serious military challenge to the Yishuv.[10] This strategic appraisal remained in force until the communal war in Palestine was already in an advanced stage.[11]

As part of his conception, Ben-Gurion ordered a major reorganization of the Hagana in order to create a regular military force that would be able to resist an invasion by the regular Arab armies.[12] Such a drastic move was more easily said than done. During the first months of the conflict most of the Hagana's personnel were only semi-mobilized, and were confined to a specific territory. Only the Palmah, the Hagana's strike arm, consisted of full-time mobilized combatants, ready to carry out orders on a national scale. In late 1947–early 1948 the Hagana underwent a major structural change, aimed at transforming its semi-mobilized brigades into fully mobilized forces. The shift was articulated in the Order of National Structure, issued by the Hagana Command in November 1947, stipulating for the transformation of the Hagana into a national army, based on compulsory mobilization of the Jewish population and charged with confronting regular armed forces. Though the Order yet again played down the military capabilities of the Palestinians, this had little effect on the actual course of the fighting, as the implementation of the Order was an arduous task which was completed only after the end of the intercommunal strife among the Palestinians.[13]

As to the Palestinian threat, Ben-Gurion did not think in terms of a communal war. He shared the dismissive views that he heard about the capabilities of the local Palestinian forces. When he summed up in his diary the quantitative assessments of the military strength of the foreign Arab armies, he ignored the military potential of the local Arab population.[14]

## PALESTINIAN PREPARATIONS

Two determining factors underlay the Palestinian response to the UN Partition Resolution: the refusal of the Arab governments to let the Palestinians fight their *own* war; and their lack of a national political and military leadership, resulting in their overwhelming dependence on the assistance of the Arab states. The Palestinians emerged from the 1936–39 Revolt with a broken leadership and without national institutions or political and military power. The Arab Higher Committee (AHC) which was under Husseini's sway, was recognized by the Arab League and the British Mandatory government as the representative body of the Palestine Arabs, but it was torn by bitter internecine strife and remained void of influence. The re-emergence of the former Jerusalem Mufti, Hajj Amin al-Husseini, as head of the AHC during 1946 effected no dramatic change in its status. The Arab leaders, particularly in Syria, Transjordan and Iraq, were unwilling to allow the Mufti to lead the struggle for Palestine: he was not invited to attend the official Arab League meetings, even those dedicated to the Palestine crisis, and the Transjordanian and Iraqi prime ministers led the opposition to his demand to establish a provisional Palestinian government.[15] In October and December 1947, in summit meetings in Alei and in Cairo, representatives of the Arab states decided to place the military campaign in Palestine in the hands of the Arab League's military committee, under the command of the Iraqi General Ismail Safwat. It was decided to provide money and rifles to the Palestine Arabs, but to entrust their distribution to the military committee, not to the AHC or the Mufti.[16]

Internally, Husseini was unable to unite the Palestinians under his leadership, and the Palestinian camp found itself in disarray. The Mufti did not balk at using violence to impose his authority, including the use of terror against political rivals, which had been so damaging to the Palestinians during the 1936–39 Revolt. Thus the Palestinians entered the crucial stage in the struggle for Palestine internally divided and with little influence on the inter-Arab and international arenas.[17] The Palestinians' military organization – or more accurately, the lack of such – reflected these shortcomings: they were incapable of mounting a sustained military campaign against the organized Jewish forces.

Ironically, the progress made during 1946 in the international diplomatic efforts to resolve the Palestine question, which made it appear increasingly likely that a Jewish state would be established, heightened the general perception that the struggle over Palestine would be determined on the battlefield. The AHC vehemently opposed the plan submitted by the Arab League at the London conference (September 1946) stipulating the establishment of a unitary independent state in Palestine. According to the League's plan, Palestine would become a fundamentally Arab state, with the Jewish minority recognized as an autonomous religious faction and granted no more than one-third of the representation on the legislative council. In contrast, the AHC demanded that the Jewish presence in the national institutions be only one-sixth, accurately reflecting the proportion of the Jewish population in Palestine before 1918. The implication was that post-1918 Jewish immigrants would not be recognized as citizens. Another AHC condition was a ban on additional Jewish immigration and a prohibition on the sale of land to Jews by Arabs.[18]

These demands were rejected by the Arab League, and the AHC proceeded to promote the military option. At the meeting of the Arab League Council in Bludan (Syria) in June 1946, a ranking member of the AHC, Jamal al-Husseini, pressured the participants to provide military aid to enable the Palestinians to thwart an imposed Anglo-American solution entailing the partition of Palestine. According to Husseini, the AHC had already recruited 30,000 Palestinians, who needed only arms and financial and political support from the Arab governments. Husseini was confident that the Palestine Arabs would easily overpower the Jews,[19] but there were no grounds for his optimism. The Palestinians' only combat personnel were the al-Najada paramilitary group, numbering a few thousand members, whose sporadic military training did not go beyond the use of a rifle. In fact, al-Najada was caught up in internal power struggles and gradually faded into oblivion upon the eruption of the hostilities in Palestine after 29 November 1947.[20]

The visit of the United Nations Special Commission on Palestine (UNSCOP) in the country, in June 1947, further increased the feeling among the Palestinians that a violent resolution was inevitable. However, apart from manpower problems, the Palestinians suffered from severe arms shortage. Their arsenal consisted of obsolete rifles, and even those were scarce. It was again the Arab League that dominated the Palestinians' military preparations. In September 1947, the League's political committee met at Sofar (Lebanon) to formulate a reaction to UNSCOP's majority recommendation to establish two states in Palestine, one Jewish and one Arab. The committee urged the Arab governments to assist the Palestinians with arms, money and manpower. In addition, a permanent technical committee was established with the role of defining the military needs for the defence of Palestine and to co-ordinate and organize inter-Arab assistance. In the final account, though, the implications of the decision to establish what would afterwards become the Arab League's Military Command for the Palestine conflict was to divest the Palestinians of responsibility for the fighting. True, the AHC had a representative on the military committee, but he was one among eight.[21] Another step in this direction was the establishment of the semi-military Arab Liberation Army (ALA), a move instigated by Syria with a view to aborting King Abdallah's plans to take over Palestine as the first step towards the implementation of his Greater Syria vision. By way of controlling the new force, the Syrians appointed Fawzi al-Qawuqji as its commander. The Mufti, who had been on bad terms with Qawuqji, had hoped to install his nephew, Abd al-Qadir al-Husseini, as commander, to no avail.[22] The Mufti's disappointment was twofold: not only was he denied command of a force that was relatively well organized, trained and equipped, but the establishment of the Arab Liberation Army neutralized the Arab League's decision to assist the Palestinians, as arms and funds were transferred to the ALA rather than given directly to the Palestinians.[23]

## COMMUNAL WAR IN PALESTINE

The Jewish and Palestinian reactions to the United Nations Partition Resolution were, naturally, very different. Ideological aspirations notwithstanding, the Jewish leadership made a clear and unequivocal political decision: to accept the idea of partition. This was the case when UNSCOP members introduced the idea to the Jewish leadership, and yet again when the committee's majority recommendation for partition was announced. As the Jewish Agency Executive put it in an internal discussion: 'Our position will be that we were and we are ready to reach a compromise, i.e. a viable state in part of the country'.[24] When the Partition Resolution was adopted by the UN General Assembly, the Jewish leadership, notably Ben-Gurion, welcomed it enthusiastically as a major success for the Zionists.[25] This is not to say that the Jewish leadership regarded the partition lines as the best possible lines. On the contrary. Moshe Shertok, Head of the Jewish Agency's Political Department called the Zionist acceptance of partition a major compromise,[26] and the Jews eventually extended the boundaries set by the UN Partition Resolution. However, this happened only after a major shift in the political and strategic situation, following the Arabs' refusal to accept the Partition Resolution and their attack on the nascent Jewish state.

That the initial Jewish acceptance of the Partition Resolution was not mere rhetoric was also evidenced by the strategic planning of the war against the Palestinians. Thus, for example, from that moment onwards, the discussions on the security of Jewish settlements in the Western Galilee were conducted on the assumption that they would be residents of the prospective Palestinian state.[27]

Similarly, the Hagana's military preparations from late November 1947 to mid-May 1948 would seem to negate the popular conspiracy theory of a Jewish–Transjordanian collusion to divide Mandatory Palestine among themselves.[28] Not only did the Zionist leadership invest great efforts to evict Transjordan's British-led Arab Legion from Palestine upon the expiry of the Mandate, if not earlier, but following a meeting on 11 May 1948 between Golda Meir, Acting Head of the Jewish Agency's Political Department, and King Abdallah, in which the latter proposed to forgo the establishment of a Jewish state in return for an autonomous Jewish province in his kingdom, Ben-Gurion summoned the Hagana's High Commanders and ordered them to regard the

Jordanian front as an active war zone. Consequently, five Hagana brigades, out of ten, and two battalions from a brigade facing the Egyptian front, were deployed along the eastern front.[29]

Be that as it may, war with the Palestinians broke out on the day after the UN resolution. The AHC retained its defiant attitude towards the Partition Resolution, and the Mufti rejected the compromise ideas put forward by Arab politicians, insisting that the only solution was the creation of a unitary Palestinian state with an Arab majority and a minority representation for the Jews in the national institutions. The only way to achieve this, the Mufti maintained, was through a military confrontation, in which he was certain the Palestinians would have the upper hand.

On 30 November 1947, the Palestinians declared a three-day strike accompanied by a flare-up of violence against Jewish targets. These developments vindicated the underlying assumptions of the Hagana's May 1946 Plan, which envisaged major unrest while the British were still in the country.[30] Accordingly, the Jewish reaction to the outbreak of hostilities was the implementation of the May 1946 Plan. The Yishuv leadership had assumed that the Palestinians would eventually accept the UN resolution and that a sharp and decisive, yet localized response to Arab attacks would prevent escalation and would eventually drive the Arab leadership into moderation.[31] Hagana intelligence experts claimed that the majority of the Palestinians had not joined in the fighting, hence nothing should be done to provoke them. This cautionary note was widely accepted by the Yishuv's military and political leadership.[32]

The Hagana's assessment that most Palestinians would be reluctant to take part in the fighting proved correct. One reason for this was the widespread opposition to the Mufti's leadership. Some Palestinian opposition leaders, mainly in the cities, critical of the Mufti for involving the Palestinians in a war without making the necessary preparations, actively supported the refusal of Syria and the Arab League to allow the Mufti to conduct the war. Others opposed his leadership over the Palestinians, recalling his brutal attempts to impose himself on the Palestinians during the 1936–39 Revolt. Notables from Beersheba, Hebron and Gaza reportedly preferred to be part of Transjordan rather than come under the Mufti's rule.[33] Another problem was the silent opposition of many Palestinians to the war. In various places, Palestinian notables negotiated ceasefire agreements with their Jewish neighbours on a local basis, and several villages signed peace agreements with Jewish leaders at the local and national level. This tendency grew with the setbacks suffered by the Palestinians during December 1947–January 1948 at the hands of the Jewish forces. Rapidly mounting financial losses also prompted the Palestinians to try and reach a truce with the Jews, as in the case of Haifa.[34] Many of the

Palestinians who did fight did so on a local basis,[35] and were often split into various groups, some better organized than others. In many places around the country, young Palestinians underwent brief military training, usually in the use of small arms – but this was of little military value.

This internal fragmentation was exacerbated by the policies of the Arab states. Their promised military and financial assistance arrived in small droves, while their governments refused to allow the Mufti to run the war. It was only after laborious negotiations that the Arab League's political committee agreed to assign limited responsibility to the Mufti's loyalists: Abd al-Qadir al-Husseini was appointed commander of the Ramallah–Jerusalem–Hebron sector, and Hassan Salame was placed in charge of the Lydda–Ramle sector. Qawuqji was assigned to the northern front, which included the Galilee and Samaria, while no decision was made about the commander of the southern sector. The League's compromise solution led to the creation of two rival power centres, one led by Qawuqji, the other by the Mufti. The inherent disharmony of the situation was further aggravated when each man tried to increase his influence in the other's territory.[36]

While the Mufti controlled the National Committees that were established in most Palestinian towns, and more significantly in rural areas, the organization, recruitment and arming of the population proceeded slowly, hampered by the internecine strife. The Mufti found it difficult to impose his authority beyond his limited circle of followers, his attempt to set the pace and character of the Palestinian reaction being unsuccessful. His plan was first to organize forces loyal to him, which in turn required an initial defensive stage before moving on to the offensive. In practice, however, young Palestinians defied the Mufti's orders, as well as those of the National Committees, and attacked Jewish and British targets at their own initiative.[37] The forces loyal to the Mufti, under the command of Abd al-Qadir al-Husseini and Hassan Salame, consisted of recruits and armed villagers who were usually assembled on an *ad hoc* basis for specific missions, and of several hundred Palestinians who received military training at the Syrian facility in Qatana.[38] Two other local commanders loyal to Husseini established their base in the Galilee. The division between the forces loyal to the Mufti and those acting independently on a local basis was manifested in their different *modus operandi*: the former took the offensive, while the latter were engaged mainly in defensive operations.[39]

The Palestinians' military inferiority was particularly striking in comparison with the better-organized Hagana, which was the armed branch of a political entity, taking orders from a central command. The chances of the local Palestinians seemed poor, and this was the assessment of the Yishuv leadership. 'If we had to deal only with the

Palestine Arabs, I think we could have already won the war', Ben-Gurion asserted in January 1948, and the Hagana experts agreed, repeating their opinion in March.[40] Hence, adherence to the May 1946 Plan was the natural result of the Yishuv leadership's political and military perception of the state of affairs in Palestine, and the continuation of the fighting did not change the Jewish approach or strategy.

By the second week of December 1947 it was clear that the militant Palestinians would not lay down their arms.[41] The Hagana responded in accordance with the May 1946 Plan, intensifying the scale and ferocity of the counterattacks, which were an important component of the plan. The same was true with regard to Palestinian attacks against Jewish transportation throughout the country, which nearly brought it to a halt. Measures were devised and implemented to relieve the pressure, all in accordance with the principles of the May 1946 Plan. The High Commissioner was urged to use British forces in order to secure transportation routes in Arab-controlled areas;[42] suggestions were raised to attack Arab transportation so severely that attacks on Jewish transportation would stop;[43] and new roads were built to bypass regions controlled by the Palestinians.[44] By the end of December, a new solution was worked out. Jewish transportation in sensitive areas proceeded in convoys protected by armed Hagana members, and the vehicles were plated with armour.[45] These solutions temporarily relieved the pressure on the Hagana and, even though Jewish–Palestinian hostilities continued, in January 1948 Ben-Gurion recounted 'the current phase of the war' as a success.[46] The Hagana's operational strategy of hitting selected targets remained unchanged, though the operations became bolder and more ferocious. Still, no territory was seized, and field forces did not initiate decisive campaigns, or attempt to break the backbone of Palestinian military power. Ben-Gurion responded to complaints from the northern part of Palestine that the situation had deteriorated by insisting that the local forces should and could stand firm and repulse Arab attacks.[47]

## TOWARDS PLAN DALET

Two developments that took place in March led to the shift in the Hagana's strategy: the blows the Palestinians inflicted on the convoys system, and the graduated British departure from Palestine which began earlier than expected.

As the war with the Palestinians continued, the Hagana Command made plans to deal with the anticipated evacuation of the country by the British, which was to be completed by 15 May 1948. Acting on the assumption that the departure of the British would be followed by an invasion of Arab forces, the Hagana Command issued Plan Dalet in March 1948.

This plan was interpreted by the Palestinian scholar Walid Khalidi, and adopted by other academics, as a Jewish master-plan for the occupation of the territories which would eventually come to comprise the Israel of 1949, at the expense of the Palestinians, and for the deportation of the Palestinians from these territories.[48]

However intriguing, this thesis is fundamentally misconceived, not least since it is predicated on a combination of a tendentious interpretation of a military document and a reading of history from the end to the beginning, as if the final stage were the inevitable result of earlier events.

The existing evidence shows that the concept underlying Plan Dalet was shaped during discussions held by Ben-Gurion with the Hagana's General Staff in February 1948, with a view to D-Day – as Ben-Gurion termed the imminent Arab invasion of Palestine.[49] A careful scrutiny of the plan shows that its conceptual framework was still grounded in the UN Partition Resolution and that its aim was to place the Jews in the best possible strategic position in the face of an imminent Arab invasion. The Hagana brigades were ordered to take over evacuated government installations, capture Arab-populated areas within the would-be Jewish state, and take over vital strategic points in border areas. As to Jewish enclaves in the prospective Palestinian state, they were ordered to guard, not to seize them.[50] As to the accusations that the plan set the guidelines for the massive deportation of the Palestinians, one could note Ben Gurion's astonishment, in May, at the flight of Haifa's Palestinians: 'How did tens of thousands flee in such haste with no justifiable reason? What was the cause? Only orders from above? ... only fear?'.[51]

Plan Dalet's working assumption was that the Hagana should facilitate the establishment of a Jewish state in accordance with the UN resolution, and secure its existence against hostile forces. As for the forces the Hagana could expect to encounter after the British left, these were likely to consist of a combination of the local Palestinian forces, irregulars who were already operating in the country, and the regular Arab armies that were expected to join the fighting after the British withdrawal – 'all acting simultaneously, according to one common operative plan'. Plan Dalet's point of departure was that the enemy's 'presumed operational targets' would be 'to cut off, and if possible to conquer, the Galilee and the Negev, a deep invasion into the heart of the country, isolation of the three major cities (Tel Aviv, Jerusalem and Haifa), and the cutting-off of supply lines and vital facilities such as water, electricity etc'. Consequently, the Hagana's operational aims would be to secure the areas where the invading forces could be met and repulsed; to ensure freedom of movement across the country through the occupation of vital strategic sites; to disable the operational arm of the (local) enemy by capturing its bases within the designated Jewish state. The plan ordered seizure of Palestinian territory in strategic areas on the borders of the Jewish state. As to the Jewish enclaves, left by the Partition Resolution in Palestinian territory, the Hagana brigades were instructed 'to defend' them.[52]

Plan Dalet was scarcely, then, what Khalidi has read into it. Rather, it was a response to developments on the military and political fronts – the ongoing fighting with the Palestinians and the expected invasion of the Arab armies – while the timetable was set by the pace of the British evacuation. Hence the shift to the offensive by the Hagana corresponded to the British evacuation of any given area of the prospective Jewish state: wherever the British forces left, the Hagana took over, by force if necessary. Hagana forces thus gained control, step by step, over the mixed towns as well as the rural areas, stabilizing a line of defence against the expected invasion along the Partition Resolution lines plus areas across the border inside the territory allocated to the Arabs.[53]

It is important to stress that the implementation of Plan Dalet was the result of the continuous Palestinian hostilities. The original intention and hope of the Jews were to carry out the Partition Resolution, alongside the Palestinians, in their UN-assigned territories. It was only when it became clear that the Palestinians would not accept the Partition Resolution, and in light of the impending invasion of the Arab armies, that the Hagana turned to the offensive.

Plan Dalet's depiction of the Palestinians as 'enemy' was a reflection of a given situation of an intense intercommunal war in which it was extremely difficult to draw a clear dividing line between combatants and non-combatants. Moreover, the plan was devised as a strategy against an invasion, rather than against the Palestinians, but the developments on the Jewish–Palestinian front made it relevant there as well. During March the tide in the struggle with the Palestinians began to change. Worried by Palestinian failures and the prospect that Jerusalem would fall to the Jews – or even worse, to King Abdallah of Transjordan, the Mufti in February 1948 instructed Hassan Salame and Abd al-Qadir al-Husseini, to fight an all-out war for the road to the city.[54] The 'war of the roads' had been underway since December 1947, but the Palestinians lacked sufficient trained and committed fighters who could stop the convoys to Jerusalem altogether.[55] Not only the failure to stop the convoys, but also the abortive attack in January 1948 on the Jewish settlements south of Jerusalem (Gush Etzion), in the midst of an Arab-populated area, made it clear to the Mufti that his forces were no match for the Jews. To rectify the situation, Salame and Husseini set up training camps near Jerusalem in January–February 1948, and in early February the Mufti and his two senior commanders travelled to Damascus, where they met the Syrian President, Shukri al-Quwaitly. At the meeting the division of labour in Palestine was reaffirmed, and it was agreed that the Mufti would receive financial assistance to pay the wages of local and foreign 'volunteers'.[56]

As the Palestinians were reorganizing their ranks, Hagana Commanders warned that a change in strategy was required. The Palestinians, they said, had regained the initiative and were dictating the terms and pace of the fighting – and that must be denied to them. The Hagana High Command therefore decided in February 1948 that its operational aims should be the 'taking over [of territory] inside the [Jewish] state, and [setting up] defence along its borders'. To accomplish this it would be necessary to increase the Hagana forces, enhance their mobility, and improve their combat ability against the Palestinians.[57] This was easier said than done. The Jews took a step in this direction by gradually adopting a policy of occupying sections of the Tel Aviv–Jerusalem road in advance of the convoys.[58] But in February the Hagana Command still thought in terms of prevention and deterrence by attacking selective Palestinian targets, with its Chief of Operations invoking the May 1946 Plan, with its limited aims.[59]

By March, the Mufti's campaign against the Jewish convoys proved successful, for a number of reasons. To begin with, the Palestinian camp was strengthened by the arrival of several hundred trained fighters recruited by Abd al-Qadir al-Husseini and Hassan Salame in Syria. Together with several hundred local Palestinians whom Husseini had trained and whose wages he paid, and assisted by Palestinians who lived in villages along the road and who could be mustered whenever a convoy passed by, this was a formidable force, probably numbering some 3,000 guerrillas. Moreover, the Palestinians could act freely since February 1948, when the British decided to avoid the problematic Tel Aviv–Jerusalem road and instead to use the Latrun–Ramalla route to enter or leave Jerusalem.[60]

Geography also provided the Palestinian forces with an advantage, which they exploited well: the eastern part of the road ran through a mountainous and densely populated Arab area, dominated by steep ridges. In late March and early April, the Palestinians succeeded in closing the road to Jerusalem.[61] Indeed, throughout the country the convoy system came under severe pressure. During one week in March five convoys were destroyed and more than 100 Hagana fighters killed.[62]

The failures in the 'struggle over the roads' convinced the Hagana Command that the May 1946 Plan did not provide an adequate response to the new situation. The convoy system seemed to be no longer viable. The roots of the problem were the Hagana's failure to appreciate the ability of the Palestinians to muster forces when a convoy approached, and its reliance on a military escort for convoys instead of seizing territory in anticipation of the convoy's journey. Moreover, the reactive strategy stipulated by the May 1946 Plan led to the dispersion of Hagana forces in protective missions all over the country. Not least, the recruitment of new soldiers to the Hagana proceeded at a slower pace than expected, and the organization was not able to amass its troops and use them as a strike force. This state of affairs was sufficient to prevent the fall of Jewish settlements, but it was inadequate for coping with the vigorous Palestinian campaign against Jewish transportation.[63]

Plan Dalet offered a direction towards a solution by setting guidelines for the seizure of strategic positions, thereby improving the Hagana's defence lines in the face of the impending invasion. This was the logic behind the first major offensive operation of the Hagana, which sought to open the road to Jerusalem. In April 1948 Jerusalem was under siege imposed by the Palestinians, cut off from the main Jewish body in the coastal plain. Ben-Gurion, seeing the grave situation in the city and the despair among its Jewish residents, feared that Jerusalem would fall. He therefore decided to commit the bulk of the Hagana field forces to open the road to the city.[64] The outcome was Operation Nahshon (5–20 April) in which for the first time the Hagana assembled three brigades to fight Abd al-Qadir al-Husseini's forces along the Tel Aviv–Jerusalem road. During the operation, in which Husseini himself was killed, Hagana forces seized the hills and ridges controlling the road and captured several Arab villages, in some of them expelling the residents and demolishing their homes.[65] The road to Jerusalem was temporarily opened and supply convoys rushed to the besieged city.

The Hagana's successes in April marked a change in its strategy, as indeed in the whole thrust of the war with the Palestinians. Abandoning the defensive strategy articulated in May 1946, the Hagana now seized the initiative. The Palestinians were unable to mount a viable response. If the Mufti's attempts to organize his forces during February–March were crowned with a certain success, the situation was reversed in April. The Palestinians lost the backbone of their command with the death of Abd al-Qadir al-Husseini and Hassan Salame's 'disgraceful' escape following a raid on his headquarters in Ramle by a Hagana commando unit in conjunction with the Nahshon operation.[66] The Palestinian setback was exacerbated by the Dir Yassin massacre, in which some 100 villagers were killed by 'dissident' Jewish forces. The massacre was a breaking point for the Palestinians, who fled in increasing numbers in the face of the Jewish military forces.[67] The failure of the attack by the Arab Liberation Army against the northern Jewish kibbutz of Mishmar Ha-emek, which was launched on 4 April and ended ten days later in ignominious defeat, was another blow to Palestinian morale and bolstered the Hagana's self-confidence.[68]

By now the Palestinians had lost all hope of withstanding the Jews on their own and looked to assistance from an Arab intervention force. Not only Amman but Tel Aviv as well knew of the Palestinians' desperate plight, and the Hagana's next moves were influenced by the defeatist mood in the Palestinian camp.[69] It now moved to the offensive against the Palestinians, who were 'untrained, disorganized and short of equipment',[70] targeting the mixed towns first and executing Plan Dalet. By 15 May the Jews had gained full control of the mixed towns that were within the partition lines (notably Haifa and Tiberias). Further territories were gained in yet another round of operations after that date. As the Arab states attacked the newly born state of Israel, Palestinian defeat was complete.[71]

## CONCLUSION

For the past century, Jewish and Palestinian history has been entwined in the territory of Palestine. The outcome of the 1947–48 War reflects that tragic entanglement, in the sense that the advantages that accrued to one side were the mirror image of the setbacks suffered by the other. In other words, the factors that enabled the Jews to win the war were precisely those that the Palestinians lacked. The Jews had a central political leadership, recognized by the majority of the Jewish population, which controlled a unified national armed organization; the national resources were subordinate to the goals defined by the national leadership, which possessed the organizational capabilities to realize them. The Palestinians, on the other hand, were sorely divided. They had neither national institutions nor a national leadership; a deep gulf existed between the rural and urban populations, as well as between tribes and families. The self-proclaimed leader was not accepted by many and was consequently unable to mobilize the majority of the Palestinians to pursue the goals he had set. Even among those who fought, many acted independently. And as if the internal divisions were not enough, the Arab governments did not recognize the Mufti's claim to leadership and reneged on their pledges of assistance. The end of the confrontation was thus inherent in its beginning, reflecting the situation of the two communities: one fundamentally leaderless and deeply divided, the other highly motivated and internally cohesive.

### NOTES

1. See, for example, Zehava Ostfeld, *Tsava Nolad*, Tel Aviv, 1994, Vol. I, pp.67–8; Meir Pail, *Min Ha-hagana Le-tsva Ha-hagana*, Tel Aviv, 1979, pp.278, 291ff; Yoav Gelber, *Gar'in Le-tsava Ivri Sadir*, Tel Aviv, 1986, Ch.2.
    Avraham Sela offers a rare exception to this rule. However, he concentrates almost exclusively on the Arab side, and his account is a social, rather than military or political

history. See Avraham Sela, 'The Palestine Arabs in the 1948 War', in Moshe Maoz and B.Z. Kedar (eds), *The Palestinian National Movement: From Confrontation to Reconciliation?*, Tel Aviv, 1996 (Hebrew).

2 See, for example, Walid Khalidi, 'Plan Dalet: Master Plan for the Conquest of Palestine', *Middle East Forum*, November 1961; Ilan Pappe, *The Making of the Arab–Israeli Conflict, 1947–1951*, London, 1992, pp.89–93; Uri Ben Eliezer, *Derekh Ha-kavenet: Hivatsruto shel Ha-militarism Ha-Israeli, 1936–1956*, Tel Aviv, 1995, pp.253–5; Nur Masalha, *Expulsion of the Palestinians*, Washington DC, 1992, pp.177–8; William Roger Louis, *The British Empire in the Middle East, 1945–1951*, Oxford, 1984, p.576.

3. David Ben-Gurion, *Zikhronot*, Tel Aviv, 1969, Vol. III, pp.42, 123, 128, 135, 167–8, 222–3.

4. Plan B explicitly assumed that 'following the policy conducted by the [Mandate] government, a [Jewish–Arab] war will not exceed the level of "small war"'. 'Plan B', September 1945, the Hagana Archives, Tel Aviv, Israel, 73/100 (hereinafter HA). See also 'The May 1946 Plan', ibid., 73/140.

5. Alan Bullock, *Ernest Bevin, Foreign Secretary, 1945–1951*, London, 1983, pp.47–8, 164–8. On the Yishuv's struggle against the British White Paper policy see Yehuda Slutski *et al.*, *Sefer Toldot Ha-hagana*, Tel Aviv, 1954–73, Vol. 3/3, annexes 32–6, pp.1921–34.

6. David Ben-Gurion, *Ba-ma'arakha*, Tel Aviv, 1951, Vol. 5, pp.135–6; idem, *Medinat Israel Ha-mehudeshet*, Tel Aviv, 1969, p.68; *Sefer Ha-hagana*, Vol. 3/3, pp.1901–14, 1921–34. Yoav Gelber claims that Ben-Gurion paid no attention to the daily security problems dealt by the Hagana even after assuming the defence portfolio; yet he fails to elaborate on the meaning of this neglect. Gelber, *Gar'in Le-tsava Ivri*, pp.20–21.

7. 'Instructions to the Hagana Command', 18 June 1947, in David Ben-Gurion, *Be-hilahem Israel*, Tel Aviv, 1975, pp.13–18. Ben-Gurion repeated his warning that a full-scale war was imminent at a meeting of the Mapai Political Committee on 8 January 1948. See Labour Party Archives, Beit Berl, Israel (henceforth LPA), 25/48.

8. David Ben-Gurion's speech at the Jewish Congress's political committee, 18 December 1946, Ben-Gurion, *Ba-ma'arakha*, Vol. 5, pp.135–6.

9. Ben-Gurion heard this from Israel Galili, Head of the Hagana's National Command, from a veteran of the Soviet Red Army, Zalman Livon, and from one of his intelligence advisers, Joseph Karkovi. See David Ben-Gurion War Diaries (BGWD), entries for 3, 8, and 9 April 1947. The references to Ben-Gurion's Diary during March–November 1947 are taken from Meir Avizohar (editor and annotator), David Ben-Gurion, *Paamei Medina*, Tel Aviv, 1994.

10. See comments by Moshe Zelitski (Carmel), Joseph Rohel (Avidar), and Israel Galili in BGWD, 17, 25, 30 April 1947. See also entry for 10 April 1947.

11. See, for example, Ben-Gurion's speech at the Security Committee, 8 June 1947, in Avizohar, *Paamei Medina*, p.295.

12. 'Instructions to the Hagana Command', Ben-Gurion, *Be-hilahem Israel*, pp.16–17; Ben-Gurion's speech at the Security Committee, 8 June 1947, Avizohar, *Paamei Medina*, p.295. On the response to the local Arab threat, see ibid. pp.297–8; on the response to external threat see ibid. pp.298–301.

13. 'Order of National Structure', November 1947, HA, 73/140; Pail, *Min Ha-hagana*, pp.161–74, 274–7, 282–91; Dov Tamari, 'Hashiva Estrategit Be-irgun Ha-hagana, 1936–1947', MA thesis, Tel Aviv University, 1995, pp.162–3.

14. Ben-Gurion, *Medinat Israel Ha-mehudeshet*, pp.70–71; Ben-Gurion's speech at the Security Committee, 8 June 1947, Avizohar, *Paamei Medina*, pp.295–8. See also BGWD, 27 June 1947, and his analysis in the protocol of the meeting of the defence committee on 19 October 1947, Central Zionist Archives, Jerusalem, Israel (hereinafter CZA).

15. From Beirut to Foreign Office, 12 October 1947, FO 371/61530/E9951; Sela, 'The Palestine Arabs in the 1948 War', pp.143–4.

16. *Behind the Curtain: A Report by an Iraqi Parliamentary Committee on the Palestine War*, tr. S. Sabag, Tel Aviv, 1954, pp.54, 55–6.

17. Record of Conversation [Between a British Officer of the Arab Legion and a Visitor from the Hebron District], 28 January 1948, Public Record Office (PRO), FO 816/116; Sela, 'The Palestine Arabs in the 1948 War', pp.130–35.

18. See a report of an interview with the Mufti: British Middle East Office (BMEO), Cairo, to BAB Burrows, Foreign Office, London, 2 October 1947, FO 371/61836/E9097; Sela, 'The Palestine Arabs in the 1948 War', pp.132–3.

19. Sela, 'The Palestine Arabs in the 1948 War', pp.133–4.

20. Sela, 'The Palestine Arabs in the 1948 War', pp.136–7. See also Haim Levenberg, *The Military Preparation of the Arab Community in Palestine, 1945–1948*, London, 1993, pp.126–54, 239–40.
21. From Amman to Foreign Office, 24 September 1947, FO 371/61529/E8873; Sabag, *Behind the Curtain*, pp.51–2; Sela, 'The Palestine Arabs in the 1948 War', p.140.
22. From Amman to Foreign Office, 20 December 1947, FO 371/61583/E12129; Sela, 'The Palestine Arabs in the 1948 War', pp.148–9.
23. From Amman to Foreign Office, 21 December 1947, FO 371/61583/E12132.
24. Protocol of Jewish Agency Executive meeting, 18 June 1947, CZA, S/100/52b. This decision reiterated earlier resolutions. See, for example, protocols of Jewish Agency Executive meetings on 21 March, 26 May and 8 June 1947. See also *The Jewish Plan for Palestine – Memoranda and Statements Presented by the Jewish Agency for Palestine to the UNSCOP*, Jerusalem, 1947, pp.67–9, 331–2, 354–5; David Ben-Gurion's letter to Paula Ben-Gurion, 2 September 1947, Avizohar, *Paamei Medina*, pp.349–52; Meeting of the Zionist Executive Committee, Zurich, 2 September 1947, ibid., p.352; BGD, 18 September 1947, ibid., pp.363–4.
25. Protocol of the Jewish Agency Executive meeting, 30 November 1947, CZA, S/100/53b; Ben-Gurion to the High Commissioner, Avizohar, *Paamei Medina*, p.13, entry for 1 December 1947; Ben-Gurion's speech to the Histadrut Executive Committee, 3 December 1947, ibid., pp.20–21; Ben-Gurion's speech to the Mapai Centre, 3 December 1947, LPA, 25/47.
26. Reply of the Government of Israel to the Proposals of the UN mediator, Count F. Bernadotte, 5 July 1948, Israel State Archives, FO 2451/1.
27. David Ben-Gurion (G. Rivlin and E. Oren (eds)), *Yoman Ha-milhama*, Tel Aviv, 1982, Vol. I, p.15, entry for 2 December 1947 (hereinafter BGWD).
28. This claim was first made by Israel Beer, a former IDF Lieutenant Colonel, imprisoned in the 1950s for treason, and adopted by a group of 'revisionist' Israeli historians. See Israel Beer, *Bithon Israel: Etmol, Ha-yom, Mahar*, Tel Aviv, 1966, pp.125–6.
29. Operations Branch/General HQ, 'Modification of Plan Dalet, 11 May 1948', Israel Defence Forces Archives (hereinafter IDFA), 922/75/1206; BGWD, Vol. I, p.411, entry for 12 May 1948.
30. The Hagana Command stated explicitly in mid-December 1947 that 'the strategic assumptions that were articulated in the May 1946, were vindicated'. GHQ/Operations Branch: 'Summary of the Enemy Organization in Light of the Recent Disturbances', 19 December 1947, IDFA, 922/75/595; *Sefer Ha-hagana*, Vol. 3/2, pp.1360–63.
31. Galili at a meeting of the Yishuv Security Committee, 13 November 1947, CZA, S25/9343; Ben-Gurion at meetings of Mapai Political Committee on 9 December 1947 and 8 January 1948, LPA, 25/47, 25/48; Yitzhak Ben-Zvi at a meeting of Mapai Political Committee, 11 October 1947, in Meir Avizohar (ed.), *Akhshav O Le-olam Lo*, Beit Berl, 1989, p.183; Ben-Gurion on equal rights for the Arab citizens of the Jewish state at a Keren Ha-yesod convention, 29 October 1947, in Avizohar, *Paamei Medina*, p.438.
32. Protocol of a Meeting on Arab Affairs, 1–2 January 1948, HA, 80/50/21; Israel Galili in *Sefer Ha-palmah*, Vol.2, January 1948, pp.xx–xxii, February 1948, pp.xxii–iv; Ben-Gurion's letter to M. Shertok and Golda Meyerson, 14 March 1948, Memoranda Files, Ben-Gurion Research Centre, Sde Boker Campus, Israel (hereinafter: BGA).
33. Record of Conversation [Between a British Officer of the Arab Legion and a visitor from the Hebron District], 28 January 1948, FO 816/116; British Legation in Amman, 'Monthly Report on Transjordan for the Month of January', 3 February 1948, FO 371/68845; from Amman to Foreign Office, 18 March 1948, No. 304, FO 816/117; Sela, 'The Palestine Arabs in the 1948 War', pp.146, 149–50.
34. The following is a partial list of intelligence reports on agreements negotiated and concluded between Jews and Arabs: a *modus vivendi* understanding between kibbutz Ma'ale Ha-hamisha and the Arab Katana village, 23 December 1947; peace agreement between the Arab population of Emeq Hefer and their Jewish neighbours, 31 December 1947; negotiations on peace in Haifa, 18 January 1948; peace talks between the Jewish head of Ben Shemen and the mayor of the Arab Lydda, 7 January 1948; agreement between the Arab village of Aqir and Jewish Eqron, 9 February 1948; ceasefire negotiated to stop the mutual shooting on Jewish and Arab transportation in Acre, 6 February 1948; truce signed between Magdiel and Bir Adas, 9 March 1948; the residents of Arab Tantura

decided to surrender to the Jews but asked that this take place after an ostensible Jewish attack upon them, 3 May 1948. All in HA, 105/54/2. See also General Sir A. Cunningham to the Secretary of State for the Colonies, 'Weekly Intelligence Appreciation', 1 February 1948, CO 537/3869.

35. HA File 105/148, for example, contains many intelligence reports on the various local Arab groups who acted on their own initiative against the Jews in their neighbourhood, and on the military training undertaken by Palestinians in various places across the country.

36. Sela, 'The Palestine Arabs in the 1948 War', pp.154, 156, 158.

37. Cunningham to Secretary of State, 'Weekly Intelligence Appreciation', 3 January 1948, CO 537/3869. One such instance was an attack on the Jewish settlements of Gush Etzion in January. The attack failed, and it was stopped under the Mufti's orders, who did not approve it in the first place. Cunningham to Secretary of State, 'Weekly Intelligence Appreciation', 16 January 1948, CO 537/3869.

38. Abd al-Qadir al-Husseini opened a training base in Tsurif, near Jerusalem, 'Tene Intelligence Report', 1 January 1948, HA, 105/148; 'Tene Information Report', 28 December 1947, ibid.

39. Sela, 'The Palestine Arabs in the 1948 War', pp.162–3.

40. 'Guidelines for Plans in Case of [British] Evacuation', unsigned document from late December 1947, IDFA, 922/75/595; Ben-Gurion speech in Mapai Centre, 8 January 1948, LPA, 25/48; see also Ezra Danin's assessment, protocol of a meeting on Arab affairs, 1–2 January 1948, HA, 80/50/21; Ben-Gurion to Shertok and Meyerson, 14 March 1948, Memoranda Files, BGA.

41. 'List of People wounded [from 1 December 1947 to 25 February 1948]', General Memoranda, BGA; see also Levenberg, *The Military Preparation*, p.179.

42. Meeting between David Ben-Gurion and Sir A. Cunningham, 1 December 1947, *Israel Documents 1948*, State of Israel, Israel Sate Archive, Political and Diplomatic Documents, 12/47–4/48 (ed. Gedalya Yogev), Jerusalem, 1979, p.16; BGWD, p.18, entry for 2 December 1947; ibid., p.43, entry for 13 December 1947; ibid., pp.49–50, entry for 16 December 1947; ibid., p.72, entry for 25 December 1947.

43. GHQ/Operations Branch, 'Summary of the Enemy Organization in Light of the Recent Events', 19 December 1947, IDFA, 922/75/595; BGWD, p.15, entry for 2 December 1947; ibid., pp.37–8, entry for 11 December 1947.

44. 'Summary of the Enemy Organization in Light of the Recent Events'; BGWD, p.63, entry for 22 December 1947; ibid., pp.71–2, entry for 25 December 1947; ibid., pp.92, 94, entry for 31 December 1947.

45. 'Summary of the Enemy Organization in Light of the Recent Events'; BGWD, pp.77, 79, entry for 28 December 1947; ibid., p.82, entry for 29 December 1947; ibid., p.94, entry for 31 December 1947. On the convoys system see *Sefer Ha-hagana*, Vol. 3/2, pp.1442–56; *Sefer Ha-palmah*, Vol. 2, pp.91–105; Amiad Brezner, *Nitzaney Shirion*, Tel Aviv, 1995, Chapter 2.

46. 'On Defence and Security Problems', 21 (or 27) January 1948, in Ben-Gurion, *Be-hilahem Israel*, p.43; BGWD, pp.183–5, entry for 25 January 1948.

47. BGWD, p.151, entry for 15 January 1948; see also various speeches by Ben-Gurion on 15 January, 21 February, 1, 6 and 7 March 1948, in *Be-hilahem Israel*, pp.34–74.

48. See note 2 above.

49. BGWD, pp.216, 270, entries for 8 and 29 February 1948. The plan's principles were presented by the head of the Hagana National Command. See Israel Galili, *Sefer Ha-palmah*, Vol. 2, pp.xxxiii–iv.

50. GHQ/Operations Branch, 'Plan Dalet', 10 March 1948, IDFA, 922/75/595; GHQ/Operations Branch, 'A Proposition for Shaping of the Borders and Establishing Border Strongholds', 11 May 1948, HA, 80/50/25. It was only in regard to Jerusalem that the plan exceeded the Partition lines, stipulating for the seizure of the city and its access roads.

51. BGWD, Vol. I, p.381, entry for 1 May 1948.

52. David Ben-Gurion at a Mapai Centre meeting on 6 February 1948, LPA, 25/48; GHQ/Operations Branch, 'Plan Dalet', I. Galili's report, 4 April 1948, HA, 80/50/18.

53. On Hagana operations during April–May 1948 see *Sefer Ha-hagana*, Vol. 3/2, Chapter 78.

54. Cable from 'Max', 4 February 1948, CZA, S/25/9007.

55. Records of the convoys plying road from the Coastal Plain to Jerusalem, and reports of attacks on convoys all over the country reached the Hagana Command on a daily basis

from December 1947. These reports are deposited in IDFA, 464/54/2. See also report by
'Benjamin', 26 February 1948, HA, 80/50/21.
56. Cable to 'Sasha' (Y. Allon) from Y. Yadin, January 1948, IDFA, 661/69/36; cable from E.
Danin to E. Shiloah, 13 January 1948, CZA, S/25/9007; Cunningham to Secretary of State,
'Weekly Intelligence Appreciation', 16 January 1948, CO 537/3869; cable from 'Adina' to
'Hilel' (I. Galili), 3 February 1948, IDFA, 464/54/2; from Amman to Foreign Office, 9
February 1948, FO 371/68366/E1889; Arab Liberation Army [unsigned paper], 13
February 1948, CZA, S25/3999; Cunningham to the Secretary of State, 'Weekly
Intelligence Appreciation', 14 February 1948, FO 816/116. On the training programme
and the 'volunteers' who have undertaken it see J. Palmon's report of 26 February 1948,
HA, 80/50/21; Yavne to Tene, 'The volunteers in Jerusalem', 3 March 1948, HA,
105/216/1; Yavne to Tene: 'The Arab force in Jerusalem', 16 March 1948, ibid.; *Behind
the Curtain*, pp.82–4; Yitzhak Levi (Levitse), *Tish'a Kabin*, Tel Aviv, 1986, pp.354–5.
57. GHQ/Operations Branch: 'Analysis of the Strategic Situation and Conclusions as to the
Distribution of the Hagana Forces', February 1948, IDFA, 922/75/595; I. Galili's notes, 29
February 1948, HA, 80/50/28; I. Galili's report, 4 April 1948, HA, 80/50/18. The
Hagana's intention to move on to the offensive was noted by the British High
Commissioner. See, for example, Cunningham to Secretary of State, 'Weekly Intelligence
Appreciation', 23 February 1948, FO 816/116.
58. BGWD, p.327, entry for 30 March 1948; I. Galili's report, 4 April 1948, HA, 80/50/18;
*Sefer Ha-palmah*, Vol. II, pp.99–101.
59. Y. Yadin's report, 26 February 1948, HA, 80/50/21.
60. 'Palestine: Withdrawal of British Administration', C.P. (48) 40, 4 February 1948, Cabinet
Files (CAB)/129; cable from the 'Moatsa' to the 'Knesset', 24 February 1948, IDFA,
464/54/2; Cunningham to the Secretary of State, 'Weekly Intelligence Appreciation', 27
March 1948, CO 537/3869; HM Minister, Amman to Secretary of State for Foreign
Affairs, 21 April 1948, No. 237, FO 816/117.
61. Cable from 'Max' to the Jewish Agency, 2 February 1948, CZA, S/25/9007; *Sefer Ha-
hagana*, Vol. 2, pp.1446–7. Constant intelligence information on the planned campaign to
cut the road to Jerusalem reached the Hagana during February–March, and is deposited in
IDFA, 661/69/36. See also 'Summary of the Situation in the Battlefield', 1 April 1948,
IDFA, 922/75/595.
62. *Sefer Ha-hagana*, Vol. 3/2, pp.1452–6.
63. 'Summary of the Military Situation', 1 April 1948, IDFA, 922/75/595; I. Galili's report, 4
April 1948, HA, 80/50/18; Tamari, 'Hashiva Estrategit', pp.162–3.
64. See the urgent letters sent to Ben-Gurion on the serious situation in the city: from David
Shealtiel (Jerusalem's military commander), 28 March 1948, HA, 80/50/25; from Leo
Kohen, 29 March 1948, General Memoranda, BGA.
65. Nahshon HQ, 'Operational Instructions', April 1948, in *Ma'arachot*, No. 263–4, June
1978, pp.29–30; IDF History Branch, 'Study on Plan Dalet', July 1963, p.13, IDFA,
922/75/595; *Sefer Ha-hagana*, Vol. 3/2, pp.1562–4.
66. Cunningham to the Secretary of State, 'Weekly Intelligence Appreciation', 10 April 1948,
CO 537/3869.
67. Cunningham to the Secretary of State, 13 April 1948, No. 956, FO 816/117; HM
Minister, Amman to the Secretary of State for Foreign Affairs, 21 April 1948, No. 234,
ibid.; B. Morris, *The Birth of the Palestinian Refugee Problem, 1947–1949*, Cambridge,
1987, pp.113–15.
68. The Egyptian Minister for Foreign Affairs asked for British assistance to rescue Qawuqji's
forces in Mishmar Ha-emek, otherwise they 'would undoubtedly be wiped out'. See Cairo
to Foreign Office, 15 April 1948, No. 467, CO 537/3904. On the 'general collapse of
[Palestinian] Arab morale', see HM Minister, Amman, to Secretary of State for Foreign
Affairs, 16 April 1948, No. 227, FO 816/117.
69. King Abdallah referred to this matter in his letter to the Secretary-General of the Arab
League, quoted in Amman to Foreign Office, 21 April 1948, No. 237, FO 371/68852;
Eliyahu Sasson's report to Ben-Gurion, BGWD, Vol. I, pp.357–8, entry for 20 April 1948.
70. Amman to Foreign Office, 21 April 1948, No. 237, FO 371/68852.
71. On the impact of the Jewish military successes on the Palestinian Arab population see Tene
intelligence reports, 24 April 1948, HA, 105/98; Cunningham to the Secretary of State,
'Weekly Intelligence Appreciation', 1 May 1948, CO 537/3869.

# Shall We Go to War? And If We Do, When? The Genesis of the Internal Debate in Israel on the Road to the Sinai War

MOTTI GOLANI

On 29 October 1956, Israel attacked Egypt. Forty-eight hours later, Britain and France joined the offensive. Like any other war, this one did not erupt out of the blue. On a broader level, the roots of the Sinai War can be traced back to the conclusion of Israel's War of Independence. This essay, however, seeks to pinpoint the genesis of the conscious process that eventually made Israel one of the initiators of this war. More specifically, it will attempt to ascertain which major figures in Israel's security establishment spearheaded this move, which had originated in the idea a that 'second round' against the Arab states was bound to occur sooner or later.

As will be shown below, the run-up to the 'war of choice' in 1956 revolved around three personalities: David Ben-Gurion, the Prime Minister and Minister of Defence from May 1948 to January 1954 and from November 1955 to June 1963, and also Minister of Defence in the interim period, from February 1955 to November 1955; Moshe Sharett, who was Foreign Minister from May 1948 to June 1956 and also Prime Minister from January 1954 to November 1955; and Moshe Dayan, the Chief-of-Staff of the Israel Defence Forces (IDF) from December 1953 to January 1958.

In December 1953, Ben-Gurion resigned. The departure of the 'founding father' of the Jewish state shocked the entire nation. Several politicians tried to fill the vacuum created by the resignation. Some of the most prominent among them, such as Pinhas Lavon, the new Minister of Defence, faded quickly into obscurity. Others became strong enough to threaten Ben-Gurion's standing, not least the new Prime

Motti Golani is a Lecturer at the Department of Eretz Israel Studies at Haifa University.

Minister, Sharett. Still others came into their own after the departure of the 'Old Man' and remained solidly entrenched in the upper echelons of the establishment until Ben-Gurion's return after a mere 14 months of retirement. Most notable among these was Moshe Dayan.

As the IDF's fourth Chief-of-Staff, Dayan had an extraordinary influence on the Israeli government, whose decisions he was supposed to carry out. Dayan was hardly an anonymous officer when Ben-Gurion appointed him to the army's top spot on 6 December 1953, one day before going into voluntary political exile in the Negev kibbutz Sde Boker. Already in 1949 Dayan had displayed political acumen as Jerusalem's Military Commander, when the truce agreements between Israel and Jordan were drawn up – first in the city itself and then in the armistice talks at Rhodes. As his military career progressed – he was head of Southern Command, Northern Command, and of the General Staff Branch before becoming Chief-of-Staff – Dayan made no secret of his views on questions which went beyond his military preoccupations.[1]

Dayan was a quintessential creation of the Labour movement. Shmuel Dayan, his father, was a member of the Knesset on behalf of Mapai (Land of Israel Workers' Party) which in various incarnations ruled Israel from 1948 to 1977. Dayan himself was a chosen candidate of the party for the first Knesset elections before officers in active service were forbidden to be members of elected political bodies. But he remained an active participant, albeit not a formal member, of certain party bodies. His activist approach to security was no secret either. It was this background that led Ben-Gurion to appoint Dayan Chief-of-Staff on the eve of his departure for a remote desert kibbutz.[2]

Dayan, then, was imposed on Ben-Gurion's successor, Moshe Sharett, who viewed the new Chief-of-Staff as a political figure who would politicize the IDF. Moreover, Sharett believed – quite rightly – that Dayan was Ben-Gurion's tool. But the real problem was that Sharett had no faith in Dayan and indeed feared him. The Chief-of-Staff's ultra-activism, as Sharett saw it, posed a concrete danger to the country. If he could not remove Dayan, Sharett wanted at least to tighten the supervision over his decisions and actions. But a 'legacy of Ben-Gurion's' was inviolable in the political reality of mid-1950s Israel.

Until February 1955, Sharett had to cope with Dayan on his own. But from the day, in that month, on which Ben-Gurion returned from his self-imposed exile to become Minister of Defence, Sharett was confronted with the seemingly impossible task of rebuffing pressure from both the Chief-of-Staff and the country's senior figure, Defence Minister Ben-Gurion.[3]

On the day of Dayan's appointment as Chief-of-Staff, Ben-Gurion also carried out another decision, naming Shimon Peres Director-General of the Ministry of Defence. The two 'youngsters' played a major role in keeping Ben-Gurion abreast of political–security developments at his home in the remote Negev. The two consulted regularly with Ben-Gurion, and their impact (together and separately) on the events that followed was immense.[4]

## THE CHIEF-OF-STAFF STEERS THE COUNTRY TOWARDS WAR

Ben-Gurion and Dayan disagreed vehemently with Sharett's policy and were disinclined to accept his authority as Prime Minister. Ben-Gurion was strengthened in his objections to Sharett's security policy and encouraged to formulate a new policy of his own by two factors: the objective security situation and Dayan's actions.[5]

Dayan found the interrelations at the top levels of government useful for his purposes. The antagonistic relations between the Minister of Defence and the Prime Minister meant that the Chief-of-Staff often became the effective Minister of Defence, particularly in 1954, when Lavon served in that capacity. At the same time, the ties between Dayan and Ben-Gurion, still in Sde Boker, became extremely close, so much so that Sharett thought the Chief-of-Staff was making efforts to remove him and engineer Ben-Gurion's return as Prime Minister. In early 1955, Sharett wrote in his diary that Zalman Aranne (the minister in charge of 'information') had told him that Dayan had suggested to a number of people that they organize a kind of alliance to replace the leadership of the party, of the Histadrut Federation of Labour, and of the government. Several months later, when Ben-Gurion had reassumed his post as Minister of Defence, Sharett asked him whether he knew about these appearances by the Chief-of-Staff and what he intended to do to restrain him. In his account, 'B-G was embarrassed and mumbled something unclear'.[6]

In 1954, Sharett repeatedly thwarted Dayan's activist initiatives, which the Prime Minister believed often transcended the wish to retaliate firmly against the robberies and murders perpetrated by Palestinian Arabs who infiltrated across the border into Israel. Dayan objected to Sharett's approach, which in his view boiled down to 'anything but war'. His attitude was different: 'Anything but forgoing Israel's vital goals, even at the price of war'. If Israel's right of navigation in the Red Sea or its plan to divert the Jordan River were vital interests, they must not be ceded, even if the Arabs resorted to war. In that case Israel should be able to pre-empt the enemy and attack first. The same was true with regard to the reprisals: they had to be painful, even at a risk of war, for otherwise they would be ineffectual.

Dayan's concept of 'basic security' was mixed inextricably with his view of 'routine security'. He believed that Israel's true problem had always been in the sphere of basic security and that everything, including routine security, had to be subordinated to it. Dayan did not speak explicitly about an Israeli-initiated war before April 1955, though that was the real thrust of his approach. In off-the-record conversations he nevertheless admitted that he preferred war over a 'peace' that would not guarantee Israel's security. In this view, a *status quo* based on the 1949 Armistice Accords, in the absence of defensible borders or access to the Red Sea, and with Israel's deterrent capability declining by the year did not amount to real peace. Although Dayan believed that the Arab–Israeli conflict could not be solved by military means, he thought that Israel needed a 'second round' against the Arabs in order to be able to negotiate future peace treaties from a position of strength. The primary target of his war aim was Egypt, the leading Arab country. Some in Israel dismissed this approach as sheer adventurism, but others supported it, as we will see.[7]

Dayan, as Ben-Gurion saw him, was 'daring almost to the point of lunacy, [but this was] balanced by deep-reaching tactical and strategic judgment'. Nor did the Chief-of-Staff hide his views from foreign officials. Visiting the United States in the summer of 1954, he explained to CIA Director Allen Dulles that Israel had very good reasons to want a war: inconvenient borders and the rapid military build-up of the Arab states. However, he was quick to add (remaining loyal to the government's line), that Israel was not conducting a policy aimed at fomenting a war.[8]

With Sharett as Prime Minister, Dayan found it impossible to implement his policy. The Chief-of-Staff did not disobey orders, though he floated threats to resign – which were ineffective, since Sharett would have liked nothing better than to see him go. Dayan, then, longed for Ben-Gurion's return to the government, and the sooner the better. But he soon found out that even Ben-Gurion, as of 1954, was not an advocate of activism to the point of war. In 1954, Israel's founding father thought that the country needed 'people not territories'. He deeply feared the reaction of the great powers to an Israeli act of aggression, and his general argument was that 'there is no last battle for Israel', and that the conflict with the Arabs must ultimately be settled by negotiations. Until then, Israel must manage the conflict, however lengthy it turned out to be, in a manner that would cause it minimal damage. So, from Dayan's point of view, Ben-Gurion needed convincing.[9]

Dayan launched his efforts to win over Ben-Gurion months before the latter returned to the Ministry of Defence in February 1955. On 8 June 1954, the Chief-of-Staff made one of his frequent consultation visits to Ben-Gurion. Their conversation on this occasion took place at Tel Ha-shomer hospital, next to Tel Aviv, where Ben-Gurion was then convalescing. The following is Dayan's account of their talk: 'And when

I told him that I aspire to a more activist policy he began cross-examining me: "What is activism? What do you want – war?"'. Dayan replied cautiously: 'I am not for initiating a war. But I am against concessions in any area, even if adamancy brings war. An Arab threat of war should not prevent any action [deemed necessary] by us'.[10]

Ben-Gurion did not react directly, but probably took Dayan's remarks as a request – made not for the first time – that he return to the government in order to support the Chief-of-Staff's policy. He explained to Dayan that he would return only if he were able to convince the party to adopt his ideas on changing the election system; otherwise he would leave politics. He was fed up, Ben-Gurion said. At this stage, then, Dayan's predilection for war was not enough to lure Ben-Gurion back to the government.

On 20 August 1954, Ben-Gurion was visited at Sde Boker by Teddy Kollek, the Director-General of the Prime Minister's Office, and Abba Eban, Israel's ambassador to the United States and the United Nations. Eban, who was working vigorously for an American–Israeli alliance, reported to Ben-Gurion on his talks with Secretary of State John Foster Dulles, in which questions relating to arms supplies and a defence pact had been raised. Ben-Gurion argued that an alliance should be concluded only if there were no other choice. Such an alliance, he explained, with a nod towards Dayan's war ambitions, would result in a war of expansion, which he opposed: 'Our problem today is Jews, not territory, at least in the present period'.[11]

TWO AGAINST ONE

Ben-Gurion returned to the Ministry of Defence on 21 February 1955. Both Dayan and Peres were instrumental in this development, because of the positions they held and because of their close personal relations with the old/new Minister of Defence. Back in office, Ben-Gurion set up a forum of three – himself, Dayan and Peres – which came to be known as the 'Small Staff'. Once a week (usually on Thursdays) Ben-Gurion convened the group, with others invited according to the subject under discussion. Here Dayan and Peres could bring systematic, persistent pressure to bear on Ben-Gurion to reconsider the option of an Israeli-initiated war.[12]

On 27 February, the Sharett government decided on a large-scale reprisal operation north of Gaza ('Operation Black Arrow'). Although it was not the first raid of its kind, its unusual scale and the large number of Egyptians killed (38 soldiers) generated widespread reverberations. At the time of the raid Ben-Gurion was not yet fully abreast of affairs in the ministry. Nevertheless, the operation in Gaza was a fitting backdrop for his return to the government and a harbinger of events to come.

Immediately after the Gaza raid the first flickering of Ben-Gurion's new approach could be discerned. Citing the impressive though unplanned results of the operation, Ben-Gurion noted that 'it is important to display our military superiority over the strongest Arab state [Egypt]'.[13]

In March 1955, the domestic political atmosphere in Israel was ripe for an about turn in security policy. The opportunity came towards the end of the month. On the night of 24–25 March, a wedding took place in Patish, a small moshav in southern Israel. As the guests crowded in one of the rooms in the private home where the celebration was being held, hand grenades were thrown into the well-lit room and shots were fired. Between 15 and 20 people, some of them children, were wounded. One of the guests, a young 22-year-old volunteer named Varda Friedman, who was working with the moshav's new immigrants, was killed. The perpetrators' tracks led to the Gaza Strip. The country was shocked, perhaps more deeply than after similar events in the past.[14]

Ben-Gurion's reaction to the Patish attack was unusual, both in terms of the 'level of retaliation' and in its clear latent potential to trigger a war. His proposal was, simply, to drive the Egyptians out of the Gaza Strip – in other words, to capture this territory. Before putting his idea to Sharett and the cabinet, however, Ben-Gurion asked Dayan three questions which implied that he was fully aware of the implications of such an action. How long would it take to capture Gaza? Was the IDF ready for a war against Egypt? Was the IDF prepared for a war against all the Arab states? There is no evidence to show that the Chief-of-Staff tried to dissuade Ben-Gurion from submitting his plan to the cabinet for approval – on the contrary.[15]

For the first time since reassuming the defence portfolio, Ben-Gurion responded to a terrorist attack with an operative proposal of his own. On 25 February 1955, when a bicycle rider was murdered near Rehovot, Ben-Gurion had been back in office for only three days and the Chief-of-Staff was ready with the Black Arrow plan. On 19 March, a member of kibbutz Jezreel was killed by marauders from Jordan. As far as is known, that incident brought no concrete reaction from the defence establishment. But by the end of March Ben-Gurion was in full control. Did he want to utilize the reprisal for Patish to strike at Egypt, which he considered the main confrontation state? It would seem so. He admitted that he wanted to take the opportunity to repay the Egyptian President, Gamal Abdul Nasser, both for Egypt's repeated violations of the Armistice Agreement and for infringing on Israel's right of passage in the Gulf of Eilat and in Suez Canal.[16]

Following the Patish incident, in contrast to the past, the Minister of Defence not only put forward an initiative for a military response, but he also defined its goal and target. The usual practice was for the army to submit a plan of action to the Minister of Defence, who would either approve it and refer it to the cabinet, or reject it out of hand. Ben-Gurion's proposal spoke for the first time in concrete terms of an Israeli-initiated war. Even at the time this trend was clear: the argument in the cabinet following the Patish murder revolved around the question of whether Israel had a reasonable *casus belli* and not around the issue of reprisal *per se*. In the event, it was now obvious that Ben-Gurion had joined Dayan in the struggle against Sharett over an Israeli-launched war.

'A GUARANTEED MINORITY'

Ben-Gurion acted quickly. Already on Friday 25 March, he convened a consultation at his residence in Tel Aviv. The next day – the Sabbath – following an additional consultation with the Mapai leadership (again at his home) the cabinet met for an extraordinary session. In the meeting Sharett clashed sharply with Ben-Gurion. No decision was taken, and the discussion continued at the regular weekly cabinet meeting the next day. Again, there was no final decision but Ben-Gurion did not relent. On 28 March he visited Patish and a day later requested another discussion by the cabinet, only for his motion to be defeated by one vote. Opposing him were Prime Minister Sharett, three Mapai ministers, and all coalition members from other parties.[17]

Ben-Gurion knew from the outset that he would not be easily able to muster a majority in the cabinet. What then made him persist? On 30 March, with the discussion at its height, he ordered Dayan to call off the army's preparations because he had a 'guaranteed minority', as he put it, in the cabinet. Can the continuation of the discussion be explained solely in terms of Ben-Gurion's wish to pit his approach against the Prime Minister's? What would have happened had Ben-Gurion been victorious? Indeed, the outcome in Sharett's favour was not as self-evident as Ben-Gurion claimed. It was not a political debate over the party's platform or about basic principles for future action. The cabinet was convened to decide whether to execute a political–strategic plan. Ben-Gurion's aim was to change Israel's basic security policy. He placed on the cabinet's agenda, for the first time, the possibility of an Israeli-initiated limited war as part of a solution to the country's security problems. Following the vote Sharett summed up: 'We were spared a disaster which might have had incalculable results'.[18]

THE DEBATE OVER THE WAY AND THE DEBATE OVER THE PACE

The debate over Ben-Gurion's and Dayan's proposal to capture the Gaza Strip, in the wake of the Patish incident, had the effect of sharpening positions. In Sharett's account of the meeting, he argued that capturing the Gaza Strip would not solve the security problem. Both the Palestinians who would flee and those who would remain in place would continue to mount attacks against Israel, and with greater ferocity. What would Israel gain by making a brief conquest which would only produce an argument over whether to withdraw? Sharett believed that war would enable Israel to defeat the Arabs – but not to make peace with them. The only way for Israel to impose peace on the Arabs, he maintained, was by conquering Cairo, Damascus and Amman.[19]

Ben-Gurion, with Dayan's backing, retorted that Israel's strength lay in self-reliance and independence of action. Only this way could it wield political influence. International factors took second place, while Egypt was bent on expansion – not peace-seeking. Only a daring act, before the opportunity was lost, could contain Cairo. The Arab world was split and would not assist Egypt. Even Nasser might choose not to respond to the capture of Gaza, since his certain defeat by Israel was likely to rock his regime.

Nor would the Western powers take action, since Egypt had no defence pact with either of them. Domestic public opinion would prevent the Americans from intervening. As for Britain, if it were to invade the Negev, 'we will throw it out [of there] in disgrace'. In the same matter-of-fact way Ben-Gurion also dismissed the economic boycott that Israel was likely to face following the proposed operation. 'Should there be an economic boycott', he said, 'we will suffer, but we will endure'. The danger to the country's morale in the case of inaction, especially in the border settlements, must also be taken into account, the Minister of Defence added. In short, Ben-Gurion seemed to think, at least in late March 1955, that with one war Israel could solve a large proportion of its security problems.[20]

In the spring of 1955, then, Ben-Gurion no longer seemed to subscribe to his approach of a year earlier whereby 'people are important to us, not territories'. Yet, as has often been the case with Ben-Gurion, the change was not unequivocal. His comment about a 'guaranteed minority' and the serious hesitations he would display in the following months reflected the continuing equivocation, distress and even fear that characterized Ben-Gurion's behaviour in the run-up to and during the Sinai War.[21]

Ben-Gurion – even Ben-Gurion – needed support, even after his position on the question of an Israeli-initiated war was accepted at a later stage. The bulk of that support came from Dayan who as Chief-of-Staff was even more convinced than Ben-Gurion of the benefits of an initiated war. In the months to come the two would play out a riveting discourse, with Ben-Gurion taking the role of inhibitor and asking the difficult questions and Dayan acting as the accelerator, driving ahead on the road to war. The roles were tailor-made for the personality, age and positions of the two protagonists as they were then. Still, their interaction depended on basic agreement between them on the need for Israel to attack. Their argument with Sharett was over the road, while between them they disagreed about the pace.

Even if Ben-Gurion wanted to test and pressure Sharett and undermine his authority, he must have realized that his demand for a move that might lead to war might be implemented. More important, the seed was sown: an Israeli-initiated (limited) war was no longer just a private idea of Dayan. It was a concrete possibility that had the support of senior cabinet members, including leaders of Mapai such as Ben-Gurion himself, Levi Eshkol and Golda Meyerson (Meir). A policy which only yesterday seemed wild and irresponsible had suddenly become a reasonable proposition.

Dayan and Ben-Gurion lost no time in taking advantage of their success. On the day the Minister of Defence's proposal was narrowly defeated in the cabinet, kibbutz Nahal Oz, adjacent to Gaza, was shelled. It was the first incident of its kind since the 1948 War of Independence. In another incident that day in the same area, two Israeli soldiers were killed when their patrol hit a landmine.[22]

Ben-Gurion demanded another cabinet meeting, which was held the next day. He brought Dayan to the meeting (a highly unusual move at the time), who painted a grim picture whereby the continuation of patrols along the Gaza Strip was tantamount to suicide for the soldiers, whereas their suspension would jeopardize the Israeli settlements in the area. Dayan stopped short of drawing the unavoidable conclusion, but at once added details about the Egyptian army's deployment in the Gaza Strip. The hint was clear. Sharett, for one, immediately grasped Dayan's drift.

Dayan then left the meeting and Ben-Gurion took the floor. Yet he did not propose what Sharett had expected – an explicit military strike – after having failed to muster a cabinet majority the previous day. Instead he suggested that Israel declare the Armistice Agreement null and void due to Egypt's repeated violations of the agreement. Yet again Sharett won the day, but by the narrowest possible margin. The vote was a tie, which meant that the proposal was neither accepted nor rejected. This was a severe warning to the Prime Minister. The new security policy espoused by Ben-Gurion and Dayan was accepted by half the cabinet. Is it still arguable, at this stage, that Ben-Gurion merely wanted to weaken Sharett's position in the cabinet?[23]

'WE HAVE NOT AVENGED THE BLOOD'

Ben-Gurion's new approach following the Patish incident resulted in an immediate change in Dayan's orders to the army. The Chief-of-Staff had long been ripe for this reorientation.[24] His opinion about a necessary revision in security policy is better seen in his deeds than in his words. The minutes of General Staff meetings reveal little about the Chief of the General Staff's view of government policy. The General Staff rarely addressed planning questions, even at the level of strategy. For the most part the generals discussed subjects related to the IDF's work plan – replenishment, training, conditions of service, and so forth. Dayan did not usually share with the General Staff his qualms about policy or planning, but at the beginning of every meeting he supplied an update. His comments suggested the spirit which he sought to imbue in the commanders. In contrast to his relative restraint before the Patish murder, immediately after the incident he explained Egypt's responsibility to the General Staff. Stating that it was essential to react, and on a large scale, he added: 'I don't know whether this [the murder and sabotage raids] is happening with the knowledge of the Egyptian army – to a certain degree it doesn't matter'.[25]

A clear expression of the change can be found in the orders concerning routine security which were issued immediately after the murder at Patish and the shelling of Nahal Oz (which reinforced the view that force should be used against the Egyptians). Already on 3 April, after the attack on Nahal Oz and the emergency cabinet meeting in its wake, Dayan asked Ben-Gurion to approve IDF artillery fire and the capture of Egyptian outposts in the event of harassment of IDF patrols. Ben-Gurion gave the go-ahead, and Dayan issued an order stating that if an IDF patrol were fired upon, the enemy was to be shelled with 81mm mortars. If complications arose, the army was to cross the border and capture the nearest Egyptian outpost. On 17 May 1955, in a consultation held with the IDF leadership at the Prime Minister's residence, Dayan reported on a series of border incidents which had been sparked at the initiative of IDF units.[26]

Although one should not necessarily ascribe moderate intentions to the Egyptians or a desire to calm the situation along the border with Israel, it is difficult to ascertain what motivated the Egyptian activity – consisting of irregular firing and laying mines – along the border of the Gaza Strip from April to June 1955. President Nasser claimed that his troops and other forces, feeling themselves threatened by the IDF's operations in Gaza, frequently reacted by opening fire. He told the head of the United Nations Truce Supervision Organization (UNTSO) that he could not order his troops to desist from such actions.[27] The IDF's reactions along the border with Egypt became especially aggressive at beginning of the spring of 1955. What is important for our purposes is that the reactions were prompted by more than the desire for single-point reprisals.

Dayan had a largely free hand on routine security. In some areas he did not seek Ben-Gurion's approval, notably in operational planning and mounting immediate reactions to border incidents. On 11 April 1955, Dayan ordered the Operations Branch of the General Staff to plan, as instantaneous responses to every Egyptian attack, a series of punitive raids on military and civilian targets deep inside the Gaza Strip which would inflict casualties and destroy the targets. As far as is known, this was the first time since the 1948 War that such an order had been issued.

However, the relative quiet which descended on the sector after the Nahal Oz incident at the beginning of April until the middle of May did not allow for a serious operation. The few border incidents, some of them initiated by Israel, did not result in casualties, which were so often the trigger of Israeli reprisals. Sharett welcomed the situation, though he also instructed Abba Eban to apprise the United Nations, in the spirit of Ben-Gurion's proposal of 3 April, that continuation of the shooting and mine-laying along the border would bring about a situation in which the armistice would *de facto* cease to exist. Although Sharett himself did not support the actions of Ben-Gurion and Dayan, he thought it advantageous to make use of their policy in order to pressure the UN and Egypt.[28]

For his part Dayan kept Ben-Gurion informed about incidents on the borders in a constant effort to prompt him to act. Surprisingly, perhaps, the Minister of Defence was less perturbed about routine security at this time than either the Chief-of-Staff or the Prime Minister. The latter two seemed to be far more preoccupied with the possible escalation that might ensue. Sharett saw the risks, Dayan the opportunities, and Ben-Gurion encouraged Dayan to go on pressing his views on Sharett.

After three IDF officers were killed on 17 May 1955 when their vehicle hit a mine on the patrol road near kibbutz Kissufim, near the Gaza Strip, a reprisal operation was approved – the first since the Gaza raid – code-named Operation Pleshet. The Egyptian army was blamed for the mining, and Dayan wanted to take the opportunity to attack Egyptian forces.[29]

It was Dayan who initiated the operation. After Ben-Gurion approved Dayan's ideas, the 'Forum of Five' of the Mapai (the ruling party) leadership met – a body authorized by the Mapai Secretariat to decide on questions of reprisal before they were brought to the cabinet. Unlike the situation in the cabinet, Sharett found himself in a minority in this forum, facing Ben-Gurion, Meyerson and Eshkol, who were in favour of the operation (the fifth member, Zalman Aranne, was not present). Since the debate following the Patish incident at the end of March, Sharett had scrupulously convened the Forum of Five for preparatory discussions on reprisals. The Prime Minister was anxious to co-ordinate positions in order to avoid a situation in which he would have to decide against his party colleagues in the cabinet, drawing on the support of the other parties in the coalition.[30]

Dayan, who took part in the discussion and guided it, did not conceal the possibility that an aggressive military response, however limited, might assume proportions exceeding the original plan. Beyond the question of the operation's effectiveness as a reprisal, the discussion was at bottom a continuation of the debate over an Israeli-initiated war. Ben-Gurion repeated the view that he would prefer to expel the Egyptians from the Gaza Strip and annul the Armistice Agreement (a step that would probably mean war). He did most of the work for the Chief-of-Staff in this instance. It was clear that the two agreed about the need to heat up the border. In the absence of a cabinet majority, Ben-Gurion explained, he would make do with a small-scale operation. Sharett, though, continued to reject both a wider operation and the proposed reprisal raid, which he thought disproportionate.[31]

On the night of 18–19 May, a company-size IDF force attacked the Egyptian army's base opposite kibbutz Kissufim. The IDF also mined roads in the area. No one was killed on either side in the operation, which was on a scale similar to that of the Gaza raid. However, the very fact that the raid was approved was a victory for the activist approach of Ben-Gurion and Dayan. While Sharett thought that he could muster a cabinet majority against the operation, he did not want to utilize that majority against his party associates this time. He took some consolation in the fact that no one had been killed in the raid. But because the Egyptians had escaped without losses, 'there are undoubtedly some amongst us who are gritting their teeth – after all, we had not avenged the blood'.[32]

As for the IDF, an order appended to the reprisal raid (Pleshet 1) by the Operations Branch of the General Staff instructed all branches of the army to go on alert to deal with a possible Egyptian reaction to the attack. The order added: 'You must be ready to capture the Gaza Strip'. It was obviously an order that could mean only war. From this time, before every reprisal raid the possibility would be examined of dragging Egypt into a war.[33]

The Operations Branch soon also circulated an order of principle on this subject. Operational order David of 24 May contained clear directives for capturing the Gaza Strip 'on the night following an Egyptian attack'. The road to war is described here in IDF vernacular, but the underlying conception is readily discernible: 'As a result of an aggressive Egyptian action' – that is, a border incident of some kind – 'a situation is liable to emerge in which the IDF will have to react swiftly by executing a potent military operation' – meaning a reprisal raid. Now came the innovative principle (which had been adduced a week earlier in Operation Pleshet): 'Following the execution [of the reprisal raid] a further development should be expected, in the wake of which the IDF will capture the entire Gaza Strip'. The relevant IDF units were ordered to submit plans for approval within two days. The order also included detailed planning guidelines, such as the method of execution and a table of forces admissions. The order was to be circulated all the way down to the company commander level – proof that it was intended for immediate implementation, if and when the cause should arise.[34]

The new orders reflected Dayan's approach. The Chief-of-Staff considered Israel's inability to maintain normal life along its borders the equivalent of failure in war. Ensuring normal life, Dayan explained in an internal IDF lecture, is worth even the price of war.[35] Sharett called this policy (propounded, he believed, by Ben-Gurion and Dayan) 'a method of irritation for its own sake in order to push matters to a volatile crisis which will supposedly culminate in deliverance'. The debate over Pleshet strengthened Sharett in his view that Ben-Gurion supported Dayan unreservedly. In this case Sharett was right. Would Dayan himself, who took no major action without Ben-Gurion's approval, have drawn up orders which could only mean that efforts should be made to escalate border incidents at the risk of war?[36]

A PUZZLING QUIET

The Egyptian response to Pleshet came on 30 May. Two kibbutzim, Ein Ha-shlosha and Nirim, were shelled; two civilians were killed and four seriously wounded. The IDF replied with artillery fire. There is no doubt that from this time the border with Egypt was no longer perceived solely in terms of infiltrations. The road to war had been shortened, though war was not yet inevitable. The fact that the Egyptians had not gone beyond shelling meant that Dayan did not have a cause to demand an attack on the Gaza Strip.[37]

Near the end of June, Nasser, who had not long before refused to commit himself to quiet on the border, directed Colonel Salah Gohar, the head of the Palestinian Desk in the Egyptian Ministry of War, to hold talks with Israel on a local settlement along the border which would put an end to the incidents. The reason may have been Egypt's expectation of an arms deal with Czechoslovakia. The 'Gaza talks', which continued until the middle of August, contributed by their very existence to calm along the border. The dynamics (known at the time as 'local commanders' agreements') were more important than the results of the talks, which were inconsequential. One fact is irrefutable: while the talks lasted there was not one attempt, either by Egypt or by Israel, to heat up the border.[38]

There is no certainty that the quiet along the frontier was due to the fact that the Israeli political leadership was then preoccupied with a political crisis (the Sharett government fell at the end of June and Sharett formed a new government based on a smaller coalition, and impending elections). Still, a review of the events until then shows that the domestic political situation in Israel had a role in ensuring the relative quiet of those months. The fairly frequent incidents between the IDF and the Egyptian army in April–May 1955 were in no small measure the result of deliberate Israeli policy. The curbing of that policy, and not necessarily for security reasons, contributed substantially to bringing about quiet on the border.[39]

This conclusion does not eliminate the need to examine Egypt's role in the tension of April–May 1955 and the calm of July–August. True, Nasser had put forward ideas for a local border settlement, but at the same time he kept up his bellicose rhetoric, and activated terrorist and intelligence squads from Jordan and Lebanon. The international situation also played a part in maintaining the relative quiet of those months. The Gaza talks had the support of the Western powers, which encouraged any settlement that would pacify the region.[40]

Did the calm in the first part of that summer reflect a change in Ben-Gurion's and Dayan's policy, or had their policy perhaps failed? Not necessarily. Even in this period Dayan continued to press Ben-Gurion to approve heightened activity, and also to persuade him to reassume the premiership. Despite his ostensibly non-political position as commander of the army, Dayan expressed his opinion – in the midst of the election campaign for the Third Knesset – that a reorganization of the Mapai leadership was needed.[41]

Ben-Gurion, while supporting Dayan's approach, consistently rejected his proposals. The reason for Ben-Gurion's restraint was the election campaign, which temporarily moderated Israel's reprisal policy and by the same token reduced the prospect of dragging Egypt into a war by means of incidents related to routine security. In any event, Ben-Gurion headed Mapai's list in the election campaign, and as such was the party's candidate to serve as Prime Minister.

Although Mapai's strength was reduced in the Third Knesset, the possibility loomed of a more activist coalition in which the 'Sharett School of thought' would no longer command a majority. In this spirit Ben-Gurion began to conduct negotiations in early August 1955 with possible partners for a government under his leadership.[42]


ANOTHER STAGE IN THE DETERIORATING BORDER SITUATION

In Israel the political situation began to emerge more clearly. As he toiled to put together the new coalition, Ben-Gurion intimated that Israeli security policy was about to change. A series of internal statements and an open clash with Sharett at a meeting of the Mapai Centre on 8 August 1955 suggest that Ben-Gurion had given Dayan the go-ahead to resume his 'policy of deterioration' towards war.[43]

One of the clearest expressions of Ben-Gurion's thrust in this direction can be seen in the intensive effort to conclude an Israeli–American defence pact. Sharett and Ben-Gurion agreed that a security agreement with the United States was an urgent necessity. The Foreign Ministry and the Israeli embassy in Washington thought that such a treaty could be signed in the near future – were Israel not to sabotage it with its own hands, particularly by its security operations. The questions of Israel's relations with the United States in general, and of a security treaty in particular, were at the centre of the coalition's negotiations with the left-wing parties, which opposed American policy and objected to a security agreement. As a result of this, at least as Sharett and his loyalists in the Foreign Ministry saw it, Israeli restraint was now more essential than ever. Apparently the Foreign Ministry had not yet grasped the connection which Ben-Gurion saw between an Israeli-initiated war and the urgent need for an alliance with the United States.[44]

From the middle of August the security conception advocated by Ben-Gurion and Dayan faced a test of unprecedented gravity. Events in the realm of routine security brought Egypt and Israel to the brink of hostilities. By the end of the month it appeared that Dayan's conception of the link between basic security and routine security had a solid foundation to stand on.

On the morning of 22 August 1955, Egyptian army outposts opened fire on an IDF patrol near kibbutz Mefalsim. In reaction, the patrol's commander crossed the border and together with reinforcements captured the Egyptian Outpost No. 41. The Egyptians responded by shelling the area of the outpost and kibbutz Nahal Oz for several hours. That the Egyptians were responsible for the renewal of tensions along the border of the Gaza Strip seemed clear. Sharett, after lengthy agonizing, accepted this conclusion and approved a reprisal raid (see below). What he did not know, however, was that on the previous night, 20–21 August, an IDF unit had been sent to attack an Egyptian military camp near Rafah. The raid was unsuccessful. Although there is no definite evidence, it is reasonable to assume that the Egyptian fire, after a lengthy period of total quiet, came in response to the abortive attack on the camp.[45]

Israel's part in the escalation of late August was also illustrated by the reaction of the patrol that was attacked near Mefalsim. In storming the Egyptian outpost the patrol's commander was following the guidelines which Dayan had sought to instil since his tenure as head of Operations Branch, certainly from the time he became Chief-of-Staff, and with greater intensity since April 1955. It will be recalled that Dayan had stated at a meeting of the General Staff in April: 'In the event of firing on a patrol ... if complications arise, to cross the border, if necessary, and to capture the nearest Egyptian outpost'. In the first General Staff meeting after the August incident, Dayan was critical of the hasty decision by the patrol commander to cross the border, but of course praised him for the execution.

The Egyptians reacted harshly to the Mefalsim incident. Between 25 and 30 August, 16 Israelis were killed along the Egyptian border and in the southern part of the country. The Egyptians resorted to shelling, light-arms fire, ambushes, and mining roads near the border; they also captured two hills inside Israel, at Sabha, south of Nitzana – far from the Gaza Strip. For the first time the Egyptians employed an organized force of terror squads which were sent deep into Israel, especially around the Nes-Tsiona–Rehovot area. Egyptian planes penetrated Israeli air space and one of them was shot down.[46]

To the IDF, neither the Egyptian army's response nor the terrorist attacks following the Mefalsim incident came as a surprise. Indeed, the Israeli High Command seemed to have anticipated this type of reaction. The head of Military Intelligence, Yehoshafat Harkabi, explained to the General Staff that the Egyptians were aware of the Israeli policy underlying the incidents: 'The Egyptians see our actions on the 22nd as having originated from above. They stated already after the Gaza [operation] that they would give tit for tat. And there will be pressure on the political–military level to adopt that line. They are beefing up their force in the region and claiming that they are preparing for war. They do not fear war but incidents'. Harkabi added that 'the tension is helping Nasser unite the ranks in the [Arab] League and with a view towards the meeting of the [UN General] Assembly. Nasser is exploiting the current tension for political purposes'. The IDF, then, had decided to resort to preventive operations even before the Mefalsim incident in order to protect the civilian population in the interior of the country. Already on 21 August, the day before Mefalsim, the Operations Branch had issued the order for Operation Catch – to apprehend Egyptian intelligence scouts who were operating in southern Israel.[47]

On 26 August Dayan ordered the army not to permit any Egyptian movement, including civilian movement, near the Gaza Strip border. The IDF should 'snipe along the line'. Immediately afterwards he called Ben-Gurion out of the coalition negotiations in order to propose an operation in the Gaza Strip. Dayan assumed that a large-scale attack would not be approved, instead suggesting a series of small operations to be carried out simultaneously. Ben-Gurion met that same day (Friday) with Sharett, who was still the head of the transition government. Sharett ordered the IDF not to act but to await developments; the subject would be brought to the cabinet at its regular Sunday meeting. Thus, on 28 August, Dayan outlined his plan to the cabinet. The ministers were not enthusiastic, Dayan later wrote in his autobiography.

Sharett was thus able to snipe away at the already reduced plan. A few 'retail raids' were decided on: four or five small squads, which would operate during two or three nights. Dayan ordered the paratroops to act immediately, but they were not ready until the following night, 29–30 August 1955.[48]

## SHARETT'S LINE OR BEN-GURION'S LINE

No sooner had the approval been given than Sharett changed his mind – as he had on more than one occasion in the past (notably in Operation Pleshet) – and tried to get the raid called off. Only two days earlier US Secretary of State Dulles had made public the Anglo-American Alpha Plan for resolving the Arab–Israeli conflict. Dulles's declaration included assurances that Israel had long wanted to hear: a guarantee of its borders and assistance in obtaining an international loan in order to pay compensation to the Arab refugees. In the background, the talks on an Israeli–American security pact continued.[49]

Sharett feared that an Israeli military operation would scuttle all these developments. The pretext for calling off the operation was found in the person of the self-appointed mediator Elmer Jackson, an American Quaker, who knew Nasser personally and had arrived in the region to try his hand at resolving the conflict. Jackson arrived in Israel in mid-August and then went on to Egypt. In Israel he apparently asked Sharett to ensure that the escalation would not continue, so as not to harm his chances.[50]

The result was that at 1.00 am on 30 August, after the Israeli squads had already set out on their mission, Colonel Nehemiah Argov, the Minister of Defence's adjutant, arrived at Dayan's forward command post in kibbutz Nir Yitzhak with Sharett's order (and Ben-Gurion's assent) not to execute the raids. Dayan obeyed and ordered the squads back.[51]

The Chief-of-Staff then rushed to Jerusalem, gave Ben-Gurion a report of the events, and handed him a letter of resignation:

> Minister of Defence, the discrepancy between the security policy which has recently been set by the government and the security policy which seems to me essential, is depriving me of the possibility of bearing the responsibility required from the Chief of the General Staff. I therefore submit my resignation from my current position and request that you bring this for the cabinet's approval ...

Having read the message, Ben-Gurion demanded a renewed discussion by the cabinet. The Chief-of-Staff's resignation brought Ben-Gurion, for the second time since the elections (the first had been in the 8 August meeting of the Mapai Centre), into an open confrontation with

Sharett: 'Either Sharett's line or Ben-Gurion's line'. Pursuing each alternately, he argued, had only caused damage. Immediately after receiving Dayan's resignation, Ben-Gurion convened the Mapai ministers in the cabinet, apprised them of the Chief-of-Staff's move, and disappeared from sight for 24 hours, even though the State President had already formally charged him with the task of forming the government. The joint protest of the Minister of Defence and the Chief-of-Staff had the intended effect. Sharett accepted, through Argov, Dayan's first proposal (of 26 August) to mount a major operation in the Gaza Strip. In the meantime, the Egyptian army and the terrorist squads which operated under its auspices were involved in additional actions, which only strengthened the view that a reprisal was necessary. Already on 30 August the cabinet (without Ben-Gurion's presence) approved Operation Elkayam in Khan Yunis, the IDF's largest reprisal raid until then.[52]

On 31 August, the IDF blew up the front of the Khan Yunis police station and a nearby gas station, sabotaged a hospital as well as buildings in the village of Ibsan, and attacked an Egyptian military position. Seventy-two Egyptian soldiers were killed and 58 wounded. The raiding force suffered one soldier killed and 17 wounded. Ben-Gurion reappeared as mysteriously as he had vanished and Dayan withdrew his letter of resignation.[53]

In early September 1955, following the Khan Yunis attack, Israel and Egypt began to mass forces along their common border. The two armies were soon exchanging artillery barrages. War seemed imminent. However, Nasser's Egypt was in the midst of an arms deal of unprecedented scope – and far-reaching implications – with Czechoslovakia, while Ben-Gurion was about to reassume the premiership and apparently did not yet feel sufficiently prepared for war. The result was that both leaders acceded to the UN's call for a ceasefire. War was averted, at least for the time being.[54]

Was this yet another internal political exercise? Probably not. Ben-Gurion was busy putting together his next government at the time. Nothing stood in the way of his return to power. The operation was a fully fledged statement of political intentions. Henceforth the internal balance of forces would be clear. The security concept of Ben-Gurion and Dayan had become the leading approach. Their long-running dispute with Sharett was not over the goal – acknowledged by all to be peace – but over how to reach it. Sharett favoured an approach that would moderate the conflict, whereas Ben-Gurion and Dayan believed in escalation as a means to achieve better results in future peace negotiations. Incidentally, the events of early September 1955 also exposed a disagreement between Ben-Gurion and Dayan – not over the goal and not over the way to achieve it, but over the pace and the timing of an Israeli-initiated war.[55]

In retrospect, it would appear that the foundations for a new Israeli security policy were laid in the spring–summer of 1955: an initiated war as a realistic and indeed preferred option. That policy bore no relation to the Suez crisis which erupted a year later. Nevertheless, the crisis over Suez in the summer–autumn of 1956 found Israel prepared for war.

## NOTES

1. Moshe Dayan, *Avnei Derekh*, Tel Aviv, 1976, p.24.
2. Ibid.; Shabtai Teveth, *Moshe Dayan*, Tel Aviv, 1972.
3. See, for example, Sharett's conclusions from the Olshan-Dori Commission (which investigated the 'Security Mishap'): 'Dayan cannot remain as Chief-of-Staff', in Moshe Sharett, *Yoman Ishi*, Tel Aviv, 1978, Vol. III, p.666. On Sharett's fears of Dayan, ibid., p.699.
4. On the central place of Dayan and Peres in Israel's preparations for war during this period, see M. Golani, 'Dayan Leads to War', *Iyunim*, 4, 1994.
5. Sharett, *Yoman*, Vol. III, p.657; ibid., Vol. IV, p.1006.
6. Ibid., Vol. IV, p.1048.
7. Dayan, *Avnei Derekh*, pp.125, 143–5; Sharett, *Yoman*, Vol. II, p.591. The term 'basic security' refers to a confrontation in the form of war against one or more Arab states; 'routine security' refers to the effort to prevent the penetration of the state by hostile elements, particularly Palestinians. The two terms were used by the defence establishment from the mid-1950s. See, for example, Memorandum by Lt. Col. Yuval Ne'eman, Head of Strategic Planning Department in Operations Branch, 6 January 1955, Israel Defence Foces Archives, 637/56/29 (hereinafter IDFA).
8. Teveth, *Moshe Dayan*, p.413; Dayan, *Avnei Derekh*, p.129.
9. Sharett, *Yoman*, Vol. III, p.639; David Ben-Gurion's Diary, Ben-Gurion Archives, Sde Boker, February–June 1954 (hereinafter BGD).
10. Dayan, *Avnei Derekh*, pp.122–3, 125.
11. BGD, 20 August 1954.
12. Ibid., 2 March 1955; IDFA, Weekly Meeting Files, Nos 822–97.
13. Sharett, *Yoman*, Vol. III, pp.816, 894. For a detailed analysis of the Gaza operation and its political context, see my article, 'Israel and the Gaza Operation – Continuity or Change?', in Motti Golani (ed.), *Black Arrow: The Gaza Operation and Israel's Reprisal Policy in the 1950s*, Tel Aviv, 1994, pp.23–34 (Hebrew).
14. On the reaction to the Patish terrorist attack see Sharett, *Yoman*, Vol. III, pp.861–6; Dayan, *Avnei Derekh*, p.143; Nathan Alterman's poem 'On a Flower Named After Varda', in Bracha Habas, *Tnuah Lelo Shem*, Tel Aviv, 1964, p.189.
15. Dayan, *Avnei Derekh*, p.143.
16. On the murder of the member of Kibbutz Jezreel, see 'Report on Routine Security for 1955–1956', History Branch, IDF, 1957 (hereinafter RS Report); General Staff meeting, 21 March 1955, IDFA, 847/62/29; Sharett, *Yoman*, Vol. III, p.865.
17. On the course of events following the murder at Patish, see Sharett, *Yoman*, Vol. III, pp.861–99; BGD, 25, 27–28 March 1955.
18. Dayan, *Avnei Derekh*, p.143; Sharett, *Yoman*, Vol. III, p.894.
19. Sharett, *Yoman*, Vol. III, pp.873–4.
20. BGD, 6 April 1955; Sharett, *Yoman*, Vol. III, pp.874–5. It was in the cabinet discussion of the events relating to Patish that Ben-Gurion, for the first time, as far as is known, used the famous expression 'UM Shmoom'.
21. Actions motivated by fear were not foreign to Ben-Gurion, and he did not disavow his fears. On 14 December 1949, after Jerusalem had been annexed to Israel and declared its capital, Ben-Gurion wrote in his diary: 'I do not always express all my fears – because I am afraid I will frighten our comrades and the movement [the party] too much; and out of fear I favour violating the UN resolution immediately and by actions'.
22. RS Report.

23. Sharett, *Yoman*, Vol. III, pp.896–9.
24. An echo of the change can be found in the Rules of Engagement issued by Operations Branch: 'Orders to Central Command', 29 April, 11 May 1955, IDFA, 637/56/14.
25. General Staff Meeting, opening remarks by the Chief-of-Staff, 28 March 1955, IDFA, 847/62/29.
26. Dayan's letter to Ben-Gurion, and to Head of Operations Branch, 4 April 1955, IDFA, 847/62/29.
27. This was probably the spirit of Nasser's conversation with Burns, the head of the UN's Truce Supervision Observers staff, though the record went through several filters. Burns reported on the conversation to Sharett on 7 June. Yosef Tekoah, the Israeli representative of the Foreign Ministry to the Armistice Commission, who was present at the Sharett–Burns meeting, conveyed its contents to the Chief-of-Staff on 9 June. See Dayan, *Avnei Derekh*, p.145. Sharett described the talk with Burns in his diary, Sharett, *Yoman*, Vol. IV, pp.1047–8. These sources are insufficient to understand Nasser's motives during this period. For our purposes what is important is the information that reached Israel.
28. Sharett to Eban, 6 April 1955, Israel State Archives, 2454/6 (hereinafter ISA); Sharett, *Yoman*, Vol. IV, pp.999–1000.
29. 'Survey of Routine Security 1951–1956', History Department Archives (hereinafter HDA), 64/2. Subsequent reference: RS Survey; 'Operational Activity of the IDF 1955–1956', HDA, 64/2 (hereinafter Operational Activity).
30. On the private reprisal perpetrated by Meir Har-Tsion and his friends, see Sharett, *Yoman*, Vol. IV, 17 April 1955, pp.941–2; and the consultation on the eve of Operation Pleshet, ibid., 17 May 1955, pp.1000–1003.
31. Sharett, *Yoman*, Vol. IV, pp.1006, 1009; RS Survey.
32. BGD, 17 May 1955; Sharett, *Yoman*, Vol. IV, 19 May 1955, p.1009.
33. 'Appendix to Operation Pleshet – Pleshet 1', Operations Branch, 24 May 1955, IDFA, 637/56/14.
34. Sharett, *Yoman*, Vol. IV, meeting on Pleshet, 17 May 1955, pp.1000–1008; directive on operational order David, oral approval of directive, Operations Branch, 24 May 1955, IDFA, 637/56/14.
35. Dayan, *Avnei Derekh*, 13 June 1955, p.145.
36. Sharett, *Yoman*, Vol. IV, 11 April 1955, pp.920, 1007.
37. RS Survey.
38. RS Survey. On the 'Gaza talks' see 'Tekoah Memorandum', 6 September 1955, ISA, 2454/7; and memoirs of E.L.M. Burns, *Between Arab and Israeli*, London, 1962, pp.69–84.
39. Even though the connection between the internal political arena and a state's external reactions is natural, it is given little explicit verbal expression. My supposition stems from a summation of the relevant events.
40. See M.B. Oren, 'Escalation to Suez: The Egypt–Israel Border War 1949–1956', *Journal of Contemporary History*, Vol. 24, 1989, pp.359–60.
41. Sharett, *Yoman*, Vol. IV, pp.1037, 1048; Dayan's comments on this subject can be found in Dayan, *Avnei Derekh*, pp.143–4.
42. BGD, 31 July 1955. A series of meetings was held with the leaders of Ahdut Ha-avoda and Mapam, neither of which participated in the previous government, as part of the negotiations to form a new government: conversation with Mapam leaders Meir Yaari and Yaacov Hazan, 7 August 1955, and conversation with Ahdut Ha-avoda leaders Israel Galili, Yigal Allon, and Moshe Aram, 12 August 1955, Ben-Gurion Archives, Sde Boker (BGA) – Records of meetings.
43. BGD, 31 July 1955. On the discussion in the Mapai Centre on 8 August see Michael Bar-Zohar, *Ben-Gurion*, Vol. III, Tel Aviv, 1978, pp.1144–5; Sharett, *Yoman*, Vol. IV, pp.1116–18; and see also the protest letter by Yavnieli, a party veteran, to Ben-Gurion against his fierce attack on Sharett at the Mapai Centre meeting, 11 August 1955, BGA – Correspondence.
44. On the discussion with the Left on the question of a security treaty with the United States, see Ben-Gurion's meetings with the leaders of Mapam and Ahdut Ha-avoda during August, see note 42.
45. For a description of the incident, see General Staff meeting, 29 August 1955, IDFA,

847/62/30. The head of the Operations Department, Colonel Narkiss, described what took place there. See also 'Events Report of Central Command', 26 August 1955, IDFA, 637/56/15. On the operation at Rafah, see summation report on routine security which was drawn up as preparation for a book on the 'reprisal operations' (unpublished), HDA, 64/9.

46. General Staff meetings, 18 April 1955, IDFA, 847/62/29; 29 August 1955, IDFA, 847/62/30.

47. Remarks by Colonel Harkabi, Head of Military Intelligence, at General Staff meeting, 29 August 1955, IDFA, 847/62/30; see 'Operation Catch' for apprehending intelligence scouts operating in southern Israel, Operations Branch, 21 August 1955, IDFA, 637/56/15.

48. Dayan, *Avnei Derekh*, pp.150–51; General Staff meeting, 29 August 1955, IDFA, 847/62/30.

49. Eliyahu Elath, *Through the Mists of Time*, Jerusalem, 1986, p.69 (Hebrew).

50. Sharett, *Yoman*, Vol. IV, p.1131; Bar-Zohar, *Ben-Gurion*, Vol. III, pp.1146–8.

51. Mordechai Gur, a company commander in the Paratroops Battalion, claimed that his force nevertheless carried out its mission that night. Mordechai (Motta) Gur, *Company D*, Tel Aviv, 1966, pp.9–14.

52. Dayan, *Avnei Derekh*, 26–31 August 1956, pp.150–52.

53. Operation Elkayam – The Battle for the Khan Yunis Police Station and Outpost 132, General Staff, HDA, H-381-1-1956.

54. See, on this, the memorandum by Yosef Tekoah, Israeli Foreign Ministry liaison to the Armistice Commissions with the neighbouring Arab states, 6 September 1955, ISA, 2454/7.

55. Sharett, *Yoman*, Vol. II, 31 January 1954, p.332.

# The 1956 Sinai Campaign: David Ben-Gurion's Policy on Gaza, the Armistice Agreement and French Mediation

## MORDECHAI GAZIT

The many books and monographs devoted to the 1956 Sinai Campaign (Mivtza Kadesh) seem to justify the conclusion that everything concerning this event has been thoroughly studied and is well known. Further research, however, still manages to highlight new facets, three of which will be discussed here.

The first pertains to David Ben-Gurion's attitude to the Gaza Strip. Contrary to the received wisdom, including the views of some of his closest associates, Ben-Gurion did not view the Strip as something which Israel should be wary of holding on to. Practically all the relevant documents are now available and it is clear that there were various phases in Ben-Gurion's position. In 1949 he declared his willingness to incorporate the Gaza Strip into Israel and to integrate its entire Arab population, both refugees and permanent residents. In 1956, after the capture of this territory, Ben-Gurion's position became more realistic. He now insisted on maintaining a hold over the Gaza Strip without annexing it. How important this territory was to Ben-Gurion can be inferred from his protracted diplomatic struggle to keep it. The Prime Minister was ready to settle for *de facto* Israeli control and dispense with the trappings of sovereignty, and even to tolerate a United Nations (UN) presence in Gaza. Unlike his attitude in 1949, Ben-Gurion now recoiled from assuming responsibility for all the Palestinian refugees in Gaza. Even so, he was prepared to pay a considerable price by giving a commitment to raise the standard of living of the permanent, non-refugee Gaza inhabitants (then estimated at 60,000) and also to absorb some of the Gaza refugees in Israel in the framework of a UN plan to resolve the refugee problem as a whole (the refugee population in Gaza

Mordechai Gazit, a former Director-General of the Prime Minister's Office, is a Senior Research Fellow at the Truman Institute for Peace Studies at the Hebrew University in Jerusalem.

was then estimated at 260,000). On one occasion Ben-Gurion went so far as to say that even international sanctions would not deter Israel from holding on to Gaza. What spurred him in his efforts to maintain this position was the issue of Israel's security and defence. He feared that an Egyptian return to the Strip, coupled with renewed terrorist raids by Palestinian refugees, would actually put Israel in jeopardy, being convinced that only Israel's presence there could obviate this danger. In the end Ben-Gurion failed to achieve this goal and was forced into ordering a complete Israeli withdrawal from the Gaza Strip.

The second observation, almost as surprising as the first, concerns the role which the 1949 Armistice Agreement was destined to play in the 'Understanding' of 1 March 1957 ending the crisis caused by the military campaign. Scrutiny of Ben-Gurion's moves in the period from November 1956 to March 1957 reveals how crucial his new stand on the seven-year-old Armistice Agreement with Egypt was to become. He seems to have been genuinely convinced that his November 1956 declaration in the Knesset that the Armistice Agreement was 'dead' was unassailable. Still, it is difficult to imagine that Ben-Gurion actually believed that by releasing himself unilaterally from the Agreement he would succeed in spiriting away the legal contention of both the UN and the United States that Egypt's right to be in the Strip was embedded in the Armistice Agreement. Furthermore, Ben-Gurion did not foresee that the UN and the US would eventually find a way out of the crisis, based on the very Agreement he had denounced. The US Secretary of State, John Foster Dulles, was to contend that if the Armistice Agreement was invalidated, then the US had nothing to latch on to in order to give Israel even a semblance of assurance to make its withdrawal from Sharm al-Sheikh and Gaza less risky. Ben-Gurion had also declared that with the Agreement's 'demise', the old armistice demarcation line had been erased, thereby enabling Israel to incorporate the Strip. It is unlikely, however, that he thought that this kind of argument would carry weight with Dulles and the UN Secretary-General Dag Hammarskjold, both strong-willed and able personalities. The two of them insisted that there was no juridical alternative to the Armistice Agreement, on which a future understanding for ending the crisis could be based.

Had Israel, in early December 1956, heeded the advice of Ralph Bunche, the UN Under-Secretary-General and recipient of the Nobel Prize for fathering the 1949 Armistice Agreement, and formally repudiated the Agreement through the UN, then the UN and the US might perhaps have been persuaded to find a legal device other than the Armistice Agreement. To assist them in this effort, Israel would have had to launch a vigorous diplomatic campaign to convince third parties to acquiesce in the suspension of the Agreement. This advice was given by Bunche when Gaza was still low on the list of UN Secretariat priorities.

More than once in December 1956 the Israeli representatives in the UN told Jerusalem that the UN had not yet come up with a Gaza policy. This might have been the right moment for Israel to seize the initiative and try to win Hammarskjold over by agreeing to have the newly created UN international force, UNEF (United Nations Emergency Forces), stationed in the Gaza Strip, with Israel remaining in charge of security and civilian matters. Israel, however, did not act upon Bunche's advice. The window of opportunity was closed, if indeed it had ever existed, and Hammarskjold would soon grasp at the hesitant hints of Mahmoud Fawzi, the Egyptian Foreign Minister, to the effect that if Egypt were allowed to return to the Strip, it might be ready to consider some changes in its Gaza policy.

What might have helped Israel to persuade the UN to find a substitute for the Armistice Agreement was President Eisenhower's attitude. The US President had pointed out to Dulles on several occasions that Gaza had never been part of Egypt. He opined that since the UN had been behind the 1949 Agreement, it was not unreasonable to assume that it could admit, perhaps even initiate, changes in the Armistice Agreement.

Events would show, however, that Dulles got his way. In the last week of February 1957 he proposed an 'Understanding' which would consist of unilateral statements made by Israel, the US, France and others in the UN General Assembly. These statements would express certain 'hopes and expectations', without anyone demurring. This was the agreed-upon diplomatic scenario.

The third new facet about the 1956 Campaign concerns French mediation efforts on the eve of the UN General Assembly meeting of 1 March 1957 when the 'Understanding' was about to be announced. American documents show that the French efforts, though highly valued by the Israeli participants, were effectively nothing but a matter of clever orchestration on the part of Dulles. The Foreign Secretary knew that Israel would only agree to leave the Gaza Strip in return for an American assurance that should the 'Understanding' collapse and Gaza become yet again a threat, Israel would have the right to take measures to defend its interests (in accordance with Article 51 of the UN Charter) with the US indicating comprehension. Dulles thought that such an Israeli expectation was perfectly justified and said so to Eisenhower and Hammarskjold. All the same, he decided that American interests in the Arab countries obliged the United States to withhold the necessary assurance to Israel on Gaza.

Instead, Dulles manipulated matters so as to have the French include a passage in their statement in the UN General Assembly to the effect that Israel might be forced to act 'if the "Understanding" broke down'. He also persuaded Hammarskjold not to take exception to either the

French or the Israeli statements voicing such warnings. Clearly, had Hammarskjold expressed dissatisfaction with the French and Israeli statements, he would have endangered the whole 'Understanding'. By making sure that Hammarskjold would go along, Dulles clinched the matter. Understandably, Ben-Gurion was pleased with the French statement, but he told the US ambassador in Israel that this did not lessen his disappointment. He had expected to hear from the Americans what the French had said.


THE STRUGGLE TO KEEP GAZA

What was the position taken by Ben-Gurion on incorporating the Gaza Strip into Israel? Some of those who worked closely with the Prime Minister affirm that he had serious misgivings about such a possibility. To prove their point, they cite remarks made or written by Ben-Gurion. Abba Eban, for example, recounts that on one occasion Ben-Gurion burst out: 'Gaza as part of Israel could be like a cancer. In return for a small sliver of territory we would take responsibility for some two hundred and fifty thousand Arabs ... Our interest in Gaza is security. To take a small territory with a vast Arab population would be the worst possible exchange'.[1]

Ben-Gurion himself confided to his diary on 10 March 1957 that:

> Gaza, in itself, is a pain in the neck, in all circumstances. Be it under Egyptian rule, Israeli rule, UN rule or combined rule. Egyptian rule would be the worst thing. It would be somewhat less dangerous if Israel alone ruled there. The danger would be of two kinds: material – how can we support 260,000 permanent inhabitants. The political danger is even greater. There can be no doubt that the refugees and others will perpetrate acts of terror. Can we crush them like the British did in Cyprus or the French in Algeria? ... The Gaza Strip is a curse and a danger under all circumstances and on its account we ought not to endanger our security in the future and become outcasts in the world ...[2]

It should be noted, however, that this entry of Ben-Gurion's was made after he had ordered the Israeli withdrawal from Gaza. In fact, Ben-Gurion's attitude on Gaza underwent changes and its later version was different from the earlier one. Mordechai Bar-On calls Ben-Gurion's attitude 'ambivalent',[3] but this description does not properly describe Ben-Gurion's position. On two occasions before the Sinai Campaign, he had expressed readiness to annex the Gaza Strip. He did so in April 1949, committing himself to absorb all Gaza refugees into Israel proper. This commitment, initially an oral one, was soon to become a formal written commitment to the UN Palestine Conciliation

Commission, given on 29 May 1949.[4] The US evinced much interest,[5] and had Egypt not immediately and discourteously rejected this proposal, the US would have arranged a meeting between Egyptian and Israeli representatives. Preparations for such a meeting were already underway.

Six years later, in March 1955, Ben-Gurion brought a proposal to the Israeli government to order the Israeli army to expel the Egyptians from the Strip. Ben-Gurion was then Minister of Defence in Moshe Sharett's cabinet, shortly after his return from his voluntary exile in Sde Boker. His proposal was supported by only four ministers besides Ben-Gurion himself. To those who were alarmed by the prospect of absorbing so big an Arab minority into Israel, Ben-Gurion said that it would be possible to open two corridors for the Gaza Arabs who so chose to leave and go to Egypt or Jordan.[6]

The third occasion where Ben-Gurion evinced willingness to keep the Gaza Strip was after it was taken by the Israeli army in the Sinai Campaign of 1956. From the earliest days after the end of fighting the Prime Minister stressed that while the Strip had been 'liberated', the Sinai Peninsula had simply been 'conquered'. In his reply to President Eisenhower's communication of 8 November 1956, Ben-Gurion expressed readiness to order the withdrawal of the Israeli forces from 'Egypt'. He used the word 'Egypt' advisedly in order to say that withdrawal from Sinai posed no problem since it was Egyptian territory in every sense, but this was not the case with Gaza. Ben-Gurion would strenuously oppose the idea of giving up the Israeli hold on the Strip which 'was not Egyptian and has never been so'.

The determined struggle carried on by Israel for four months to maintain its control over the Strip, if only de facto, does not leave a shred of doubt that Ben-Gurion had kept his assessment from the days of Israel's War of Independence that Egyptian presence in Gaza was one of the greatest fiascos of that war and a danger to Israel's security. He considered the US to be the main culprit for this, reminding the US ambassador to Israel (on 31 December 1956) that in 1948, when Israeli forces were about to expel the Egyptians from Gaza, the US administration intervened and prevented this from happening.[7] He was thinking of the sharply worded demand of President Truman (31 December 1948) to end the fighting and withdraw the Israeli forces from al-Arish in Sinai. The objective of the Israeli forces was to occupy Gaza after completing its encirclement from the south. Ben-Gurion told the American ambassador that unlike in 1948 this time he had made up his mind that Gaza was not to revert to Egypt. UN support for Gaza's return to Egypt would be a 'fatal mistake'. The Egyptian presence in Gaza was, he said, a 'political anomaly which has no moral validity'.

It is not irrelevant to mention here that proof of Ben-Gurion's consistent interest in controlling Gaza resurfaced a decade after the Sinai Campaign. In 1967, Ben-Gurion, then already retired, again expressed his opinion that Gaza was a problem that Israel ought to confront squarely and courageously. In a detailed declaration on 19 June 1967 regarding the future of the territories occupied in the Six Day War, he stated: 'The Gaza Strip will remain in the State of Israel and Israel will make efforts to settle the refugees on the West Bank, which will be autonomous, or in any other Arab country, with the consent of the refugees and the ... assistance of the State of Israel'. He offered to give the West Bankers an outlet to the sea in Haifa, Ashdod or Gaza. He also offered the Kingdom of Jordan an outlet 'of the kind granted to the West Bank'.[8] It is quite clear that Ben-Gurion would not have proposed Gaza as an outlet to the sea just as he proposed Haifa and Ashdod to the Palestinians and Jordanians, had he not seen it as a territory which Israel could dispose of freely.

On 2 August 1967 Ben-Gurion told students that Gaza was part of Israel.[9] When he said somewhat later that in return for real peace he would be ready to give back all the occupied territories, except for Jerusalem and the Golan Heights, it is an open question whether he meant to include Gaza. What is certain is that by 1972 he had made up his mind in favour of Israel's keeping considerably more than just Jerusalem and the Golan. He explained that five years had elapsed since the war, and 'if the Arabs were not ready to make peace, we are not committed to giving back [the territories]. We cannot take it upon ourselves to retain all we have occupied, but there are territories where this (i.e., keeping them) is possible'.[10] In his interview he did not mention Gaza specifically, but it is quite certain that having to give back Gaza in 1957 still rankled with Ben-Gurion for years, and undoubtedly until 1972.[11]

On 2 November 1956 the Gaza Strip was taken. Five days later Ben-Gurion declared in the Knesset that so far as Israel was concerned, the 1949 Armistice Agreement with Egypt was 'dead and would not come to life again'. With the death of the Armistice Agreement, he added, the armistice demarcation lines had also breathed their last breath.[12] Henceforth the line dividing the Strip from Israel was no longer in existence. This is what Ben-Gurion was telling President Eisenhower indirectly on 8 November when he said that Israel did not intend to annex Sinai. In putting it this way, he was implying that while Israel's non-annexationist intentions towards Sinai were clear, Gaza was a wholly different issue. Several days later the Prime Minister recalled in the Knesset a speech he had made to soldiers in which he said that one of the objectives of the war was to 'liberate this piece of our homeland [*moledet* in Hebrew] seized by the invader'. The allusion to Gaza was unmistakable.[13] Soon thereafter Ben-Gurion was even more explicit: 'Israel would on no account agree to Egyptian invaders returning to the Gaza Strip'.[14] This formulation was carefully chosen. Ben-Gurion had changed his mind since 1949, when he proposed to annex the Strip and its inhabitants. He had now reached the conclusion that straight annexation, with all that went with it, was undesirable and might prove dangerous. Instead, Israel should insist on remaining in effective control of Gaza and on not letting the Egyptians return. Nor could he permit the entry into the Strip of the newly established UN force (UNEF); further, the Israeli civilian administration ought to be maintained and the police should be under Israeli control. Israel would not assume responsibility for the upkeep and resettlement of the Gaza refugees. The Israeli administration would, however, improve the economic condition of the 60,000 permanent Gaza residents.[15] The general question of the Arab refugees would have to be dealt with by the UN. The Knesset approved Ben-Gurion's statement.[16]

Early in November 1956 the US and the UN were already requesting Israel to leave Gaza. This was a firm demand, presented with a tone of finality. On 2 November the UN General Assembly, with US support, adopted a resolution demanding Israel to withdraw. Israel consented and began a gradual withdrawal of its forces from Sinai, but not from Gaza. During the first weeks Israeli efforts focused on the question of the freedom of navigation in the Gulf of Aqaba (Eilat). In the UN Secretariat, as well as in Washington, the issue of Gaza was still dormant. At one of the meetings between the Israeli representatives and Dulles, the former understood the US Secretary as saying that Gaza had never been part of Egypt and that he did not know what future arrangements would be made there. This pleased Ben-Gurion who expressed his delight to the US ambassador in Israel. Washington, however, was quick to put things right. True, Dulles had said that Gaza had never been Egyptian, but he had also said that it had never been on the Israeli side of the demarcation line. The matter of future arrangements was indeed open, but the US supported the UN General Assembly resolution which urged Israel to withdraw from Gaza.[17]

The US administration did not enter into more detailed talks with Israel until February 1957; and when it did so, this was apparently because Congressional and public opinion had become sympathetic to the Israeli case.[18] Parallel with Israel's talks with Dulles, its diplomats also conducted negotiations with the UN Secretary-General. It emerged that even the UN Secretariat was then less concerned with the Gaza question than with the issue of maritime freedom of passage. Ralph Bunche, one of Hammarskjold's deputies, told Abba Eban, the Israeli ambassador to the UN and the US, that opinions in the UN Secretariat were divided as to whether the organization should assume direct responsibility for Gaza.

The Secretariat wanted to preserve UN rights on Gaza but without having to exercise them. The UN was concerned that if it assumed full responsibility, it would have to carry it forever with the US having to foot the bill, a difficult proposition at a time when the US Congress was reluctant to assume additional financial burdens. Eban reported to Jerusalem, possibly because Bunche had told him so, that if Israel showed itself willing to absorb a considerable number of the Gaza refugees, it would thereby 'make it possible [for the UN] to acquiesce in our [Israel's] staying on [in Gaza]'.[19] Two weeks later Bunche told Eban that he had some ideas concerning Gaza's future, but in the meantime it was desirable that the present 'nebulous situation' continue.[20]

Ben-Gurion himself unwaveringly adhered to his position that Israel must not leave Gaza. On 25 December he cabled Eban that 'under no circumstances shall we let the Egyptians return to Gaza. In my view, we should not annex the Strip formally, but our security requires that no Egyptian or UN force be in the Strip ... We shall gladly discuss with the US how to solve the general refugee question and that of Gaza'.[21] This position was endorsed by the government on 31 December.

Ben-Gurion's strong determination to control Gaza was expressed in yet another cable to Eban in which he said that Israel would not leave Gaza and Sharm al-Sheikh even if the US were to impose sanctions on the Jewish state.[22] In the meantime, the UN Secretariat continued to waver. On 10 January Eban reported that Hammarskjold 'still had no inkling on how to resolve the Gaza question'.[23] By the second week of January 1957 Bunche had made up his mind. He told an Israeli diplomat that Israel must evacuate Gaza and let UNEF replace it. Israel could announce its withdrawal, coupled with a statement that it would re-enter the Strip if the Egyptian army or an Egyptian civilian administration entered; if UNEF left before appropriate arrangements had been made; or if UNEF failed to prevent infiltration.[24] In less than six weeks Bunche's proposal became the basis for the 'Understanding' that made the Israeli withdrawal possible, but Bunche got no credit for the idea. Instead, the credit went to the Americans and the French.

Meanwhile, exchanges between Hammarskjold and Israeli representatives began to be short tempered. The Secretary-General was unbending: the UN could not 'accept a presence of Israeli security forces in Gaza'. Israel's insistence on remaining in Gaza would be resisted. It was incumbent on him, as UN Secretary-General, to report to the UN General Assembly to the effect that under the existing circumstances in Gaza the UN could no longer maintain its aid programme for the refugees there. For his part Bunche pointed out that the UN could not co-operate with Israel in Gaza any more because there was no support for doing so among UN members.[25]

On 3 February, Eisenhower sent Ben-Gurion a strongly worded message: 'Continued ignoring of the judgement of the nations ... would almost surely lead to invoking of further UN procedures which could seriously disturb the relations between Israel and other member nations, including the United States'.[26] Although the hint at sanctions was clear, Ben-Gurion remained defiant: Israel would not permit Egypt to return to Gaza, Israel's administration would continue there in co-operation with the UN and the local population. Israel expressed readiness to discuss modalities. In lieu of the Armistice Agreement, no longer relevant from Israel's point of view, it was necessary to negotiate a non-aggression or peace agreement.[27] Eban's protestations to Ben-Gurion were of no avail. He remained unmoved.[28] In his reply to Eisenhower, the Prime Minister commented on the implied threat of sanctions, pointing out that none were 'ever invoked against Egypt which, for eight years past, has violated resolutions of the Security Council and provisions of the Charter'. By the Security Council resolution, he meant the September 1951 UN ruling that Israel had the right to free passage in the Gulf of Eilat and the Suez Canal.[29]

While these exchanges were taking place, the US was busy working out its position in detail. Dulles told Eisenhower that he and his advisers did not see 'how we can at this time commit ourselves or anybody to rewrite the Armistice Agreement. Under it, the Gaza Strip is turned over to Egypt for administration and policing'. Even the stationing of UNEF there had 'to be worked out on a voluntary basis' (that is, Egypt would have to give its consent freely). What the US could do for its part was to give Israel an assurance 'outside the context of the UN'. Such assurance would refer to the question of freedom of maritime passage. More specifically, the US was 'thinking of giving an assurance that we and a group of maritime nations will assert the view that [the Gulf] is an international waterway ... and if it is blocked we would consider it an act of aggression'.[30] This assurance would take care of the Gulf problem, but not of Gaza.

Dulles then outlined the American position in a special *aide-mémoire* (11 February)[31] which constituted a turning point in the US–Israeli dialogue. All it said with respect to Gaza, however, was that the UN General Assembly had 'no authority to require of either Egypt or Israel a substantial modification of the Armistice Agreement' which gave Egypt 'the right and responsibility of occupation'. Israel should promptly withdraw from Gaza whose future should be 'worked out through the efforts and good offices of the UN'. The US *aide-mémoire* urged the UN to move UNEF into Gaza 'and to be on the boundary between Israel and the Gaza Strip'.[32]

Ben-Gurion welcomed the American initiative but found it wanting; Israel was ready to withdraw its military forces from Gaza but insisted that its civilian administration and police remain. He suggested that a special Israel–US working group consider a plan for the administration of Gaza after Israel's evacuation.[33] The US rejected this proposal. The Americans felt that Israel tended to 'charge the US with responsibility for every knotty problem the UN encountered'.[34] Dulles told Eisenhower that Israel assumed that the US 'was acting for all the world and all they [the Israelis] have to do is to sit down and negotiate with us'.[35] This US reaction makes it impossible to know what direction US policy might have taken on Gaza had Hammarskjold not suddenly discovered that the Egyptian Foreign Minister, Mahmoud Fawzi, was ready to consider a UN administration in Gaza 'at the right time'.[36] The Egyptians had stated their concession in veiled terms, but it sufficed to prompt the Department of State to tell its embassies around the world that the US favoured immediate Israeli withdrawal from the Strip and a UN take-over. The future status of the Gaza Strip would be left to the UN.[37] Israel's detailed reply (on 15 February) to the American *aide-mémoire* of 11 February left the US position unchanged. Even the Israeli offer not only to pay compensation to the Arab refugees but also to make a contribution to a UN programme for solving the Gaza refugee problem through the 'settlement of a part of the refugee population of Gaza [in Israel]'[38] had no effect.

Dulles was disappointed by the Israeli reply. He told Eban that the US had already made its policy clear in its *aide-mémoire* and would not enter into separate consultations with Israel over an arrangement that would then be submitted to the UN. Such an approach was not only 'unacceptable' but would be 'deeply and properly resented by the UN'.[39] Ben-Gurion did not give in. He cabled Eban: 'The Egyptians must not be permitted to return to Gaza'.[40] He took this strong line in full awareness of its consequences at the UN General Assembly, which was about to convene again, and where sanctions against Israel were to be discussed. On 20 February Eisenhower made a broadcast to the American nation, warning that the UN had no choice but to exert pressure on Israel to comply with the withdrawal resolution.[41] He spelt out this warning in a communication to Ben-Gurion saying that if Israel did not immediately withdraw there could be 'no assurance that the next decisions soon to be taken by the UN will not involve serious implications. He, Eisenhower, would greatly deplore the necessity of the US taking positions in the UN and of the UN itself having to adopt measures which might have far-reaching effects upon Israel's relations throughout the world'.[42]

Well aware of the seriousness of the situation, Ben-Gurion was reassured by private messages from an American personality close to Eisenhower telling him that the US assurance as made known to Israel amounted to a firm moral commitment by the US administration, one which Israel could trust.[43] On 21 February the Israeli cabinet decided to request the US to agree to separate the Gulf and the Gaza issues. Israel urged that the freedom of navigation assurance become operative immediately, with the future of a Gaza arrangement left open for further negotiation. Israel stated again that the Egyptians must be prevented from returning to Gaza directly or indirectly.[44] A meeting between Dulles and Eban took place on 22 February. The Israeli and American reports on this meeting are not quite identical. According to the American report, the Israeli representatives had informed them that Israel had changed its position and had agreed to withdraw its army and let UNEF in, even though the UN was unable to promise that UNEF would remain on 'Egyptian soil until peace had been established'. This report has Dulles saying that the UN General Assembly could not 'rewrite' the Armistice Agreement which constituted the basis for Egypt's rights in Gaza. In seeking to deny Egyptian rights under the Armistice Agreement, 'Israel was asking for more than the UN could give'.[45]

The Israeli account, prepared by Eban and his deputy Reuven Shiloah, described Dulles's position in less negative terms. It said that the Foreign Secretary agreed that after Israel's military evacuation of Gaza, an international administration would be established without Egypt's participation, while the Israeli civilian authority would continue. It is possible that the Israelis mistook Dulles's remark that he believed that 'Egypt would acquiesce in some change' for implying acquiescence in the Israeli demands. They were likewise encouraged by Dulles's stating that 'it is impossible to persuade Egypt to renounce its rights, but it is possible to persuade it not to insist on their implementation in practice'.[46]

Ben-Gurion was much upset by the statement of his representatives in Washington to the effect that Israel was ready to withdraw its army and permit the entry of UNEF. He cabled immediately to say that the cabinet had not agreed to UNEF's entry 'not before and not after the arrival of the working group [proposed by Israel]. It was only agreed that we would discuss everything [with the working group]'.[47] He continued to insist on separation between the issues of free passage in the Gulf and Gaza, confiding to his diary that 'Eban did not convey the cabinet instructions to Dulles. The conversation [Eban–Dulles] shook me. AE [Abba Eban] conveyed to them a message of his own, undoubtedly without evil intent'.[48] Jerusalem first instructed Eban to tell Dulles that a mistake had been made in conveying the cabinet's decision, but then decided to leave the matter at that.[49]

The shock felt by Ben-Gurion when he was told about the mistaken message to Dulles indicates that he was still set on keeping Gaza even at this late moment and in spite of the harsh American warnings. Israel was ready for no more than a token concession: to let some UN observers, but not UNEF, into Gaza. This was not good enough for Dulles and Hammarskjold. The Secretary-General would 'do his best' to ensure quiet in the region after Israel's withdrawal, but his action would be based entirely on the assumption of Egypt's return to Gaza.

Against this backdrop, the talks with Dulles and Hammarskjold were likely to have reached a deadlock had Dulles not proposed on 26 February to involve the French in the efforts to persuade Israel to evacuate the Strip. He discussed the idea with Eisenhower, with the French – who immediately agreed – and lastly with the Israelis.[50] The French involvement was useful in inducing Israel to leave Gaza, but the French role was in fact considerably more modest than some Israeli participants assumed. It was Dulles who pulled the strings without the French and Israelis realizing it.

## BEN-GURION AND THE ARMISTICE AGREEMENT

On 7 November 1956, shortly after the fighting in Sinai had ended, Ben-Gurion told the Knesset that the Armistice Agreement with Egypt (signed on 24 February 1949) 'was dead and buried and would not come to life again'. With the Agreement, said Ben-Gurion, the armistice demarcation lines between Israel and Egypt had breathed their last. He explained that the 'Egyptian dictator [Nasser] had for many years ridden roughshod over the Agreement ... violated UN Security Council resolutions and the UN Charter. Furthermore, the Egyptian President's innumerable declarations that a state of belligerency existed between Egypt and Israel, had distorted the essence of the Agreement'.[51]

Ben-Gurion may have chosen his words advisedly when he announced the 'death and burial' of the Agreement, but the fact of the matter is that he did not make a formal, legal statement to the effect that the Government of Israel had decided to cancel the Armistice Agreement because the Egyptians had grossly violated its provisions. In the end, as will be shown shortly, his unilateral non-formal declaration stood him in good stead. At one of the talks between Eban and Hammarskjold in December 1956, Bunche, who was present, told Eban that in his view Israel for its own good should 'formalize' its declaration on the repudiation of the Armistice Agreement. The way to do this was to ask the Secretary-General to convene a meeting between Israeli and Egyptian representatives as provided for by Article 12 of the Agreement. This article laid down that either of the two parties had the right to request the convening of the parties at a conference for the purpose of considering changes in or suspension of any of its provisions. It was incumbent on both parties to participate in such a meeting. Israel could declare that it requested the meeting in order to repudiate the

Agreement. Should Egypt refuse the Secretary-General's invitation, Israel could then state that it had exhausted all procedural possibilities open to it and considered itself no longer bound by the Agreement. It is evident that Bunche was sure that his advice was sound since he repeated it on several occasions, arguing that Israel stood to gain if it acted in this vein.

Bunche's idea was discussed at a meeting with Golda Meir in New York. The participants were in favour of following his advice and not leaving the suspension of the Agreement in doubt. They did not think, however, that Israel should refer to Article 12 as Bunche had recommended, since from its point of view that article was in an agreement that Israel no longer accepted. Another way should be found.

No action, however, followed this meeting. The legal adviser to the Israel Ministry for Foreign Affairs considered Bunche's idea a 'trap' designed to revive the Agreement, since it suggested having recourse to Article 12.[52] Hammarskjold's attitude was firm and perfectly clear from the start, inspired as it was by the UN General Assembly resolution of 2 November 1956 urging the parties to observe the Armistice Agreement. Hammarskjold referred to the armistice demarcation lines in his report of 22 February 1957, in which he pointed out how the crisis should be resolved. He outlined Egypt's position, saying that:

> ... the Government of Egypt, recognizing the present special problems and complexities of the Gaza area and the long-standing major responsibility of the UN there ... and having in mind also the objections and obligations of the Armistice Agreement, has the willingness and readiness to make special and helpful arrangements with the UN and some of its auxiliary bodies ... [including] UNEF ... The arrangement for the use of UNEF in the area would ensure its deployment on the armistice line at the Gaza Strip and the effective interposition of the Force between the armed forces of Egypt and Israel.[53]

The report made it crystal clear that Hammarskjold preferred the Egyptian case to the Israeli case presented by Ben-Gurion in his Knesset statements.[54] Israel repeatedly put forward its contention that Egypt had systematically violated the Agreement. The quintessence of the Agreement was the end of the state of belligerency between the two states and the call for action towards achieving peace. Egypt, however, claimed that the Agreement could exist side by side with a state of war. Israel completely rejected this interpretation which it considered to have brought about the death of the Agreement. A new kind of relationship was needed. Israel also denied having asserted that there was a state of belligerency between it and Egypt. The relations between Israel and Egypt, even in the absence of the Armistice Agreement, were based on the UN Charter, which denied the existence of a state of belligerency between UN members.

Hammarskjold did not go along with this argument. He told Eban that not only Egypt but Israel as well had violated the Agreement. Despite recent events, he viewed the Agreement as an asset not to be ignored in any effort to re-establish satisfactory relations between the two countries.[55] In another talk with Eban several days later, Hammarskjold said that 'the UN cannot put away anything on the shelf of history unless this is done legally; this is why the UN believes that it is committed to the Armistice Agreement'.[56]

The US view was identical. On 9 February 1957, just before the US set out its position in a special *aide-mémoire* (dated 11 February), constituting in more than one sense a turning point, Dulles told Eisenhower that he could not commit the US or anybody to 'rewrite' the Armistice Agreement. Under its terms the Gaza Strip was 'turned over to Egypt for administration and policing'. The US wanted UNEF to control Gaza, but that had 'to be worked out on a voluntary basis'.[57] Dulles was clearly convinced that because of the Armistice Agreement his hands were tied with respect to Gaza. The US *aide-mémoire* stated that the UN General Assembly 'has no authority to require of either Egypt or Israel a substantial modification of the Armistice Agreement'. The Agreement 'gives Egypt the right and responsibility of occupation [of Gaza] ... we believe that Israeli withdrawal from Gaza should be prompt and unconditional, leaving the future of the Gaza Strip to be worked out through the efforts and good offices of the UN'.[58]

Israel's reply to the US *aide-mémoire* disappointed Dulles.[59] It agreed to withdraw its army but not its civilian authority and police. Nor did Israel agree to let UNEF in. It proposed the setting up of a working group which would come to Gaza to study the problem and make recommendations to the UN General Assembly. Dulles, however, insisted that the Armistice Agreement could not be ignored.[60]

On 14 February, in an almost desperate effort to make the US change its position, Israel agreed to UNEF's entry into the Strip, but continued to insist on its civilian administration and police staying there. It also demanded that free navigation for Israel in the Gulf become operative immediately, even while the Gaza issue was still being negotiated. Israeli legal experts argued that once the Israeli army was no longer in Gaza and UNEF had taken over, no one could contend that the state of belligerency between Israel and Egypt remained in force. UNEF was the best guarantor that there would be no more fighting. The State Department's legal experts accepted the soundness of the Israeli argument, namely that once UNEF had entered the Strip, the Israeli civilian authorities 'would be at the behest of the United Nations' force ... [and] would have no power except that derived from the UN. If the

Israeli administration were simply carrying out instructions of UNEF, it would seem that there would no longer be a question of military occupation or the exercise of belligerency'. However, the US experts added that Israel was wrong in assuming that its civilian administration in the Strip did not require UN approval. As Dulles saw it, Israel could not 'stipulate no Egyptian participation [in the Strip]'. He said again that the UN could not rewrite the Armistice Agreement, 'certainly not without the concurrence of both parties'.[61]

When Dulles reported to Eisenhower what Israel insisted on and why he had to refuse, Eisenhower said that the armistice had been proposed by the UN which therefore had some leeway. Dulles countered by pointing out that the Armistice Agreement had been agreed upon by both states and thus the UN could not 'unilaterally dissolve it, it was a question of national pride'.[62] He did, however, give some ground when he told Eisenhower that Israel could get some of what it wanted on the basis of Egyptian acquiescence. Eisenhower stuck to his guns saying that 'Gaza has never been ceded to Egypt and has never been part of it, so [it is] not the same as lower Sinai'.[63]

Obviously, Eisenhower had been persuaded by Ben-Gurion's argument that Gaza was legally quite distinct from Sinai. However, in Dulles's memorandum to Eisenhower of 26 February 1957, which constituted the basis of the 'Understanding' announced three days later, he stated that 'under the Armistice Agreement Egypt has a right of occupancy and there is no way in which the UN or Israel can take this right away without Egypt's consent and Egypt does not consent, although it acquiesces in the exercise of administrative functions through a United Nations Commission ...'.[64] In talks with Eban, Dulles warned Israel that there was a 'definite link between Gaza and the Gulf of Aqaba'. The US would feel able 'to give assurance with respect to Aqaba only if Israel complied with UN resolutions relating to Gaza and did not assert rights incompatible with the terms of the Armistice Agreement'. The US legal argument went as follows: if the Armistice Agreement were abolished, the state of belligerency would be in force again and this would spell the end of the Gulf of Aqaba arrangement. In 1951 the UN Security Council ruled that the Egyptian interference with Israeli shipping must stop because there existed the Armistice Agreement which put an end to the state of belligerency between the two states. Thus the affirmation by the UN of the absence of belligerency formed the only legal basis for the Gulf arrangement. Israel could not obtain freedom of navigation without leaving Gaza and letting the Egyptians return there, as was their right under the Armistice Agreement.

Dulles and his advisers rejected the Israeli argument that the UN Charter banned the state of belligerency and therefore the Armistice Agreement was not needed to obtain this result. Dulles claimed that without the Armistice Agreement 'chaos' would ensue. The US and Israel would be on an 'uncharted sea'. The assurances the US was prepared to give Israel were conditional on its complete withdrawal and were based on the premise that the Armistice Agreement was valid, and along with it, the legal framework that it provided.[65]

As a general rule, the US did not think that it was wise to repudiate agreements even when they were not satisfactorily implemented. Korea was a case in point; violations by the North Koreans had not induced the US to repudiate the agreement. The very existence of an agreement, even if violations continued, had a restraining influence. In Korea the agreement established the demarcation line and other matters of importance, which survived the violations. This was why the US would not support a position in favour of repudiating the Egyptian–Israeli Armistice Agreement. On the contrary, the US would try to rehabilitate it and would expect Egypt to co-operate.

The US legal adviser, Herman Phleger, argued that renunciation of the Armistice Agreement might boomerang. Since Israel was actually observing the main principles of the Armistice Agreement, it should also be able to benefit from its rights under it. Those countries that were ready to support Israel all adhered to the legal doctrine based on the Armistice Agreement and the 1951 UN Security Council resolution. Israel should, therefore, do nothing that would make it difficult for the US and others to identify with it.[66]

Dulles took the same position in talking to the French Foreign Minister, Christian Pineau, who arrived in Washington: if Israel insisted on considering the Armistice Agreement null and void, 'a serious problem would arise in that it would revive [the state of belligerency] to full vigour and it would be difficult to assert rights of innocent passage into the Straits of Aqaba'.[67]

In its statement in the UN, on 1 March 1957, after Israel had announced its readiness to withdraw, the US referred to the Armistice Agreement and urged Egypt and Israel to base their relations on 'full observance of the Armistice Agreement … so that the Agreement will become fully operative'.[68] Clearly, therefore, in the end Israel accepted the US scenario, or at least acquiesced in it though it revived the Armistice Agreement which Ben-Gurion had declared dead only three months earlier. In return, as a trade-off, the US supported some of Israel's most vital policy interests. In a long exchange between Ben-Gurion and Hammarskjold in Jerusalem two months later (May 1957), with Meir and Bunche also present, the Prime Minister expounded his position again. By that time the Egyptians had already returned to Gaza. Ben-Gurion asserted that he continued to consider the Armistice Agreement 'dead', but not its principles. He could not understand why the UN had permitted the Egyptians to return to Gaza, and was puzzled why the international organization had not first insisted that the Egyptians abide by their obligations under the Armistice Agreement. Since the UN, unlike him, viewed the Agreement as valid, argued Ben-Gurion, it should not have exempted Egypt from declaring an end to belligerency and acceptance of the 1951 Security Council resolution concerning navigation. In reply, Bunche pointed out that that resolution itself was based on the Armistice Agreement which Ben-Gurion no longer recognized as binding. Ben-Gurion said that the resolution clearly rejected the Egyptian allegation that there was a state of belligerency between Egypt and Israel. The Egyptians had no right to return to Gaza as long as they clung to that interpretation. Bunche said that Egypt's right to be in Gaza derived from the Armistice Agreement which Israel had never formally repudiated. In saying this Bunche was in essence echoing what he had repeatedly told Eban in December 1956, namely, that Israel ought to give the UN formal notice that it wished to repudiate the Armistice Agreement.[69]

While it is impossible to state with any certainty that Israel erred in not giving formal notification to the UN that it considered the Armistice Agreement null and void, it would appear that this Israeli omission made it easier for the UN to ignore Ben-Gurion's Knesset statement and to act throughout the negotiation period as if the Armistice Agreement remained in force as before.

## LAST-MINUTE FRENCH MEDIATION

As the crisis between Israel and the US–UN reached its climax in the last week of February 1957, it became clear that Dag Hammarskjold was not going to budge. In his 22 February report to the General Assembly, he outlined the elements which would provide the basis for ending the crisis, and as far as he was concerned this was his final word on the subject. He firmly rejected Israel's demand that Egypt should not return to Gaza, arguing that Egypt's rights were based on the Armistice Agreement. Hence, the UN efforts to ensure quiet in the region after Israel's withdrawal would be made in a manner fully consistent with the safeguarding of Egypt's rights.[70]

Israel objected. It would compromise on one point only, namely agreement to some UN observers being posted in Gaza. The stationing of UNEF was out of the question. Israel would, however, be prepared to report regularly to the UN on its administration of the Strip.[71] Israel also expressed readiness to withdraw immediately from Sharm al-Sheikh, the last place in Sinai it still held, on condition that the principle of freedom of navigation be implemented concurrently with its withdrawal. The unresolved Gaza issue would go on being discussed. Dulles rejected the Israeli proposal but, at the same time, advised Eban, almost pleaded with

him, to meet with the French Foreign Minister, Christian Pineau. Pineau
and France's Prime Minister, Guy Mollet, were then visiting
Washington. By way of explanation Dulles added that Pineau 'had some
ideas which might be helpful ... [and] commended themselves to the
President and to M. Mollet'.[72]

What is known about the French role in the last days of February
(just before the 'Understanding' was to be announced on 1 March) is
gleaned from the Israeli and American documents, the French
documents being still classified. Pineau's book of memoirs on the Suez
Campaign adds little to what is known about the French role.[73] Still it
does perhaps provide a clue to the question as to why Dulles asked the
French to play a part. According to Pineau, the Foreign Secretary asked
him to find a suitable formula in consultation with Hammarskjold,
acceptable to both Egypt and Israel. Dulles explained that he was asking
this of France because his own hands were tied, having to take Arab
interests into account. Pineau does not add anything beyond that on his
talk with Dulles. He does not even mention the high-level
Eisenhower–Mollet meeting of 28 February, in which he and Dulles
took part.

Pineau talked to Hammarskjold immediately thereafter, telling him
that it was vital that UNEF's deployment in Gaza and Sharm be for an
unlimited duration. When Hammarskjold asked whether this would
satisfy Israel, Pineau said it would not since Israel would fear that Egypt
might demand the removal of UNEF at any time. Hammarskjold then
asked: 'and what if Egypt agrees?'. Since Pineau does not explain what
it was that Egypt had to agree to, it would appear that Hammarskjold
wanted to find out what the positions of France and Israel would be if
Egypt were to give a clear undertaking not to demand UNEF's
departure. It is, however, most unlikely that Hammarskjold would be
prepared at this late stage (26–27 February) to ask Cairo for such a
commitment. As he saw it, everything had already been settled. Fawzi
and Nasser had given their tacit agreement to let UNEF deploy in Gaza
and Sharm with the understanding that UNEF would be told to leave
only after giving a prior warning. This being the case, it is not at all clear
what Pineau achieved in his talk with Hammarskjold, except perhaps a
secret meeting with Fawzi, arranged by the UN Secretary-General at the
latter's residence. Pineau narrates that the meeting was recorded in the
form of a procès-verbal (memorandum of conversation) signed by all
three present. Unfortunately, he does not say what was in the
memorandum. So much for Pineau's account.

Brian Urquhart, an assistant of the UN Secretary-General, published
a biography on Hammarskjold which makes extensive use of classified
UN material. Urquhart mentions the meeting between Pineau and
Fawzi, hosted by Hammarskjold, apparently without attaching much

importance to it. The memorandum of conversation between Pineau–Fawzi–Hammarskjold is not mentioned at all. Urquhart says that Hammarskjold showed Pineau the text of the 'Understanding' reached by Dulles and Golda Meir the previous day. According to Urquhart, Hammarskjold was referring to the text of the statement which Meir was about to make at the UN General Assembly on 1 March. After reading the text, Pineau said that the thrust of Meir's statement was that Egyptian forces were not to return to Gaza. Hammarskjold reacted, saying that he could not get a promise of such a thing from Cairo. He hoped that Egypt would not insist on restoring the Egyptian administration in Gaza but he could not be certain. He estimated that Egypt would not want to see its presence reduced to a mere token.[74] According to Urquhart, Pineau did not remonstrate with Hammarskjold on being given this information. If we are to believe Urquhart's account, and there are sound reasons for doing so, it emerges that Pineau was in fact unable to get anything at all out of Hammarskjold. To Hammarskjold the understanding between the UN and Egypt was already a *fait accompli* announced on 22 February, and that was that.

What indeed was the role Dulles envisaged for France? The US documents provide a clear answer. When Israel informed the US that it had reached a deadlock in its talks on 25 February with Hammarskjold, Dulles lost no time. He talked to Eisenhower and suggested that he persuade Prime Minister Mollet, whom he was about to see on 26 February, to exert 'some French *pressure* on the Israelis to withdraw',[75] in accordance with the joint US–UN position on Gaza. Dulles attached considerable importance to France's talking to Israel. France was a country which had stood by Israel before, during and after the Sinai Campaign. He saw clearly, however, that France would not succeed in persuading Israel unless it could offer it something the US could not. This would have to take the form of a US public acknowledgement that Israel had the right to defend its interests in the Gaza Strip, if the arrangements made by the UN were to break down or if Egypt were to encourage raids from the Strip into Israel.

The US documents also reveal that Eisenhower and Dulles agreed that Israeli scepticism about what Hammarskjold had obtained from the Egyptians was perfectly natural. As we have seen, Eisenhower told Dulles that Gaza had 'never been ceded to Egypt'.[76]

Dulles, for his part, immediately told Hammarskjold that Ben-Gurion was indeed justifiably concerned over the UN's inability to give a firm promise that conditions in Gaza would not revert to what they had been. Consequently, he told Hammarskjold that he ought to convince Israel that, though it must accept what he had proposed in his 22 February report, the Secretary-General would let Israel's announcement of readiness to withdraw contain a caveat '[that] if it [the arrangement] did not work out ... [the] Israelis would reserve their rights so they would not be any worse off'. Dulles also told Hammarskjold that while Ben-Gurion could not 'get what he wants exactly, he can get [a] practical assurance'. Hammarskjold promised to help.[77]

The importance of this American document is in its demonstration that it was the US and not France who proposed that Israel should announce its withdrawal decision together with a clear warning as to what it would do if the Gaza Strip arrangement broke down. The Americans knew that this proposal removed the last stumbling block, the Sharm al-Sheikh issue having been settled by them two weeks before. The US had taken a very firm position on this issue by stating that it considered the Gulf of Aqaba international waters and that no nation had the right to prevent passage there and through the straits giving access to the Gulf.

Thus Dulles resolved the tricky Gaza issue by letting France acknowledge Israel's right to act in the defence of its interests in Gaza, namely, the right to invoke Article 51 of the UN Charter. The French acknowledgement would achieve two purposes. First, it would carry great weight with Israel, and second, it would obviate the need for the US to take a similar public stand on Israel's side on Gaza. Dulles felt that the public support that the US had given Israel on Sharm al-Sheikh had come close to exhausting America's credit in Egypt. He could do no more publicly. Quietly, however, he not only talked to Hammarskjold but also asked the US ambassador at the UN, Cabot Lodge, to cover the same ground with Hammarskjold.

Like the first American conversation with Hammarskjold, the second one also took place before Dulles's meeting with Pineau. Lodge was instructed to ask Hammarskjold to tell Eban specifically that 'neither Israel nor Egypt would be giving up any rights by agreeing to the type of arrangement for Gaza he [the Secretary-General] had in mind. Israel could still assert whatever rights they had if the arrangements there turned out to be unsatisfactory'. Although Hammarskjold promised to 'try his best with Eban'[78] he apparently did not do so. However, what is of interest here is not whether Hammarskjold did accommodate the US on this, but that Dulles was almost desperately searching for third parties to tell Israel what he himself was unwilling to tell it. On 26 February, in a memorandum to Eisenhower he said that Israel continued to insist on 'guarantees' (the quotes are Dulles's) that 'Egypt will never return to Gaza'. The memorandum also said that Israel should withdraw on the basis of what Hammarskjold had been able to get from the Egyptians, including their acquiescence to there being in Gaza a 'UN administration which for an undefined period of time will be designed to provide solid protection and civilian administration ... '. But [in return] Israel would have 'a case for seeking relief by its own action' should something go wrong with the Gaza arrangement.[79]

It is on the basis of this memorandum that Dulles talked to Eisenhower, just before his meeting with Guy Mollet, suggesting that he invite French 'pressure' on Israel. Fifteen minutes after his talk with Eisenhower, Dulles met with Pineau and let him read his memorandum to the US President, but was quick to take it back (the US document states: 'This copy [of the memorandum] was subsequently returned to the Secretary by Mr. Pineau at the Secretary's request'.) Dulles told Pineau that the Israelis insisted that it should be made clear that the UN would indeed take on the Egyptian role in Gaza, but he also told him truthfully that this Israeli condition could not be fulfilled. Dulles explained: 'the UN could not substitute itself for the Armistice Agreements ..., any administration in Gaza required the acquiescence of Egypt'. He admitted that theoretically, as Israel justifiably feared, Egypt's acquiescence could be withdrawn at any time. In those circumstances Dulles saw only one way out, namely to urge Israel to 'take a chance' on the arrangement despite its inherent weakness. If the arrangement collapsed Israel would have 'world sympathy behind her'. At this point Pineau asked Dulles if this would satisfy Israel and whether a clarification could be added to the withdrawal statement to the effect that Israel reserved its rights which it would exercise if something went wrong. Dulles must have been quietly pleased with this question because it showed that Pineau saw eye to eye with him. The Frenchman then summed up what were to be called the 'French suggestions': (1) UNEF and a UN administration should be established for an indefinite duration, with the tacit acquiescence of Egypt (a suggestion which was identical with the US–UN line); (2) Israel would reserve its rights with regard to the termination of this arrangement (again, this was in line with the Dulles memorandum to Eisenhower); (3) Other countries would take note of this arrangement without approving or disapproving it (it was Dulles who proposed this point by saying that it was important that some other countries should state their hope that the UN administration should go on until the conclusion of a peace settlement and that if Egypt returned to the Gaza Strip earlier this would create a new situation calling for consultation).

The detailed, four-page-long report of the Dulles–Pineau meeting, seen in the context of the US position, wrapped up as it was on the eve of this conversation, leads almost inevitably to the conclusion that Dulles succeeded in cleverly steering Pineau towards accepting, in effect endorsing, the American line. The American documents do not reveal that Dulles kept one vital point hidden from Pineau, namely that the US itself would not state publicly what it urged France to state: recognition of Israel's rights to take independent military action should the Gaza arrangement break down. Since Dulles let Pineau read the memorandum to the President, Pineau might have thought that the US, too, would announce support for Israel if such a contingency arose. After all, the memorandum stated so explicitly ('... Israel will have a case for seeking relief by its own action'). This impression of Pineau's must certainly have been reinforced by Dulles telling him that it was not good enough, as Pineau suggested, merely to state that 'other countries take note of this [the Gaza] arrangement, without approving or disapproving it', suggesting instead that this point be amplified to say that other countries 'should also express the hope that the UN administration should last until conclusion of a peace settlement', etc.

In talking with Eban, after seeing Pineau, Dulles took the same line. He approved the draft of the Israeli statement in which the latter reserved its right to take military action if the arrangement collapsed, but did not reveal to his Israeli interlocutor that the US itself would not support publicly this part of the Israeli declaration. Dulles let Eban glance quickly through the statement the US would deliver at the UN General Assembly,[80] but did not give him a copy for thorough perusal.[81] There was no reason for Eban to suspect that Dulles had ulterior motives in not giving him a copy of the US statement. The Secretary of State had been an active participant in the drafting of the Israeli statement as a whole, the language Israel used on Gaza was unequivocal and agreed to by Dulles: 'if conditions are created in the Gaza Strip which indicate the return to the conditions of deterioration which existed previously, Israel would reserve its freedom to act to defend its rights'.[82]

A State Department circular telegram sent to a number of US diplomatic missions on 28 February stated as a matter of fact that 'Israel will also make clear that, in withdrawing, it reserves its right under Article 51 of the Charter to defend its interest re any possible future incursions from Gaza ...'. In a conversation with Dulles just hours before Israel made its statement, the Secretary of State referred to 'a plan that we prepared together with Mollet and Pineau intended to prevent the return of Egypt to Gaza, both militarily and in a civilian capacity'.[83] The use of the word 'plan' (*accord commun* as the French called it) to describe what the US had agreed with France could only strengthen Eban's belief that there existed no difference between the French and the American positions.

Clearly, therefore, Dulles was less than candid with Israel and France. Eban had reported confidentially to Jerusalem that 'on the whole, Dulles accepts' all Pineau's positions.[84] As for Pineau, he was convinced that Dulles and he were in complete agreement on Gaza. He was naturally disappointed with the US statement in the General Assembly on 1 March which omitted any reference to Israel's rights in Gaza. In a reception in New York, a day later, Pineau accused the US ambassador at the UN, Cabot Lodge, of changing the agreed statement and said that he viewed this as 'the kind of thing which made Franco-American relations bad'.[85]

Of course, Ben-Gurion, for his part, was also upset by the American statement. Even after another message from Eisenhower (2 March), designed to reassure him, he told the US ambassador in Israel that he would like to receive from the US 'a little more on Gaza'. He, too, was certain that there had been last-minute changes in the US statement and was sorry that 'it was the French who said what I had hoped to hear from you'.[86] Dulles, however, refused to give any further clarification. This time he was frank in explaining to both Pineau and Eban that there in fact existed 'a difference of opinion regarding Gaza'. He said he saw no use in spreading that difference on the record as would have to be done if the US undertook to continue the exchange.[87]

Dulles derived whatever benefit he could from this refusal. The Americans could now truthfully tell the Arabs that no secret US undertaking to Israel existed. Everything was part of the public record. Cabot Lodge assured Fawzi that the US position was identical with Egypt's, based as it was on the Armistice Agreement.[88] On 1 March Dulles met with diplomats from nine Arab states, telling them that Israel 'had endeavoured to obtain more extensive commitments from the US, but we had declined to give them'.[89]

In fairness to Dulles it should be added that he did tell Eban that the US did not altogether exclude the possibility that in certain circumstances Israel would have the right to use force to oust Egypt from Gaza (3 March). The difficulty as he saw it, however, was not to recognize this right in principle but to determine 'how long Israel would have to wait after the return of Egypt and how imminent the danger must be, before [invoking] the right of defence'.[90]

On 6 March Dulles wrote to Cabot Lodge: 'We naturally could not object to Israel in the future exercising its "rights", but we refused to agree in advance as to what its rights might be under various hypothetical conditions'.[91]

In conclusion, it may be argued in Dulles's defence that throughout the talks he had made it unmistakably clear that the US supported Egypt's right to return to Gaza even though the US would much prefer it if Egypt did not avail itself of that right. Dulles would, however, have incurred less French and Israeli criticism had he forewarned them a day or two before the General Assembly meeting as to what the US would say on Gaza in its statement and what he would refrain from saying.

NOTES

1. Abba Eban, *An Autobiography*, Jerusalem, 1977, pp.245–6.
2. David Ben-Gurion's Diary, entry for 10 March 1957, Ben-Gurion Archives, Sde Boker (hereinafter BGD).
3. Mordechai Bar-On, *Sha'arei Aza*, Tel Aviv, 1992, p.372.
4. Mordechai Gazit, 'Ben Gurion's 1949 Proposal to Incorporate the Gaza Strip with Israel', *Studies in Zionism*, Vol. 8, No. 2 (1987).
5. Moshe Sharett, *Yoman Ishi*, Tel Aviv, 1978, pp.872, 874, 875, 878; BGD, entry for 3 April 1955. The vote took place on the same date.
6. Michael Bar-Zohar, *Ben Gurion*, Tel Aviv, 1981, Vol. III, p.1140 (Hebrew).
7. Foreign Relations of the United States (hereinafter FRUS), Washington, DC, 1955–57, Vol. XVII, p.5.
8. *Ha-aretz*, 19 June 1967 (reprinted in ibid., 10 June 1988).
9. *Maariv*, 2 August 1967.
10. Ibid., 21 January 1971 and 3 May 1972.
11. *Ha-aretz*, 8 September 1972, interviewed by R. Priester.
12. *Divrei Ha-Knesset*, Vol. 21, 7 November 1956.
13. Ibid., 14 November 1956, p.260.
14. Ibid., 17–19 December 1956, p.513.
15. Ibid., p.829ff.
16. Ibid., p.851.
17. FRUS, 1955–57, Vol. XVII, p.5ff.
18. Israel State Archives (hereafter ISA), Foreign Ministry (FM)/2448; selected documents on exchanges between the Israeli Government and the US, the National Defense College.
19. FM/2448, Eban in telegram to Herzog, 6 December 1956. Eban was given similar advice by delegates from various (other) nations (ibid., Eban to Herzog, 13 December).
20. Ibid., Eban to Ben-Gurion, 19 December 1956.
21. Ibid., 12 December 1956. In a telegram of 24 December to Nahum Goldmann Ben-Gurion said 'I am surprised ... in particular because you quote me as being ready to leave Gaza'.
22. Ibid., Ben-Gurion to Eban, 7 January 1957.
23. Ibid., Eban to Golda, 10 January 1957.
24. Ibid., M. Kidron to Herzog, 13 January 1957.
25. Ibid., Eban to Jerusalem, 14 January 1957; Kidron to Herzog, 21 January; Rafael to Herzog, 21 January.
26. FRUS, 1955–57, Vol. XVII, pp.82–4.
27. ISA, Ben-Gurion to Israeli Foreign Minister Golda Meir, 8 February 1957.
28. Ibid., 10 February 1957.
29. FRUS, 1955–57, pp.109–112.
30. Ibid., pp.115–16.
31. Ibid., pp.132–4. The text was released on 17 February.
32. Ibid., p.132–3.
33. Ben-Gurion's telegram of 12 February 1957, ISA, FM/2459; FRUS, 1955–57, p.135.
34. FRUS, 1955–57, p.148.
35. Ibid., p.157.
36. Ibid., p.149.
37. Ibid., p.152.
38. Ibid., pp.168–9.
39. Ibid., p.162. See also Herzog's telegrams to Meir and Eban of 15 and 16 February, ISA, FM/2459.
40. Ibid., Ben-Gurion to Eban, 18 February 1957.
41. M. Medzini (ed.), *Israeli Foreign Relations, Selected Documents 1947–1974*, Jerusalem, 1976, p.596.
42. FRUS, 1955–57, pp.226–7.
43. ISA, FM/2459, 21 February 1957. The American involved was General Walter Bedell Smith.
44. Ibid., telegram containing the cabinet instructions of 22 February 1957.
45. FRUS, 1955–57, p.264.

46. ISA, FM/2459, telegrams of 25 February.
47. Ben-Gurion's telegrams, ibid.; HZ/2459, Herzog telegram to Eban of 25 February.
48. BGD, entry for 25 February 1957.
49. ISA, FM/2459. Herzog said in one of the telegrams of 26 February that 'there is no need to convey to Dulles the message concerning the mistake that had occurred'.
50. FRUS, 1955–57, pp.283–4, 285, 289, 293.
51. *Divrei Ha-Knesset*, Vol. 21, 11 November 1956, p.197ff.
52. ISA, FM/2448/8, 7 December 1956.
53. FRUS, 1955–57, pp.243–4.
54. One of the most detailed ones were in *Divrei Ha-Knesset*, Vol. 21, 23 January 1957, pp.827–9.
55. ISA, FM/2448, Eban–Hammarskjold conversation, 25 January 1957.
56. Ibid., 4 February 1957.
57. FRUS, 1955–57, p.115.
58. The text of the *aide-mémoire* is in FRUS, 1955–57, pp.132–4.
59. Ibid., pp.163–8.
60. Ibid., pp.158–65. The Israeli response can be found there, pp.165–70.
61. Ibid., pp.254–67.
62. Ibid., p.268.
63. Ibid., pp.272–3.
64. Ibid., pp.282–3.
65. Ibid., pp.291–5.
66. ISA, FM/2448/8, Eban to Jerusalem, 9 March 1957.
67. FRUS, 1955–57, p.296.
68. Ibid., pp.327–9.
69. ISA, FM/2448/11, May 1957.
70. Ibid., Eban to Jerusalem, 26 February 1957.
71. Ibid., telegram from Jerusalem to Golda Meir and Eban, 26 February.
72. FRUS, 1955–57, p.293; ISA, FM/2459, Eban to Jerusalem, 26 February.
73. Christian Pineau, *1956, Suez*, Paris, 1976, pp.209–32.
74. Brian Urquhart, *Hammarskjold*, New York, 1972, p.212.
75. FRUS, 1955–57, pp.283–5 and editor's footnote, p.285.
76. Ibid., pp.272–3.
77. Ibid., pp.274–5.
78. Ibid., p.278.
79. Ibid., pp.282–3.
80. Ibid., pp.285–9.
81. Ibid., p.312.
82. Ibid., p.316.
83. ISA, FM/2459/3. At a meeting at the Israel Embassy in Washington on 9 March Eban said that the paragraph on Gaza in the Israeli statement was written by the French. He could not know then that a day before the arrival of the French on the scene, Dulles had received Eisenhower's blessing for the moves that were to follow.
84. ISA, FM/2459, 3 March 1957.
85. FRUS, 1955–57, p.339.
86. Ibid., pp.348–9.
87. Ibid., p.357.
88. Ibid., p.360.
89. Ibid., p.332.
90. Ibid., p.353.
91. Ibid., pp.375–6.

# The 'Tranquil Decade' Re-examined: Arab–Israeli Relations During the Years 1957–67

## MENACHEM KLEIN

The view that relations between Israel and the Arab states were tranquil in the decade that separated the second and third rounds of wars was developed by Israeli figures who played a key role in the 1956 War and remains a pervasive argument in the conventional Israeli discourse. In the words of David Ben-Gurion, Israel's first Prime Minister and Minister of Defence, the Sinai Campaign 'has enhanced security on the borders and for some time has deterred our neighbours from challenging Israel'.[1] Given this view it is not surprising that Ben-Gurion, in his history of Israel, titled the study of the decade 1957–67 as 'Years of Peace'.[2]

Similarly, Moshe Dayan, the Israeli Chief-of-Staff during the 1956 War has argued that 'the main change in the situation achieved by Israel ... was manifested among her Arab neighbours. Israel's readiness to take to the sword to secure her rights at sea and her safety on land, and the capacity of her army to defeat the Egyptian forces, deterred the Arab rulers in the years that followed from renewing their acts of hostility'.[3] Mordechai Bar-On, who served at the time as Dayan's director of office, noted a similar view in his war diary: 'Security issues will not disappear from Israel's policy agenda during the upcoming years, but the Sinai Campaign has temporarily removed them from the top of the country's list of urgent priorities, and has moved them to the periphery of the state matters'.[4] For Shimon Peres, then Director-General of the Ministry of Defence under Ben-Gurion, this evaluation remained true for more than 30 years, stating in 1990 that 'we got rid of the fedayeen; we had eleven years of tranquillity; the Straits of Tiran were opened; the brilliance of the Israeli army and of Dayan emerged and received world recognition'.[5]

Menachem Klein is Senior Lecturer in Political Studies at Bar-Ilan University.

To a certain extent, Israeli academic writing on this period is more cautious. In his doctoral dissertation Bar-On reflected: 'The main accomplishment of the 1956 War in the Sinai was the respite it afforded. For ten years following 1956 Israel enjoyed a period of relative calm'.[6] This view has been reiterated by Itamar Rabinovich who has concluded that 'in the Arab–Israeli conflict the Sinai Campaign produced eleven years of relative calm.'[7]

This essay takes issue with this view. It claims the post-Sinai decade was not quiet at all. To the contrary, in the minds of the country's policymaking elite, apprehensions of renewed conflict heightened in the years following the 1956 War. The change of leadership which ensued after 1964, when Levi Eshkol replaced Ben-Gurion, led to a new, seemingly more relaxed, perception of the conflict. The new elite did not believe that the danger of war was imminent. Still, in actual fact, the Arab–Israeli conflict became more intense during these few years prior to the outbreak of the 1967 War.

By way of substantiating this claim, this essay will focus on the two main arenas in which conflict between Israel and the Arab states occurred throughout this period: in relations between Israel and Syria, and between Israel and Egypt. It will conclude with a possible explanation as to why the view of a quiet decade came to prevail in the academic and political discourse.

## ISRAEL'S CONFLICT WITH SYRIA

The decisive Israeli victory over Egypt in the 1956 War had almost no effect on the Israeli–Syrian front. Conflict between the two countries ensued within a year of the termination of the Sinai War. In August 1957, the United States and Israel began to worry about pro-Soviet encroachments on Syria. Their apprehension was due to several developments: the increasing instability in Syria; the continuing hostility between the Communist and Ba'th parties; the growing Soviet intervention in the area; and the number of border skirmishes with Israel.[8]

Israel acceded to an American request not to respond to Syria regarding these developments. At the same time, however, Israel pressured the United States to carry out an anti-Syrian plan by means of some third, pro-Western, party. According to the American plan, Turkish or Iraqi forces concentrating along Syria's borders, would instigate a Syrian response. This, in turn, would lead to a Turkish or Iraqi invasion of Syria that would result in a change of regime in Damascus. Though Israel was not meant to take part in such an invasion, it did concentrate troops along its border with Syria, apparently in the expectation that such favourable sequence of events would occur.[9]

Syria at the time was riven by numerous *coup* attempts, and Israel sought to exploit the situation by supporting a group of Syrian officers affiliated to the country's former President Adib Shishakli, then exiled in Paris. Working independently, the intelligence services of Israel and the United States were in contact with Shishakli. They encouraged him to lead this group of officers in their attempt to regain control of Syria. This plan came to nought as some of the officers leaked information to Syria's intelligence service.[10]

The conflict with Syria was not short lived. Already at the start of the 1950s, the issue of cultivating lands in the demilitarized zones controlled by Israel was a matter of contention in Israeli–Syrian relations. Israel viewed the demilitarized zones as areas under its sovereignty. Syria contended, however, that these were ownerless areas controlled by the United Nations, and as such it systematically disrupted Israel's attempts to develop them as United Nations efforts to settle this dispute consistently failed.

Also, during the 1960s, skirmishes involving sniper fire became steadily more serious. On 30 January 1960, for example, in response to Syrian fire, Israel troops fought Syrian forces in the village of Tawfiq; on 17 March 1962, the Israel Defence Forces (IDF) clashed with Syrian troops in the village of Nuqeib; and on 13 November 1964, Israel's Air Force (IAF) became embroiled for the first time in this theatre. By 1965 the question of the demilitarized zones had become connected to two other areas of controversy which caused conflict between Syria and Israel: the Arab attempts to divert the Jordan River, and collaboration between Syria and Fatah.

In 1959 the Arab states initiated a plan to divert the resources of the Jordan River in response to an Israeli decision unilaterally to implement the Johnstone Programme, which had been drafted in 1955 for a planned, joint use of the resources of the Jordan River by Syria, Lebanon, Jordan and Israel. Israel began in 1964 to draw water from the Sea of Galilee in accordance with this plan; in retaliation Syria, the main power behind the Arab plan, began to divert the Jordan's resources, in the hope of causing the river to run dry thus denying Israel of this precious water source. At the beginning of 1965 an argument about whether, and how, to respond to the Syrian actions intensified in Israel. Moshe Dayan (then a member of the Knesset) and Golda Meir, the then Minister of Foreign Affairs, contended that Israel ought to seize control of those parts of the Golan Heights in which Syria's efforts to divert the Jordan were concentrated, even at the risk of a wider confrontation with Syria.

Nevertheless, Prime Minister and Minister of Defence Levi Eshkol, together with the IDF's Chief-of-Staff Yitzhak Rabin, Mossad Director Meir Amit and the Ministers Yigal Allon and Israel Galili, believed that

Israel should not be drawn into armed conflict, especially in view of the likely American and British opposition to such actions. Acting on Rabin's advice, the political and security leadership opted to attack the Syrian equipment by means of tank fire and air attacks rather than through armed capture of territory.[11]

The second source of Syrian–Israeli tension, namely, the former's collaboration with Fatah, derived from a common interest in the intensification of the conflict with Israel. While Syria wanted to damage Israel's use of resources and water in the Israeli parts of the Jordan and the Sea of Galilee, Fatah (founded in 1959) intended to bring about a general war as early as possible, so as to liberate Palestine in the short term. By the mid-1960s, however, this Palestinian position was not perceived in Israel as a new, distinctive factor in the dispute. Instead, in the Israeli view Fatah was a puppet organization of Syria in a manner that recalled the Egyptian-backed fedayeen organizations of the 1950s.[12] The 'Rabin Doctrine' of 1965 thus constituted an attempt to resolve the mounting Syrian and Palestinian acts of hostilities, without leading to a full-scale war. Rabin argued that Israel should attack military and strategic targets in Syria since the Syrian regime was responsible for both Fatah raids and the encroachments on water resources and the cultivation of lands. At the same time, Rabin rejected attacks against Lebanon and Jordan, as he believed they sought to restrain Fatah's actions, though he did not rule out strikes against specific targets inside these countries which assisted Fatah.

The Rabin Doctrine became the focal point of a heated debate, with the Director of the Mossad, Meir Amit, arguing that Israel's responses to Syria were excessive. Still, he and the head of the Intelligence Branch, Major General Aharon Yariv, were the only senior officials calling for a more moderate Israeli response. Most opponents of the Rabin Doctrine, such as Major General Ezer Weizman, then head of the IDF Staff Branch, took the opposite tack.

This ongoing security debate was compounded by uncertainty as to how Egypt would respond to Israel if it persisted in the implementation of the Rabin Doctrine. Rabin argued that Egypt would not become embroiled in a conflict, a view contradicted by Yariv who argued that Egypt would not be able to stand aside, were Israel to initiate sustained actions against Syria.[13] In any event, all parties to the debate reasoned that Fatah was not an independent factor in the conflict; nor were the Palestinians seen as an explosive element which might detonate and cause a struggle between Israel and Syria to be transformed into a regional confrontation.

The debate over the Rabin Doctrine was not confined to security circles, but spilled over into the political arena. After Ben-Gurion's secession from Mapai in 1963, parties split over the issue: Rafi and

Gahal joined forces on the one hand, and on the other side Mapai and Ahdut Ha-avoda supported each other. This was also a political struggle in which the new political–security elite clashed with the old establishment. The new leaders of the 1960s, Eshkol, together with minister Galili and Allon, Mossad Director Meir Amit and IDF Chief-of-Staff Yitzhak Rabin, disagreed with former Prime Minister and Defence Minister Ben-Gurion, and his young disciples Moshe Dayan and Shimon Peres. This group formed the Rafi Party and found itself disillusioned, marginalized and removed from the centres of influence and power. But they nevertheless set out to oppose what they termed 'security impasses', a codeword for the views and actions of the new leadership.

The Rafi leadership used its experience and reputation to criticize (even de-legitimize) the Rabin Doctrine, using Israeli casualties caused by Fatah to promote an atmosphere of insecurity in the country. For its part, the new leadership, anxious to establish its credentials, was acutely sensitive to such charges. This shift in Israel's political landscape, as well as the divisiveness of the debate about military policy, provides the backdrop for the importance attributed by Israel to border skirmishes with Syria and to Fatah infiltrations. Between January 1965 and the June 1967 War, 14 Israelis were killed and 72 were wounded due to Fatah operations.[14]

From May to June 1966 and throughout the year which preceded the Six Day War, Israel prepared a series of wide-ranging retaliation acts against Syria which had escalated its attacks against Israeli civilian targets. Though these plans were not implemented, it is doubtful whether they would have curbed the escalation in the conflict with Syria during October–November 1966. As shall be shown below, the matter was transformed from a two-sided dispute into a regional confrontation. In October 1966, Rabin described his policy *vis-à-vis* the Syrians as follows: 'The response to Syria's actions should be targeted against the terrorist operations and against the regime … in essence, the Syrian problem involves clashes with the ruling power. In this sense, the situation can be compared to relations which obtained between Israel and Egypt in 1955–56'.[15]

Accordingly, in October the Israeli Chief-of-Staff attempted to gain his government's approval for a limited but vigorous air operation against Syria that was to involve the deployment of 80 planes, the targeting of primary Syrian headquarters and artillery bases, and the capture of a number of fortifications on Syria's front line. All this was to be achieved within a 24-hour period. A few weeks later, the objectives of this operation were amplified. The goal now became the capture of a large portion of the Golan Heights, and the stationing of the IDF there for an unspecified period. Rabin's plan, however, was put on hold, as Eshkol decided to attempt a political resolution.[16]

Following the killing of three soldiers by a mine laid by Fatah operatives, a large IDF contingent retaliated in daylight against the village of Samu in Jordan, which was located near the mine zone. Property damage and injuries to civilians were considerable; also, a Jordan Legion force was surprised by an Israeli ambush and sustained heavy losses (14 dead, 37 wounded, three prisoners), and a plane was shot down.

This Israeli operation was conducted despite pleas for restraint by King Hussein, who promised to pursue the Fatah contingent responsible for the strike. Rabin and Eshkol rejected this appeal. They declared publicly that Hussein lacked the ability to impose law and order, and so Israel was forced to act as it did.[17] The operation ruptured Hussein's contacts with Israel, and also encouraged Syria and Fatah to persist in their militant policies, as they watched Israel punish a regime for which they had nothing but contempt.

A string of pro-Palestine Liberation Organization demonstrations erupted on the West Bank, and Hussein launched a campaign of invective against Egypt for failing to come to his aid and for hiding behind United Nations Emergency Forces in Sinai (UNEF). The Egyptian position, it should be recalled, was indeed formulated by President Gamal Abdel Nasser; still there were high officers in the Egyptian army who thought differently, and who wanted to heed Hussein's entreaty. Abd al-Hakim Amer, the head of the army, on his way to Pakistan from a visit to the Soviet Union, called upon Nasser to remove UNEF from the Sinai, to seize and close the Straits of Tiran, and to brace Egypt for a defensive operation on the eastern part of the Sinai.[18] In November–December 1966, Nasser rejected these measures. In May 1967, as is well known, he did precisely that, thereby leading to war the following month.

In short, the Samu operation sealed a process by which the Israel–Syria dispute was converted into a regional conflict. An examination of this conflict in the period between the 1956 and 1967 wars reveals that until 1965 the struggle on the Syrian–Israeli border was continuous, if generally sporadic. Latent in this struggle was its possible transformation into a general confrontation; this took some time and in actual reality occurred rather late. Yet in the minds of Israel's leaders, the fear of such an escalation had existed already in 1963. Between 1965 and the Six Day War the Israel–Syria struggle became especially sensitive and contentious, as the sporadic local outbreaks of armed violence became frequent, planned initiatives often spreading over a wide stretch of land which encompassed most of the Israeli–Syrian border.

## THE CONFLICT BETWEEN ISRAEL AND EGYPT

From 1955 Israel viewed Nasser's Egypt as its main enemy. The following year it joined forces with Britain and France in a combined war effort with the aim of toppling his regime.[19] As part of the arrangements which brought about Israel's withdrawal after the war, Egypt consented that commercial agents and Israel-bound ships would have free passage in the Suez Canal. This agreement was upheld in the two years between April 1957 and March 1959; but afterwards, and through October 1959, several boats whose destination or port of origin was Israel were detained. Israel was unsuccessful in its bid to get UN forces to enforce the agreement and make Egypt live up to its obligation; and the faith of Israeli leaders in agreements that were built upon hopes and expectations, rather than formal and contractual rules, was shattered. This development especially influenced Foreign Minister Meir's attitude and approach to conflict resolution. When she led a failed struggle in the United Nations in 1956–57 to prevent a withdrawal from the Sinai, Meir suffered from feelings of isolation and rejection. These feelings encouraged a view of the Arab–Israeli conflict as a struggle between a force of light which seeks peace, and a force of darkness that rebuffs hands outstretched in hopes of peaceable agreement. The added political failure strengthened this bleak perception and Meir went so far as to claim that she had been informed by an Arab leader that no Arab leader had in his heart any measure of readiness to make peace with Israel.[20]

The Israeli fears were further exacerbated by the establishment of the Egyptian–Syrian United Arab Republic (UAR) in 1958. All of a sudden, Israel started to fear that perhaps the grim prospect of Arab pincers encroaching from the north and south might become a fact. The entire Middle East seemed to be falling into Nasser's lap. Israel viewed Abd al-Karim Qassem's *coup* in Iraq in July 1958 as a gain for Nasser, and Ben-Gurion made manifest these anxieties when he stated that the *coup* represented one of the gravest tragedies in the post-war world.[21]

In the aftermath of the *coup*, Israel asked the United States to influence Iran and Turkey to intervene to try to restore the pro-Western regime and the Baghdad Pact in Iraq.[22] At the end of 1958 the United States feared that Qassem would effect a turnabout and join forces with the Communists; and so America began to plan a counter-revolt. By now Israel had changed its position claiming that the new regime should be left standing, since it formulated a neutral policy towards Nasser.[23]

Still more worrying to Israel than the internal affairs of Iraq was the possibility of a pro-Nasser *coup* in Jordan. Israel prepared itself at least twice in 1958–63 for the possibility of capturing either the West Bank as a whole or some portion of it in response to such a development. The first such state of alert occurred in July 1958, one week after the overthrow of the monarchy in Iraq.[24] The second instance occurred in 1963, in the wake of the Ba'th *coups* in Syria (February) and in Iraq (March), and the signing of an accord between these states and Egypt in April.

Debates and preparations in Israel differed in focus from the discussions that ensued in the United States and Britain. Instead of contemplating how Hussein might be saved, the Israelis wondered how they should respond once Hussein was removed from power, or fell into Nasser's hands. Intelligence data arriving in Israel was interpreted as though Hussein would imminently lose power or be swept up in the wave of unity which was washing over the entire Arab world. The infiltration of Egyptian, Iraqi and Syrian forces into Jordan was already envisaged by Israeli leaders and they planned for a scenario whereby Egypt usurped the Jordanian Legion.

The nightmare of total Egyptian encirclement of Israel appeared to be on the brink of realization. Ben-Gurion attempted to obtain authorization for some response from the United States and France; but the Americans evaluated the situation differently, judging that Hussein's position was stable and that the United States was ultimately responsible for the stability of the Hashemite Kingdom. The United States asked Israel that even in the event of a widespread pro-Nasser movement taking hold in Jordan, there was to be no intervention in the internal affairs of its neighbour.[25]

Israel's response to the events of 1958 and 1963 derived from the excessive gravity it attributed to each sign of Arab unity shown subsequent to the formation of the United Arab Republic. Israeli leaders viewed the UAR as a stable, structurally sound unit. They were not aware of the internal dissent and complications which split the body. Israel's fear became greater after February 1960 when Egypt secretly moved 500 tanks and two infantry divisions into the Sinai (the Rotem alert), in violation of UN resolutions on demilitarization. Israel learned about the Egyptian entry from American intelligence sources only after six days. Even after the collapse of the UAR in 1961, Ben-Gurion and other leaders acted as though the advent of Arab unity was still a reality, though at this point, Israeli intelligence reasoned that such unity did not constitute a real threat.

Similarly, while the formation of a union between Egypt, Syria and Iraq in April 1963 was in actual fact a paper agreement not destined to last any significant period of time, the Israelis viewed the pact as though it were geared towards the destruction of Israel. Responding to the creation of the union, Ben-Gurion sent urgent cables to 60 heads of state around the world, demanding that they guarantee Israel's security and that they sever all aid to any country which refused to acknowledge the existence of its neighbour.

Beyond this, while President Kennedy did not accept Ben-Gurion's grim evaluation of the situation, the Israeli leader pressed the White House to bring about the demilitarization of the West Bank and to sign a treaty with Israel which would insure the latter against the possibility that Hussein would be deposed or join forces with the UAR.[26]

In the 1957–63 period, Israel's leadership developed a long-term view which accompanied its short-term responses to immediate threats and perceived situations. The necessity for the evolution of this long-term policy derived from the fear that as the years passed Israel would not be able to stand up to its enemies, due to the demographic asymmetry between them. Acting in the international sphere, Ben-Gurion repeatedly attempted to extract from the United States both a formal commitment towards Israel's security, and a bilateral agreement against pro-Soviet Arab states, especially Egypt and Syria. Ben-Gurion also asked the United States for a supply of top-rate, sophisticated weaponry, and he even called for Israel's entry into NATO.

These efforts came to nothing as Washington tended to isolate the Arab–Israeli dispute and to deal with it at some remove from the superpower conflict. The Americans simply did not perceive the threats to Israel with the gravity which Ben-Gurion attributed to them; and the United States tried to strengthen its position in the Middle East not by making a pact with the Israelis, but rather by using its leverage to effect a pro-Western bloc in the Arab world.[27]

The new long-term Israeli policy also concerned activity in the regional sphere. The Israelis sought collaborative, anti-Nasserist agreements with moderate countries which were also believed to be threatened and targeted in schemes hatched by the Egyptians – namely, Jordan, Morocco, Lebanon, Sudan, Tunisia and even the Qassem regime in Iraq and the Saudi regime. Tacit co-operation of sorts was sought separately with each of these states. Essentially they were designed to allow Israel to support any attempts to liquidate signs of Nasserist encroachment, as well as to facilitate Jewish emigration to Israel. Because of their common borders with Israel, in the cases of Jordan and Lebanon, these collaborative agreements also provided for *ad hoc* solutions to bilateral problems that arose along the ceasefire zones.[28] To supplement these collaborative arrangements, in 1957–58 Israel prepared what it termed 'an alliance with the peripheral states' – Turkey, Iran, Ethiopia – that is, non-Arab, pro-Western states which bordered the Arab Middle East. In actual fact, a full-blown alliance was not the object of Israeli policy. Instead, the Israelis sought anti-Nasserist collaboration with each one of these states in intelligence, operational and political spheres.

The development of nuclear capabilities was another policy Israel followed in order to cope with the threat posed by Nasser. Common fears shared by France and Israel led to the signing of an agreement in October 1957 by which France provided Israel with a nuclear reactor. This was a novel twist in the Israeli–Arab dispute, as Ben-Gurion had originally opposed adding a nuclear element to the conflict. This resistance dissipated at the end of the 1950s and the beginning of the 1960s as his fears about the nature of the conflict, and about the policy responses of the United States, mounted.

In particular, in this period he became a proponent of an Israeli nuclear programme, owing to his evaluation both of Nasser's growing strength, and of the lopsided imbalance of power that obtained between Israel and its many Arab neighbours and enemies. Ben-Gurion decided that only a nuclear capability would guarantee the future existence of the state, as Israel would otherwise be engulfed by an abundance of manpower and capital in the Arab world, as well as by the advance of certain Arab states in scientific and military spheres. Israel, Ben-Gurion reasoned, could not keep pace over the long haul in a conventional arms race with these powers. The fact that Ben-Gurion actually manoeuvred to deflect American attempts to restrain Israel's nuclear arms build-up testifies to the seriousness with which Israel's elder statesmen viewed the Arab threat.[29]

With Ben-Gurion's departure from politics and the formation of a new government in Israel at the end of 1963, Israel's policy altered. As they began to view the Arab threat in somewhat different terms, and to work towards a new policy orientation in relations with France and the United States, Israel's statesmen determined to compensate a slow-down in the nation's new nuclear arms policy with an accelerated build-up of the country's strength in terms of conventional weaponry. This change did not alleviate the anxieties of all Israeli leaders. As early as Ben-Gurion's last days in office, the Egyptian response to Israel's new nuclear policy – the development of surface-to-surface missiles that could be capped with biological, chemical and radiological warheads – worried Israel's policymakers.

In 1962–63 Israel attempted to derail Egypt's attempt to develop the missiles by sending Mossad agents to track down German scientists who were working on the project. Israel's endeavours were only partially successful at best; and the Mossad estimated in 1966 that the Egyptian missile programme was, as far as Israel was concerned, approaching a dangerous level. This was the background to Yigal Allon's threat in April 1966 to damage the dams of the Nile and thus flood Egypt.[30]

The policy directives and inclinations outlined above indicate that Israeli statesmen were guided by a particular view of the Egyptian ruler. Indeed, throughout the 1950s and into the 1960s, Israeli leaders viewed Nasser as though he were a demonic force. On more than one occasion, Ben-Gurion compared Nasser to Hitler, and he made a habit of calling

Nasser the Egyptian tyrant. Ben-Gurion thought Nasser to be a strong man and politician, and a patriot of sorts; and he viewed Nasser as a dangerous force, and as the most troublesome of Israel's enemies.[31] Golda Meir's approach was no less riddled with pessimism. She viewed Nasser as a fearsome, monstrous figure who would never be willing to come to terms with Israel. During a conversation with President Kennedy, she expressed the fear that Nasser would recapitulate his threat to perpetrate a Holocaust, emphasizing that Nasser and his ambitions undermined all Israeli efforts to establish a sovereign state. Meir argued that Nasser was harmful not only to Israel but also to Egypt as the Egyptian people must really have longed for a peaceful settlement with Israel so as to deal with their own weighty internal problems.[32] This view was shared by Major General Yehoshafat Harkabi, head of IDF Intelligence 1954–59, who viewed Nasser as the 'source of evil' and argued that:

> Were Nasser to die, this would only benefit Israel ... Nasser reasoned that Israel must be annihilated so that 1956 would not repeat itself, and I believed that he was turning his eyes towards the destruction of Israel. His speeches struck in me a chord of fear. I myself was astonished by him, by his powerful charisma and ability to electrify the Arab world, and I thought – in the end, all of this would be turned against Israel.[33]

Israel's military leadership occasionally discussed the idea of sponsoring Nasser's assassination. In the end, however, nothing came out of such thoughts. As Peres's biographer reflected: 'Many Israelis believed honestly that if they were rid of the militant, nationalist President, all of their problems would be over'. It would seem that the obstacle that thwarted this plan was political in nature, and not an issue of principle; more precisely, it was impossible to carry out such a deed without being held culpable for the act before the international community.[34]

A change in Israel's perception of Nasser was brought about by the shift in the country's leadership in 1963. Throughout the 1957–64 period, Rabin viewed Nasser as a triumphant ruler; after 1964, however, he saw the Egyptian as a stricken leader whose successes were already behind him due to the collapse of the UAR in 1961 and Egypt's military involvement since 1962 in the civil war in Yemen.[35] Eshkol saw Nasser as an ambiguous figure,[36] while Aharon Yariv, the director of the intelligence branch since 1963, saw Nasser as 'enemy number one, and the only individual capable of forming an effective front, despite his entanglement in Yemen, and despite the failure of the unification talks in 1963. Though his timetables have been thrown out of synch, this dangerous man will be ready by 1970'.[37] To be sure, Yariv's estimate of Nasser was more pessimistic than that of Rabin and Eshkol; nevertheless, he also did not perceive Nasser as an actual, present threat. In contrast to the estimations of its predecessor, the new political–security establishment in Israel did not search for a way to harm Nasser directly. As Meir Amit has said: 'I did not reckon that the way to rid oneself of a problem was to liquidate a person. I did not follow this line of thought; nor was I really searching for this sort of solution, though we did reason that if he were to descend from the stage, our situation would improve'.[38]

Amit and Eshkol thus operated on two different levels. First, they did not refrain from aiding other forces which were intent upon harming Nasser. Second, they took advantage of the threat Nasser posed to moderate Arab states; they endeavoured to strengthen Israel's ties with these states, as well as with Iran, Turkey and Ethiopia. In other words, throughout the tenure of Eshkol and Amit, Israel changed a basic foreign policy approach, ceasing any direct intervention in the internal affairs of the Arab states. In policy situations where Israel might be asked to lend support, and in cases where it had an interest in helping a foreign ruler maintain control, Israel's agents did not themselves strike against opposition elements. At the same time, they gave indirect support to the elimination of unwanted forces by providing intelligence information.

Efforts by Israel's leaders to find a way to discuss matters with the Egyptians peaceably also reflect perceptions of their neighbours and assumptions that motivated policy directives. In other words, the character of discussions held between the Israelis and the Egyptians in the 1957–67 period is a measure of the character of the conflict. Ben-Gurion, it will be recalled, viewed the threat posed by the Arabs and Nasser to be especially ominous, and he thus maintained that the Arabs must undergo a radical transformation if they were to seek peace with Israel. They must, he believed, relinquish any belief in the possibility of exterminating Israel. This view led Ben-Gurion to demand a meeting between himself and Nasser. At the same time, he did not predicate such an encounter upon the momentous transformation he expected as a precondition of peace. Throughout the years 1961–63, Ben-Gurion turned to mediators such as O-Nu, Prime Minister of Burma, Tito, the President of Yugoslavia and the *Sunday Times* journalist James Hamilton in an attempt to arrange a meeting with Nasser.[39] Second, Ben-Gurion did not offer the Arabs any sort of positive reinforcement. As a matter of fact, he tendered only forms of negative reinforcement so as to pressure the Arabs toward frustration and despair. He thus spurned Yigal Allon's policy proposal, set out in 1959, that interim arrangements ought to be sought with the Egyptians, for the short-term purpose of preventing misunderstandings which could lead to an escalation of tension and war, and which would in the longer term lead to bona fide security arrangements.[40]

Allon's policy view was, for its time, utterly radical in terms of its projection of a thaw in Egyptian–Israeli relations; with respect to the balance and symmetry in power relations between the two countries which it envisaged; and in terms of the fact that it endorsed the use of positive incentives. As Ben-Gurion virtually dictated Israel's position to the country's power elite, Allon's plan was scrapped, and remained an entirely academic notion.

The efforts to initiate dialogue between Israel and Egypt were influenced only in limited measure by the formation of Eshkol's government, and the changes in the perception of the Arab threat which accompanied it. During Eshkol's tenure, the Mossad was entrusted with the responsibility of maintaining contacts with states which did not have formal diplomatic ties with Israel; certain overtures to Nasser were part of this Mossad effort, yet during the 1963–67 period they did not achieve much. The change in policy brought about by the new leadership was not comprehensive, as Israel's leaders doubted that the basic Arab position had changed. Still influenced by Ben-Gurion's doctrine, they continued to wait for a radical transformation of the Arab view.

While the new elite believed that the danger posed by Nasser was latent, rather than a present emergency, this more moderate view did not stimulate a political breakthrough. In this context, the most conspicuous failure was the breakdown of contacts with Egypt in 1965. General Isam al-Din Halil, one of the senior advisers to Marshal Amer, the Egyptian Minister of War, mediated in Paris between the director of the Mossad, Amit and Deputy Minister of the Treasury Zvi Dinstein, and the Egyptian Minister. It would seem that issues such as Egypt's economic and social ills during this period, along with Amit's desire to slow down the arms race were topics of discussion during this meeting; and after the discussion, the two were invited to Cairo for a meeting with Amer himself. Yet Eshkol decided to veto the trip as Amit and Isar Harel, his predecessor (and rival) at the head of the Mossad, believed that the invitation was an Egyptian trap.[41]

CONCLUSION

This essay has argued that the decade which stretched between the second and the third Arab–Israeli wars was far from tranquil in character. To be sure, no general war between Israel and its neighbours ensued in this period. Still, the chasm between this and a definition of the era as a 'tranquil decade' is wide. If this is the case, then why has such a conception of the period become widely accepted? Beyond the tendency to evaluate the Arab–Israeli conflict in terms of consecutive outbreaks of full-blown war, the notion of a 'tranquil decade' may well have evolved as a cover for Israel's failure to attain its long-term objectives in 1956. By claiming that the 1956 War led to an easing of the Arab–Israeli conflict for ten years, Israeli leaders sought to portray the war as a limited operation aimed mainly at stopping the string of Egyptian-based fedayeen attacks against Israel's civilian population and at securing free passage in the straits of Tiran, at a time when the war's real long-term objective was the toppling of Nasser's regime.

## NOTES

1. David Ben-Gurion, *Israel: Years of Challenge*, London 1963, p.189.
2. David Ben-Gurion, *Israel – A Personal History*, New York, 1971, p.445. Similarly, Michael Bar-Zohar, one of Ben-Gurion's biographers, wrote that 'the Sinai Campaign brought Israel rich dividends, first and foremost ten years of peace. One after another, her borders fell silent'. See *Ben-Gurion: A Biography*, New York, 1977, p.258.
3. Moshe Dayan, *Diary of the Sinai Campaign*, New York, 1967, p.207. See also his *Story of My Life*, New York, 1976, p.259.
4. Mordechai Bar-On, *Etgar Ve-tigra: Ha-derech Le-sinai 1956*, Beersheba, 1991, p.331.
5. Shimon Peres, 'The Road to Sevres: Franco-Israeli Strategic Cooperation', in Ilan S. Troen and Moshe Shemesh (eds), *The Suez–Sinai Crisis*, London, 1990, pp.148–9. The term 'tranquil decade' was also used by Meir Amit, the IDF's head of the Staff Branch in the 1956 War, in a 1986 interview. See Yosef Evron, *Suez 1956 Be-mabat Hadash*, Tel Aviv, 1986, p.177. See also Daviv Shaham, *Israel 40 Ha-shanim*, Tel Aviv, 1991, pp.147, 158; Chaim Herzog, 'The Suez–Sinai Campaign: Background', in Troen and Shemesh, *The Suez–Sinai Crisis*, pp.3–14; and Yitzhak Rabin, 'The Sinai Campaign and the Limits of Power', ibid., pp.238–48.
6. Mordechai Bar-On, *Sha'arei Aza: Mediniyut Ha-huz Veha-bitahon Shel Israel 1955–1957*, Tel Aviv, 1992, p.382.
7. Itamar Rabinovich, 'The Suez–Sinai Campaign: The Regional Dimension', in Troen and Shemesh, *The Suez–Sinai Crisis*, p.170.
8. Meir Avidan, *Hebetim Iqaryyim Be-yahasei Israel Ve-artzot Ha-brit Bi-shnot Ha-hamishim*, Jerusalem, 1982, pp.83–4.
9. David Eishenhower, *Waging Peace 1956–1961*, New York, 1965, pp.119–20, 200, 286–93; Townsend Hoopes, *The Devil and John Foster Dulles*, Boston, 1973, pp.119–20; Moshe Zak, 'Zalafim Mul Mazilim', *Maariv*, 28 October 1983; Patrick Seale, *The Struggle for Syria*, London, 1966. See also Muhammad Heikal's weekly column in *al-Ahram*, 12 June 1965.
10. Nadav Safran, *Medinat Israel Ve-yahaseha Im Artzot Ha-brit*, Tel Aviv, 1979, p.326; Gideon Raphael, *Be-sod Leumim*, Tel Aviv, 1981, p.75; Michael Bar-Zohar, *Ben-Gurion*, Tel Aviv, 1977, p.1318. The notes here and below relate to the longer Hebrew version of Bar-Zohar's biography of Ben-Gurion.
11. See *Ha-aretz* and *Maariv*, March–April 1965; Yitzhak Rabin, *Pinqas Sherut*, Tel Aviv, 1979, pp.121–9; *Divrei Ha-Knesset*, Vol. 45 (1966), p.1020.
12. Or as Moshe Dayan called them in the Knesset, 'a few dozen bandits'. *Divrei Ha-Knesset*, Vol. 47 (1967), p.32.
13. Author's interviews with Aharon Yariv, Meir Amit, and Yitzhak Rabin in 1982.
14. Yehoshafat Harkabi, *Fatah Ba-estrategia Ha-arvit*, Tel Aviv, 1969, pp.66–7.
15. Moshe Gilboa, *Shesh Shanim Shisha Yamim*, Tel Aviv, 1969, p.60.
16. Amir Oren, 'Dog-fight Ve-underdog Ve-lo Od Dog-matim', *Davar*, 19 February 1993, p.9; Jon Kimche, 'Zahal Bein Ha-derg Ha-medini Veha-tzvai', *Maariv*, 18 February 1983, p.15.
17. See *Divrei Ha-Knesset*, Vol. 47 (1967), pp.290–93; David Kimche and Dan Bavli, *Sufat Ha-esh: Milhemet Sheshet Ha-yamim, Meqoroteha Ve-tozoteha*, Tel Aviv, 1968, p.72.
18. Gilboa, *Shesh Shanim*, p.76; Richard B. Parker, *The Politics of Miscalculation in the Middle East*, Bloomington, 1993, p.91.
19. J.A. Sellers, 'Military Lessons: The British Perspective', in Troen and Shemesh, *The*

*Suez–Sinai Crisis*, pp.17–53; Julian Amery, 'The Suez Group: A Retrospective on Suez', ibid., pp.306–9.

20. Golda Meir, *Hayyai*, Tel Aviv, 1975, pp.220–25; *Divrei Ha-Knesset*, Vol. 28 (1960), p.176; Brian Urqhart, *Hammarskjold*, New York, 1972, pp.303–6; author's interview with Mordechai Gazit in 1982.

21. *Divrei Ha-Knesset*, Vol. 26 (1958), p.2341. On Israel's readiness in December 1958 to attack the Syrian and Egyptian air forces following the heightening of tension on the Israel–Syria border see Amir Oren, 'Nifgeu Bi-teunat Imunim', *Davar*, 4 June 1993, p.9; Moshe Sharett, *Yoman Ishi*, Tel Aviv, 1978, p.2309.

22. Israel's policies during the first stage of Qassem's *coup* were founded upon faulty intelligence reports overestimating the power of the pro-Nasserist section among the rebels. American intelligence discerned that Qassem had defeated the pro-Nasser faction in his camp, but Israeli intelligence was oblivious to this. The author's interview with Yehoshafat Harkabi, 1982; Eishenhower, *Waging Peace 1956–1961*, pp.270–71, 288.

23. Author's interview with Harkabi and Yehuda Tagar in 1982; Avidan, *Hebetim Iqaryyim*, pp.90–92.

24. Bar-Zohar, *Ben-Gurion*, 1333–4, 1342; Uzi Narkis, *Ahat Yerushalaim*, Tel Aviv, 1975, pp.28–31, 51–3.

25. Moshe Zak, 'Ha-sibuchim Ba-derech Le-rabat Ammon', *Maariv*, 11 July 1980, p.21, and 'Kol Ha-pgishot Im Hussein', *Maariv*, 31 March 1980, p.19, and 'Ha-misdaron Le-aza Hifrid Bein Ben-Gurion La-melech Abdallah', *Maariv*, 17 October 1986, pp.22–3.

26. Yehoshafat Harkabi and Mordechai Gazit in an interview with author, 1982; *Divrei Ha-Knesset*, Vol. 40 (1963), p.1268; Bar-Zohar, *Ben-Gurion*, pp.1550–52. The American intelligence assessment was comparable to that of the Israeli intelligence. See Mordechai Gazit, *President Kennedy's Policy Towards the Arab States and Israel, Analysis and Documents*, Tel Aviv, 1983, pp.49–52, 120–21.

27. *Divrei Ha-Knesset*, Vol. 22 (1957), pp.2039–41; Bar-Zohar, *Ben-Gurion*, pp.1319–41.

28. Gazit, *President Kennedy's Policy*, pp.92, 109; Menachem Klein, *Praqim Beyachasey Israel v-Ha'aravim Bein Hashanim 1957–1967*, Truman Institute,The Hebrew University, Jerusalem, 1986, pp.69–71; Avner Yaniv, *Politica Ve-estrategiya Be-Israel*,Tel Aviv, 1994, pp.164–7, 172–8; Yaron Tzur, 'Ha-nasih, Ha-diplomat Veha-iska, *Ha-aretz*, 18 November 1994; Avraham Peleg, 'Mumhim Yardenim Biqru Be-Israel Le-diyun al Tochniyot Yam Ha-melach', *Maariv*, 27 May 1983, p.19. For a study of the contacts made by Israel with moderate opposition groups in radicalized Algeria, see Raphael, *Besod Leumim*, pp.75–6, 78–81. On the Mossad and the Israeli embassy in Paris contacts with the Tunisian regime in 1961 see David Ariel to Yaacov Karoz, 24 February 1961 and David Ariel to the Israeli Embassy, Paris, 17 February 1961, Israel State Archives, 3759/2.

29. American pressure in this regard began in 1960 when the existence of the Dimona reactor was exposed, and the US even sent jets to gather intelligence about the reactor. See *Maariv*, 21 July 1963.

30. Amit's interview with the author, 1982; Yigal Allon, 'Kochot Ha-magen Ha-israelim Meha-etmol La-machar', *Ma'arachot*, No. 174–5 (March–April 1966), p.79.

31. Gazit, *President Kennedy's Policy*, pp.125–9; Bar-Zohar, *Ben-Gurion*, pp.1524, 1553.

32. Author's interview with Harkabi in 1982.

33. Ibid.

34. Matti Golan, *Peres*, Tel Aviv, 1982, p.122. For a description of plans drawn up by French and Israeli intelligence officers to assassinate Nasser immediately after the 1957 withdrawal from the Suez Canal, see Oded Granot, 'Qtzinei Modi'in Israelim Ve-tzorphatim Tichnenu Le-hitnaqesh Be-Abdel Nasser', *Maariv*, 24 October 1986, p.16.

35. Rabin in a 1982 interview with the author.

36. *Divrei Ha-Knesset*, Vol. 41 (1965), pp.2–3.

37. Yariv in a 1982 interview with the author.

38. Amit in an interview with the author, 1982.

39. Bar-Zohar, *Ben-Gurion*, pp.1525–6; Gilboa, *Shesh Shanim*, p.31; Golan, *Peres*, pp.121–2.

40. Yigal Allon, *Masach Shel Hol*, Tel Aviv, 1960, pp.355–6.

41. Uri Dan, *Mivtz'a Gome*, Tel Aviv, 1981, pp.16–17; Meir Amit in an interview with the author, 1982, and also in an interview published in *Yediot Aharonot*, 11 May 1979.

# Israel's Nuclear Programme, the Six Day War and Its Ramifications

## SHLOMO ARONSON

The main thesis of this essay is that, ironically enough, during the 1967 Middle East crisis, the Israeli cabinet believed the country's nuclear programme to figure most prominently on the Arab list of Israeli targets. The irony lies obviously in the fact that Israel's initial effort to acquire the ultimate deterrent had aimed at driving the Arabs to accept the Jewish state within its 1949 boundaries. But this strategy, initiated by Prime Minister David Ben-Gurion, was contested by members of the Israeli elite for several reasons, including fear of American pressure and/or Soviet reaction. Parallel to Ben-Gurion's nuclear endeavour, a strategy of conventional pre-emption was developed already during his own tenure, later to be established as a doctrine by his political rival, Yigal Allon, and implemented during the May 1967 crisis. The Israeli cabinet deliberated beforehand whether the Egyptian challenge at the time was not aimed at its nuclear project, hence an Israeli pre-emptive war might in fact play into Arab hands seeking to destroy its nuclear option.

Following the Israeli conventional pre-emptive operations in June 1967, the Arabs adopted conventional war aims leading to the 1973 Yom Kippur War. Israel's nuclear option (which survived the 1967 crisis unscathed), together with the peace negotiations between Israel and its neighbours following the 1973 War, the active regional role played by the United States, and changes in the Arab world and in the former Soviet Union, may explain the current peace process in the region, and some domestic Israeli difficulties in this regard anchored in the results of the Six Day War.

### DAVID BEN-GURION AND THE BOMB

The attention given by Israel's founding father, David Ben-Gurion, to the atomic bomb was grounded in three observations. First, that the

Shlomo Aronson is Professor of Political Science at the Hebrew University in Jerusalem.

Jews of Europe were trapped between Hitler, who had destroyed them, and the Allies, who could not rescue them or refused to absorb them owing to various political reasons, some of them legitimate. Second, that in the nuclear age, at the height of the Cold War, similar reasons led the West to refuse to do Israel's fighting for it. Third, Israel's War of Independence (1948–49) established the newly born state within improved Armistice Demarcation Lines (ADLs) in a partitioned Palestine, which must remain partitioned in principle, however constrained its borders were, while the conventional variables (manpower ratio, Arab territorial, political and economic potential) would prevent the Arabs from accepting Israel unless the bomb was acquired by Israel first, while pan-Arab leaders of the time would seek the bomb anyway.

Hence the bomb was perceived by Ben-Gurion as a must, which had to be acquired before the Arabs developed a means of mass destruction or won a series of conventional rounds which they could afford thanks to their conventional political–economic superiority. At the same time, the acquisition of the bomb by Israel would allow the Arabs to retreat from their conventional political obligation to obliterate the Jewish island in the midst of the Arab ocean. Since Israel enjoyed an edge over the Arabs in terms of technological know-how and connections abroad, and since there were no established international means of enforcement such as the International Atomic Energy Agency (IAEA) and the Non-Proliferation Treaty (NPT) at the time, Israel had a window of opportunity to join the club this way or the other.

The moral–political justification of such an unprecedented endeavour was anchored in the asymmetrical character of the Arab–Israeli conflict, and in historical–cultural givens in the Arab–Muslim coalition. The asymmetry was not just a matter of Arab numbers, vast territories, economic muscle, and strategic importance at the height of the Cold War. It was also a matter of official Arab policy and the declared Arab aim to destroy Israel, whereas Israel did not want to destroy the Arab states. The Arabs obviously had their genuine fears, political calculations, domestic necessities and the need for support from the Palestinian Diaspora. If the Arabs wanted to destroy Israel, then the Jewish state was justified in seeking to deter them through the threat of insufferable damage. This asymmetry would still persist if the Arabs acquired the bomb or other means of mass destruction – because for Israel the only objective would be national survival whereas for Arabs the obliteration of Israel – by whatever means – might mean a series of unmitigated disasters in the nuclear age.

Moreover, Arab–Muslim political culture and its ensuing behaviour – or several patterns of behaviour – were viewed by Ben-Gurion as removed from Western traditions of mass-industrial war fighting. True, the Arabs had very good reasons not to accept Israel and to try to obliterate it; but this did not necessarily mean preparedness on their part for enormous damage to their earthly existences for the sake of transcendental goals or values. Arab interests, Arab rights and Arab honour were at stake since Israel's birth and before, but the political–strategic means aimed at (re)gaining them were conventional not only in terms of numbers and political muscle but also in the conceptual sense. Hence, reasoned Ben-Gurion, the bomb might give them the ladder for a climb-down from their commitment to the destruction of an unconventional Israel: not merely because of its immense power of destruction but because of its revolutionary nature, which could justify Arab concessions without being viewed as surrender to Jewish (conventional) sword. This required Israel to behave prudently with regard to several conventional issues such as boundaries (partition of Western Palestine), rule over occupied Arabs (none), and the use of conventional force (retaliatory acts). Obviously, it is arguable that such a world view could only encourage the Arabs to acquire, or even to use the bomb. Nor could Israel ignore the American interest in maintaining the nuclear club as closed as possible, given that this was the only weapon which could conceivably threaten a superpower especially when acquired by small and contested entities. Also, the Soviet wrath in this regard, since Israel was viewed as effectively part of the West, was expected to complicate superpower relations still further. For its part Britain took a position similar to that of the United States.

## THE 1956 SUEZ CAMPAIGN

France's situation was unique at the time, because it found itself in confrontation with the Arab majority in Algeria, supported by other Arab factors spearheaded by Egypt's pan-Arab President Gamal Abdel Nasser. In Europe, France tried to retain its strategic–political edge over West Germany by building a nuclear infrastructure, but the typical infighting between the numerous political parties of the Fourth Republic did not allow a final decision to acquire an independent nuclear military force, or share such an effort with other European powers, or to agree with them on the establishment of a European Common Market. Such decisions, and the decision to give Israel what premier Guy Mollet called 'the royal gift', namely, a complete nuclear infrastructure, resulted from the 1956 Suez Campaign, or rather from its failure.

The initial negotiations on French–Israeli military collaboration against Egypt entailed a French promise in the nuclear sphere, since Ben-Gurion was not ready to join the Anglo-French coalition in its bid to recover the Suez Canal and thus pre-empt Egypt's growing conventional threat only. Yet the campaign's complete fiasco as far as the two

European powers were concerned, leading to US–Soviet co-operation against both of them (and Israel), including American economic pressure and public Soviet threat to use nuclear weapons against Paris and London (while threatening Israel's very survival), triggered a string of consequent French decisions.

The first such decision was the creation of the European Atomic Energy Community Treaty (Euratom) as a first step towards establishing European co-operation in this area, in the face of superpower monopoly and British dependence on the United States despite London's possession of its own nuclear force; and the creation of the European Economic Community (EEC) by signing the Treaty of Rome of 1957. Another decision was to create a French military nuclear force; and while the foundations of such a force were already in place, the French Socialist Party needed the Suez Campaign – and Gaullist support – to undertake this initiative. Finally, in October 1957 Mollet's socialists and their radical partners signed a contract with Israel giving the Jewish state a complete nuclear infrastructure. The domestic and foreign political reasons for this move were probably rooted in socialist–radical desire to legitimize their own decision to 'go nuclear', by making Israel – a socialist ally deserted by France in the wake of the Suez Campaign, isolated and threatened by a triumphant Nasser – a nuclear partner. It was hoped that Israel would emerge soon as a powerful French ally in its struggle over Algeria. Besides, France's European partner, West Germany, was morally obliged to Israel, refusing to cut off its reparation payments to the Jewish state under American pressure, following the occupation of Sinai and Gaza by Israel in 1956.

Israel thus had some breathing space until both territories were returned to Egypt in early 1957 and UN forces were placed along the ADL in Gaza and in the Red Sea straits leading to Eilat. American promises to keep the straits open were also given, but the presence of the UN force in the straits and along the Gaza Strip depended on continuing Egyptian goodwill.

THE AMERICAN INTERVENTION: PHASE ONE

The nuclear treaty of October 1957 between Israel and France remained secret, of course, and was honoured – at first – by General Charles de Gaulle when he assumed power in 1958. The General, however, who rejected any foreign sharing in an independent French nuclear power, first killed Euratom, then manoeuvred to make West Germany his own ally, while reaching his initial decisions to leave Algeria in due course (1962).

De Gaulle's nuclear programme benefited in the meantime from the French–Israeli connection, since Israel's Weizmann Institute was reported to have calculated the parameters of the French bomb using American computing systems which were denied from France at the time. Soon after he had his own bomb, de Gaulle froze the nuclear treaty with Israel, claiming that the secret had been exposed and that the Western press would make it public soon. De Gaulle's main motive, in my opinion, was his fear that the Israeli and French military establishments, which at the time worked closely together, and which viewed the Sahara as a testing ground for nuclear weapons and France's early generation of missiles, might endanger his decision to withdraw from Algeria. Late in 1960, following the general elections in the United States, Ben-Gurion announced in the Knesset that a nuclear reactor for peaceful use was being built at Dimona, in the Negev desert, thus resolving the issue of secrecy and declaring the project's peaceful purpose. This in turn allowed the resumption of the French role in the reactor's construction, but de Gaulle was reported to have refused to deliver the most vital part needed to build bombs: a plutonium separation plant. If Israel wanted the reactor to be completed, it should conduct itself with restraint and refuse any co-operation with rebellious elements in the French army regarding Algeria. This was indeed done in 1962, and the Dimona reactor was reported to have been completed in 1963. Even the separation plant was supplied, either behind the General's back or with his tacit consent. At that stage David Ben-Gurion resigned from both his offices (Prime Minister and Minister of Defence) under heavy American pressure, directly related to Dimona.

The American efforts in this regard succeeded at first in making the Israeli nuclear programme look publicly as if it had no military ramifications. But this happened in 1960, while the Dimona reactor was still under construction. To ensure its peaceful use, the United States demanded from Ben-Gurion adequate safeguards (such as IAEA inspections, which were promptly refused) or American inspection visits, especially when the reactor was reported to have been completed in 1963. This demand, however, was linked by the Americans to Egyptian concessions pertaining to Nasser's own efforts to produce missiles armed with unconventional warheads with the help of German and Austrian scientists. The Egyptian missile effort proved in the meantime to have been both costly and ineffective, hence Ben-Gurion could have expected the main bulk of the American pressure to fall upon Israel's shoulders. Having lost his central role in his own political party Mapai, since 1960, due to a variety of domestic and foreign political reasons, Ben-Gurion refused to risk a confrontation with the United States on the Dimona issue, once the Kennedy administration produced an Egyptian concession – by itself meaningless – on the missile issue. He tried hard to legitimize Dimona *vis-à-vis* the Kennedy administration by quoting alarming developments in the Arab world, but resigned his post when the domestic crisis seemed to be coupled with irresistible American pressure on the Dimona issue.

## THE AMERICAN INTERVENTION: PHASE TWO

It is not known whether Kennedy's efforts were also prompted by Soviet intervention, at least behind the scenes, to curb the Israeli nuclear project already during Ben-Gurion's time. That this might have well been the case is indicated by Ben-Gurion's letters urging the superpowers to guarantee Israel's existence in the face of growing Arab hostility and competition between the pan-Arab regimes in Damascus and Cairo, with Iraq involved in both countries.

Having failed to secure either objective – the reactor's legitimacy in American eyes, or superpower guarantees – Ben-Gurion resigned his offices as Prime Minister and Minister of Defence. The premiership was assumed by the then Minister of Finance, Levi Eshkol, with Golda Meir as his Foreign Minister. Meir, Ben-Gurion's domestic rival, and Eshkol, a compromiser by reputation, whose main interest lay in Israel's economic development, quickly became American targets regarding the nuclear programme, and were given assurances about the US guarantee to Israel's ADLs, in order to freeze the nuclear project after Ben-Gurion's departure.

But while he was seeking Egypt's concessions with regard to its own unconventional programme, President Kennedy was assassinated and his successor, Lindon B. Johnson, was less interested in the Israeli endeavour. Johnson, however, retained Kennedy's national security staff, which in my view slowly drove Israel to the Six Day War, without either realizing this process or admitting it at a later stage, to this very day.

The components of the package leading to the war were as follows:

• Early in his first tenure, Eshkol's cabinet not only continued the Dimona project, but ordered two dozen intermediate range ballistic missiles (IRBMs) in France, as well as a number of short-range missiles. The missiles were to be developed first, with the delivery date reportedly being 1967, but the US administration put enormous pressure on Israel not to deploy them.

• Eshkol tried hard to legitimize Dimona in his talks with the Americans in 1964, arguing that although American security guarantees were welcomed the United States might be involved elsewhere in times of emergency for Israel (as was indeed the case with Vietnam). Eshkol's arguments, including a promise not to expose Israel's missile capability for the time being, were reported to the American missions all over the Arab world, to Moscow and to the IAEA in Vienna.

- Two Arab summit conferences were convened – for the first time – in 1964 and in 1965, to deal with various issues concerning Israel. The first such issue was the Israeli Negev irrigation project, based on diverted water from the Sea of Galilee. Countermeasures were agreed upon in 1964, and at the same time a Palestine Liberation Organization (PLO) was set up under Egyptian auspices (with Ahmad Shuqairi as chairman) to compete with the Fatah guerrilla organization based in Syria under Yasser Arafat. Having thus created a (competing) Palestinian guerrilla outfit to fight Israel under the nuclear threshold, as the Syrians and Arafat perceived the Algerian and the Vietnam wars against the nuclear French and American powers, and the Egyptian-controlled PLO, the Arab leaders dealt with the Israeli nuclear threat thoroughly in a closed summit in 1965. Following the latter summit Egypt, and other Arab states, made the Israeli atomic programme an official *casus belli*, should Israel actually 'go nuclear'. The American ambassador in Egypt, John S. Badeau, had come close to justifying this *casus belli* already in 1964, when he cabled Washington that Nasser did not intend to attack Israel (notwithstanding his public rhetoric) unless it became clear that Israel had or was shortly to obtain nuclear weapons. Nasser's objectives were described as the destruction solely of the Dimona reactor, leading to immediate withdrawal behind the Egyptian line. The CIA's or the State Department's analysts saw in the Israeli nuclear threat – and its removal – an utmost Egyptian national interest, since the obvious target of the Israeli bomb would be the Aswan High Dam, whose destruction would only be possible by using a nuclear warhead, while Egypt could not retaliate by using the same device because of Israel's peculiar boundaries. These made Israel less vulnerable to a nuclear attack, even one which might cause terrible harm to its Arab neighbours. The Egyptian threats thus triggered an ongoing American effort to prevent the threatened war by removing its alleged cause – which at the same time was not ready yet (missiles included) – and which was viewed by Israel as the ultimate reason for Egypt not to wage wars altogether any more.

At this stage – 1965 – the Americans intervened by offering Israel conventional aid, and by demonstrating to Egypt their own involvement as a safeguarding power at Dimona. By so doing, the United States gave Egypt a *casus belli* if it could prove, at least to itself, or to the Soviets – or if it were charged by other Arabs of negligence in this regard – that Israel had indeed gone nuclear.

The direct supplies of American jets and tanks – which the United States had hitherto avoided giving to Israel – promised in 1965, were linked to Israel's concessions in the nuclear sphere. However, the Israeli government allowed American inspection visits only at Dimona and thus could hardly satisfy the Egyptians or other Arab leaders; this at the same time angered Ben-Gurion and his younger aides Moshe Dayan and Shimon Peres. In 1965 Ben-Gurion resorted to a general campaign against Levi Eshkol, for a combination of domestic and political–strategic reasons, including the American inspection deal later on, and Eshkol's strained relations with de Gaulle's France, the would-be supplier of the Israeli IRBMs. It is still unclear whether Eshkol had indeed yielded to the American pressure not to receive or deploy the IRBMs when ready, in exchange for the promised American hardware, but Ben-Gurion blamed him publicly for major incompetence with regard to an essential security issue. At about the same time Ben-Gurion also created his own party which remained in opposition after the 1965 elections, and which helped immensely to damage Eshkol's reputation in security matters from then to the crisis of May 1967.

## THE ROAD TO WAR: PHASE ONE

Egypt's *casus belli* regarding Dimona since 1965 remained a hollow threat, or so it seemed to knowledgeable Israelis (the threat itself remained censored by the military), mainly because since 1962 the Egyptian army had found itself bogged down in a civil war in Yemen, thus severely limiting its freedom of action elsewhere. However, the war in Yemen also strained Nasser politically, exacerbated his relations with Saudi Arabia and Jordan, while in early 1966 a more radical version of the Ba'th pan-Arab party assumed power in Damascus. The Syrians allowed Arafat's Fatah to launch guerrilla raids into Israel (via Jordan), and engaged it in series of direct military actions along the common ADL, pertaining to the Arab water diversion operation and to Israel's cultivation of demilitarized zones in the vicinity of the ADL. For its part Egypt's hands were tied by the presence of the UN buffer force which had effectively sealed the border since 1957. Israel thus exchanged blows with Syria, and in early 1966 it was reported by the *New York Times* that it had ordered nuclear IRBMs from France. The report coincided with a visit by the Egyptian Chief of Staff, Abdel Hakim Amer, to France, in which he was told that the Israelis had obtained the bomb. But did they obtain credible delivery means? Or did they possess a credible arsenal at this stage? Not yet, but they might obtain the missiles later in 1967, as one may conclude both from the *New York Times* report, and from a public statement quoting the Soviet Minister of Defence, Andrei Grechko, who had reportedly 'pledged protection' to Egypt following a visit to the country in late 1966, when and if Israel built or acquired nuclear weapons.

It is hard to assess the impact of this 'nuclear guarantee' on Israeli decision-makers, but the 'conventionalists' among them such as Yigal

Allon might have felt that their own strategy of conventional deterrence and pre-emption had now proved to be far more justified than before. Conventional deterrence required action, and thus in November 1966 Israel launched a major retaliatory act against the Jordanian village of Samu (in the south of the West Bank), where Fatah guerrillas had encamped on their way from Syria to Israel. The Samu operation was unprecedented in scope, compared to Ben-Gurion's times. Launched in daylight, it involved armour and eventually aircraft. They fought the Jordanian army, which came to support the Palestinians, causing heavy Jordanian casualties and a Palestinian uprising in the West Bank. King Hussein was forced to crush the rebellion by military means, but at the same time he bitterly blamed Egypt for hiding behind the UN buffer and doing nothing to make good Nasser's own threats against the Jewish state.

In the meantime the Syrian–Israeli clashes escalated further, with the Israeli air force intervening, pursuing Syrian aircraft into Damascus itself, where two were shot down. Early in 1967 Lieutenant General Yitzhak Rabin, the Israeli Chief-of-Staff, appeared to have threatened the Syrian regime in public. Here was new evidence to suggest perhaps that Rabin and several ministers in Eshkol's cabinet, notably Allon, did plan a major operation against Syria, the main (and only) source of trouble in the region, as Egypt was viewed by the IDF (Israeli Defence Forces) to be totally immersed in Yemen and hence not ready for war.

True, the PLO organs and Chairman Shuqairi personally publicly urged Nasser to go to war at once, before Israel went nuclear. But the Egyptian President had repeatedly warned everyone in the Arab world that he would not fight before he was ready – a warning which the Israelis interpreted in terms of his involvement in Yemen – only to be forced to weigh it afresh in terms of Soviet support, which he might have gained in May 1967.

Otherwise the marching of Egyptian troops into Sinai since mid-May 1967 could have been interpreted as a show of force to relieve the Israeli pressure over Syria. But soon enough all the parties lost control over a process of escalation, which they had hoped to be able to control.

THE ROAD TO WAR: PHASE TWO

The manning of Egypt's fortified positions along the Israeli ADL in Sinai, which had remained empty since 1956, and the appearance of the Palestinian Liberation Army (PLA), under Egyptian command, in the Gaza Strip alarmed the Israelis. Yet the main source of their anxiety was the reconnaissance flights by Egyptian aircraft over the Dimona reactor on 17 May, which coincided with Nasser's decision to remove the UN buffer from the ADL along the Gaza Strip and the UN presence in the

Red Sea straits. All of a sudden, Israeli decision-makers were reminded of the 1965 *casus belli* regarding Dimona, while they had no credible delivery means for whatever limited nuclear weapons they might have had possessed at the time, except a number of subsonic French-made, light bombers.

Hence Chief-of-Staff Rabin was given permission to call up reserves, at least to seal off the open boundary in the Negev. Once the reserves were mobilized, and the Egyptians removed the UN buffer, an uncontrolled wave of enthusiasm engulfed the Arab world, and Nasser seemed to have recovered his mythical grasp over its masses. He then escalated the crisis by closing the Red Sea straits, defying a declared Israeli *casus belli* since 1957.

For the IDF this meant the failure of Israel's conventional deterrence posture, requiring immediate action. But the political level was divided, expecting the Johnson administration to open the straits owing to the obligations made following the Suez Campaign, to Eshkol's 'special relations' with the Americans, based on the Dimona inspection tours, and possibly to Israel's acceptance of the American demands prohibiting the deployment of the French IRBMs, if ready.

Thus the political echelons decided to wait until the Americans intervened to open the straits, only to hear Nasser proclaiming the coming extinction of Israel now that the 1956 *status quo* was re-established. The Israelis had now to plan how to pre-empt such Egyptian actions as a direct limited attack from Sinai, PLA raids from Gaza, or the closure of the straits to Israeli shipping, that would still fall short of a general war. Yet an Israeli resort to a shooting war in response to these developments might give Nasser what he actually wanted: a prolonged battle along the Egyptian fortification line in Sinai until the political intervention of the Eastern Block and the non-aligned nations would stop the war, coupled with the freedom to attack Dimona – a far-reaching step which might be justified, possibly with Soviet backing, only if Israel attacked Egypt first. At any rate, no one would shed many tears – except Israel itself – if its nuclear reactor disappeared, so the only course, which should have been pursued by Israel, was the removal of the Red Sea blockade, to which Washington was formally committed.

While the Johnson administration was contemplating if and how to do that, at the height of the Vietnam War, a rapid escalation of tension in the Arab world seemed to dictate Israeli pre-emption sooner rather than later, at a time when almost the entire Israeli reserve army had been called up. King Hussein buried the hatchet and joined Nasser, placing his army under Egyptian command, and an Iraqi expeditionary force entered Jordan – in defiance of yet another Israeli *casus belli*. While the IDF's High Command pressed for action now, Eshkol's government still waited for American help, thus rapidly losing its public standing.

Under heavy pressure to yield the Defence Ministry – which he held in personal union with his office as Prime Minister – to somebody else now that a war seemed inevitable, Eshkol was faced with public and partisan pressure to recall Ben-Gurion, or at least appoint Moshe Dayan Minister of Defence while creating a broad government of national unity. Dayan was finally appointed, and in defiance of Ben-Gurion's views opted for war early in June 1967.

## THE WAR: IMMEDIATE AND LONG-RANGE IMPLICATIONS

Eshkol's refusal to allow Ben-Gurion's return to the Ministry of Defence was anchored, on top of the personal rivalry between the two, in his argument that Ben-Gurion, because of his independent nuclear policy, was not acceptable to the Americans – who owed Eshkol several things regarding Dimona; hence Eshkol's readiness to go on waiting and to forgo pre-emption. Paradoxically, Eshkol's policy was rather close to that of his nemesis, as Ben-Gurion would not pre-empt if this endangered the nuclear programme, ran the risk of many casualties, and involved no prior understanding with a great power as in 1956. Dayan and Peres, however, realized that their mentor's option was dead, and hence manoeuvred to use his political party to negotiate with Eshkol their own participation in a proposed government of national unity, which was created in early June, with the participation of Menachem Begin, the hitherto ostracized leader of the Israeli Right. Ben-Gurion was in fact deserted by his younger lieutenants, who later in 1968 had his party – without him – align itself with Eshkol's Mapai and Allon's nationalist Left in the framework of Israel's Labour Party. This was just one result of the Six Day War – launched against Egypt on 5 June 1967, with Dayan playing a decisive role, but expanding later to Jerusalem, the West Bank, and the Golan Heights.

The Syrians, ironically enough, were pretty cautious during the war, limiting themselves to the 'usual' shelling from the Golan and some air activity. Eshkol, however, and then Dayan, decided to remove the Syrian threat to northern Israel from the Golan Heights, which were subsequently occupied in the final stage of the 1967 War, thus giving Damascus concrete war aims – as the Sinai did for Egypt in the 1973 Yom Kippur War.

The Israeli nuclear option, however, survived the 1967 War, and had to be reckoned with in 1973. By this time Israel had lost its French connection and had to rely on aircraft to carry its growing arsenal. Hence, in 1973 the Arabs could wage a limited war aimed at the recovery of occupied territory, once Soviet anti-aircraft guns and missiles effectively neutralized the Israeli air force – and their war aims were short of the destruction of Israel.

The painful effects on Israel of the 1973 War, however, bolstered the Israeli reliance on nuclear deterrence, IRBMs included, thus explaining – among other reasons – the active American involvement in the peace negotiations which started after the Yom Kippur War, leading to the Israeli–Egyptian peace agreement of 1979, based on the complete return of Sinai to Egypt.

The case of Jerusalem, the West Bank and the Gaza Strip, also occupied in the 1967 War, has remained the core of the conflict, especially following the restructuring of the PLO in 1968 with Yasser Arafat as its chairman. Until 1967 Arafat and others had been speaking for the dispersed Palestinians. The occupation of the West Bank and Gaza in 1967 made them, during a long process which started then, the main spokesmen of the Palestinians in the occupied territories as well, thus creating two different foci in Palestinian politics. The exiled Palestinians, whose primary interest was to return to their homes in pre-1967 Israel, and the occupied Palestinians, were effectively two different groups in terms of their immediate interests; and, following the *intifada* of the 1980s, Arafat was finally able to speak on the latter's behalf with the Israelis. Arafat's final decision to recognize Israel and negotiate a settlement with it was dictated, *inter alia*, by his previous decision to support Saddam Hussein in his 1991 Kuwaiti misadventure. As a result, Arafat found himself totally isolated in the Arab world, without aid from the disintegrating USSR, and had to change course, also regarding Israel.

Iraq's nuclear programme was one of the causes of the Kuwaiti misadventure, and also a main target of the Western allies during the ensuing Gulf War. The Iraqi nuclear programme had first been contemplated in 1968, possibly as a response to the NPT, which came into being then, while using the treaty as a shield for its own violation; possibly as Iraq's long-range response to the Israeli nuclear challenge, facing a potential, similar, Iranian challenge.

The ending of the Gulf War without clear results regarding Iraq's return to the nuclear path, and Iran's growing nuclear infrastructure thus threaten the Israeli nuclear monopoly, which seemed to have been secured following the Six Day War. But its founding fathers, Ben-Gurion and Peres, had always calculated that an Arab or Muslim bomb would emerge one day, the main issue for them being the fundamental asymmetry of the conflict.

For some theoreticians there is no way to make such adversaries behave 'rationally' once the Israeli nuclear monopoly is broken, because the nature of the conflict was, and will always be, a 'given' and at a high level indeed. For Ben-Gurion, however, such views were pure sophistry, and misconceived. The nuclear issue was not theoretical, but was rather anchored in the culture and history of the entities involved. The level of the conflict was dictated by conventional variables, and was therefore not constant; nor were suicide attacks sponsored by Arab leaders inevitable if Israel maintained the partition of Palestine, refused to rule over Palestinians, and secured enough support among third parties. Ironically, the results of the Six Day War made several of these preconditions hard to meet in Israel itself.

## NOTES

This article is a shorter and slightly revised version of a monograph, published in 1999 by the Mediterranean Studies Programme at King's College London. Readers wishing to inform themselves about my primary and secondary sources are advised to consult the original work.

PART II:
CHANGING PERSPECTIVES ON NATIONAL SECURITY

# Towards a Paradigm Shift in Israel's National Security Conception

## URI BAR-JOSEPH

The concept of 'national security' refers, traditionally, to the protection of the territorial and political integrity of the state and its national interests from the use of force by an adversary. The national security conception[1] of any state is the product of the given reality of external environment and internal resources (the 'operational milieu') as perceived and processed in the minds of her political and military elite (the 'psychological milieu'). Consequently, revisions in national security conception can be the result of changes in the operational milieu, the psychological milieu, or both.[2]

Zionism was born without any national security conception. It started to formulate such a theory only in the 1920s, following the first military clashes between the pre-state Yishuv and the Arab community in Palestine, and this crystallized into (what I will later term as) the Zionist national security paradigm, during the 1930s and 1940s.

Since then no fundamental changes have taken place in the psychological milieu of Israel's national security. Its operational milieu went through one radical shift, in 1948, when the conflict ceased to be a local struggle between Jews and Arabs in Palestine and became a conflict between the Israeli state and the Arab world.

Consequently, Israel's present national security conception is, to a large extent, the product of the psychological and operational milieus of the Jewish Yishuv and the war of 1948. During the last decade, however, certain cracks have appeared in these two environments. This essay discusses these changes and their implications for Israel's national security conception.

Two arguments stand at the core of this essay: (a) that Israel is nearing the stage where its present national security conception will become obsolete because of radical changes in its operational milieu; (b) recent changes in Israel's national security's psychological milieu

Uri Bar-Joseph is Lecturer in Political Science at Haifa University.

facilitate the build-up of a new theory which will better suit the new strategic environment. Consequently, the first part of this essay, which focuses on the operational milieu, briefly describes the existing national security conception and then elaborates on the main shifts in Israel's strategic environment which call into question the validity of the present theory. The second part starts with a description of the dominant beliefs which make up the core of the psychological milieu and then analyses how they have changed in recent years. Finally I will outline possible implications, the most important of which is the likely transformation of the Israeli Defence Forces (IDF) from a conscript to a professional all-volunteer army.

## THE OPERATIONAL MILIEU OF ISRAEL'S NATIONAL SECURITY CONCEPTION

### The Traditional Conception

The following elements are at the core of the Israeli national security conception, and have been since the early 1950s:[3]

1. The massive disproportion between Israeli and Arab national resources (chiefly in terms of territory, manpower and gross national product (GNP)) prevents Israel from ending the conflict by military means, while allowing the Arabs to do so. Consequently, Israel is a territorial and political *status quo* power and the only goal of the IDF, as implied by its name, is to defend the country against an aggressive Arab world.[4]

2. The most fundamental and dangerous threat to Israel's existence is an all-out co-ordinated Arab surprise attack. Hence, Israel should always maintain the ability to defend itself under the conditions of such a worst-case scenario, known as *mikreh ha-kol* (the all-out case).

3. As derived from the above, Israeli national security doctrine rests on three pillars: *deterrence* (as implied by the defensive goals of its national security conception); *strategic warning* (on any development which might endanger its national existence); and *decision* (the military ability to win a decisive victory if deterrence fails).

There are two primary operational implications of this doctrine. First, the build-up of the capability needed to provide a high-quality strategic warning and a quick response to external threats. This explains why the Military Intelligence branch (DMI), the Air Force (IAF) and the Navy are regular forces while the ground forces are based on reserve manpower. Second, a capability to maintain operational initiative in war scenarios and in the battlefield, in order to be able to win a decisive victory within a short period of time.

*The Changes in the International System and its Implications*

The cracks in the operational setting of the Israeli national security conception are, primarily, the product of political changes at the international and regional levels. In addition, it is influenced by certain developments in military technology and the proliferation of non-conventional weapon systems to the region.

The end of the Cold War, the collapse of the Soviet Union, and the transition of the international system from a bipolar to a unipolar system under American hegemony, have changed significantly the operational milieu of Israel's national security. After 1955, when the USSR became an active participant in the Arab–Israeli conflict, Arab military ability to launch a war against Israel increased significantly, and a political solution to the conflict became far more difficult.

The disappearance of the USSR from the scene has had the following implications for Israel's national security: first, the superpower political and military umbrella, under which Soviet regional clients could have sheltered from the risks involved in initiating a crisis and even a war with Israel, has disappeared. Indeed, from 1956 the Soviets had acted to limit Israel's freedom of action – either through verbal warnings or by actual military intervention in their client's favour – in each of the Arab–Israeli wars.[5]

This is most true of Syria, the Soviets' closest regional ally since the mid-1960s. Without the Soviet safety net any Syrian military move against Israel will involve considerable threats to Syrian strategic assets, first and foremost, the capital Damascus which is within Israeli military reach. Hence, Syrian ability to initiate such a war against Israel has decreased significantly since the end of the Soviet Union.

Secondly, from 1955, for almost four decades, the USSR was the main supplier of arms and military instruction and advice to Israel's chief enemies. The collapse of the Soviet Union does not mean an immediate cease of arms transfers to the Arabs. However, because of increasing economic constraints, the Russian military–industrial complex is constantly losing its ability to develop and produce the next generation's weapon systems. Consequently, traditional Soviet clients, and Syria is the most important case from the Israeli perspective, will have to choose in coming years between one of three options: (a) to continue to rely on outdated Russian or Chinese military supplies and thus to increase further their technological inferiority *vis-à-vis* the IDF; (b) to make a transformation to sophisticated (and expensive) Western, primarily American weapons, with the political concessions involved and the risk of being militarily vulnerable during the transition period which may last more than a decade; and (c) to give up the conventional military build-up and concentrate on the development of a non-conventional capability as a means to deter Israel.

Notably, each of these options will leave former regional clients of the USSR conventionally far weaker than Israel in the foreseeable future as Arab clients sum up the lost political, diplomatic, economic and scientific support which enabled them to bear the cost involved in their enduring rivalry with Israel.

### Regional Changes and their Implications

Since 1990 the Middle East has experienced two main developments which are, to some extent, the product of the systemic changes discussed earlier. The first development was the 1991 Gulf War. The second is the Arab–Israeli peace process which has yielded, so far, a Jordanian–Israeli peace agreement, a number of Palestinian–Israeli partial agreements, the beginning of formal Syrian–Israeli negotiations, and a major improvement in Israel's relationship with most other Arab states.

The main implications of these developments for Israeli national security have been:

- A sharp decrease in the magnitude of the Iraqi conventional threat, because of Iraq's (for the time being unrecoverable) military losses in the war; the peace treaty with Jordan which hampers advancement of Iraqi forces towards Israel; and Iraqi apprehension of rising threats from its own neighbours, primarily Iran, which decreases the likelihood of an Iraqi military initiative against Israel in the foreseeable future.

- A decrease in other Arab states' motivation to initiate a war against Israel, primarily because the political option provides them with a more realistic alternative to attain an acceptable *status quo*. Notably, Israel's strategic deterrence, its ability to persuade the opponent to avoid launching a war, have failed only twice throughout the conflict with the Arabs: in 1969 with the Egyptian initiation of the War of Attrition and in 1973 at the start of the Yom Kippur War. Since in both cases the balance of forces was clearly in favour of Israel, while the balance of interests favoured the Arabs, one can conclude that an acceptable political solution makes Israeli deterrence more likely to work than a relative increase in its military power.

- A growing Arab willingness to accept Israel as a legitimate actor in regional politics is another new factor. Though Israel was an important actor in the regional arena since its birth, it had always had to act latently since no Arab state was ready to be its open ally. This norm was broken to some extent during the Gulf War, when Saudi fighters participated in Israel's defence against Scud attacks, and other traditional enemies such as Syria joined a coalition in which Israel was a latent participator.

As Israel has normalized its relationship with a growing number of Arab states in recent years this process has gained momentum. Though the Arabs, primarily Egypt, have made it clear that they will reject Israeli attempts to become the dominant regional actor, they have also left the impression that they accept an Israeli role as legitimate not only in the regional economic arena but also in the political and military spheres as well.

### Modern Military Technology and the Proliferation of Non-conventional Weapons

Two developments concerning arms, which have occurred in recent decades, are also significant. The first involves the military technology revolution (the Revolution in Military Affairs (RMA)) and the introduction of sophisticated conventional weapon systems into the region. The second is the rapid proliferation of non-conventional weapons by regional actors, especially in the aftermath of the Gulf War.

From the military technology perspective, sophisticated conventional wars of the future will rely, primarily, on 'the combination and integration of high-quality target intelligence and acquisition methods, on effective and rapid command and control, and on high-kill probability precision fire power capable of destroying targets, on land, at sea or in the air, either by day or at night'.[6]

One example of the impact of this technological revolution on the way wars of the future may be conducted is the complete destruction of Syrian air defence batteries in the Beqa valley during the June 1982 war in Lebanon, without any losses to the IAF. Another is the Gulf War, where the Iraqi ground forces enjoyed a numerical superiority but the US-led coalition forces had superb air, ground and naval weapon systems. The combination of this technological and human superiority led to an unprecedented, in terms of loss ratio, Iraqi defeat.[7]

The rapid proliferation of non-conventional weaponry in the region revolves, primarily, around the Syrian acquisition of ballistic missiles armed with conventional and chemical warheads, Iranian nuclear efforts, and Iraq's attempts to maintain its non-conventional capabilities despite American and international pressures. As indicated, such efforts show that these regional powers seem to believe that the next war in the Middle East will not be a classic conventional confrontation between large-scale ground forces supported by air power. Instead they consider non-conventional weapons as the most effective answer to the dire strategic situation in which they have found themselves in the wake of the collapse of the USSR, the second Gulf War and the Arab–Israeli peace process.

The development of such capabilities makes the recurrence of large-scale conventional wars far less likely. And while it is probably true that the main goal of this non-conventional potential is to deter Israel from exploiting its strategic superiority if war erupts, it is important to note that such acquisitions will limit Israel's freedom of manoeuvrability in any future conflict, as they can be used for offensive purposes as well.

*Implications for Israeli Security*

From Israel's perspective there are three main conclusions to be derived from the discussion so far:

1. Because of the global and regional changes of the last decade, the Arab political motivation and military capability to launch a conventional war against Israel has diminished significantly. Consequently, the traditional threat to Israel's existence – the 'all-out case' of co-ordinated surprise attack by the neighbouring Arab countries, which dominated Israeli strategic thinking from the early 1950s – has almost disappeared.

2. The source of the main threat to Israel's existence in the foreseeable future will be the non-conventional arsenals held by regional powers that do not participate in the peace process. If one of these states succeeds in obtaining an operational nuclear capability, Israel will face, for the first time since 1948, the threat of annihilation.

3. The source of the main threat to Israel's existence in the future will not come from Egypt and Syria, its traditional enemies, but from the second-circle Arab states (primarily Iraq and Libya) or third-circle states (Iran and, perhaps, Sudan).

THE PSYCHOLOGICAL MILIEU: THE ZIONIST NATIONAL
SECURITY PARADIGM

*The Zionist National Security Paradigm*[8]

The realization that the fulfilment of the Zionist goals involved dealing with individual and collective security challenges began during the Second Aliya and gained momentum after the British occupation of Palestine, primarily during the 1921–22 clashes between the Arab and Jewish communities in Palestine. The practical response was the establishment of the Hagana, which, combined with British assistance, was aimed at providing Jews protection against Arab violence.

More interesting, in the context of this essay, is the psychological milieu of Jewish national security in Palestine which crystallized in response to rising security threats. The consolidation of a set of beliefs on Jewish security in Palestine gained momentum during the 1936–39 'disturbances'[9] and matured during the three decades that follow, reaching its most explicit and extreme ('ideal type') form between 1967 and 1973.

At the centre of this psychological milieu stand three fundamental beliefs.

## The Primacy of Security

This belief, which became especially dominant after the establishment of Israel, holds that almost every national problem is a security problem, or at least involves security aspects. Its prime proponent was Israel's first Prime Minister David Ben-Gurion. For Ben-Gurion, immigration absorption and the build-up of settlements were security issues, so too was his famous aspiration that Israel should become 'a light unto the nations'. As he explained it, besides its moralistic value, Israel as a beacon for other nations had an important security function, providing as it did external support which was so essential to ensure its existence.[10]

Such subordination of all private and collective aspects of life to security demands bordered on 'security Bolshevism' and is typical of the Second Aliya generation. Nevertheless, since Ben-Gurion was well aware that moral, economic or social values were very important in ensuring Israel's existence, he did automatically rank values of physical security above other values.

Consequently, when security considerations collided with the rule of law principle (for example, the Tobiansky affair), Ben-Gurion supported the latter.[11] Similarly, despite being so identified with Israel's security demands, under Ben-Gurion the defence budget almost never exceeded ten per cent of Israel's GNP. Only after he was replaced by Levi Eshkol did the defence budget rise above this level.[12]

Another aspect of the tendency to view every national challenge through the security prism is the inclination to focus on the security dimension of every problem as the prime justification to solve it. A typical example is the 'integration of the exiles' – one of the most basic and desired goals of the Zionist ethos. Already in the 1940s, security frameworks were used to promote this goal when socially and economically weak youngsters of Sephardic origin were recruited to serve with elitist Ashkenazi youth in the Palmach.

Similarly, in the 1950s the justification for compulsory service relied not only on security needs but also on the belief that the army was the most effective vehicle to integrate new immigrants with longer-established Israelis.[13]

## Resort to Force as a Panacea to Security Problems

Some sections of the Zionist movement were always aware that military solutions had their own limitations. Other ideological streams – especially the activist ones on the right and the left – tended to view the use of force as almost the only means to solve all sorts of security problems.

The belief that force is a panacea, and that the use of brute force alone could and should solve all security problems was dominant especially in the early 1950s and after the 1967 War, and coincided with the belief in 'self-help' (see below). A typical example of this way of thinking, and its outcome, can be seen in the case known as 'the Unfortunate Business'.

In 1954 Britain and Egypt reached an agreement on the evacuation of the British army from its camps in the Suez Canal zone. The accord reflected the realities of the post-1945 international system and was one stage in an historical process that resulted in the dismantling of the British Empire. Since it was perceived to weaken Israel's balance of forces *vis-à-vis* Egypt, Benyamin Givli, the chief of Military Intelligence (with *post factum* approval from the Defence Minister Pinhas Lavon), decided to conduct sabotage acts in Egypt to halt this process of withdrawal.

The result was the total fiasco that later came to be known as the Lavon affair. The important point, in terms of this essay, is the absurd way of thinking which brought about such a fiasco. As Yehoshafat Harkabi, who became the chief of Military Intelligence in the aftermath of this failure, wrote, 'the gap between the network [ability] and the mission it was to achieve was shuddering ... The two were in two different levels, without any linkage between them'.[14]

Others, such as Prime Minister Moshe Sharett thought so too. But since Givli's frame of mind focused only on active ways to stop the British evacuation he opted for action despite its poor chance of success.

The technological panacea is also another aspect of this way of thinking as the rise of new threats, such as the introduction of ballistic missiles armed with non-conventional warheads, result in the demand to use new military technologies. The *Arrow* (Hetz) anti-ballistic-missile defence system is a good example of a technological answer to a major new challenge.

In contrast, the *Katyusha* threat to northern Israel constitutes a typical terrorist challenge, namely a minimal military threat with a maximum psychological effect. But in the name of the drive for total security (see below), Israel has developed, with American aid, highly sophisticated and costly weapon systems which will shoot down *Katyushas* on their way to Israel. Most experts agree that the solution to Israel's security problems in the north is political – a comprehensive agreement with Syria which will also include Lebanon. But such a solution (assuming that Syria is serious about peace in the first place) involves difficult political decisions, including the handing of the Golan Heights to Syria. Hence, looking under the 'technological light' is a far more convenient (though probably ineffective) solution, especially if one believes that security problems can be solved by military means alone.

## Self-Help

The principle of 'self-help' stands at the centre of the realist and neo-realist school in international relations. The premise underlying this approach is that in an anarchic international system, where there is no formal power that can ensure the state's existence, states will tend to rely on their own military power rather than on external guarantees such as peace agreements, defence pacts or arms control regimes, to ensure their survival. Such a tendency leads, however, to the 'security dilemma'; that is, the condition in which states, unsure of one another's intentions, arm for the sake of insecurity and in doing so set a vicious circle in motion. Having armed for the sake of security, states feel less secure and buy more arms because the means to anyone's security is a threat to someone else who in turn responds by arming.[15]

Although the tendency towards 'self-help' is of universal nature, it became extremely dominant in the Zionist national security paradigm. A thousand years of Jewish traumatic history in the Diaspora, culminating in the Nazi Holocaust, created a siege mentality and a fundamental mistrust of Gentiles. During its short history of existence, Israel had gone through a number of traumatic events including the Arab invasion of 1948, the May–June 1967 crisis, and the 1973 Yom Kippur surprise, which magnified further this sense of insecurity.[16] As Henry Kissinger has noted,

> Israel's margin of survival is so narrow that its leaders distrust the great gesture or the stunning diplomatic departure; they identify survival with precise calculation, which can appear to outsiders (and sometimes is) pettifogging obstinacy. Even when Israeli leaders accept a peace proposal, they resist fiercely, which serves the purpose of showing that they are not pushovers and thereby discourages further demands for Israeli concessions. And their acceptance is usually accompanied by endless requests for reassurances, memoranda of understanding, and secret explanations – all designed to limit the freedom of action of a rather volatile ally five thousand miles away that supplies its arms, sustains its economy, shelters its diplomacy, and has a seemingly limitless compulsion to offer peace plans.[17]

The suspicion of others has had a major impact on the Israeli reluctance to give up territories deemed essential for the state's security, so long as the Arabs were not seen to have abandoned their aim of subverting the Jewish state. Under these circumstances, ending the conflict on the basis of the 'territories for peace formula', which became increasingly feasible after 1967, turned out to be far more difficult. An additional 25 years of conflict and violence were needed to convince most Israelis that peace, even at the cost of relinquishing elements of 'self-help' is a more effective way to get out of the 'security dilemma'.

## THE IMPACT OF THE ZIONIST REVOLUTION CONTEXT

The three beliefs discussed above are heightened by the classic characteristic of every revolution, that ranks the collective rather than the individual's good at the centre of the individual and collective being. Zionism, as a revolutionary national movement, had never argued (as the nineteenth-century national–romantic European movements did) that the individual's ultimate fulfilment is through sacrificing himself to promote national goals. But as a national movement which faced existential threats it adopted elements of self-sacrifice, as expressed by Yossef Trumpeldor's last words – 'it is good to die for our country' on which generations of youngsters were educated. And in this ideological atmosphere the tendency to stick to the three beliefs that constitute the core of the Zionist national security paradigm was enhanced.

### The Changes in the Collective Belief System

Although the Zionist revolution is not yet over, there are many indications that Israel is nearing the third stage in the history of the Zionist enterprise, a stage termed by some as the post-Zionist era.[18] The goal of the first stage of the Zionist enterprise – to build a Jewish state – was achieved in 1948. The goal of the second stage was to ensure the safety of that state. After five decades of conflict with the Arab world, a peace agreement with Syria, which is possible in the foreseeable future, will bring the second stage of the Zionist revolution to a successful conclusion as well.

This will mean the opening of the third stage of Israel's history, which will be characterized by a significant reduction in external threats and a normalization of relations between Israel and most Arab states.

We have already discussed the main changes in the operational milieu of Israel's national security which indicate the probable emergence of the third stage. Now it is time to discuss the changes which announce its coming in the psychological milieu.

### The Primacy of Security

It will be recalled that the primacy of security in Israeli life has stood at the centre of the traditional national security paradigm. This belief has gone through considerable changes during the last two decades. Though still dominant, security demands are considered today as one – and not automatically superior – of a number of societal values.

One dimension of this change is the creation, through a number of Supreme Court rulings, of a new balance in the triangular relationship between security needs, the rule of law and the public's right for information. The principal decision which established the new balance was taken in 1988 when the Supreme Court overruled the banning of a newspaper article which criticized the director of the Mossad.[19]

This precedent lessened the military censor's tendency to use his authority to ban the publication of similar information.[20] The new balance of forces between the censors and the media was officially recognized in May 1996, when the two signed a new, and far more liberal agreement, in which the censor gave up some of its draconian powers, including its right to close down a paper, and the media gained the right to appeal to the Supreme Court to overrule censorial decisions.[21]

Another dimension is the opening of security organs to external oversight. A good example is the recent change in the status of the General Security Service (SHABAK). Until the mid-1980s SHABAK's supervision was, almost exclusively, in the hands of the Prime Minister's Office. Since then, the legislative and judicial branches have become far more active in its supervision and so have the media and human rights organizations. The Law of the SHABAK, which was presented to the public in early 1996,[22] will frame the service's legal status, subordination and activities, within a well-defined legal setting.

Despite these changes, it is important to note that polls show that the majority of the Israeli public,[23] and large segments of the political elite,[24] still believe in the primacy of security. But with a peace process which is expected to decrease the security burden, and if the new balance between security demands and other societal values proves to benefit both security and society, it is quite probable that public belief in the primacy of security will also change.

*Resort to Force as a Panacea for Security Problems*

In the quarter of a century since their brilliant victory in the Six Day War, Israelis have undergone the traumatic experiences of the Yom Kippur War and the Lebanon War, the failure to stop the *intifada* by military means or the Iraqi Scuds from landing during the Gulf War. These events have certainly taught Israelis the limits of military power in solving security problems.

A good expression of this are the public opinion polls which show a growing popular support for political solutions to Israel's most fundamental security problems. In 1986, 30 per cent of Israelis believed that Israel should give up the territories as long as Israel's security was provided for. In 1991, 51 per cent favoured this solution, and in 1993 the figure was 54 per cent.

At the same time, the percentage of Israelis who supported the annexation of the territories fell from 34 per cent in 1986 to 15 per cent in 1993. Similarly, in 1987, 33 per cent of the Israeli public favoured negotiations with the Palestine Liberation Organization (PLO) while 66 per cent were opposed. In 1994, 60 per cent were in favour of such negotiations and only 40 per cent were against. Finally, in 1987, 53 per cent of Israelis supported the idea of an international peace conference, while 48 per cent were opposed. In 1993, 89 per cent supported this idea, while only 11 per cent were against.[25]

The reduction in the belief that the use of force is a panacea for security problems is also evidenced in Israel's security policy. For example, in contrast to past practice where the objective of Israeli force was to coerce the Arab side to return to the previous ceasefire regime, Israel's political goals in the struggle against Hizbullah in Lebanon are far less ambitious and are aimed at limiting the war to Lebanese territory and preventing further escalation. Given the losses Israel has suffered, even in attempting to achieve these limited goals, a unilateral withdrawal from Lebanon has become the most feasible option. Similarly, restraint has been shown by both Labour and Likud governments in their responses to Palestinian provocation since 1992–93.

*Self-Help*

Along with the growing awareness that military force is not a panacea for security problems, and as a logical result of this view, the Israeli public have begun to change their views on the relationship between Israel and the rest of the world. The belief that the whole world opposed Israel began to fade away with the collapse of the Soviet Union. This view gained momentum following the 1993 and 1995 accords with the PLO, when a number of Arab states initiated diplomatic, economic and tourist connections with Israel, thus minimizing Israel's sense of isolation in the region.

A typical expression of the public's change of mind was given in a poll which showed that, in 1991, 49 per cent of Israelis believed that the Arabs' final goal was to destroy Israel and its Jewish population. In 1996 this constituency had fallen to 28 per cent.[26] Another indication is public attitude towards the establishment of a Palestinian state in the occupied territories. In 1987 only about 21 per cent supported such a solution.[27] In 1996, before the May elections, 48 per cent supported it.

*The End of the Zionist Revolution*

The last, and perhaps most important, change involves Israel's new order of priorities, which reflects the notion that the Israeli public is becoming ready for the post-Zionist stage in the nation's life. At the centre of this change is the relationship between the collective and the individual. The days when the individual was subordinate to the collective are over. Instead, there is a growing tendency in Israeli society to rank the good of the individual higher than that of the collective. The main implication of this change is the increasing reluctance to serve in the army, especially in frontline units.

This tendency is expressed in a number of ways. The 1996 annual report by the State Comptroller assessed the indicators for motivation for service in regular and reserve army units. It revealed that there was an increase in the number of recruitment refusals; a decrease in the readiness of individuals to volunteer for frontline units; a change in the sources of motivation to serve in elite units – away from patriotism and towards an individuals desire for self-fulfilment; and a general decrease in reservists motivation to serve.[28]

This change in priorities finds a vivid expression also in current security policy. Shortly after Moshe Dayan became Chief-of-Staff in 1953 he issued an order that any commander whose unit failed to reach its operational goal without suffering at least 50 per cent casualties was likely to see his military career come to an end.[29] In contrast, the emphasis in IDF operational activities in Southern Lebanon in recent years was on loss avoidance, even at the cost of a failure to obtain operational goals.

Similarly, the 'Grapes of Wrath' operation of spring 1996 did not start with a brilliant military move in the best Israeli tradition, but rather with an orderly evacuation of the civilian population from the Upper Galilee. This care for the individual stands in clear contrast to the classic Zionist ethos which opposed the evacuation of settlements in combat zones even when under physical attack (for example, Gush Etzion and Jewish settlements in the Negev in 1948).

IMPLICATIONS

Shortly before he died in 1980, Moshe Dayan suggested a new conception for Israeli national security: a decrease in the conflict's intensity (through territorial concessions) added to a valid deterrence against a decisive war (namely a nuclear capability) plus conventional forces sufficient to fight a limited conventional war. This, Dayan argued, would provide reasonable security at a reasonable cost.[30] Adding to this formula one more factor – an American–Israeli defence pact – gives a fair indication of the probable conception of Israeli national security after it achieves peace agreements with Syria, Lebanon and the Palestinians.

The completion of the peace process with all neighbouring states will create a new operational milieu for Israel's national security. There are likely to be two main changes. The first will be a total disappearance of the classic conventional threat – a massive, Arab attack against the Jewish state. This change will be the outcome of a reduction in Arab motivation to initiate war against Israel (as a result of a new and accepted *status quo* following the signing of peace treaties); an effective Israeli deterrent which will rely on a perceived (perhaps even an open) nuclear arsenal; a defence pact with the United States; and an Arab inability to surprise Israel strategically because of demilitarized zones in Egypt (Sinai) and between the Syrian and Israeli armies.

The second factor will be the continuation, perhaps even escalation, of non-conventional threats from second- and third-circle states which, at present, include Iraq, Iran and Libya. If the present trend continues, at least one of these states will be able to threaten Israel with an effective arsenal of ballistic missiles armed with non-conventional (in the case of Iraq and Iran probably nuclear) warheads, within the next decade.

The changes in the operational milieu necessitate a paradigm shift in Israel's national security conception. The changes in her psychological milieu make the adaptation to these new realities possible. Consequently, the combination of the two is likely to yield a paradigm shift, the first of its kind, in the Zionist national security conception.

The most radical element in this shift will probably be the transformation of the IDF from a conscript army to a volunteer professional army. The logic behind such a change is compelling as Israel's present military forces (artillery, tanks, soldiers) constitute a formidable and costly body that is prepared to fight conventional threats that are ceasing to exist.[31] These resources can be diverted into Israel's economy to make it stronger, but are quite useless against the menace of ballistic missiles carrying non-conventional warheads. As such, a smaller, more sophisticated and more professional army is the prerequisite for successfully meeting the new challenges of the future.

## NOTES

1. I prefer to use the term 'conception' here since it encompasses a wider view of what national security is all about. Alternative terminology routinely used in this connection, such as 'strategy' (which refers mainly to the military aspects of national security), or 'doctrine' (which refers to a number of principles which stand at the core of national security), is too narrow and technical for this purpose.
2. The terms 'operational' and 'psychological' milieu were offered already in the 1950s. See, Harold and Margaret Sprout, *Man–Milieu Relationship Hypotheses in the Context of International Politics*, Princeton, 1956 and idem 'Environmental Factors in the Study of International Politics', *Journal of Conflict Resolution*, Vol. 1, No. 4 (1957), pp.309–28. For a classic discussion of the impact of perceptions in relations between states, see Robert Jervis, *Perception and Misperception in International Politics*, Princeton, 1976.
3. Some of the works on Israel's national security conception available in English are Michael I. Handel, *Israel's Political–Military Doctrine*, Cambridge, 1973; Yoav Ben-Horin and Barry Posen, *Israel's Strategic Doctrine*, Santa Monica, 1981; Avner Yaniv, *Deterrence Without the Bomb: The Politics of Israeli Strategy*, Lexington, 1987.
4. The only major exception to this rule is Israel's 1982 initiative in Lebanon. As is clear today, the strategic results of this initiative make it far less likely that a similar undertaking will occur in the future.
5. For a discussion of this Soviet role in 1956, 1967, 1969–70, 1973 and 1982, see among

others, John D. Glassman, *Arms for the Arabs*, Baltimore, 1975; Efraim Karsh, *The Cautious Bear: Soviet Military Engagement in Middle Eastern Wars in the Post-1967 Era*, Boulder, 1985; and Uri Bar-Joseph and John Hanna, 'Intervention Threats in Short Arab–Israeli Wars: An Analysis of Soviet Crisis Behaviour', *Journal of Strategic Studies*, Vol. 11, No. 4 (December 1988), pp.437–67. For a first-hand (and first-time) account of Soviet action during the 1973 War see Victor Israelyan, *Inside the Kremlin During the Yom Kippur War*, University Park, Pennsylvania, 1995.

6. Zeev Bonen, 'Sophisticated Conventional War', in *Advanced Technology and Future Warfare*, Tel Aviv, 1996, p.19.

7. For a short discussion of the role of sophisticated military technologies in Israel's military doctrine, see Saadia Amiel, 'Deterrence by Conventional Forces', *Survival*, Vol. 20, No. 2 (1978), pp.58–62; Amnon Yogev, *Model Bitkhoni Atidi Le-medinat Israel*, Tel Aviv, 1986. For a thorough discussion of the impact of American technological superiority in the Gulf War, see Department of Defense, *Conduct of the Persian Gulf War, Final Report to Congress*, Washington DC, 1992; Edward Luttwak, 'Air Power in US Military Strategy', in Richard H. Shultz and Robert Pfaltzgraff (eds), *The Future of Air Power in the Aftermath of the Gulf War*, Maxwell, 1992, pp.17–38; Eliot Cohen, *Gulf War Air Power Survey*, Washington DC, 1993.

8. A paradigm is 'a set of rules, standards, and examples of scientific practice which is shared by a coherent group of scientists, the commitment to which and consensus produced by it being prerequisites to the genesis and continuation of a research tradition'. See Christopher Lloyd, *Explanation in Social History*, Oxford, 1986, p.75. In the context of this paper this term refers to a set of principal beliefs on Israeli national security. While it is true that this set is less coherent and crystallized than a paradigm in the hard sciences, I nevertheless prefer its use here for three reasons: (a) it encompasses the beliefs, historical lessons and rules of behaviour shared by all those who define themselves as Zionists; (b) it is a necessary condition for the construction of a collective and consensual conception of national security; and (c) changes in Israel's national security operational and psychological milieus cast doubt, very much like Kuhn's 'puzzles', on the validity of the existing paradigm and indicate the rise of a new one, i.e., a paradigm shift. See Thomas S. Kuhn, *The Structure of Scientific Revolutions*, Chicago, 1970.
   Two more points are appropriate here. First, I use the term 'Zionist' rather than 'Israeli' national security paradigm since the set under discussion was born before 1948. Second, the beliefs I introduce below are presented in a sort of a Clausewitzian 'ideal type' mode. In reality, of course, there are many nuances to each of these beliefs. Presenting them in a rather simplistic and abstract form, however, will make the discussion of the changes in these beliefs far more clearly explicit. For a discussion of the use of this methodology by Clausewitz, see Michael Handel, *Masters of War: Sun Tzu, Clausewitz and Jomini*, London, 1992, pp.25–6.

9. For an interesting though somewhat problematic thesis on this subject, see Uri Ben-Eliezer, *Derekh Ha-kavenet: Hivazruto Shel Ha-militarizm Ha-israeli, 1936–1956*, Tel Aviv, 1995.

10. David Ben-Gurion, *Yihud Ve-yeud*, Tel Aviv, 1971, pp.162, 263.

11. Shabtai Teveth, *Kitat Yorim Be-bet-Jiz*, Tel Aviv, 1992, pp.67–71; Yechiel Gutman, *Taltela Ba-SHABAK: Ha-yoetz Ha-mishpati Neged Ha-memshala Mi-marashat Tobianski ad Parasht Kav 300*, Tel Aviv, 1995, p.163.

12. Zvi Offer and Avi Kobber (eds), *Mehir Ha-bitahon*, Tel Aviv, 1984, p.172.

13. For a critique of this belief see Victor Azarya and Baruch Kimmerling, 'New Immigrants as a Special Group in the Israeli Armed Forces', in Moshe Lissak (ed), *Israeli Society and Its Defence Establishment*, London, 1984, pp.128–48.

14. Yehoshafat Harkabi, *Edut Ishit: 'Ha-parash' Mi-nkudat Reuiti*, Tel Aviv, 1994, p.27.

15. Kenneth N. Waltz, *Theory of International Politics*, New York, 1979, p.186.

16. For a good discussion of this subject see Michael Handel, 'The Evolution of Israeli Strategy: The Psychology of Insecurity and the Quest for Absolute Security', in Williamson Murray, MacGregor Knox and Alvin Bernstein (eds), *The Making of Strategy: Rulers, States and War*, New York, 1994, pp.542–4.

17 Henry Kissinger, *White House Years*, Boston, 1979, pp.583–84.

18. For some of the meanings of post-Zionism see Uri Ram, *The Changing Agenda of Israeli Sociology: Theory, Ideology and Identity*, New York, 1995 and Amos Elon, 'Israel and the

End of Zionism', *New York Review of Books*, 19 December 1996, pp.22–30.
19. V. Schnitzer, *The Chief Military Censor*, **BGZ** 88/680, P.D.42 (4)617.
20. Moshe Negbi, *Hofesh Ha-itonut Be-Israel: Ha-hebet Ha-huki*, Jerusalem, 1995, pp.45–6.
21. *Ha-aretz*, 23 May 1996.
22. *Ha-aretz*, 24 January 1996.
23. Asher Arian, *Security Threatened: Surveying Israeli Opinion in Peace and War*, Cambridge, 1995, pp.234, 278.
24. Michal Shamir, 'Political Intolerance among Masses and Elites in Israel: A Re-evaluation of the Elitist Theory of Democracy', *Journal of Politics*, Vol. 53, No. 4 (1991), p.1036.
25. Arian, *Security Threatened*, pp.274–8.
26. Asher Arian, *Daat Qahal Be-Israel Be-nosei Bitahon*, Tel Aviv, 1996, p.9.
27. Asher Arian, 'Opinion Shift in Israel: Long-Term Patterns and Effects of Security Events', in Daniel Bar-Tal, Dan Jacobson and Aharon Klieman (eds), *Concerned with Security: Learning from the Experience of the Israeli Soldier* (forthcoming), p.17.
28. State Comptroller, *Doch Shnati* 46 (Annual Report 46), Jerusalem, 1996, pp.843–51.
29. Moshe Dayan, *Story of My Life*, London, 1976, pp.182–3.
30. *Ha-aretz*, 22 August 1980.
31. Ephraim Kam (ed.), *The Middle East Military Balance: 1994–1995*, Tel Aviv, 1996, pp.250–51.

# Patterns of War Initiation in the Arab–Israeli Conflict: A Note on the Military Dimension

## DAVID RODMAN

The Arab–Israeli conflict has spawned more episodes of violence than any other enduring conflict in the post-Second World War era.[1] Over the past half-century, this conflict has regularly given rise to intercommunal unrest, terrorism, border skirmishes and war. While most of the conflict's episodes of violence fall well short of war on the violence spectrum, war itself has not been uncommon. Indeed, Arabs and Israelis have fought a total of six wars: the 1948–49 War of Independence; the 1956 Suez War; the 1967 Six Day War; the 1969–70 War of Attrition; the 1973 Yom Kippur War; and the 1982 Lebanon War.[2]

These wars have not lacked their chroniclers. Military historians have traced their battlefield histories, addressing such issues as the nature, scope and results of the fighting, while diplomatic historians have probed their political backgrounds and consequences. Although some of these works, especially those of certain military historians, are comprehensive in the sense that they cover all of the Arab–Israeli wars, they are not comparative in the sense that they search for patterns that hold across these wars.[3] Only a relative handful of works look explicitly for such patterns.[4]

Perhaps the primary reason for the dearth of comparative analyses is that the Arab–Israeli wars are quite different from each other in a number of readily apparent respects. Not only do their particular diplomatic backgrounds and consequences vary, but they also display evident dissimilarities with respect to duration and intensity. The 1956, 1967 and 1973 wars lasted a relatively short period of time, from just a few days to a few weeks. In contrast, the 1948–49, 1969–70 and 1982 wars dragged on for a relatively long period of time, from a few months to over a year. The 1956, 1967 and 1973 wars resulted in heavy losses in men and equipment on a daily basis, especially among the Arabs. The 1948–49, 1969–70 and 1982 wars certainly had their share of

David Rodman is a New York-based writer and commentator.

destructive days, but losses in men and equipment on a daily basis proved to be considerably less severe.

A comparative analysis of these wars, however, can yield insights that improve the state of knowledge about the Arab–Israeli conflict. One of the most obvious observations to emerge from a comparative analysis is that Arabs and Israelis have each initiated three wars. The Arabs began the 1948–49, 1969–70 and 1973 wars, while the Israelis began the 1956, 1967 and 1982 wars. This observation raises a few important questions about Arab and Israeli decisions to initiate war. Have Arab decisions to initiate war been predicated on a particular military strategy? Likewise, have Israeli decisions to initiate war been predicated on a particular military strategy? And have these strategies been similar to – or different from – each other?

The purpose of this essay is to propose answers to these questions. One caveat, though, must be borne clearly in mind: a country's decision to initiate a war is at least as much influenced by political as by military considerations – that is, such a decision is also based on domestic, regional and global political variables. Indeed, a compelling set of political circumstances must emerge before a country thinks seriously about war initiation. To put it another way, the mere existence of conditions that, from a military viewpoint, favour war initiation is not by itself sufficient to lead to war initiation. In 1967, for example, Israeli leaders would not have thought about war initiation if a number of Arab countries had not first engaged in a series of very provocative actions that directly threatened Israel's security. Similarly, in 1973, Egyptian and Syrian leaders would not have thought about war initiation if they had not been deeply disturbed by the prevailing territorial and diplomatic *status quo*. In short, a country's decision to initiate a war is always complex, and what follows is not intended to deny this reality.

Whatever the political variables that influence such a decision may be, however, they fall beyond the purview of this article, which examines only the military aspect of Arab and Israeli decisions to initiate war.[5] To this end, the first part of the essay defines war and war initiation in the context of the Arab–Israeli conflict. The second part proceeds to discuss the general concept of military strategy, including brief sketches of Arab and Israeli strategies. The third part then demonstrates how these Arab and Israeli strategies influenced national decisions to initiate specific wars. Finally, the last part of the essay summarizes patterns of Arab and Israeli war initiation behaviour.

WAR AND WAR INITIATION

Hedley Bull captured the fundamental essence of the concept of war when he wrote that, 'War is organized violence carried on by political units against each other'.[6] Violence may certainly be disorganized and may certainly be carried on by entities other than political units, but such violence does not amount to war. Nevertheless, his definition leaves open the question of how to distinguish between war and other forms of 'organized violence carried on by political units'. Terrorist incidents and border skirmishes, for example, also satisfy Bull's definition of war, even though these sorts of episodes are clearly quite different from war.

War may be distinguished from other types of ordered, politically motivated violence in two ways. First, it can be differentiated from them on the basis of objective, measurable criteria, such as the amount of force employed by the combatants, the size of the military units deployed by the combatants and the number of deaths suffered by members of those units. A war involves a much greater use of force and much heavier casualties than, say, a terrorist incident or a border skirmish.[7] Second, war may be distinguished from other forms of organized political violence on subjective grounds as well. Disagreements about isolated cases notwithstanding, knowledgeable observers of warfare – historians, political scientists, anthropologists and so on – have been able to achieve a remarkable degree of consensus about which episodes of violence qualify as war – and which do not – across different temporal and spatial domains.

With respect to the Arab–Israeli conflict, the 1948–49, 1956, 1967, 1969–70, 1973 and 1982 wars comprise the complete universe of Arab–Israeli wars. These episodes of violence differ from others in the Arab–Israeli conflict on the basis of objective criteria, such as the amount of force employed in them by the combatants and the number of deaths suffered in them by members of their armed forces. Furthermore, knowledgeable observers agree that these episodes of violence are different from other episodes, such as terrorist incidents and border skirmishes.

The concept of war initiation, like the concept of war, is not as straightforward as it may first appear. It can be defined in a number of ways. A political unit – in the modern world, generally a country – whose action, even if non-violent itself, begins a chain of events that eventually leads to war could be labelled as the initiator of war. Similarly, a political unit whose action, even if non-violent, constitutes a *casus belli* under international law could also be labelled as the initiator of war. Egypt is frequently cited as the initiator of the Six Day War because its blockade of the Straits of Tiran in mid-May 1967 constituted a *casus belli* under international law.[8] In this essay, however, war initiation is defined in terms of the actual use of force.[9] Simply put, the political unit that 'fired the first shot' in a war is defined as the initiator of that war. Hence, since the Arabs fired the first shots in 1948–49, 1969–70 and 1973, they initiated these three wars. Since the Israelis fired the first shots in 1956, 1967 and 1982, they initiated these three wars.

## ARAB AND ISRAELI MILITARY STRATEGIES

Broadly speaking, attrition and manoeuvre constitute the two most basic types of military strategy.[10] An attrition strategy is based on the principle of defeating decisively an opponent by engaging it in a static or slow-moving campaign in which its armed forces are gradually whittled away to the point of complete destruction. As John Mearsheimer says: 'Little emphasis is placed on achieving the battlefield equivalent of a knockout punch. Instead, victory follows a series of set-piece battles and is not expected to be quick. The process is protracted, and success ultimately comes when the [opponent] can no longer continue to fight'.[11] Conversely, a manoeuvre, or a 'blitzkrieg', strategy is based on the principle of defeating decisively an opponent by effecting a deep penetration into its rear areas in a fast-moving campaign in which its armed forces are routed rather than destroyed. As Mearsheimer remarks:

> The concept of blitzkrieg stands in marked contrast to the view of war as a series of 'bloody and destructive' battles that grant victory to the side with the greatest 'physical and moral strength' ... The blitzkrieg's ultimate success results from the paralysis of the [opponent]. Large elements of the [opponent] forces may still be intact at the conflict's end, but the [opponent] is no longer able to coordinate them and thus to [fight].[12]

While knowledgeable observers of warfare have correctly noted that pure attrition and pure manoeuvre strategies are ideal types that do not occur in the real world, it is still possible to classify strategies as either primarily attrition or primarily manoeuvre.[13] Two examples drawn from the Second World War will suffice to illustrate this truism. The Allied campaigns in North Africa and Western Europe fall into the category of attrition warfare, since their principal *modus operandi* was to exploit the Allies' superiority in men and equipment to engage and destroy German (and German-allied) forces in slow-moving 'battles of annihilation', even though on certain occasions the Allies attempted (with limited success) to engage in manoeuvre warfare. On the other hand, the German attacks on France and the Soviet Union fall into the category of manoeuvre warfare, since their principal *modus operandi* was to drive deep behind French and Soviet lines in order to bring about the collapse of the French and Soviet armies, even though the Germans occasionally engaged in massive battles of annihilation against French and Soviet forces.

Attrition and manoeuvre strategies result in different costs. Specifically, an attrition strategy is a more expensive proposition for a country's armed forces, involving as it does the higher human and material costs associated with a more protracted and destructive military campaign. For this reason, it may safely be assumed that, ideally, a country's armed forces would prefer to adopt a manoeuvre strategy; however, reality may push a country to adopt an attrition strategy. First, not every country necessarily has the option to adopt a manoeuvre strategy, which is not easy to employ, since it depends upon the availability of high-quality human and material resources. Second, a country might simply come to the conclusion that its capabilities and attributes, relative to those of its opponent, make an attrition strategy attractive to it. A combination of internal and external variables, in short, may influence a country to adopt an attrition strategy.

*Arab Military Strategy*

Israel's Arab opponents are an excellent case in point. A combination of internal and external variables led Arab leaders to adopt an attrition strategy, and it has convinced them to maintain this strategy ever since that time.[14] Internally, these leaders early on reasoned that, since the Arab countries would always have a much greater reservoir of manpower than their Israeli opponent, attrition warfare would effectively wear down Israel's ability to fight. The Arabs could simply afford to absorb many more casualties than the Israelis. Later, after direct experience of the superiority of Israeli manpower, Arab leaders would cite another virtue of attrition warfare: Because attrition warfare, with its emphasis on set-piece battles, is much less dependent than manoeuvre warfare, with its emphasis on the 'fluid battlefield', on high-quality manpower capable of independent and rapid initiative, it would serve to reduce the impact of the considerable qualitative superiority of Israeli manpower. The longstanding Arab quantitative superiority in equipment, according to Arab leaders, has favoured attrition warfare as well. Not only would Arab countries be in a better position than Israel to sustain the high losses of aircraft, armoured vehicles, artillery tubes and so on that are the inevitable product of attrition warfare, but this mode of warfare would also reduce the impact of whatever qualitative advantages were enjoyed by the Israel Defence Forces (IDF).[15] Furthermore, Arab leaders reckoned that their societies would be in a better position than Israel's to withstand the psychological and economic strains of attrition warfare. With the Jewish people's extreme sensitivity to casualties, attrition warfare would sap Israel's will to fight to a much greater extent than it would the will of Arab societies. Additionally, since a mobilized IDF, always dependent on reserve forces, would bring the Israeli economy to a virtual standstill, attrition warfare held out the prospect of eventually destroying the Israeli economy. Arab economies, largely independent of the mobilization of the armed forces, would not be similarly affected by such extended warfare. Externally, Arab leaders concluded, attrition warfare would provide the Arab world with opportunities to increase foreign support for itself – and to weaken foreign support for Israel – by bringing its much greater (in comparison to Israel) economic and political power to bear on vital foreign countries. Swifter manoeuvre warfare would not permit these economic and political pressures to build up on foreign countries. In sum, according to Arab leaders, attrition warfare has offered a better alternative to the Arabs than manoeuvre warfare.

*Israeli Military Strategy*

Israel's military strategy has constituted a mirror image of Arab strategy. Israel adopted a manoeuvre strategy based largely on the same set of internal and external variables that led the Arabs to adopt an attrition strategy, and it has stuck to this strategy since that time as a consequence of these variables.[16] Internally, Israeli leaders early on arrived at the conclusion that the IDF's quantitative inferiority in manpower necessitated a manoeuvre strategy. Israel would simply be less able than the Arabs to absorb the heavier casualties produced by attrition warfare. Moreover, an attrition strategy would minimize the impact of the qualitative superiority of Israeli manpower, while a manoeuvre strategy would maximize this impact. Likewise, the IDF's quantitative inferiority in equipment would place Israel in a worse position to absorb the heavier material losses associated with attrition warfare; and whatever technological advantages the IDF possessed over Arab forces would also be minimized by employing an attrition strategy, while they would be maximized by employing a manoeuvre strategy. From a societal perspective as well, Israeli leaders reasoned that the IDF should adopt a manoeuvre strategy. First, the lower human losses associated with manoeuvre warfare would cushion, to some extent, any psychological blow to Israeli society caused by war. Second, the less protracted nature of this type of warfare would mean that the Israeli economy could start to function normally again more quickly. Geography, too, had a major influence on Israel's choice of a manoeuvre strategy. The country's lack of defensible frontiers and territorial depth in its first decades convinced Israeli leaders that battles must not be fought on Israeli soil. Instead, fighting must occur on Arab territory. The best way to accomplish this end would be to embrace manoeuvre warfare, which would permit the IDF to carry the war deep into Arab territory. Externally, Israel's lack of alliance partners, coupled with the Arab world's considerable influence on the international community, convinced Israeli leaders that wars must be short. The longer an Arab–Israeli war dragged on, they assumed, the more likely that outside powers would intervene to the detriment of Israeli interests. In sum, according to Israeli leaders, manoeuvre warfare has offered a better alternative to Israel than attrition warfare.

## THE ARAB–ISRAELI WARS

Whichever strategy a country adopts, it may be hypothesized that it is more likely to initiate war at times when it perceives that its chosen strategy is favoured. A country that adopts an attrition strategy, in other words, is more likely to initiate war at times when it believes that conditions favour attrition warfare, while a country that adopts a manoeuvre strategy is more likely to initiate war at times when it believes that conditions favour manoeuvre warfare. It is now appropriate to examine whether war initiation in the Arab–Israeli wars conforms to this behavioural pattern.

### The 1948–49 War of Independence

On the eve of the War of Independence, Arab knowledge about the Yishuv's military capabilities could best be characterized as very spotty.[17] Arab leaders had some idea of how many men the Yishuv could put into the field. They did not, however, truly know anything about the quality of the Jewish forces – their level of training, their state of morale, their officers' effectiveness and so on. The crude abilities of Arab countries in the late 1940s to gather and process information ensured that such intangibles would not affect Arab military decision-making. Besides, Arab leaders initially had an extremely dismissive view of Jewish martial prowess – a view informed, to a great extent, by outright prejudice. Even had information about these intangibles been available, therefore, it is quite unlikely that it would have influenced their decision-making. Arab leaders were also aware that, on the eve of war, the Yishuv had no heavy weapons ready for combat – no genuine combat aircraft, no genuine tanks and no modern artillery tubes.[18] They knew that Jewish forces could field only a handful of non-combat aircraft, some hastily improvised 'armoured' vehicles (actually civilian buses and trucks covered with armoured plates) and light weapons, mainly small mortars, machine guns, rifles, pistols and grenades. Arab leaders, in short, believed that the Yishuv was militarily weak. Moreover, they were aware of the fact that Palestinian (and foreign Arab) irregulars, who had been waging a campaign to cut Jewish supply and communications lines and to overrun isolated Jewish agricultural settlements since late 1947, had managed to inflict significant losses on the Yishuv. To this already encouraging picture, Arab leaders added the knowledge that their own military forces – whose quality they overrated – were equipped with modern combat aircraft, armoured vehicles and modern artillery tubes, albeit in limited numbers. Finally, Arab leaders believed that their traditional colonial patrons, especially the British, would come to their assistance in a war, supplying them with arms, while the Jewish forces could not count on similar support from foreign governments.[19] Arab leaders, then, convinced themselves that the military forces of the newly created state of Israel would eventually be overwhelmed and destroyed in an attrition campaign that featured a series of set-piece battles of annihilation. The belief that conditions favoured the success of attrition warfare surely influenced their decision to opt for war in May 1948.

## The 1956 Suez War

In the War of Independence, Israel lost approximately one per cent of its pre-war population – about 6,000 soldiers and civilians from an initial total of 600,000 people – in what was, at least until its final stages, a draining war of attrition. Equipment losses proved correspondingly heavy. Although the IDF finally won a great victory of which the Israeli public was justifiably proud, the heavy loss of life constituted a serious psychological blow to the new country, born as it had been out of the ashes of the Holocaust. Furthermore, the Yishuv's already shaky economy had been shattered by the war, with productive activity essentially grinding to a halt. The new country's territorial dimensions, too, did not augur well for its future security. While much land not originally allocated to the country had been captured, Israel now had indefensible borders and no strategic depth.[20] Moreover, the country emerged from the War of Independence with no allies that could be relied upon to provide it with military, diplomatic or economic assistance during a future round of fighting. Based on Israel's experiences in that war, in fact, Israeli leaders thought that, in a future war, foreign powers would – if granted an opportunity – intervene in ways that would harm the country's vital interests. Given these national circumstances, Israeli leaders of the immediate post-independence years concluded that Israel simply could not afford another round of attrition warfare. This feeling, combined with the IDF's successful application of manoeuvre warfare in the last stages of the War of Independence, especially against the Egyptian army in the Negev and Sinai, convinced Israeli leaders that the IDF had no alternative but to be built for manoeuvre warfare. However crude by later Israeli standards, the IDF did indeed adopt a manoeuvre strategy by the mid-1950s.[21] It indoctrinated and trained its units for this brand of warfare. What it still needed was the modern aircraft, armour and artillery necessary to implement a blitzkrieg. Fortunately for it, the French agreed to supply the IDF with this equipment, particularly from the summer of 1956 onwards. By the autumn of that year, Israeli leaders were confident that the IDF could launch a successful blitzkrieg against Egypt, its most visibly threatening foe at the time, across the Sinai. All that was now required was the right political scenario – one that would permit the IDF to effect a blitzkrieg without leaving Israel completely isolated in the world community. This scenario became a reality in October 1956, with the conclusion of a British–French–Israeli war pact. The IDF was unleashed against Egypt soon after.

## The 1967 Six Day War

The IDF's blitzkrieg in the Suez War turned out to be tremendously successful. At the cost of fewer than 200 dead, and correspondingly small equipment losses, the IDF completely shattered Egyptian forces in the Sinai in a matter of days. Not only were many thousands of Egyptian troops killed, wounded or captured, but significant quantities of Egyptian armoured vehicles, artillery tubes and small arms also fell into Israeli hands. In a larger sense, at least in the near term, the IDF's blitzkrieg removed the Egyptian threat, without causing serious harm to Israel. Not surprisingly, then, Israeli leaders became even more firmly convinced that a manoeuvre strategy was ideal for the IDF.[22] They had now seen how such a strategy maximized Israel's strengths, especially its superior manpower, and minimized its weaknesses, especially its limited resources. The Israel Air Force (IAF), which had performed very well in the Suez War, received a bigger role in Israeli planning. At the outset of the next war, it would destroy an opponent's air power on the ground, thereby furnishing Israel with air superiority. Once air superiority had been guaranteed, the IAF would fly close air support and battlefield air interdiction missions in order to assist the IDF's land forces in their advance. To this end, the IAF got a considerably larger share of the Israeli defence budget than it had in the past, principally to purchase more and better aircraft, to improve the air base infrastructure necessary to handle these aircraft, and to train more and better air and ground crews. Likewise, the IDF's tank formations, which had also performed very well in the Suez War, received a much bigger role in Israeli planning. They now became the lead element in the land component of the IDF's manoeuvre strategy. Rather than support the infantry, the infantry would support them. Between 1956 and 1967, the IDF purchased more and better tanks as well as improved the quality of the manpower and training within tank formations. By 1967, the IDF had thoroughly prepared to execute a classic blitzkrieg strategy – a strategy very similar to the one used by the Wehrmacht against the French and Soviet armies in the early days of the Second World War. Before the Six Day War, therefore, Israeli leaders were confident that the IDF could unleash an even more devastating blitzkrieg against Egypt than the one unleashed in the Suez War, despite their knowledge that the Egyptian army had steadily improved quantitatively and qualitatively since that war.[23] Furthermore, since Israel's fundamental territorial, economic and diplomatic position had not changed in the inter-war years, a manoeuvre strategy remained imperative in the eyes of Israeli leaders.[24] Once again, all that was necessary for the IDF to launch a blitzkrieg was for the correct set of political circumstances to emerge – that is, a tangible Arab threat to Israel coupled with an ensuing Israeli diplomatic effort to convince the United States that the eventual use of force to eliminate this threat would be justified. That set of circumstances, which began to materialize in mid-May 1967, had come together by early June 1967, ushering the IDF into battle.

### The 1969–70 War of Attrition

Contrary to Arab decision-making on the eve of the War of Independence, Egyptian decision-making on the eve of the War of Attrition stemmed not from ignorance of – and contempt for – Israeli military capabilities, but rather from first-hand knowledge of – and healthy respect for – those capabilities.[25] In both the Suez and Six Day wars, the Egyptian army had been thoroughly defeated in manoeuvre warfare campaigns, which prompted Egyptian leaders to conclude that Egypt simply could not compete with Israel in this form of warfare. Rather, Egypt had to wage attrition warfare if it had any hope of achieving its political aims through war. What it needed to initiate attrition warfare, however, was an environment that would compel Israel to engage in this form of warfare. The post-Six Day War environment, Egyptian leaders concluded, provided Egypt with a perfect opportunity to induce Israel to fight on Egyptian terms. Since Israel had conquered the Sinai in the Six Day War, the Suez Canal now stood between the two countries. Although not an impassable geographical barrier, as the Egyptian crossing and Israeli counter-crossing in the Yom Kippur War would demonstrate, this obstacle was excellent for waging a static, attrition campaign. It would be exceedingly difficult, Egyptian leaders reasoned, for the IDF to respond to an Egyptian attrition campaign with a swift, manoeuvre campaign across the canal. Additionally, because the Egyptian army had recovered from its personnel losses in the Six Day War and had been generously re-supplied with equipment by the Soviet Union, it once more had a considerable quantitative edge, especially in artillery, over the IDF. It would be better able than the IDF, therefore, to sustain losses in a 'trench' war. Furthermore, an attrition campaign would compel the IDF to mobilize a significant portion of its combat units, putting both psychological and economic pressure on Israel. Finally, since the Soviet Union was firmly supportive of Egypt, while the United States had interests at stake in both Israel and Egypt, an extended attrition campaign had the potential to elicit the intervention of the superpowers on behalf of Egypt's effort to 'liberate' the Sinai without having to sign a peace accord with Israel. It was this mix of circumstances that motivated the Egyptian leadership's decision to initiate the War of Attrition in early 1969.

*The 1973 Yom Kippur War*

Egyptian and Syrian decision-making prior to the Yom Kippur War bears strong similarities to Egyptian decision-making before the War of Attrition.[26] Leaders of both countries realized that their armies would suffer grave reverses in a manoeuvre warfare campaign against the IDF. Thus, conditions would have to be ripe for attrition warfare before they could consider embarking on a war to achieve their political aims. Specifically, this meant that they would have to find a way to neutralize the IDF's superior air and armoured forces. State-of-the-art, Soviet-supplied anti-aircraft and anti-tank missiles offered this prospect, making attrition warfare feasible. To mire the IDF in an attrition campaign, Egyptian and Syrian leaders devised an ingenious plan. The Egyptian and Syrian armies would first launch a surprise assault in the Sinai and on the Golan, respectively, capturing slices of Israeli-controlled territory. Then they would fortify their new positions with very large numbers of anti-aircraft and anti-tank missiles in order to defeat the inevitable Israeli counterattack. Not only would Israel suffer heavy losses in men and equipment in the subsequent attrition campaign, causing psychological and economic distress to the country, but the superpowers would also be dragged into the war to terminate the fighting. Egyptian and Syrian leaders, in short, were convinced that, by inflicting pain on Israel and by drawing the superpowers into the Arab–Israeli conflict, they could achieve their political aims of regaining the 'occupied territories'. All of the military pieces necessary to implement this plan were in place by autumn 1973. Hence, the Egyptian and Syrian decision to go to war in October of that year.

*The 1982 Lebanon War*

In 1982, in contrast to 1956 and 1967, Israeli leaders recognized that the IDF could not launch a classic blitzkrieg.[27] Unlike the generally flat and dry desert terrain of the Sinai, southern Lebanon's terrain is mountainous and often muddy, which makes rapid armoured penetrations quite difficult. On this occasion, however, Israeli leaders did not feel that the capability to engage in a classic blitzkrieg was of the utmost importance. Israel still had a manoeuvre warfare option available to it. The IDF, after all, had enormous quantitative and qualitative advantages over PLO forces. Moreover, it also had the capability to put armoured, artillery and infantry forces behind PLO lines via amphibious and airborne assaults, thereby putting PLO forces under pressure from a number of directions. Even if an invasion of Lebanon sparked a larger war with Syria, Israeli leaders believed that the IDF's superiority would allow it to achieve all of Israel's military objectives quickly – and with minimal losses – in a blitzkrieg-like advance. Put differently, Israeli leaders were thinking in terms of a very brief and relatively painless war.[28] Israeli war initiation, therefore, simply awaited the correct political circumstances, especially American approval for an Israeli operation. By June 1982, these political circumstances had materialized, prompting the invasion of Lebanon.

CONCLUSION

Arab and Israeli behaviour has thus far been consistent with the hypothesized relationship between war initiation and military strategy. Each of the three wars initiated by the Arabs was begun at a time when Arab leaders perceived that conditions favoured their chosen strategy of attrition warfare. Likewise, each of the three wars initiated by the Israelis was begun at a time when Israeli leaders perceived that conditions favoured their chosen strategy of manoeuvre warfare. The validity of this relationship is further reinforced by pointing out that Arab leaders had no plans to initiate war in 1956, 1967 and 1982, at least in part because they believed that conditions were not ripe for the success of attrition campaigns. Egyptian leaders may have been eager for battle in 1967, but they were content to allow the IDF to attack first. They believed that the Egyptian army could block the initial Israeli assault, thereby turning a manoeuvre campaign, which they could not win, into an attrition campaign, which they could win. Similarly, Israeli leaders had no plans to initiate war in 1969–70 or 1973, at least in part because they perceived that conditions favoured attrition rather than manoeuvre warfare. In 1948, because Israel was invaded immediately upon its birth, Israeli leaders had no choice about whether to initiate war; but, had they had such a choice, it is safe to assume that they would not have initiated war, recognizing that the Arab world's greater resources would not have augured well for an Israeli victory in an attrition campaign. All in all, then, while the decisions of Arab and Israeli leaders to initiate war have never been made solely on the basis of military thinking, these decisions have clearly been influenced by perceptions about whether their chosen strategies were favoured.

NOTES

1. It does not follow, of course, that the Arab–Israeli conflict has therefore been the most destructive conflict of the post-war era. This conflict, in fact, has not been one of the more destructive enduring – or, for that matter, passing – conflicts in the post-war world. Many other conflicts have witnessed far more death and destruction.
2. The Arab–Israeli wars are most commonly known by their 'Israeli' names; consequently, these names will be used throughout this article. The 1991 Gulf War, which pitted a Western–Arab coalition against Iraq over the latter's invasion, occupation and annexation of Kuwait, does not fit the definition of an Arab–Israeli war, even though Israel became a target of repeated Iraqi ballistic missile attacks during this war. These missile attacks, which were intended to spark a wider Arab–Israeli war, ultimately failed to do so, after all.
3. For one of the best comprehensive battlefield histories of the Arab–Israeli conflict see a

prominent American military historian's two-volume survey: Trevor N. Dupuy, *Elusive Victory: The Arab–Israeli Wars, 1947–1974*, New York, 1978 and Trevor N. Dupuy and Paul Martell, *Flawed Victory: The Arab–Israeli Conflict and the 1982 Lebanon War*, Fairfax, 1986. Also see Martin van Creveld, *The Sword and the Olive: A Critical History of the Israeli Defense Force*, New York, 1998 and Chaim Herzog, *The Arab–Israeli Wars: War and Peace in the Middle East from the War of Independence through Lebanon*, New York, 1984. For diplomatic histories of the Arab–Israeli conflict that tackle more than a single war see, for instance, Michael Brecher, *Decisions in Crisis: Israel, 1967 and 1973*, Berkeley, 1980 and Avner Yaniv, *Deterrence Without the Bomb: The Politics of Israeli Strategy*, Lexington, 1987.

4. For two works that have discovered patterns see John J. Mearsheimer, *Conventional Deterrence*, Ithaca, 1983 and David Rodman, 'War Initiation: The Case of Israel', *Journal of Strategic Studies*, Vol. 20, No. 4 (1997), pp.1–17.

5. For one effort to address both the political and military variables affecting Israeli decisions to initiate or not to initiate war see Rodman, 'War Initiation'.

6. Quoted in John A. Vasquez, *The War Puzzle*, Cambridge, 1993, p.23.

7. For efforts to define war based on objective, measurable criteria see Melvin Small and J. David Singer, *Resort to Arms: International and Civil Wars, 1816–1980*, Beverly Hills, 1982; and Vasquez, *The War Puzzle*.

8. On this point see Itamar Rabinovich, 'Seven Wars and One Peace Treaty', in Alvin Z. Rubinstein (ed.), *The Arab–Israeli Conflict: Perspectives*, New York, 1984, p.50.

9. This definition, it should be noted, carries no normative overtones. It is not the intention of this essay to assign blame on legal, moral or historical grounds to either side for the outbreak of various wars. Because this essay grapples with the connection between war initiation and military strategy, it is appropriate to define the former concept in a manner that makes sense from a military rather than a legal, moral or historical point of view.

10. Mearsheimer also includes a 'limited aims' strategy in his useful typology of military strategies. A limited aims strategy seeks to capture a portion of an opponent's territory – usually for use as a political bargaining chip – through a surprise assault. The essence of this strategy is to avoid heavy fighting with an opponent. Since neither Arabs nor Israelis have genuinely expected to be able to avoid heavy fighting in their wars, this strategy is beyond the purview of this article. For Mearsheimer's typology of military strategies see *Conventional Deterrence*, pp.13–66.

11. Ibid., p.34.

12. Ibid., pp.36–7.

13. One may consult for example the writings of Martin van Creveld and Edward Luttwak for the real-world distinction between attrition and manoeuvre strategies.

14. Not much has been written about general Arab military strategy. Some information on this strategy, however, may be gleaned by consulting the following sources: J. Bowyer Bell, 'National Character and Military Strategy: The Egyptian Experience, October 1973', *Parameters*, Vol. 5, No. 1 (1975), pp.6–16; van Creveld, *The Sword and the Olive*; Dupuy, *Elusive Victory*; Muhammed Heikal, *The Road to Ramadan*, London, 1975; Haim Levenberg, *The Military Preparations of the Arab Community in Palestine, 1945–1948*, London, 1993; Mearsheimer, *Conventional Deterrence*, pp.155–64; and Anwar Sadat, *In Search of Identity*, New York, 1978.

15. Today, the IDF's qualitative superiority in equipment over its Arab opponents is taken for granted. Actually, this superiority is of relatively recent origin. The Israel Air Force (IAF) did not achieve superiority until the late 1960s, when it began to receive American A-4 *Skyhawk* and F-4 *Phantom* aircraft. On the ground, Israeli superiority is an even more recent phenomenon, emerging only in the years after the Yom Kippur War.

16. Much has been written about general Israeli military strategy. The following accounts offer informative introductions to this strategy: Michael Handel, 'The Evolution of Israeli Strategy: The Psychology of Insecurity and the Quest for Absolute Security', in Williamson Murray, MacGregor Knox, and Alvin Bernstein (eds), *The Making of Strategy: Rulers, States, and War*, New York, 1994, pp.534–78; Yoav Ben-Horin and Barry Posen, *Israel's Strategic Doctrine*, Santa Monica, 1981; Ariel Levite, *Offense and Defense in Israeli Military Strategy*, Boulder, 1989; Bard E. O'Neill, 'Israel', in Douglas J. Murray and Paul R. Viotti (eds), *The Defense Policies of Nations: A Comparative Study*, 3rd ed., Baltimore,

1994, pp.497–541; and Yaniv, *Deterrence Without the Bomb*.

17. For Arab preparations for the War of Independence consult van Creveld, *The Sword and the Olive*; Dupuy, *Elusive Victory*; Amitzur Ilan, *The Origin of the Arab–Israeli Arms Race: Arms, Embargo, Military Power, and Decision in the 1948 Palestine War*, New York, 1996; Dan Kurzman, *Genesis 1948: The First Arab–Israeli War*, New York, 1970; Levenberg, *The Military Preparations of the Arab Community in Palestine*; Netanel Lorch, *The Edge of the Sword: Israel's War of Independence, 1947–1949*, New York, 1961; Edward Luttwak and Dan Horowitz, *The Israeli Army*, New York, 1975. These sources also provide a sense of Arab strategy in – and attitudes about – the war.

18. The extent to which they were informed about the increasingly successful Jewish efforts to acquire these types of arms in foreign countries is unclear.

19. On the Arab belief in foreign assistance see Ilan, *The Origin of the Arab–Israeli Arms Race*. That this belief was not entirely without foundation is demonstrated by a number of British measures intended to assist the Arab war effort, despite Great Britain's official neutrality in the War of Independence.

20. For Israel's overall situation in the wake of the War of Independence see, for example, S.N. Eisenstadt, *The Transformation of Israeli Society*, Boulder, 1985; Howard M. Sachar, *A History of Israel: From the Rise of Zionism to Our Times*, New York, 1979.

21. Before the Suez War, the IDF based its military strategy on mechanized infantry rather than tanks. Nevertheless, this strategy's emphasis on speed, mobility and casualty avoidance clearly marked it as a manoeuvre strategy. For the IDF's emphasis on manoeuvre warfare by the mid-1950s see Luttwak and Horowitz, *The Israeli Army*; S.L.A. Marshall, *Sinai Victory*, Nashville, 1985; Mearsheimer, *Conventional Deterrence*, pp.136–40.

22. For the development of Israeli manoeuvre strategy between 1956 and 1967 see Martin van Creveld, *Command in War*, Cambridge, 1985 and *The Sword and the Olive*; Luttwak and Horowitz, *The Israeli Army*; Mearsheimer, *Conventional Deterrence*, pp.143–53; Gunther Rothenberg, *The Anatomy of the Israeli Army*, New York, 1979.

23. It is worth noting that Israel wished to avoid a land war with Jordan and Syria in 1967, whatever transpired on the Egyptian front. Israel simply did not want to get involved in a three-front war. Additionally, the hilly terrain in Jordan and Syria, along with the extensive fortifications of the Jordanian and Syrian armies, meant that the IDF would have to employ an attrition strategy against these states. Israel, of course, fought and defeated both of them, but only after they initiated land warfare.

24. In 1967, Israel was still without defensible borders and strategic depth; it was still vulnerable to economic collapse in a long war; and it was still unable to count on foreign support in such a war.

25. For Egyptian military strategy in the War of Attrition see Yaacov Bar-Siman-Tov, *The Israeli–Egyptian War of Attrition, 1969–1970: A Case Study of Limited Local War*, New York, 1980; Jon D. Glassman, *Arms for the Arabs: The Soviet Union and War in the Middle East*, Baltimore, 1975; Heikal, *The Road to Ramadan*; David A. Korn, *Stalemate: The War of Attrition and Great Power Diplomacy in the Middle East, 1967–1970*, Boulder, 1992; Jonathan Shimshoni, *Israel and Conventional Deterrence: Border Warfare from 1953 to 1970*, Ithaca, 1988.

26. For Egyptian and Syrian military strategy in the Yom Kippur War see Hassan el Badri, Taha el Magdoub and Muhammed Dia el Din Zohdy, *The Ramadan War, 1973*, Dunn Loring, 1978; Anthony H. Cordesman and Abraham R. Wagner, *The Lessons of Modern War (Vol. 1): The Arab–Israeli Conflicts, 1973–1989*, Boulder, 1990; Dupuy, *Elusive Victory*; Glassman, *Arms for the Arabs*; Heikal, *The Road to Ramadan*; Mearsheimer, *Conventional Deterrence*, pp.155–64; and Sadat, *In Search of Identity*.

27. For Israeli military strategy in the Lebanon War see van Creveld, *The Sword and the Olive*; Cordesman and Wagner, *The Lessons of Modern War*; Dupuy and Martell, *Flawed Victory*; and Richard A. Gabriel, *Operation Peace for Galilee: The Israeli–PLO War in Lebanon*, New York, 1984.

28. That Israeli leaders apparently failed to consider that an IDF operation in Lebanon could deteriorate into a prolonged attrition campaign is indicated in Amos Perlmutter, *Israel: The Partitioned State, a Political History Since 1900*, New York, 1985, pp.313–30.

# Israel's Nuclear History

## EDWIN S. COCHRAN

Despite its small size, Israel's formidable military capabilities qualify it as a mid-level power in the global context and as the pre-eminent power in the Middle East. The technological basis for Israel's military superiority over other regional actors is a well-developed military–technical base whose capabilities far exceed those of any of Israel's potential adversaries.[1] This 'impressive scientific and technological infrastructure ... has become a main bulwark of national security, and indeed of national survival'.[2] Israel has consistently used its technological superiority to offset the quantitative advantages of the Arab states and to deter and defeat their numerically superior forces.[3]

An integral part of Israel's technological 'bulwark of national security' is its regionally unique nuclear capability. In the literature of nuclear proliferation, Israel is generally considered to be an undeclared, second-generation nuclear power,[4] and is widely reported to have produced enough fissionable material to fabricate 60–300 nuclear weapons, including enhanced radiation variants.[5]

Beginning with the government of David Ben-Gurion, the nation's first Prime Minister, Israel has implemented a strategy of 'deliberate ambiguity' concerning its nuclear capabilities and intentions. While it has developed an impressive nuclear infrastructure, the Israeli government has not formally admitted possessing nuclear weapons nor is there conclusive evidence that Israel has ever conducted a nuclear test. It has also consistently refused fully to open its nuclear facilities to international inspection or to join the Nuclear Non-Proliferation Treaty (NPT).[6]

Israel's deliberately ambiguous nuclear strategy serves as a paradigm for the concept of 'opaque' nuclear proliferation, and provides a model for other states seeking to develop a nuclear weapons capability without violating perceived international non-proliferation norms. Official secrecy is the backbone of Israel's nuclear strategy. There is little 'official' evidence available – most of the relevant documents remain classified and Israeli government officials are loath to admit that such a programme even exists. Nevertheless, over the past 30 years a body of

The views expressed in this article are those of the author and do not reflect the official policy or position of the Department of Defense or of the US Government.
Edwin S. Cochran is an officer in the United States army.

literature largely based on interviews with past policymakers combined with journalistic accounts has emerged which 'appears to reveal a central, convergent core of "received wisdom" on the subject'.[7]

This essay, based on a survey of the relevant literature and interviews with knowledgeable Israeli sources, provides an account of Israel's development as a nuclear power. For purposes of analysis, it divides Israel's nuclear history into five distinct phases: 1948–53, the period of early Israeli efforts in the nuclear field; 1953–67, an era marked by nuclear collaboration with France and the emergence of Israel's nuclear strategy of deliberate ambiguity; 1967–80, when Israel achieved a regional nuclear monopoly; the decade of the 1980s, when Israeli leaders actively sought to maintain that monopoly; and the 1991 Persian Gulf War and its aftermath, which presented Israeli leaders with new security challenges. It concludes with a discussion on the historical nature of Israel's nuclear programme and the evolution of its nuclear strategy of deliberate ambiguity.

PHASE I: 1948–53

Israeli leaders have long recognized the importance of science and technology to the security of their nation. Even before the founding of the state, Zionist leaders considered the mastery of science essential to the survival of the Jewish people. In his autobiography Chaim Weizmann, Israel's first President, wrote that for Jews living in the Russian Pale of Settlement 'the acquisition of knowledge was … not so much a normal process of education as the storing up of weapons in an arsenal, by means of which we hoped later to be able to hold our own in a hostile world'.[8]

Nuclear research and development in Israel began soon after the founding of the state. These early efforts seem to have been concerned with the development of a basic nuclear infrastructure, and not to have been linked to a firm timetable for weapons development. According to knowledgeable Israeli sources, the programme's original intention was the development of nuclear energy for peaceful purposes.[9] Israel's early leaders clearly recognized the possibilities which the exploitation of nuclear power offered to a nation which lacked readily available fuel resources. Weizmann, a renowned organic chemist in his own right, was also a long-time friend of both Albert Einstein and the great British experimental physicist Ernest Rutherford. And Weizmann actively encouraged the development of nuclear science in Israel,[10] expressing his hope that Israel would become 'a centre of the new scientific development which would get the world past the conflict arising from the monopolistic position of oil'.[11]

In 1948 a Research and Planning Branch was established within the Israeli Ministry of Defence. One of this organization's first tasks was to determine the amount of uranium ore contained in the Negev Desert's phosphate deposits. A survey subsequently conducted by the Israeli Army Science Corps revealed that the Negev's phosphate deposits contained from 0.01 to 0.1 per cent uranium, providing Israel with an estimated national reserve of 30,000–60,000 tons of uranium.[12]

A year later, in 1949, a Department of Isotope Research was established at the Weizmann Institute of Science, Israel's leading scientific institution. The department's facilities included separate laboratories for the conduct of research in the fields of applied nuclear physics, electronics, nuclear magnetic resonance, spectroscopy and the production of deuterium ('heavy water'), used as a coolant in nuclear reactors. This latter research effort was led by Professor Israel Dostrovsky, who had conducted similar work at the University of London. By the end of 1949 at least two other Israeli universities, the Hebrew University in Jerusalem, and the Israeli Institute of Technology (Technion) in Haifa, had active nuclear research programmes.[13]

Also in 1949, the first group of Israeli students went abroad to study nuclear science, most likely under the sponsorship of the Ministry of Defence. This group included several men, notably Amos de Shalit, who would figure prominently in the future Israeli nuclear programme.[14] Initially sent to Holland, Switzerland, Britain and the United States, all eventually obtained academic appointments in the United States.[15]

In 1952 Israel's nuclear programme began to emerge as a co-ordinated effort with the establishment of the Israeli Atomic Energy Commission (IAEC). Subordinate to the Department of Research and Planning within the Ministry of Defence, the IAEC remained a secret organization from its founding on 13 June 1952 until its existence was made public on 19 November 1954.[16]

Subordination of the IAEC to the Ministry of Defence probably reflected several factors. First, Israel was in a virtually continuous state of war with its neighbours, and the defence establishment was best suited to maintain the nuclear programme's security. Second, of all the new state's institutions, the Israeli military probably had the greatest degree of technical and managerial expertise, skills essential to the management of a complex nuclear development programme. Finally, there was the almost unlimited influence of David Ben-Gurion.

Ben-Gurion, who served, with the exception of one brief interlude, as Israel's Prime Minister and Minister of Defence from 1948 to 1963, was the driving force behind Israel's nuclear programme. By centralizing control of Israel's nuclear programme in his office, Ben-Gurion both provided it with political legitimacy and insulated it from unwanted interference. He also initiated the great tradition of secrecy surrounding the Israeli nuclear programme, informing neither his cabinet, nor the

Knesset, nor the Israeli intelligence community of the initial decision to develop nuclear weapons.[17]

Ben-Gurion's greatest concern following the Israeli War of Independence was the possibility of a second Holocaust, this time at the hands of the Arabs. From his perspective, such fears were well founded. A war of destruction against the Jews in Palestine had been a traditional goal of local Arab leaders. In their opposition to Jewish immigration, they had forced the British to close the gates of Palestine to Jewish refugees almost completely during the 1930s. Later the most influential Palestinian leader, Hajj Amin al-Husseini, the one-time Mufti of Jerusalem, went so far as to collaborate with Hitler and enthusiastically supported his 'final solution of the Jewish Question'.[18]

So traumatic was the impact of the Holocaust on the Jewish people as a whole, and so self-evident the need for an independent state that would protect Jews from future disasters of such magnitude, that Ben-Gurion included it as a justification for a Jewish state in the Israeli Declaration of Independence.[19] Two specific aspects of the Holocaust have left a lasting impression on those responsible for Israel's security. First, the Holocaust focused their attention on the basic question of physical survival. Unlike their counterparts in other countries, Israeli leaders believed, and continue to believe, that it is inadequate to define security merely as the safeguarding of political values, institutions and a way of life. For the leadership of Israel, security means the very existence of a people. Second, the experience of the Holocaust has driven Israeli leaders to the conclusion that physical security is too important to be left to others. Israel must strive to be as self-reliant as possible in matters of defence and security because in times of extreme peril sympathetic friends may be unable or unwilling to intervene.

The primary lesson that Ben-Gurion took from the Holocaust was that other nations would not sacrifice their interests to fight a 'Jews' war'. As he wrote in his 1948 war diary, Israel had to secure its existence before the Arabs recovered, modernized their armed forces, and possibly even united.[20] Israel's only security, he repeatedly warned, would come through self-defence and self-reliance. Ben-Gurion's initial concern was the immense quantitative superiority of the Arabs over Israel. 'What is Israel?', he mused. 'One dot. A spot. How can it survive in this Arab world?'. Ben-Gurion also believed that it would be only natural for the Arabs to seek to acquire nuclear weapons. For him, the main issue was to ensure that Israel, with its more advanced scientific skills and contacts abroad, gained and kept the lead in a potential nuclear arms race.[21]

The task of disciplining Israel's nascent nuclear programme and focusing its efforts on weapons development fell to two of Ben-Gurion's most trusted subordinates, Professor Ernst David Bergmann, the first chairman of the IAEC, and Shimon Peres. Both shared Ben-Gurion's conviction that Israel needed a nuclear capability to solve its 'security problem'.

Ernst Bergmann was the scientific 'father' of Israel's nuclear programme. Before the Second World War, Bergmann had been on the fringe of a group of eminent scientists, including Ernest Rutherford in England and Marie Curie in France, who were on the cutting edge of what would become an international race to unravel the mystery of nuclear fission. Following the war, he maintained his active contacts in the French nuclear weapons programme.

In Israel, Bergmann became chairman of the Weizmann Institute's chemistry department. As well as serving as chairman of the IAEC, he also held the portfolios of Scientific Adviser to the Minister of Defence and Director of Research and Planning within the defence ministry. As one colleague recalled, 'He was in charge of every kind of nuclear activity in Israel. He was the man who completely understood it [nuclear fission] and then explained it to other people'. Bergmann (the son of a rabbi who was an ardent Zionist, a refugee from Nazi Germany, and a friend of Chaim Weizmann) was deeply affected by memories of the Holocaust. 'I am convinced', he wrote, 'that the State of Israel needs a defence research programme of its own so that we will never again be as lambs led to the slaughter'. It was Bergmann who originally made Ben-Gurion aware of the potential of nuclear weapons.[22]

It was Ben-Gurion's protégé Shimon Peres who, as Director-General of the Israeli Ministry of Defence from 1953 to 1959 and as Deputy Defence Minister from 1959 to 1965, provided the administrative acumen required to manage Israel's nuclear programme. Peres was responsible for building Israel's nuclear infrastructure as well as arranging for its funding, partially from private sources in the United States. He was also responsible for developing Israel's long collaborative relationship with France.[23]

PHASE II: 1953–67

Throughout the 1950s and 1960s France and Israel maintained a close co-operative relationship. France was Israel's primary source of military equipment and high-technology items; indeed following the 1956 Suez Campaign, France was Israel's sole source of military assistance. This collaboration was a pragmatic, two-sided affair involving trade-offs in nuclear technology, avionics and missiles. Israeli military technicians apparently made significant contributions to a number of French weapons systems including the Mirage series of fighter aircraft and short-range ballistic missiles.[24]

It was also early in this period (1953–54) that the first Israelis sent abroad to study nuclear science returned home, and in 1954 a full

Department of Nuclear Physics was established at the Weizmann Institute. That same year a deuterium production facility became operational at Rehovot. Israel's nuclear programme may also have benefited from the immigration of American and European scientists, some of whom may have been involved in the United States and French nuclear programmes.[25]

In 1953 the IAEC entered into a technical exchange agreement with the French Commissariat of Atomic Energy (CEA). As part of this agreement, Israeli scientists were given access to basic French nuclear technology and training, possibly including detailed information from the results of early French nuclear tests in the Sahara Desert. This technical exchange agreement marked the beginning of an extended period of French–Israeli nuclear collaboration from which both countries apparently reaped significant reward.

Much remains unclear about the exact nature of French–Israeli nuclear collaboration between 1953 and 1967, when the Six Day War led to a virtual severing of their previously close military ties. The full rationale for French nuclear assistance to Israel – that is, whether the technological trade-offs and temporary convergence of aims *vis-à-vis* the Arabs was the whole story – is not known, nor is the extent to which French decisions in this area might have been a contentious issue among successive groups within the governments of the Fourth and Fifth Republics.

There was certainly a convergence of interests between the two governments at the time. France was faced with the Algerian revolt, which was sustained by Egyptian President Gamal Abdel Nasser. He, in turn, was regarded by Israel as an arch enemy because of his advocacy of total war by the Arab world against the Jewish state. Further impetus to French–Israeli nuclear co-operation may have come from the impasse in France's relations with the United States over French nuclear development. This was highlighted by Secretary of State John Foster Dulles's rebuff of President Charles de Gaulle's bid for a special nuclear relationship with the United States similar to that enjoyed by Great Britain.[26]

French–Israeli co-operation entered the scientific realm when France sought Israeli experience in nuclear physics to support development of its *force de frappé*. Israel offered France its knowledge of deuterium production and extraction of uranium from low-grade ores, both reportedly of considerable help to the French in decreasing their reliance on American technology. The Israelis, for their part, welcomed all the assistance they could get in the way of weapons and equipment.

Another factor in the French–Israeli nuclear relationship may have been the personal ties that linked many French scientists to Israel. Since a large number of French atomic scientists in the post-war period were

Jewish, numerous unofficial contacts were easily established over the years. There is also the fact that many Left-leaning French scientists had close associations with leading members of the Socialist party and with Leon Blum who, in turn, had close ties to Israel and the socialist Labour party that held power. Others, like Frederic Joliot-Curie, the High Commissioner of the French Commissariat of Atomic Energy, had played an important role in the Resistance, where many French sympathies towards the nascent Jewish state were forged.[27]

France was not the only external source of support for Israel's nuclear programme. In 1955, before French–Israeli collaboration reached its peak, Israel received its first nuclear reactor from the United States. This was the five megawatt 'swimming pool' type reactor which is still in operation at the Nahal Soreq Nuclear Research Centre at Yavne, south of Tel Aviv. Israel acquired the Nahal Soreq reactor under the aegis of the Eisenhower administration's 'Atoms for Peace' Programme. This initiative marked a change in the focus of United States non-proliferation policy from denial of information to promotion of the peaceful aspects of nuclear research. This change of focus was articulated by President Eisenhower in a December 1953 speech at the United Nations in which he made clear the United States' willingness to make available to co-operating countries the peaceful applications of nuclear energy 'as widely as expanding technology permits'.[28]

Under the terms of the agreement governing construction of the Nahal Soreq reactor the United States contributed $350,000 towards the project's total cost, which was estimated at approximately $3 million. The United States also provided training for Israeli scientists and technicians at American nuclear facilities and provided the Israelis with a technical library consisting of some 6,500 reports on nuclear research.

Finally, the United States provided the reactor's fuel, 90 per cent enriched uranium–aluminum alloy. In return, Israel agreed to receive the fuel on a loan basis only, to pay four per cent interest on its value, to return the fuel to the United States after burn-up, and to pay for the reduction of its U-235 content. The United States may also have sponsored the conduct of nuclear research at the Weizmann Institute during this period. A substantial part of the institute's operating budget was provided by the United States National Institutes of Health and by the United States air force which, along with the navy, reportedly funded classified nuclear research at the institute.[29]

The greatest boost to the Israeli nuclear programme came in 1957, when France agreed to construct a reactor and associated research facilities near the town of Dimona in the Negev Desert.[30] Although the French–Israeli agreement concerning construction of the Dimona nuclear facility (officially known as the Negev Nuclear Research Centre, or NNRC) remains secret, some idea of its scope was suggested by Professor Francis Perrin, French High Commissioner for Atomic Energy from 1950 to 1970, when he stated:

> In 1957 we agreed to build a reactor and a chemical [separation] plant for the production of plutonium. We wanted to help Israel. We knew the plutonium could be used for a bomb but we considered also that it could be used for peaceful purposes. It was kept a secret because of the Americans. We had an agreement with them whereby French scientists connected with work on nuclear weapons in Canada (during World War II) could return to France and use their knowledge, but only on condition the secrets would be kept. We considered we could give the secrets to Israel provided they kept them to themselves.[31]

There was no clear consensus within the Israeli political elite at this time concerning the development of nuclear weapons. The decision to build the Dimona reactor reportedly led to a fierce debate among Israeli scientists and political leaders, resulting in the resignation of six of the original seven members of the IAEC (including Israel Dostrovsky, whose work in deuterium production had been so important to inducing the French–Israeli relationship in the first place). Ernst Bergmann continued to hold the title of chairman of the IAEC, although he had no commission over which to preside. There was apparently no inquiry concerning the resignations, nor were any new commissioners appointed. Bergmann continued to act within the framework of the defence ministry and, since Ben-Gurion was also Minister of Defence, control over Israel's nuclear programme remained effectively centralized in his office.[32]

Construction at Dimona continued in secret until 1960, when it was detected by an American U2 overflight. When queried by the Eisenhower administration, Ben-Gurion initially claimed that the facility was a 'textile plant'. Later, in a speech before the Knesset on 21 December 1960, he admitted that a nuclear reactor was indeed under construction in the Negev, but insisted that it was intended only for peaceful scientific and industrial purposes, and to train operators for future nuclear power stations.[33]

Construction of the basic facilities in Dimona was apparently completed sometime around 1960–61, though the reactor itself did not become operational until 1964. In order to initiate reactor operations, the Israelis would have had to obtain large quantities of both deuterium and uranium. The reactor would have required at least 18 tons of deuterium to cool it at its initial power-rating of 24 megawatts. Although the deuterium plant at Rehovot had already been working for some ten years before the Dimona reactor became operational, its production capacity was limited and it probably manufactured only enough deuterium occasionally to 'top up' the reactor. As such Israel acquired its initial supply of deuterium (20 metric tons) in 1959 from the Norwegian company Norsk Hydro.[34] Israel also acquired 'a few tons' of deuterium from France, which may have originally obtained the material from Norway or the United States and then illegally re-exported it to Israel.[35]

The Dimona reactor would also have required 20 to 25 tons of uranium to meet its initial fuel requirements. By 1964, Israel had already produced approximately ten tons of uranium as a by-product of its phosphoric acid industry. The Israelis were able to obtain the balance on the world market, primarily from western European and African sources. Four tons initially came from France, and an additional ten from South Africa. Additional supplies came from Belgium and the French-controlled mines in Gabon, Niger, and the Central African Republic. Israel also purchased 13.6 metric tons of uranium from Argentina.[36]

Controversy at the highest levels of the Israeli government over the acquisition of nuclear weapons continued well after the IAEC commissioners' resignations. Sometime in 1962, Ben-Gurion convened a meeting of his closest advisers in an effort to reach consensus on the issue. Moshe Dayan and Shimon Peres presented the arguments in favour of accelerated nuclear development, emphasizing the element of deterrence and the possibility of reducing expenditures on conventional weapons.

Israel Galili and Yigal Allon presented the opposing view that Israel should not base its national security on nuclear weapons. Galili and Allon were formidable figures. Galili had served as Chief of the General Staff of the Hagana during the Israeli War of Independence and afterwards became a leading politician, deeply involved in security affairs. Allon had served as commander of the Palmach – the elite corps of the Hagana – and, like Galili, continued to be involved in matters of national security. Both were leaders of Ahdut Ha-avoda, one of Israel's socialist parties.

In general Galili and Allon drew a distinction between the nuclear situation between the United States and the Soviet Union and the likely form of such relationships in the Middle East. Whereas the superpowers possessed a wide range of instruments of power which allowed them to exhibit flexibility and control during crises and to avoid nuclear escalation, this would not necessarily be the case in the Middle East. In the end, Ben-Gurion was at least partially convinced by their arguments. Israel, he and his advisers decided, would not base its security exclusively on nuclear weapons, but would continue to seek some sort of nuclear capability.[37]

This decision regarding Israeli nuclear policy may also have reflected elements within Israel's relationship with the United States. Nuclear non-proliferation was given a high priority by the Kennedy administration, which took office after construction of the Dimona reactor was made public in 1960. President Kennedy was concerned that a nuclear-armed Israel would not only destabilize the Middle East, but would also complicate American arms control initiatives with the Soviet Union. Kennedy's concern over nuclear weapons production at Dimona led to tensions in American relations with Israel. Former Secretary of State Dean Rusk recalled how he told 'Israel [sic] more than once that they would lose [United States political support] and our nuclear umbrella if they introduced nuclear weapons and a threat to use them into the Middle East. But in the sixties we got no cooperation at all from Israel when we sent people to look at that Dimona reactor'.[38]

Resolution came in 1962 with the negotiation of a simultaneous agreement whereby the United States would sell Israel Hawk surface-to-air missiles, and in turn the Israelis would permit regular American inspections of Dimona. This degree of American concern with Israeli production of nuclear weapons seems to have ended with President Kennedy's death, American inspections of Dimona eventually became pro forma and ended altogether during the Johnson administration.[39]

In 1966, for unspecified reasons, Israel awarded its State Security Prize (presented to those who have contributed significantly to the state's national security) to Ernst Bergmann, its leading nuclear physicist. The award to Bergmann increased speculation abroad that Israel might be developing nuclear weapons. Bergmann implied as much when he said 'it's very important to understand that by developing atomic energy for peaceful purposes, you reach the nuclear [weapons] option. There are no two atomic energies'.[40]

PHASE III: 1967–80

While Israel may have been close to developing nuclear weapons in 1966, the final decision to develop a full nuclear capability was apparently made in the aftermath of the 1967 Six Day War. Despite their resounding victory, the post-war diplomatic and security situation left Israeli leaders with a profound sense of insecurity. French–Israeli political and military co-operation came to an abrupt halt in 1967 with President de Gaulle's reversal of French Middle East policy. De Gaulle's return to power had already brought various 'slow-downs' in the relationship. Indeed,

> [H]e conveyed his doubts to [French Foreign Minister] Maurice
> Couve de Murville about the closeness of the relations that had been

established by the general staffs of the two countries during the Suez expedition and the Algerian war. The high-ranking Israeli officers had entry into all the departments in which French defence plans were drawn up, particularly in the areas of information [intelligence] and nuclear research; the atomic station at Dimona ... where uranium was turned into plutonium, was sort of an annex of Marcoule and Pierrelatte [France's nuclear installations].[41]

Abandoned by their French ally, the Israelis were now dependent on limited military aid from the United States while Egypt and Syria received massive shipments of tanks, aircraft and small arms from the Soviet Union. In addition to this feeling of isolation, the wartime capture of Egyptian nerve gas stocks (as well as the knowledge that Egyptian troops had used gas while fighting in Yemen) prompted Israeli fears that the Arabs might in the future wage a genocidal chemical campaign against the Jewish state. Surrounded by seemingly implacable enemies and almost entirely dependent on the United States for military hardware, Israeli leaders were haunted by doubts about their nation's ability to survive another war.

This sense of foreboding was not restricted to the Israeli leadership. Memories of the Holocaust had sharpened the sense of danger felt by the Israeli public as a whole during the Six Day War. In a discussion by young members of kibbutzim a few days after the war one participant commented:

It's true that people believed that ... we would be exterminated if we lost the war. They were afraid. We got the idea – or inherited it – from the concentration camps. It's a concrete idea for anyone who has grown up in Israel, even if he personally didn't experience Hitler's persecution, but only heard or read about it. Genocide – it's a feasible notion. There are the means to do it. This is the lesson of the gas chambers.[42]

General Moshe Dayan played the central role in moving Israel from nuclear potential to nuclear production. Strongly influenced by Ben-Gurion, Dayan was one of Israel's leading proponents of nuclear weapons and a declared nuclear deterrent strategy. Nominated as Minister of Defence on the eve of the Six Day War, Dayan remained the highest authority on defence matters in Prime Minister Golda Meir's cabinet until after the 1973 Yom Kippur War. While the 1967 War seemed to demonstrate that Israel could attain superiority over its enemies with conventional forces, Dayan believed that the continuing war of attrition (mainly on the banks of the Suez Canal), demonstrated the inadvisability of Israel's reliance on conventional forces in the long run.[43] In 1967, Dayan announced on French television that Israel had 'the possibility[sic] of manufacturing the bomb now'. Six months later, in Canada, Dayan stated, 'Israel possesses the scientific and technical capability to produce an atomic bomb should the Arab states threaten to use such a bomb, but Israel will never be the first to launch nuclear warfare in the Middle East'.[44]

Dayan's comments concerning Israel's nuclear capabilities and intentions were fundamentally consistent with those which would be made by other Israeli leaders over the next 30 years. This continuity is found in the repeated formulation that Israel: (1) does not possess nuclear weapons; (2) will not be the first to introduce nuclear weapons into the Middle East; but, also, (3) has the capacity to manufacture such weapons.

Reiterated by successive Israeli governments, this official position was first articulated by Prime Minister Levi Eshkol in 1964. This formulation remains ambiguous in that Israeli leaders have offered no clear, or publicly stated, criterion for either the 'possession' or 'introduction' of nuclear weapons. On 5 October 1968 Eshkol added what would become the third element in the formulation of deliberate ambiguity when he stated, 'Israel has the knowledge to make atomic bombs'.[45]

Also in 1968, Israeli leaders formulated the justification for their nation's consistent refusal to accede to the NPT. The official Israeli government position on the NPT is that it endorsed the treaty in principle when it voted in favour of the United Nations resolution commending the text and that it is engaged in a 'deep, thorough, prolonged study to establish its attitude toward the treaty'.[46] Publicly stated reasons for not acceding to the NPT have all involved some aspect of Israel's security situation. During the NPT debate at the United Nations in May 1968 the Israeli delegate stated:

> For obvious reasons, my country has a special sensitivity to the security aspect. We are involved in an unresolved conflict in which our security is being threatened and which thrice in two decades erupted into armed conflict, is marked by a massive and unchecked arms race of conventional weapons which, by any standards, have a vast capacity to kill and destroy. We cannot know what dangers and threats may confront us in the future. It is only natural that we should give earnest scrutiny to the security provisions intended to accompany and compensate for the restrictions that non-nuclear powers would voluntarily assume under the treaty.[47]

Having made the decision fully to develop a nuclear weapons capability, the Israeli government may also have tasked its intelligence services to obtain additional fissile material, either for accelerated reactor operations at Dimona or for weapons fabrication. In 1968 the Mossad allegedly diverted 200 tons of uranium oxide, *en route* from Antwerp to Genoa, to Israel.[48]

Also, sometime in the early 1960s, the then Deputy Minister of Defence Shimon Peres established a new intelligence agency, the Bureau of Scientific Relations (Lishka Le-Kishrei Mada, or Lekem). This organization's mission was to conduct both overt and clandestine collection of scientific and technical intelligence. The clandestine acquisition of nuclear-related materials and technology may have significantly aided Israel in developing as many as ten nuclear warheads by the mid-1970s, up to 100 by the mid-1980s, and as many as 200 by 1990.[49]

Following the 1973 Yom Kippur War, Israel is believed to have expanded its nuclear programme to include the development and deployment of tactical nuclear weapons. Again, it was the memory of the Holocaust which shaped Israeli leaders' decisions regarding their country's nuclear capabilities. For the Israeli people the perceived danger of annihilation was even more acute in 1973 than it had been in 1967. In the words of Israeli historian Leni Yanil, 'the events of May 1967 had revived the memory of the Holocaust. But the Yom Kippur War gave the prospect [of annihilation] even greater focus'.[50]

Although the war resulted in Arab military defeat it was also a partial Arab political and strategic victory, particularly for Egypt. It demonstrated that Egyptian troops could successfully execute a major operation and resist counterattacks from Israel's best forces, at least until moving out of their prepared positions to aid Syria. The sudden advance of Egyptian forces across the Suez Canal and the Syrian attack on the Golan Heights achieved both tactical and strategic surprise.

Israel, in contrast, took days to mobilize and deploy its ground forces and Egypt and Syria achieved major initial successes, rekindling Israeli fears of the destruction of the Jewish state. It was in response to such fears that Minister of Defence Dayan may have at least tentatively suggested the arming of Israel's existing nuclear weapons.[51] Early Arab operational successes, especially the near-breakthrough by Syria on the Golan Heights, were reportedly the impetus for the Israeli development of tactical nuclear weapons following the war. These reportedly included nuclear-capable artillery systems as well as atomic demolition munitions (nuclear landmines).[52]

Expansion of Israel's nuclear programme following the Yom Kippur War is widely reported to have included collaboration with several other countries, particularly South Africa. Unconfirmed reports claim that Israel and South Africa conducted at least three joint nuclear tests. It was the third such alleged test which may have been detected by a United States Vela satellite near Prince Edward's Island in the South Pacific Ocean on 22 September 1979. The Israeli government offered no comment on the event and, despite extensive analysis of the available data, there is no conclusive evidence that such an event took place.[53]

During the 1970s, international perceptions of Israel's status as a nuclear power became less opaque. In December 1974 Israeli President Ephraim Katzir told a meeting of American and European science writers in Jerusalem that Israel had both the capability and the will to build nuclear weapons. 'We now have the potential', he told them. 'We will defend this country with all possible means at hand. We have to develop more powerful and new weapons to protect ourselves'. When asked whether Israeli nuclear activities should be a matter of international concern Katzir replied, 'why should this worry us? Let the rest of the world worry about it'.[54]

The world had, in fact, become aware of Israel's nuclear programme. As one former United States diplomat said of the first meeting of the London Nuclear Suppliers Group in early 1974, 'Israel [as a nuclear power] was a given, not an issue'.[55] Regional responses to Israel's nuclear programme, however, lacked this sense of unanimity. The positions taken by Arab governments on Israel's nuclear programme reflected varying national assessments of both Israel's nuclear capability and of appropriate responses to the Israeli acquisition of nuclear weapons.

In general, Arab responses to Israel's nuclear programme during this period fell into four categories: attempts to gain nuclear weapons or a nuclear security guarantee from the Soviet Union; development of chemical and biological weapons as a counter to Israel's nuclear weapons; demands that Israel accede to the NPT; and threats to develop their own nuclear weapons.[56]

Arab attempts to garner nuclear support from the Soviet Union were not wholly successful. Egypt apparently sought to obtain nuclear weapons, or at least assistance in developing a nuclear infrastructure, when Soviet–Egyptian relations were at their height. Egypt may have also requested a security guarantee from the Soviet Union in the event of Israeli deployment of nuclear weapons. The Soviets reportedly denied both requests. According to former Egyptian Minister of Foreign Affairs Ismail Fahmy, 'the Soviet Union refused to supply Egypt with nuclear weapons or to provide her with a guarantee against Israeli use of such weapons against Egypt'.[57]

Syria may have been more successful in securing a Soviet nuclear guarantee. Unconfirmed reports at the time indicated that such a guarantee was provided in a secret clause to the Soviet–Syrian Treaty of Friendship signed in October 1981. Syrian Minister of Defence Mustafa Tlas had earlier warned Israel and the United States of the dangers involved in a nuclear attack on Syria. 'Our friends the Soviets', he said, 'will not let us down should we face a war of destruction waged by American imperialism and Zionism'. Several months later Tlas stated that 'the Soviet Union will defend Syria should we face an Israeli nuclear threat'.[58]

Arab leaders also used Israel's nuclear programme as a justification for their own efforts to acquire chemical and biological weapons. This was particularly true of the Egyptian leadership prior to the negotiation of peace with Israel in 1979. Shortly after the 1973 Yom Kippur War Egyptian Minister of War General Abd al-Ghani Gamassy told the People's Assembly that chemical and incendiary weapons could be as effective as nuclear weapons. Two years later, in a speech before the national conference of the Party of Socialist Unity, Gamassy stated, that 'in the field of nuclear research Israel is far ahead of us … [I]f Israel should decide to use a nuclear weapon in [sic] the battlefield, we shall use the weapons of mass destruction which are at our disposal'. A year later Gamassy reiterated this position when he stated that 'the introduction of nuclear weapons and their use in the Middle East will create a new and serious situation, and Israel will be held responsible. Israel must not forget that there are also other types of weapons of mass destruction'.[59] Gamassy later added that 'weapons of mass extermination are not limited to nuclear weapons … Egypt has enough of the other types of weapons of mass extermination and it has the capability of retaliating to an Israeli nuclear blow by making use of these weapons'.

Arab states, particularly Egypt, made repeated demands that Israel accede to the NPT. In 1976 Egyptian Foreign Minister Fahmy demanded Israeli accession to the treaty as a precondition for a comprehensive regional peace agreement. Fahmy called on Israel to 'commit itself not to produce or acquire nuclear weapons; it must sign the [NPT] and agree to international inspections of her activities in the nuclear field … Egypt is ready to accept the same conditions'.[60]

These demands were repeated by President Sadat during a television interview on 24 February 1977. In 1978 the Egyptian government proposed that both nations renounce nuclear weapons and also accept limits on conventional forces as part of their 1979 peace treaty. Egypt's position, as articulated by the then Secretary of State for Foreign Affairs Butros Ghali, was that 'if Israel wishes to emphasize its pursuit of peace to Arab public opinion, it must sign the NPT'.[61]

Beginning in 1978, both Egypt and Iraq adopted a variant on the demands that Israel accede to the NPT by calling for the establishment of a Middle East nuclear-weapons-free zone (NWFZ). This demand was first presented at the United Nations in the form of resolutions which were subsequently adopted by the General Assembly. Israeli accession to the NPT and the establishment of a Middle East NWFZ have, from that point onwards, became standard Arab prerequisites for a comprehensive regional peace settlement.

Throughout the 1970s the most frequent Arab rhetorical response to potential Israeli acquisition of nuclear weapons was to threaten that this would lead the Arabs do the same. In 1974 Egyptian President Sadat warned that 'if Israel intends to introduce nuclear weapons into the area, we too will find a way of acquiring such weapons'. Also in 1974, Foreign Minister Fahmy told the United States Senate Foreign Relations Committee that 'it must be completely understood that should Israel produce nuclear weapons, Egypt will have the right to acquire this weapon in order to maintain her strategic integrity'. While in 1976 Syrian President Hafez Asad declared that Israel's nuclear capability gave Syria two options, either to prevent Israel from acquiring a nuclear capability, or to acquire the weapons themselves. And Asad was in no doubt that 'it seems that the second alternative is the more promising one for the Arabs'. A year later Asad reiterated: 'If Israel possesses this weapon, then we will possess it [also]'.[62]

Arab leaders' behaviour, however, did not match their rhetoric. Most notable was the absence of a unified Arab effort to counter Israel's perceived nuclear capability. Inter-Arab political rivalries effectively precluded the formation of a coalition with the objective of developing nuclear weapons. Due to the deep divisions in the Arab world the progress of any one Arab state towards the attainment of a nuclear weapons capability would have been (and remains) a source of concern to other Arab states.

### PHASE IV: THE 1980S

By 1980 Israel had emerged as the only state in the Middle East with the capacity to manufacture nuclear weapons. The focus of Israeli nuclear strategy for the next decade was the maintenance of this regional nuclear monopoly. In December 1981 Foreign Minister Yitzhak Shamir stated:

> The third element in our defence policy for the 1980s is our decision to prevent access to nuclear weapons for both confrontation states and potential ones. Israel cannot allow the introduction of nuclear weapons. For us it is not an issue of a balance of terror, but a question of continued survival. Therefore, we shall have to prevent this danger from the outset.[63]

This policy of denial was the foundation of the so-called 'Begin Doctrine' – that Israel would pre-empt any Arab attempt to develop nuclear weapons. This policy was most dramatically illustrated by Israel's air strike on the Iraqi Osiraq nuclear reactor at al-Tuweitha on 7 June 1981. According to Arye Naor, Menachem Begin's cabinet secretary, the Prime Minister had first brought a proposal linked to the attack before the Israeli cabinet as early as October 1980.

Begin linked this proposal directly to the Iraqi nuclear effort by arguing that 'three ... Hiroshima-type bombs would suffice to destroy

Israel'. Begin's assessment reflected the strategic constraints imposed by Israel's geography. Israel's population and industrial base are concentrated on a 60-mile coastal strip less than 20 miles wide, running from just north of Tel Aviv to immediately north of Haifa. Iraq, Begin said, might be tempted to use its nuclear capability 'once she had developed it'.[64]

Other aspects of Israel's nuclear strategy, including the nature of statements by Israeli leaders concerning Israel's nuclear position, non-accession to the NPT, and the degree of official secrecy surrounding Israel's nuclear programme remained constant throughout the 1980s. One of the most significant public statements concerning Israel's nuclear capability during this period was made by Minister of Science Yuval Ne'eman in 1984. 'We decided from day one to create the necessary infrastructure so that if someday we decided to make nuclear weapons, we would not have to depend on anyone else', he said. When asked directly if Israel possessed nuclear weapons, Ne'eman replied:

> That's technically accurate but could be misleading in terms of the length of time required to make one. If we were to cross the threshold, we would provide every justification for third parties to arm the Arabs. So we have every interest to create the infrastructure, in order not to be caught unprepared, and then stop. We say we have not crossed the nuclear threshold. How close we are, we don't say. We've had the same situation now for twenty-one years.[65]

Ne'eman's statement was particularly revealing in light of his own career within the Israeli scientific and defence communities. Ne'eman had held virtually every position of any consequence related to Israel's strategic programmes: Deputy Director of Military Intelligence; scientific adviser to, and chairman of, the Israeli Atomic Energy Commission; chairman of the National Commission for High Energy Physics; and chairman of the Israeli Space Agency. Ne'eman was also founder and leader of the ultra-nationalist Tehiya Party.

On 2 November 1987 the Israeli Representative to the United Nations First Committee, Shalheveth Freier, again explained his government's reasons for not acceding to the NPT. 'The NPT alone does not inhibit local wars, and local wars are the bane of the Middle East', he said. 'For all the value of the NPT, let me tell you which of its deficiencies are pertinent in the Middle East conflict'. Freier then went on to explain Israel's perception of the inadequacies of the safeguard system. Quoting from a statement made by International Atomic Energy Agency Director Hans Blix on 11 December 1981, Freier stated:

> The safeguards do not, of course, reveal what future intentions [a] state may have. It may change its mind on the question of nuclear

weapons and wish to produce them despite possible adherence to the NPT. Neither such adherence nor full scope safeguards are full guarantees that [a] state will not one day make nuclear weapons.

Freier then quoted a statement made by Libyan leader Colonel Gaddafi on 22 June 1987: 'The Arabs must possess the atom bomb to defend themselves, until their numbers reach one thousand million ... and until they liberate Palestine'. Pointing out that Libya was not a signatory to the NPT, Freier discussed the 'qualifications' put on accession to the treaty by other Arab nations who had expressly stated that their obligations under the NPT did not imply recognition of Israel.[66]

Finally, the Israeli government continued to enforce the high degree of official secrecy surrounding its nuclear programme. In June 1980 it reportedly prevented the publication of a manuscript entitled *None Will Survive Us: The Story of the Israeli A-Bomb* by two Israeli journalists, Eli Teicher and Ami Dor-On. Brigadier General Yitzhak Shani, Israel's chief military censor, prohibited its publication 'wholly or partially, in Hebrew or in translation, since its publication would be damaging to the defense of Israel'. The authors were further warned that disclosure of the information contained in their manuscript would bring them a sentence of 15 years to life in prison.[67]

In 1986 the veil of secrecy which had surrounded Israel's nuclear programme from its inception was lifted, if only briefly and partially, as a result of the 'Vanunu Affair'. Mordechai Vanunu, a disaffected nuclear technician, had worked at the Negev Nuclear Research Centre from 1976 until 1985. In January 1986 he left Israel with hand-written notes concerning the centre's operations and 57 photographs which he claimed to have taken inside some of its most sensitive areas. Vanunu provided at least a portion of this material to the London *Sunday Times* which then published it on 5 October 1986 under the headline 'The Sunday Times Reveals: The Secrets of Israel's Nuclear Arsenal'.[68]

On 23 September 1986, prior to publication of Vanunu's information, the Israeli embassy in London issued a denial of the *Sunday Times'* story. The Israelis characterized Vanunu as merely a minor technician with only limited knowledge of the NNRC's operations. Subsequently, Vanunu was (allegedly) lured to Italy where he was kidnapped by an Israeli intelligence team and forcibly returned to Israel. There he was tried in camera, convicted of treason, espionage, and exposing state secrets, and sentenced to 18 years of solitary confinement in an Israeli prison. The Israeli State Prosecutor specifically charged that Vanunu had revealed classified information that 'caused serious damage to the security of the state'.[69]

Despite the apparent damage to security, the Vanunu scandal may have actually enhanced the ambiguity and uncertainty surrounding

Israel's nuclear efforts. As one Israeli academic said of the Vanunu Affair: '[I]t does not really hurt security. The point of nuclear deterrents [sic] is that the other side should known that you have nuclear bombs in order not to have to use them. Let the Arabs know, and even better that it is not you who tell them but it comes in a roundabout way. Like a report in the Sunday Times'.[70]

## PHASE V: THE 1990S

Israel entered the 1990s with its regional nuclear monopoly intact and as the only regional actor with a coherent nuclear strategy. Israel's deliberately ambiguous nuclear strategy had served three ends: reassuring the Israeli people 'in times of gloom'; making the Arabs 'think twice' before engaging Israel; and relieving 'any country that does not want to take up a definite position [concerning Israel's nuclear capability] from having to do so'.[71]

One of the salient features of Israel's development as a nuclear power has been the lack of public debate on the subject. Israel is a democracy with a tradition of free and open debate over virtually every aspect of its national security policy. The fact that no public debate over the production of nuclear weapons or their proper role in the nation's security strategy has taken place is perhaps indicative of public support, as a whole, for the government's nuclear strategy of deliberate ambiguity.[72] The Israeli public views the degree of secrecy surrounding Israel's nuclear programme as part of the concept of the 'sacredness of security' (kidush ha-bitahon). This has effectively limited the nuclear debate in Israel to elites within the military, the civil government, academia and the press.[73]

The 1991 Persian Gulf War, however, served to heighten the Israeli public's awareness of the nuclear issue.[74] While most Israelis believe that their country possesses nuclear weapons, there is no clear consensus regarding their role in Israel's security strategy.

Israelis provided the following responses to a 15 February 1991 Gallup poll which asked the following question: 'Under what conditions, if any, should Israel use nuclear weapons?': nine per cent were opposed to the use of nuclear weapons under any conditions; 41 per cent favoured the use of nuclear weapons only to prevent the annihilation of Israel; eight per cent favoured the use of nuclear weapons only if Israel suffered 'very extensive' casualties; and 42 per cent favoured the use of nuclear weapons in response to their use by Iraq.[75]

Israel's nuclear programme may in fact have played a major, though unspoken, role in the Persian Gulf War. At least one analyst believes that 'the prospect of a nuclear war in the Middle East unleashed by Israel and beyond the capacity of the [United States] to control was a real, but little publicized element of the 1990–91 crisis in the Persian Gulf'.[76] Following the invasion of Kuwait, Iraq declared its chemical arsenal to be a first-strike weapon intended for use against Israel. The Israeli government, taking such threats seriously, distributed gas masks to its citizens and articulated a policy of deterrence that remained consistent throughout the war.

Israel communicated explicit warnings during the critical period between November 1990 and 15 January 1991 that were widely interpreted to mean that any Iraqi action above the non-conventional threshold would provoke the use of nuclear weapons in response. In a public warning to Iraq, Prime Minister Shamir pledged that Israel would respond to any non-conventional aggression with a 'terrible blow'. On 5 December 1990, one month before the war began, Israeli Foreign Minister David Levy declared that 'Israel's low profile will change if and when Saddam Hussein threatens the very existence of the state of Israel. Israel will have no choice but to defend itself ... and not with a low profile, but with the highest possible profile'.[77]

In a speech to the Knesset on 18 February 1991 Yitzhak Rabin, then Labour MK stated:

> What did we tell [the Arabs]? If you send missiles on Tel Aviv, Damascus will be turned into ruin. If you send missiles on Haifa – not only Damascus, but also Aleppo will cease to exist. They will be destroyed root and branch. Without dealing with missile launchers, we will destroy Damascus. The same applies to Baghdad. We told the Iraqis, if you send a missile, Baghdad will turn into dust ... Israel should preserve its deterrent power simply by saying that in the event of a single land-to-land missile strike on Tel Aviv, then Damascus, Aleppo, and Baghdad will exist no more.[78]

The following month, on 8 March 1991, Israeli air force commander General Herzl Bodinger stated that 'we know that Iraq had surface-to-surface missile with chemical warheads, but they nevertheless refrained from using them. In my opinion, the only reason was that they were afraid of the power of the response'.[79]

More recent statements by Israeli leaders concerning their country's nuclear capabilities have retained their earlier sense of ambiguity. On 25 October 1993 Deputy Defence Minister Mordechai Gur, in response to an Egyptian reporter's question concerning Arab demands that Israel open its nuclear facilities to international inspection, stated: 'I don't know what facilities they are talking about. But I advise Israel not to give up any of its military strength in favour of any of the neighbouring countries because this will only endanger Israel'.[80]

At the same time as the Persian Gulf War, Israeli leaders' perceptions of the threat posed to their nation by other regional actors apparently evolved from a focus on the quantitative superiority of their closest neighbours to the acquisition of weapons of mass destruction by the nations on their periphery. This change of focus became evident as early as October 1991, when at least three Israeli political leaders made public statements concerning the proliferation of weapons of mass destruction in the Middle East.

Labour Knesset member Moshe Shahal foresaw nuclear proliferation in the region as inevitable, stating that 'I believe that the Middle East will achieve a nuclear option within a decade and the battle, if, God forbid, it comes, will see the entry of non-conventional weapons'. The Minister of Defence, Moshe Arens, declared that '[t]he Middle East is marching toward a nuclear weapons era, [and] that is the reality we will have to live with and prepare [militarily] for'. Ezer Weizman (latterly President of Israel) said: '[T]he nuclear issue is gaining momentum [and the] next war will not be conventional'.[81] In this regard, Israeli leaders perceive the greatest threat to their state as emanating from Iran and Iraq.

Iran's 'Islamic foreign policy' includes a vehement anti-Israeli stance and its leadership regards Israel as a 'cancerous growth in the Middle East'. The Iranian government has intentionally isolated itself from the regional peace process, viewing the endorsement of any sort of settlement with Israel as an intolerable affront to Islam and as a negation of Iran's 'Islamic identity'. In December 1990 the Iranian President Hashemi Rafsanjani called for the establishment of a pan-Islamic army for the annihilation of Israel.[82]

Iran is assessed as having an active chemical and biological weapons programme, and Israeli leaders have expressed particular concern over the possibility of Iranian development of nuclear weapons. On 8 June 1992, for example, Major General Uri Saguy, chief of Israeli Military Intelligence, stated:

> Iran is conducting a nuclear fusion project which might cause us to be concerned about our existence and basic security if and when that process becomes ... irreversible ... [W]ith time that potential [for nuclear weapons] will become real and by the end of the decade ... it will be possible for Iran to achieve an independent nuclear capability.[83]

On 15 June 1992 Major General Herzl Bodinger, commander of the Israeli air force, discussing the efforts of other regional actors to acquire nuclear weapons, stated:

> The intelligence information that we have is that these countries, especially Iran, strive very hard to get this ability. We think,

according to the information that we have, that if nothing is done within a decade or so Iran will have an ability [sic] of nuclear weapons.[84]

Eighteen months later an Israeli air force officer identified only as 'Colonel A' told the *Israeli Air Force Review*: 'Iran will have [North] Korean Nodong missiles in a year which could be deployed in the West of the country and reach Israel ... There is no doubt that Iran is trying to obtain the capacity to produce chemical and nuclear weapons'. The colonel also stated that the Iranians were trying to develop aircraft and missiles 'directly threatening' Israel, and at the same time were continuing a long-term nuclear research programme. More recently, in February 1995, a senior Israeli military official stated that 'the biggest problem [for Israel] in the next decade is [Iran] with nuclear weapons. That's the worst case our planners must currently look at'.[85]

Iraq had traditionally figured in Israeli threat calculations to the extent to which it could bolster the Arab eastern front by dispatching expeditionary forces through Jordan. During the Iran–Iraq War, however, Israeli military planners gained an appreciation of Iraq as a threat to Israel in and of itself. When that war ended in 1988, the Israeli Chief-of-Staff, Lieutenant General Dan Shomron, and his staff concluded that Saddam Hussein's ambitions for pan-Arab leadership, combined with either real or perceived pressures from Islamic fundamentalists, made Israel the next likely target for Iraqi aggression.[86] They were proved at least partially correct during the 1991 Gulf War when the Iraqis declared that their chemical arsenal was intended for use against Israel.

Israeli leaders are especially sensitive to the fact that, aside from their own, Iraq's nuclear programme was the most advanced in the Middle East prior to the Gulf War. They are also concerned by Iraq's chemical and biological warfare capabilities, and its demonstrated willingness to employ chemical agents. Israeli defence planners do not consider Hussein's defeat to be the end of the Iraqi threat to Israel. They believe that Iraq possesses both the will and the ability to recover its military capabilities and they foresee the re-emergence of an Iraqi threat in the long term.[87]

Perceptions of the nature of the external security threat played a major role in the Israeli decision to refuse to join the NPT yet again in 1995. On 20 November 1993, in a letter to United Nations ambassadors, Shalheveth Freier stated:

> The Israelis wish to test whether a desire for peace exists on the part of the Arab states, and are ready to take substantial risks to this end. The Israelis do not know ... whether such a desire on the part of the Arab states does exist, or whether the present negotiations, and the

concessions extracted from Israel, simply serve as a means of attrition on preparation for a further onslaught at an opportune moment ... Israel must continue to be wary and ... nothing has happened so far which justifies any relaxation of its defense posture.[88]

The reluctance of successive Israeli governments to accede to the NPT and their practice of keeping the matter under constant review have reflected both their perceptions of the threat to the Jewish state and their own national character. States such as Iran or Iraq have the licence eventually to opt out of the NPT or simply to disregard their treaty commitments. Israel believes that it would not have such an option since, as a democracy, it would be expected by both the international community and its own citizens to abide by its commitment to the NPT.

Despite its long resistance to accession to the NPT, the Israeli government has defined the terms under which it would willingly become a signatory to the treaty. Essentially, Israeli accession to the treaty is contingent upon the establishment of a Middle Eastern NWFZ which, in turn, requires a comprehensive regional peace settlement. As Shalhevet Freier put the Israeli position:

Israel [cannot] accede to [the] NPT until after a credible NWFZ in the Middle East is in place. If Israel were to accede [to the NPT] now, it would be doing its security a fateful disservice. Everyone would applaud, and that does not count for much, and the Arab states would be happy to think that they could press onwards [towards Israel's destruction] with all means at their disposal, with nothing to worry about ...

Stable and proven peace is a prerequisite for a Middle East NWFZ. Peace must include all the confrontation states, including Iran. Also, a Middle East NWFZ will not be supervised by the International Atomic Energy Agency; rather, the non-proliferation regime must be based on mutual verification by the contracting parties.[89]

Thus, the Israeli approach to the process (a comprehensive peace settlement, followed by establishment of a regional NWFZ culminating in accession to the NPT) is fundamentally the opposite of that taken by the Arab states, especially Egypt, whereby Israel's accession to the NPT would be followed by establishment of a Middle East NWZF culminating in a comprehensive regional peace settlement.

## CONCLUSIONS

Two conclusions may be drawn from this account of Israel's development as a nuclear power. The first concerns the historical nature of the Israeli nuclear programme; the second – the evolution of Israel's nuclear strategy of deliberate ambiguity.

The historical record, at least that portion which is publicly available, indicates that since the government of David Ben-Gurion Israeli leaders have sought some form of nuclear capability. While there was no clear consensus among the Israeli political elite concerning nuclear weapons at the time of the programme's initiation, the development and maintenance of a nuclear capability appears to have emerged as a consistent, though unspoken, element of Israeli security strategy since the 1967 Six Day War.

The Israeli rationale for development of a nuclear capability has been based on two interrelated factors: the perception of the external threat to its existence and the historical experience of the Jewish people. Unlike other nations which may seek to develop a nuclear capability for reasons of international prestige or as a way to achieve regional hegemony, Israel has done so in order to ensure its national existence. Originally concerned with the unmitigated hostility and overwhelming conventional superiority of their immediate Arab neighbours, the Israeli threat perception is currently focused on the development of weapons of mass destruction by nations on their periphery, particularly Iran and Iraq. At the same time, memories of the Holocaust continue to impress upon Israeli leaders the necessity for self-reliance in matters of national security. This continuing shared memory of the destruction of European Jewry has played a consistent role in Israeli leaders' decisions regarding development of their country's nuclear capabilities.

Israel's nuclear strategy of deliberate ambiguity does not result from the execution of a well-planned design. Instead, it has developed over time in response to a variety of international, regional and domestic considerations. This strategy of deliberate ambiguity has served different functions at different times. Originally, it served to conceal Israel's efforts to develop a nuclear infrastructure. Later, it helped avert conflict with United States policymakers when Israel's nuclear programme became a focus of American non-proliferation policy. Deliberate ambiguity also served to deny the Arab states a clear picture of Israel's nuclear capabilities and has effectively forestalled the development of a potentially contentious domestic debate in Israel concerning the acquisition of nuclear weapons and their proper role in Israeli security strategy. As it now exists, deliberate ambiguity provides Israeli leaders with a coherent strategic framework governing their country's nuclear capabilities and intentions.

## NOTES

The author would like to thank Shalheveth Freier, Shlomo Aronson, Avi Beker, Yair Evron, Ariel Levite, Ze'ev Schiff and Gerald Steinberg for their helpful comments.

1. Bard E. O'Neill, 'Israel', in Douglas J. Murray and Paul R. Viotti (eds), *The Defense Policies of Nations: A Comparative Study*, Baltimore, 1982, p.432; Edward B. Atkeson, 'The Middle East: A Dynamic Military Net Assessment for the 1990s', *Washington Quarterly*, Vol.16, No.2 (1993), p.120.
2. Israel Ministry of Science and Development, *Scientific Research in Israel*, Jerusalem, 1989, p.i.
3. Gerald M. Steinberg, *Arms Control and Israeli Security: A Realistic Approach*, Policy Paper No.9, Tel Aviv, May 1993, p.7.
4. See, for example, Avner Cohen and Benjamin Frankel in Benjamin Frankel (ed.), *Opaque Nuclear Proliferation: Methodological and Policy Implications*, London, 1991, pp.17–18.
5. In 1986, Mordechai Vanunu, a former technician at the Dimona nuclear reactor, told the *Sunday Times* that Israel could manufacture 100–200 nuclear weapons. Frank Barnaby, *The Invisible Bomb: The Nuclear Arms Race in the Middle East*, London, 1988, p.25. In 1993, the Russian Foreign Intelligence Service released a report crediting Israel with possession of 60–100 weapons. 'A New Challenge After the Cold War: Proliferation of Weapons of Mass Destruction', Report by the Russian Foreign Intelligence Service, Moscow, 1993. Translation by Joint Publications Research Service, JPRS Report – 'Proliferation Issues 5 March 1993', pp.24–5. See also William Windrem, *Critical Mass: the Dangerous Race for Super-weapons in a Fragmenting World*, New York, 1994, p.308; Anthony H. Cordesman, *After the Storm: The Changing Military Balance in the Middle East*, Boulder, 1993, p.244. In 1994, Burrows and Windrem reported that Israel has actually produced a total of 300 nuclear weapons, but has retired many of the older ones.
6. Peter Pry, *Israel's Nuclear Arsenal*, Boulder, 1984, pp.30–33. See also Edwin S. Cochran, 'Deliberate Ambiguity: An Analysis of Israel's Nuclear Strategy', *Journal of Strategic Studies*, Vol.19, No.3 (September 1996), pp.321–42.
7. National Security Archive, *U.S. Nuclear Non-Proliferation Policy, 1945–1991*, Vol.1, Washington DC, 1991, p.24; Robert Harkavy, 'The Imperative to Survive', in Louis Rene Beres (ed.), *Security or Armageddon: Israel's Nuclear Strategy*, Lexington, 1986, pp.103–4.
8. Chaim Weizmann, *Trial and Error: The Autobiography of Chaim Weizmann*, London, 1950, p.18.
9. For this view see the author's interview with Mr Shalheveth Freier (former Israeli ambassador to the United Nations First Committee), 18 May 1994. In an interview with the veteran Israeli defence correspondent, Ze'ev Schiff, 23 May 1994, the latter agreed that this was so, but added that the consideration of nuclear weapons began 'much earlier' than is generally realized.
10. Fuad Jabber, *Israel and Nuclear Weapons: Present Option and Future Strategies*, London, 1971, p.15; Richard Rhodes, *The Making of the Atomic Bomb*, New York, 1986, pp.86–8, 173; Robert E. Harkavy, *Spectre of a Middle Eastern Holocaust: The Strategic and Diplomatic Implications of the Israeli Nuclear Weapons Program*, Denver, 1977, p.5. Although a proponent of nuclear science, Chaim Weizmann played no role in Israel's subsequent nuclear programme. Author's interview with Shlomo Aronson, 16 May 1994, and with Shalheveth Freier, 18 May 1994.
11. Weizmann, *Trial and Error*, p.444.
12. Harkavy, *Spectre of a Middle Eastern Holocaust*, p.5; Barnaby, *The Invisible Bomb*, p.5.
13. Taysir N. Nashif, *Nuclear Warfare in the Middle East: Dimensions and Responsibilities*, Princeton, 1984, p.15; Barnaby, *The Invisible Bomb*, pp.4–5; Stephen Green, *Taking Sides: America's Secret Relations with a Militant Israel*, New York, 1984, p.149.
14. Christopher S. Raj, 'Israel and Nuclear Weapons: a Case of Clandestine Proliferation', in K. Subrahmanyan (ed.), *Nuclear Myths and Realities: India's Dilemma*, New Delhi, 1981, p.92. De Shalit eventually headed the Physics Department at the Weizmann Institute of Science. This scientist, who died in 1969, was considered by many to have been a quantum researcher in the same class as Oppenheimer and Bohr. See Seymour M. Hersh, *The Samson Option: Israel's Nuclear Arsenal and American Foreign Policy*, New York, 1991,

pp.25–6, 144.

15. Leonard Beaton and John Maddox, *The Spread of Nuclear Weapons*, New York, 1962, p.170.

16. Ravi Shastri, 'Israeli Nuclear Strategy and Deterrence in West Asia', *Strategic Analysis*, Vol.13, No.1 (August 1989), p.38; Nashif, *Nuclear Warfare*, p.15; Jabber, *Israel and Nuclear Weapons*, p.19.

17. Louis Toscanao, *Triple Cross: Israel, the Atomic Bomb, and the Man Who Spilled the Secrets*, New York, 1990, p.100.

18. Shlomo Aronson, *The Politics and Strategy of Nuclear Weapons in the Middle East: Opacity, Theory, and Reality, 1960–1991 – An Israeli Perspective*, Albany, 1991, p.46.

19. Jay Y. Gonen, *A Psychohistory of Zionism*, New York, 1975, p.149.

20. Quoted in Aronson, *The Politics and Strategy of Nuclear Weapons*, p.51.

21. Hersh, *The Samson Option*, p.22; Burrows and Windrem, *Critical Mass*, p.281.

22. Hersh, *The Samson Option*, pp.23–6; Weizmann, *Trial and Error*, pp.356–7; author's interview with Aronson, 16 May 1994.

23. Author's interview with Freier, 18 May 1994; Raj, 'Israel and Nuclear Weapons', p.96; Hersh, *The Samson Option*, pp.66–7.

24. Thus, for example, the Jericho-1 (or YA-1), is an Israeli adaptation of the French Dassault MD620 missile design. For this period of French–Israeli political and military co-operation see Sylvia Crosbie, *A Tacit Alliance: France and Israel from Suez to the Six Day War*, Princeton, 1974; Roger F. Pajak, *Nuclear Proliferation in the Middle East: Implications for the Superpowers*, Washington DC, 1982, p.31; Harkavy, *Spectre of a Middle Eastern Holocaust*, pp.6–7; Barnaby, *The Invisible Bomb*, p.22.

25. Ernest W. Lefever, *Nuclear Arms in the Third World: U.S. Policy Dilemma*, Washington DC, 1979, p.70; Beaton and Maddox, *The Spread of Nuclear Weapons*, p.170; Barnaby, *The Invisible Bomb*, p.5.

26. Pajak, *Nuclear Proliferation in the Middle East*, p.31; Harkavy, *Spectre of a Middle Eastern Holocaust*, pp.5–6.

27. Crosbie, *A Tacit Alliance*, p.115.

28. Pajak, *Nuclear Proliferation in the Middle East*, p.14.

29. Green, *Taking Sides*, p.151.

30. Jabber, *Israel and Nuclear Weapons*, pp.25–32; Pajak, *Nuclear Proliferation in the Middle East*, p.31. Actual construction of the reactor was undertaken by the French nuclear firm Saint-Gobain Techniques Nouvelles (SGN).

31. *Sunday Times*, 12 October 1986.

32. Harkavy, *Spectre of a Middle Eastern Holocaust*, p.5; Yair Evron, *Israel's Nuclear Dilemma*, Ithaca, 1994, pp.5–10; Green, *Taking Sides*, pp.150–51.

33. Michael Bar-Zohar, *Ben-Gurion: The Armed Prophet*, Englewood Cliffs, 1968, pp.266–7.

34. The Norwegian government allowed the sale on the condition that the deuterium would be used only for peaceful purposes and that the Israelis would allow inspections to verify compliance. The Norwegians exercised their right of inspection only once, in 1961, when the deuterium was still in storage. In 1964 the Weizmann Institute purchased an additional seven kilograms of deuterium from Norsk Hydro, and the Israeli government itself bought 100 kilograms in 1968. Between 1959 and 1968, Norsk Hydro sold a total of 21,107 kilograms of deuterium to the Israelis. See, Barnaby, *The Invisible Bomb*, p.9; Leonard Spector, *Nuclear Ambitions: The Spread of Nuclear Weapons, 1989–1990*, Boulder, 1990, p.153.

35. Spector, *Nuclear Ambitions*, p.105. Israel also obtained 3.9 tons of deuterium from the United States under the bilateral agreement concerning construction of the Nahal Soreq reactor. Barnaby, *The Invisible Bomb*, pp.9–10.

36. Barnaby, *The Invisible Bomb*, p.11; Spector, *Nuclear Ambitions*, pp.152–3.

37. Yair Evron, 'Opaque Proliferation: The Israeli Case', in Benjamin Frankel (ed.), *Opaque Nuclear Proliferation*, pp.46–7 and note 7, p.62.

38. Cited in John Newhouse, *War and Peace in the Nuclear Age*, New York, 1988, p.271.

39. For a detailed discussion of US–Israeli nuclear disagreements during the Kennedy administration, see Avner Cohen, *Israel and the Bomb*, New York, 1998, Chapters 6–9. See also, McGeorge Bundy, *Danger and Survival: Choices About the Bomb in the First Fifty years*, New York, 1988, p.510; Lewis A. Dunn, 'Four Decades of Nuclear Non-proliferation: Some Lessons from Wins, Losses, and Draws', *Washington Quarterly*, Vol.13,

No.3 (Summer 1990), p.10; Hersh, *The Samson Option*, pp.111–13.

40. James Feron, 'Israelis Honour Atom Scientist', *New York Times*, 14 May 1966, p.3.
41. Jean Lacouture, *De Gaulle: The Ruler, 1945–1970*, New York, 1992, p.435; Pry, *Israel's Nuclear Arsenal*, p.19.
42. Leni Yanil, *The Holocaust: the Fate of European Jewry, 1932–1946*, New York, 1990, p.8.
43. Uri Bar-Joseph, 'The Hidden Debate: the Formulation of Nuclear Doctrines in the Middle East', *Journal of Strategic Studies*, Vol.5, No.2 (June 1982), pp.214–15.
44. Toscanao, *Triple Cross*, p.100. According to Avner Cohen (*Israel and the Bomb*, p.274), a few days before the war Israel had '"improvised" two deliverable nuclear "primitive" nuclear devices'.
45. Savita Pande, 'Israel and the Non-Proliferation Regime', *Strategic Analysis*, Vol.16, No.2 (1993), p.148; Cochran, 'Deliberate Ambiguity', p.326.
46. Statement by the Israeli Foreign Minister to the Knesset, 17 December 1968, cited in Pande, 'Israel and the Non-Proliferation Regime', p.151.
47. Ibid., p.152, quoting a statement by the Israeli representative to the First Committee of the United Nations General Assembly, 29 May 1968.
48. Barnaby, *The Invisible Bomb*, p.11. For an account of this operation see Elaine Davenport, Paul Eddy and Peter Gilman, *The Plumbat Affair*, Philadelphia, 1978.
49. Jeffrey T. Richelson, *Foreign Intelligence Organizations*, Cambridge, 1988, pp.193–4; Cordesman, *After the Storm*, p.242.
50. Yanil, *The Holocaust*, p.18.
51. Evron, *Israel's Nuclear Dilemma*, p.72. Evron maintains that Prime Minister Meir rejected this recommendation.
52. The Israeli army has reportedly developed a nuclear projectile for its 175mm self-propelled gun system. Israel is reported to have fielded three nuclear-capable artillery battalions of 12 guns each, and to have stockpiled three nuclear projectiles per gun. Michio Kaku, 'Contingency Plans: Nuclear Weapons After the Cold War', in Phyllis Bennis and Michel Moushabeck (eds), *Altered States: A Reader in the New World Order*, New York, 1993, p.66. See also, Cordesman, *After the Storm*, p.244; Hersh, *The Samson Option*, p.319.
53. Michael Dunn, 'Israel', in Gregory R. Copeland (ed.), *Defense and Foreign Affairs Handbook*, Washington, 1985, p.319; Barnaby, *The Invisible Bomb*, pp.14–21.
54. Pande, 'Israel and the Non-Proliferation Regime', p.148; *Maariv*, 2 December 1974.
55. Newhouse, *War and Peace in the Nuclear Age*, p.271.
56. Shai Feldman, *Israeli Nuclear Deterrence: A Strategy for the 1980's*, New York, 1982, p.67.
57. *Al-Sha'ab*, 17 February 1981.
58. *Tishrin*, 5 August 1980; *al-Qabas*, 5 October 1980.
59. *Al-Ahram*, 25 July 1975; *Akhbar al-Usbu*, 14 October 1976; *Yediot Aharanot*, 5 October 1976.
60. Feldman, *Israeli Nuclear Deterrence*, p.67.
61. *Associated Press*, 26 April 1976; *Maariv*, 17 May 1979.
62. Feldman, *Israeli Nuclear Deterrence*, pp.67–70; *Middle East News Agency (MENA)*, 16 August 1974.
63. Cited in Aronson, *The Politics and Strategy of Nuclear Weapons*, p.179.
64. Ibid., p.167.
65. Charles Hardenberger (ed.), *The Arms Control Reporter, 1991*, Brookline, 1991, p.453.
66. Pande, 'Israel and the Non-Proliferation Regime', p.153.
67. Raj, 'Israel and Nuclear Weapons', p.88; Israel Shahak, 'The Israeli Myth of Omniscience: Nuclear Deterrence and Intelligence', *Arab–American Affairs*, Vol.36 (1991), p.77.
68. Barnaby, *The Invisible Bomb*, pp.vi–vii. The *Sunday Times* investigative team allowed Barnaby to interview Vanunu for two days. Barnaby subsequently used this information as the basis for his book *The Invisible Bomb*.
69. For a full account of the 'Vanunu Affair' see Toscanao, *Triple Cross*. See also Norman Moss, 'Vanunu, Israel's Bombs, and U.S. Aid', *Bulletin of the Atomic Scientists*, Vol.46, No.4 (1992), p.617.
70. For these comments by Baruch Knei-Paz see Shastri, 'Israeli Nuclear Strategy', p.43.
71. Author's interview with Shalheveth Freier, 18 May 1994.
72. Interview with Avi Beker, 15 May 1994.
73. Author's interview with Avi Beker, 15 May 1994 and Yair Evron, 22 May 1994.

74. Author's interviews with Aronson, 16 May 1994, and Schiff, 23 May 1994.
75. *Yediot Aharanot*, 16 February 1991.
76. Geoffrey Aronson, 'Hidden Agenda: US–Israeli Relations and the Nuclear Question', *Middle East Journal*, Vol.46, No.4 (1992), p.617.
77. Ibid., p.619.
78. Cited in Shahak, 'The Israeli Myth of Omniscience', p.96.
79. *Yediot Aharanot*, 8 March 1991.
80. See 'Gur Interviewed on Peace, Nuclear Facilities', *MENA*, 25 October 1993. Translation by Foreign Broadcast Information Service (FBIS), Daily Report: Near East and South Asia, 29 October 1993, p.34.
81. Shahal's Speech in Knesset, 14 October 1991, cited in Aronson, 'Hidden Agenda', p.621; Arens's and Weizmann's statements as brought in *Yediot Aharanot*, 23 October 1991.
82. Frank E. Blair (ed.), *Countries of the World and Their Leaders Yearbook*, 1992, Vol.1, Detroit, 1991, p.683; Louis Rene Beres, 'Israel, Iran, and the Prospects for Nuclear War in the Middle East', *Strategic Review*, Vol.21, No.2 (1993), p.53; Atkeson, 'The Middle East', p.120.
83. 'Intelligence Official on Iran, Arafat Allegations', TA0806150892, Tel Aviv, IDF Radio in Hebrew, 8 June 1992, in FBIS Daily Report – Near East and South Asia, 9 June 1992. For assessments of Iran's non-conventional programmes see Cordesman, *After the Storm*, pp.419–23; Evron, *Israel's Nuclear Dilemma*, pp.28–30; W. Seth Carus, 'Proliferation and Security in Southwest Asia', *Washington Quarterly*, Vol.17, No.2 (1994), p.135; Beres, 'Israel, Iran, and 'The Prospects for Nuclear War in the Middle East', p.52.
84. 'Bodinger – US "Not Doing Enough"', YA15006185792, Jerusalem, Kol Israel in English, 15 June 1992, in FBIS Daily Report – Near East and South Asia, 16 June 1992.
85. 'Israeli Colonel Says Teheran to Have DPRK's Nodong-1 "Within Year"', NC2012101093, Paris APF in English, 20 December 1993, JPRS Report – Proliferation Issues, 18 January 1994; Michael Parks, 'Israel Looks Past Borders, Arms for Long-Range War', *Los Angeles Times*, 5 February 1995.
86. Laura Zitrain Eisenberg, 'Passive Belligerency: Israel and the 1991 Gulf War', *Journal of Strategic Studies*, Vol.15, No.5 (September 1991), pp.304–5.
87. Geoffrey Kemp, *The Control of the Middle East Arms Race*, Washington DC, 1991, p.73; Cordesman, *After the Storm*, pp.494–516; Evron, *Israel's Nuclear Dilemma*, pp.25–8; Eisenberg, 'Passive Belligerency', pp.321–2.
88. Letter from Shalheveth Freier to those UN ambassadors who had voted against the Israeli Nuclear Armament Resolution in the General Assembly, 20 November 1993.
89. Ibid.; author's interview with Freier, 18 May 1994.

PART III: TOWARDS PEACE

# Jewish–Non-Palestinian-Arab Negotiations: The First Phase

## ELIEZER TAUBER

Most of the studies on the first phases of the Arab–Israeli conflict concentrate on Jewish–Palestinian relations during that period, and the attitudes of the Zionist movement and the Palestine Arabs towards each other. It is the intention of this essay to focus on various negotiations held in this period between Zionists and non-Palestinian Arabs living in the neighbouring countries. The time-limit of the essay will be from the Young Turk regime, when the various Arab nationalist movements started to strive for the preservation of Arab rights, until the beginning of Mandatory rule over the Fertile Crescent, which signalled a new phase also for the Arab–Israeli conflict. Furthermore, by way of learning how Arab–Jewish negotiations in that period integrated into the nationalist aspirations of each of the movements, the essay will concentrate only on negotiations held between representatives of political organizations, leaving out the various contacts made on the individual level.[1]

During the oppressive rule of Sultan Abdul Hamid II and the discriminating regime of the Young Turks, many Syrian and Lebanese activists emigrated from, at times fled, the Ottoman Empire. The most important centre of Syrian and Lebanese nationalist activity outside the Empire during the Young Turk regime was in Egypt, then under British occupation. In late 1912 several Syrian and Lebanese émigrés residing in Cairo founded the 'Ottoman Party for Administrative Decentralization'. Ostensibly, the party worked for the granting of a decentralized regime to all of the provinces of the Ottoman Empire. Its real goal, however, was to strive for the improvement of living conditions in Greater Syria and the achievement of some measure of autonomy. The party's president was Rafiq al-Azm, a Muslim from Damascus who had emigrated to Egypt some two decades before that. Other prominent members were the party's secretary, Haqqi al-Azm (Rafiq's cousin), the Muslim thinker Rashid Rida, and the editor-in-chief of *al-Ahram*, Da'ud Barakat.

---

Eliezer Tauber is Professor of Middle Eastern History at Bar-Ilan University.

While the party's headquarters was in Cairo, it also had branches throughout Syria, Mount Lebanon and Palestine. At first, the party operated strictly in the open. However, following the military *coup* in Istanbul in January 1913, which returned the nationalist circles of the Young Turks to power (after the liberal circles had ruled the Empire for half a year), the party despaired of all possibility of introducing changes into the Empire by legal means. Shortly thereafter the party leaders decided to strive for transforming Syria and Mount Lebanon into an independent principality. At this juncture, however, the party did not have any means for implementing such a grandiose plan.[2]

In early 1913 some of the party leaders reached the conclusion that the Zionist movement could be a potential ally in their struggle against the Young Turks. It all started with an article Da'ud Barakat wrote in *al-Ahram* in February, in which he emphasized the necessity of reaching an understanding between Arabs and Zionists. He considered the Zionists an essential element that could bring capital and knowledge to the region. Several days later Haqqi al-Azm wrote in the same newspaper that the Syrians agreed to Jewish settlement in their country, since Syria needed money and laborious people, and the Jews were the best for this purpose. He pointed out that until then the Syrians had opposed Jewish immigration only because most of the immigrants kept their former nationality and were sympathetic towards the Young Turks. Were the Zionists to become Ottoman subjects and be loyal to the country and to its language, they would be welcome. Otherwise, Arab history was going to be smudged by the things the Arabs would do to the Jews.[3]

In early April, Ibrahim Salim al-Najjar, another member of the Decentralization Party, sent a letter to Sami Hochberg, a leading Zionist activist in Istanbul and the editor-in-chief of *Le Jeune Turc* (where al-Najjar had used to work in the past). He argued that since the Ottoman government refused to reform the empire, it was advisable for the Zionists to reach an understanding with Arab reformists and to support their demand for a decentralized regime, thus precluding the eventuality of an Arab Muslim–Christian union in Syria against the Jews. Al-Najjar asked Hochberg to forward his message to Victor Jacobson, the representative of the Zionist Organization in Istanbul. Hochberg forwarded the message to Jacobson, who in turn forwarded it to the Central Zionist Office in Berlin, recommending that Hochberg should travel to Egypt and enter into negotiations with the Decentralization Party. The Central Zionist Office approved of the venture.[4]

Hochberg set out for Cairo, where he met members of the Decentralization Party and also a representative of the Reform Society of Beirut then present in Cairo (see below). He reached the conclusion that both organizations had not yet formed a distinct policy towards the Jewish immigration into Palestine. The Christian members of the organizations revealed positive attitude towards Jewish immigration, since they considered the Jews an additional minority that could help them counterbalance Muslim overwhelming majority in the region. Among the Muslim members, there were those who favoured Jewish immigration because of its potential economic advantages. Others, however, voiced reservations, such as that the number of Jewish immigrants should be limited to several thousands per year and that there should be limits to Jewish land acquisition from the Arab fellahin. There were also those who entirely opposed Jewish immigration.[5]

Hochberg made it clear to the party representatives that if they wanted the Zionist movement to join their demands, they would have to take the Zionist demands into account and adopt them. To include the Zionist demands in the party platform, however, required the convening of a general conference of party representatives in all branches throughout Syria and Palestine. This could be done only after the general Arab congress that was about to convene in Paris with the participation of most Arab political organizations operating at the time.[6] For the time being, therefore, the party reached an *entente verbale* with Hochberg, to the effect that since in principle it was favourable to Jewish immigration into Syria and Palestine and to an entente with the Zionists, the party would strive for a rapprochement between the Arab and Jewish worlds. By means of oral propaganda and through the Arab press, it would dissipate all the prejudices existing in the Arab world about Jewish immigration that had hitherto prevented an Arab–Jewish rapprochement. In exchange, *Le Jeune Turc* would take upon itself to support the cause of the Arab movement, so long as it was compatible with the unity and integrity of the Ottoman Empire. The journal would do its best to convince European newspapers with which it had contacts to do the same. The entente was considered by its partners an exchange of services, with the intention of reaching a comprehensive agreement in the future.[7]

In late April, the party declared publicly that it had been founded on the basis of genuine equality of all Ottoman nationalities, regardless of religion or nationality. The Jews should have equal rights in the Ottoman Empire, and should not be denied the common rights enjoyed by all the Ottomans in general and the Syrians in particular. Furthermore, the party's president, Rafiq al-Azm, published an announcement in favour of Jewish immigration, in which he declared *inter alia* that the party had decided to safeguard the rights of the Jewish nationality. They realized all too well the precious aid that could be rendered by Jewish capital, manpower and intelligence for a rapid development of their provinces to refuse them. It was also agreed that al-Najjar would write several articles in this spirit, that would later be published under the names of various party members.[8]

The Decentralization Party was not the only organization which strove for improving the conditions in the Arab provinces of the Ottoman Empire. Such activity also took place within the Empire, though given the circumstances at the time, the demands raised by Arab activists were of a more moderate nature. In early 1913 a new movement began to operate in the Arab provinces of the Ottoman Empire, calling for administrative reforms that would improve the living conditions in these provinces. In Beirut, a Reform Society was formed, embodying both Muslims and Christians, which in addition to the demand to implement various administrative reforms in the province sought European advisers to supervise the implementation of these reforms.

However, the Reform Society of Beirut managed to operate freely only for a short time. The Young Turks, who advocated centralized regime, could not allow the existence of a reform society seeking administrative autonomy, and in April the *vali* (governor) of Beirut issued an order for its closure. The people of Beirut responded with civil disobedience and a general strike. Anarchy seemed to overcome the city; the *vali* arrested some of the activists. Finally, through the mediation of the British Consul-General in the city, the *vali* consented to free the prisoners in exchange for a promise by the people of Beirut to keep the calm.[9]

The events of April 1913 in Beirut served as a proof for Arab activists that no remedy could be found from within the Empire. Therefore, it was decided to convene a congress in Paris in June, with participation of the various existing Arab organizations, that would pronounce Arab demands from the Ottoman Empire. The intention was to give international publicity to the Arab question, thus putting pressure on the Ottoman authorities to grant the demands of the Arab reformists. Among the delegations supposed to participate in the congress was also a five-member delegation representing the Reform Society of Beirut. The first of them to sail to Egypt, in early May, on his way to Paris, was Ahmad Mukhtar Bayhum, a prominent Muslim member of the Reform Society. In Cairo, he met Hochberg and took part in the discussions about the entente with the Zionists. Furthermore, he persuaded Hochberg to sail for Beirut in order to reach a similar entente with his own society. This Hochberg did, and the entente reached in Cairo was endorsed by the Beirut Reform Society, two of whose members, the Muslim Ahmad Hasan Tabbara and the Christian Rizq Allah Arqash, published announcements in the spirit of Rafiq al-Azm's statement. Arqash declared, *inter alia*, that the intercommunal union existing in Beirut also embodied the Jews, and that Jewish immigration to Syria and Palestine had to be welcomed. It would be a crime against the fatherland to stop this immigration, he argued, since it could benefit the region by its capital and new working methods.[10]

In June, the congress of the Arab organizations opened in Paris, with the participation of 21 representatives from various places in Greater Syria and two from Iraq. Although the congress was supposed to be of an all-Arab character, in practice its distinct human make-up turned it into a Syrian-oriented congress. Its discussions dealt with administrative decentralization and its application to the Syrian provinces of the Ottoman Empire. Its resolutions demanded administrative reforms, recognition of Arabic as an official language, the broadening of the general council's authority in the *vilayet* (province) of Beirut, and financial aid to the *sanjaq* (district) of Mount Lebanon.[11]

Among those present in the congress hall was also Sami Hochberg. He prepared himself for the third session of the congress, at which Ahmad Hasan Tabbara of the Reform Society of Beirut was supposed to speak about immigration to Syria, a topic which obviously was of interest to the Zionist movement. Before the congress began, Hochberg had warned its participants that if the congress accepted an anti-Jewish resolution, the Arabs would lose all possible assistance from the Jewish world and would set the Jews against them instead of with them. Hochberg especially tried to influence Tabbara, requesting a 2,000-franc credit from the Central Zionist Office in Berlin to invite the principal members of the congress to a good meal before the day of discussions about immigration.[12]

The third session of the congress opened on 21 June at 2.30 pm, and Sheikh Ahmad Hasan Tabbara began his speech on 'Migration to and from Syria'. Statistics about emigration from Syria were followed by an analysis of its causes. He contended that the emigration was against the emigrants' will. Born as Ottomans, the Arabs wanted to remain such, but they also wanted reforms. They did not want to secede from the Ottoman Empire, but the Empire was marching towards its ruin. The call for reforms emanated from Beirut and the entire Arab nation was responding to it. It would be wrong to retreat, because the life of the nation depended on reforms. It was imperative that the Ottoman government respond and grant reforms on the basis of decentralization for every province. As for immigration into Syria, Tabbara noted that Syria could hold four times as many inhabitants, and that organized immigration would benefit the country. Hochberg could be satisfied.[13]

In the discussion following Tabbara's speech, the speakers expressed opposition to Turkish immigration into Syria. (Following the Balkan War many Muslim Turks fled the battlefields and moved to other regions of the Empire.) They demanded a resolution about this, but Abd al-Hamid al-Zahrawi, the congress's president (representing the Decentralization Party), maintained that it was preferable to defer a resolution concerning the Turkish immigrants to a later stage of the

congress. At this juncture, Khayrallah Khayrallah, one of the
participants, announced that he was against Turkish immigration and
that only immigration of rich people could benefit the country. At that
moment Bayhum, of the Reform Society of Beirut, shouted: 'Jewish
immigration – yes! But Turkish immigration – no!'. His statement was
accepted with astonishment by the audience. There were some whispers,
but no one spoke against it.[14]

Shortly after the congress, al-Zahrawi and Bayhum told Hochberg
that in their opinion Jewish immigration to Syria and Palestine would
improve the situation in these provinces. There were, however, two
conditions: that the Jews should become Ottoman subjects, and that
Arab fellahin would not be expelled from lands bought by the Jews.
They expressed their willingness to arrive at a secret agreement with
Hochberg about this, which would constitute the basis of a final
agreement to be signed with the leaders of the Zionist movement.
Hochberg also interviewed al-Zahrawi for his journal *Le Jeune Turc*. He
asked him why the Jews were not explicitly mentioned in the congress
resolutions, to which al-Zahrawi responded that all the resolutions
relating to the rights and duties of the Syrians included the Jews as well.
The Jews were their brethren in race, being Syrians who had left their
country in the course of time. All the Jews in the world were but Syrian
emigrants, the same as the Syrians living in Paris and America, for
example. Al-Zahrawi also reminded Hochberg of the pro-Jewish
statements delivered earlier by Rafiq al-Azm and Rizq Allah Arqash.[15]

The Ottoman government, perplexed by the international
reverberations of the congress, decided to reach an understanding with
its participants in order to placate them. A Young Turk emissary arrived
in Paris and came to an agreement with the congress members about
reforms that the Ottoman government had to implement in the Arab
provinces. But the agreed-upon reforms remained on paper. The
Ottoman government never really intended to keep to its promises and
evaded implementing the reforms, which led to the final break between
the Turks and the Arab activists.[16]

When the hopes pinned by the Decentralization Party on the Paris
agreement were dashed, it decided to try again to enter into a treaty
with the Zionist movement. In late September, Da'ud Barakat told a
Zionist representative in Cairo that, by way of preventing future
misunderstandings, it was desirable to revive the entente that had been
achieved between the party and the Zionist movement. An accredited
Zionist representative should arrive in Cairo to enter into negotiations
with Rafiq al-Azm, the party's president, in this regard. In early 1914,
Rafiq and Haqqi al-Azm and Rashid Rida approached the representative
of the Jewish National Fund in Cairo, expressing their will to make
contacts with international Zionism in order to arrive at an agreement

that would lead to the accomplishment of the desires of both movements. They stated their faith in the effective help the Zionists would be able to extend to them to achieve their goals.[17]

However, at this stage the relationship between the party and the Zionist movement began to deteriorate. Apparently, the very fact that the Zionist leadership disregarded these approaches was taken by the party leaders for disrespect towards them on the part of the Zionists. In March, Rashid Rida wrote in his periodical, al-Manar, that it was imperative for the Arab leaders to achieve one of the two: either to reach an agreement with the Zionist leaders that would accommodate the interests of both parties, or to join forces against the Zionists and use every means to fight them, including armed bands.[18]

In early April, Nisim Malul, a Jewish member of the Decentralization Party and a Zionist, employed by the Cairo newspaper al-Muqattam as its Jaffa correspondent, interviewed the Zionist leader Nahum Sokolow. Sokolow called for unity among Arabs and Jews in a joint struggle for Palestine. He explained that the Jews were only returning to their home after living in exile for a long time. They did not intend to harm the Arabs but to live by their side. Jewish presence would benefit the Arabs, since the Jews would develop the country by means of their money, education and modern inventions. They would prove their intention to approach the Arabs by (a) learning the Arabic language; (b) sending physicians to cure diseases prevalent among the Arabs; (c) launching shelters for the needy, especially among the Arabs; and (d) opening branches of the Anglo-Palestine Company that would lend money to the local populace.[19]

It seems that Rafiq al-Azm considered Sokolow's words regarding sending doctors and opening shelters arrogant and offensive, since several days later he published a response in al-Muqattam, in which he uttered his disbelief in Sokolow's statements regarding the Jewish will to integrate in the country. In practice, the Jews were endangering the Arabs, who considered their refusal to forgo their former nationalities a potential pretext for a foreign force to conquer the country. If the Jews wanted to be welcome in the country they had to become Ottoman subjects, to teach Arabic in their schools, to admit Arab students to these schools, and to associate Arabs in their economic and commercial enterprises. For the time being, they had done none of this.[20]

At this juncture, Ibrahim Salim al-Najjar, too, started to write against the Zionist movement and Jewish immigration into Palestine. In an article in al-Ahram, he surveyed a journey to Palestine he had made several months earlier, which convinced him that the Jews were about to become the majority in Palestine. The Jews, al-Najjar said, were gripping the economy of Palestine by the throat. They dissociated themselves from the local populace, organized in their own organizations out of the government's reach, and their settlements actually became a state within a state.

Al-Najjar claimed that the Ottoman authorities had effectively acquiesced in the Jews' actions. He attacked the Zionist leaders for ignoring the 'entente' reached with the Decentralization Party in 1913, which in his view had become a dead letter because the Zionists had reached the conclusion that the party was weak and it was preferable to negotiate with the Ottoman government. Malul responded to al-Najjar in two sharp articles in *al-Muqattam*, where he refuted his allegations concerning the Jewish presence in Palestine. He also pointed out that al-Najjar had quit the Decentralization Party, and therefore was in no position to declare that the Zionists had withdrawn from the 'entente' with the party.[21]

In late April, the party's secretary, Haqqi al-Azm, sent a letter to Malul, warning him that the ongoing press campaign was liable to effect unpleasant consequences for both Arabs and Jews. He was of the opinion that Sokolow's words proved that he was mocking the Arabs the same way the Young Turks were. He was especially angered by Sokolow's statement that the Jews were returning to their own land. Sokolow's words that the Jews would approach the Arabs by opening shelters or hospitals were rejected by him as preposterous. The Arabs would arrive at an understanding with the Jews only if the latter did not jeopardize the Arabic language by their Hebrew, and on condition that they reneged on their foreign nationalities.[22]

Nisim Malul, one of the main advocates of Jewish–Arab rapprochement in that period, decided personally to try to solve the crisis and by late May he arrived in Cairo. He went straight to the café where the party leaders used to meet and was warmly welcomed. Rafiq al-Azm attended the beginning of the conversation which followed but then retired. The main part of the conversation was conducted by Haqqi al-Azm, who mentioned an article published by Jacobson in *al-Muqattam* the previous day in response to the article written by Rafiq al-Azm in early April. Jacobson had called for understanding and co-operation between Jews and Arabs in Palestine, and supported the idea that the Jews should become Ottoman subjects. Malul confirmed that this was the Zionist stand, though he pointed out that it was the foreign diplomats who put obstacles in the process, delaying the Jews from renouncing their foreign nationalities. He also explained the importance of Hebrew for the Jews, keeping them from extinction after their religious connection had weakened. Haqqi al-Azm then brought up the entente reached with Hochberg, and claimed that the Zionists were ignoring it, preferring to make contacts with the Young Turks. He also told Malul that Rafiq al-Azm intended to publish an anti-Zionist article the next day in response to Jacobson's message. Malul answered that this argument in the press was harmful and proposed instead (a) to discuss the entire relationship between the two sides in a Zionist–Arab congress; (b) to invite Sokolow to Cairo for consultations; and (c) to prevent further publications of this type since they were poisoning the atmosphere and preventing rapprochement. Haqqi al-Azm agreed and advised him to locate Rafiq al-Azm and prevent the publication of the article. Malul immediately went to the party club, waited there until 1.30 am but al-Azm did not turn up.[23]

The next day, Rafiq al-Azm's article appeared in *al-Muqattam*, attacking the Zionists for being assisted by the Ottoman government and urging the Arabs to resist them. He rebuked the Zionists for their methods in buying lands and reproved the Ottoman government for not preventing it. At this juncture, Malul tried to save the situation by persuading Rafiq al-Azm to publish another article in which he would rectify the bad impression caused by his previous article. Convinced by Malul's arguments, the next day al-Azm published another article in *al-Muqattam*, expressing his opinion that if both sides agreed to relent a little, they would be able to reach an understanding. The Arabs wanted the Zionists to prove their good intentions in practice and not only in bare words. He also pointed out that his party was ready to hold an Arab–Zionist congress in Cairo. Two days later, *al-Muqattam*'s editorial office announced the closure of the press debate, and that no more articles on the issue would be published until the proposed Arab–Zionist congress took place, so as to allow its discussions to be held without pressure. The announcement, ostensibly published by the newspaper's editorial office, was in fact worded by Malul.[24]

In June, Najib Shuqayr, a member of the Decentralization Party, met Sokolow in Istanbul and delivered him an invitation from Rafiq al-Azm to come to Cairo. Sokolow did not arrive. At the same month, another party member, As'ad Daghir, met Richard Lichtheim, Jacobson's successor as representative of the Zionist Organization in Istanbul, and intimated to him that he would not be opposed to a limited Jewish immigration into Palestine. Describing himself as a friend of the Jews, he, however, pointed out that the Arabs were afraid that Jewish economic superiority would eventually drive them out of Palestine. Lichtheim forwarded the message to Jacobson in Berlin, following which Jacobson delivered several proposals to Daghir: (a) since the Jews had knowledge, capital and influence, while the Arabs possessed land, power and material wealth, it was advisable that the two peoples arrive at an understanding; (b) the Arabs should accept the Jews as brothers, conditional upon their becoming Ottoman subjects; (c) in exchange, the Jews would invest their material and cultural resources in the service of the Arab cause, and support the Arab parties financially (three million liras were offered, according to Daghir); (d) a Jewish–Arab congress should be held in Cairo. Daghir forwarded the proposals to Cairo.[25]

In the meantime, Malul was continuing his talks in Cairo. He persuaded Shibli Shumayyil, a member of the supreme committee of the Decentralization Party, to write a pro-Zionist article in *al-Ahram*, in which Shumayyil described the campaign against the Zionists as superfluous and detrimental. Malul also met Rashid Rida, who, while admitting that the Jews were beneficial to the country, demanded that also the Arabs should share the benefits. Rida further stated that the party leaders were suspicious that the Jews had contacts with the Ottoman government, at a time when the Arabs intended to free their lands from the Turks. Since there were only three to four million Turks, and 20 million Arabs, Rida warned, it was preferable for the Jews to reach an understanding with the Arabs, as Arab victory was guaranteed. Rida's figures were of course imaginary. Malul, at any rate, denied any connections between the Zionists and the Ottoman government.[26]

At this point, however, the short-lived rapprochement between the Decentralization Party and the Zionist movement was over. It seems that there existed a basic distrust on the part of the party activists towards the Zionists, suspecting them of collaborating with the Ottoman government and of operating in Palestine under Ottoman aegis. Under such circumstances, the party leaders saw no point in continuing the dialogue with the Zionists. It might even be that some of them believed that the entire dialogue was a mere stratagem on the part of the Zionists, meant to enable them to peacefully carry out their plans. If such was the case, then the only way to handle the situation was by using force against the Zionists.

In a letter to the head of the party branch in Beirut, Haqqi al-Azm opposed the idea of an Arab–Jewish congress and claimed that the Zionists intended to expand to Syria and Iraq. The Zionists had to be stopped by means of threats and persecution, by persuading the Arab population to destroy their farms and burn their settlements, and by organizing bands to execute this. A secret society established in Egypt for this purpose was also mentioned by him in this respect. In July, Haqqi al-Azm published an article in the same spirit in *al-Iqdam* (edited by the anti-Zionist Palestinian party member, Muhammad al-Shanti), in which he attacked the Ottoman government for doing nothing against the Zionist peril. The Ottoman government was bribed by the Zionists, he believed. However, in the end, the alliance with the government would not help the Zionists, and they would be forced by the Arabs to leave Palestine with great losses.[27]

Rafiq al-Azm, more moderate than Haqqi al-Azm, wrote in late July in a letter to As'ad Daghir regarding Jacobson's proposals of June. He argued that, while in principle these proposals were all fine, the Zionists had to understand that if their ideas were not amenable to the Palestinian Arabs, the negotiations between the Zionists and the party would become meaningless.[28] At the very same month that Rafiq al-Azm wrote this, Richard Lichtheim, the representative of the Zionist Organization in Istanbul, wrote to the Zionist Actions Committee in Berlin that 'Die grosse Frage ist nun: Was haben wir zu bieten?'.[29] By this, these two men in fact touched two key questions: was there a point in any negotiations between Zionists and non-Palestinian Arabs? and was there anything to talk about? However, for the time being there was no imperative need to answer these questions, since by August 1914 the First World War intervened and turned the pre-war negotiations wholly irrelevant.

During the war, the Ottoman authorities executed several dozens of Arab activists, among them some of those involved in the negotiations with the Zionists, such as Ahmad Hasan Tabbara and Abd al-Hamid al-Zahrawi. Others, who had long lived in Egypt, such as Rafiq and Haqqi al-Azm, Rashid Rida, Da'ud Barakat, and Ibrahim Salim al-Najjar, or had fled the Empire at the beginning of the war, like Rizq Allah Arqash, were sentenced to death *in absentia*. In order to justify the executions, the Ottomans published a series of incriminating documents which belonged to the Decentralization Party and had fallen into their hands. In some of the documents the negotiations with the Zionists were partly exposed.[30]

The Decentralization Party itself disintegrated during the war, and its remaining activists turned to establish new organizations that would be better suited for the changing circumstances. The next time the Palestine question occupied the minds of the Syrian and Lebanese activists in Cairo was in November 1917, with the publication of the Balfour Declaration concerning the establishment of a Jewish national home in Palestine. As soon as the declaration became known in Cairo, Fawzi al-Bakri (an activist from Damascus) and Sulayman Nasif (a Lebanese lawyer) went to the British Arab Bureau bearing a telegram signed by them and by Rafiq al-Azm and Faris Nimr (one of the owners of *al-Muqattam*), in which they asserted to Balfour that Palestine was an integral part of Syria. They also demanded from the British that the Syrians should have the same rights in Palestine as the Jews, in all fields. The British first promised to send on the telegram to London, but after they had kept it for almost a month they informed the senders that their telegram would not be sent, and also recommended to them to desist from this method of protest.[31]

But the Syrian activists were not ready to give up. In mid-December, a delegation of Muslim Syrians left Cairo for Aqaba, headed by Haqqi al-Azm, to persuade Amir Faisal to protest against the British policy towards Zionism. Much as Faisal expressed his misgivings about the Balfour Declaration, he refused to protest against it to the British. Apparently, Faisal well understood that he was in no position to criticize the British, upon whose assistance the entire military effort of the Arab Revolt was dependent. Haqqi al-Azm tried to persuade him that in his status as an Arab leader he was obliged to protest, and certainly his father, Hussein, the 'King of the Arab Nation', was obliged to protest. But Faisal stood by his refusal. An attempt by the Syrians to appeal to Hussein himself, through his Cairo representative, had the same result, with Hussein pointing out that he was well aware of the British plans for the Jews in Palestine. This attitude of Hussein and Faisal towards the Balfour Declaration caused the Syrian activists in Cairo to reach the conclusion that Hussein was totally under British control, and that he had even committed himself to the British not to interfere in their policy regarding Palestine.[32]

In the meantime, in London, Mark Sykes, an expert in Arab affairs on behalf of the British government (and a partner to the Sykes–Picot agreement), was busy bringing about an Arab–Armenian–Jewish understanding. Professing the realization of the national aspirations of these three peoples, and believing that they should co-operate for attaining their goals, he set up a combined committee which included Syrian, Armenian and Zionist (Chaim Weizmann) representatives. In mid-November Sykes sent a letter to several of the Syrian leaders in Cairo, who then got together in the framework of a 'Syria Welfare Committee',[33] proposing to them to co-operate with the Armenians and the Jews in the interests of the liberation of their country. He pointed out that all that the Zionists wanted was to be given the right to settle in Palestine and to conduct their national life there.

Following his request, Gilbert Clayton, Director of British Intelligence in Cairo, also joined in the attempts to convince the Syrian activists of the benefit of joining the Arab–Armenian–Zionist tripartite entente designed by Sykes. The members of the Syria Welfare Committee discussed the matter and reached the conclusion that their best policy was to co-operate with the Jews on the lines suggested. They informed Clayton that being aware of the strength and status of the Jews, they were interested in disseminating propaganda in Palestine in favour of Syrian–Jewish brotherhood. This could be achieved by sending a delegation on their behalf to Palestine. Concurrently, they also began contacts with representatives of the Zionist movement in Cairo.[34]

In January 1918, the members of the Syria Welfare Committee, among them Sulayman Nasif, Rafiq and Haqqi al-Azm, Fawzi al-Bakri and Faris Nimr, sent a reply letter to Sykes, stating that if all that the Zionists wanted was to settle in the country and enjoy the same rights and duties as the local people, they accepted favourably his proposals for Arab–Armenian–Zionist co-operation. For their part, they were ready to send a delegation to Palestine to preach in this spirit. Sykes answered their letter in mid-February, informing them in the name of the

London–Syrian–Armenian–Zionist committee of the impending arrival in Egypt of a Zionist delegation headed by Chaim Weizmann.[35]

In the end, nothing came of Sykes's plan. Contributing to its demise was also Hussein's refusal to send a representative to attend this committee, on the ground that he was the sole spokesman of the Arab nation. Nevertheless, the contacts between the Zionists and Syrians in Cairo continued. In March, the Zionist delegation headed by Weizmann arrived in Egypt and met with the representatives of the Syria Welfare Committee – Sulayman Nasif, Faris Nimr and Sa'id Shuqayr. Prior to the meeting Nasif had compiled a list of demands, whose main ones were: (a) that the Arabs would enjoy equal rights in the government of Palestine; (b) that Arabic should be the official language there; (c) that until war's end no sale of land in Palestine should be permitted. Weizmann agreed to the demands and even added that he had personally asked Balfour that until the end of the war no purchase and sale of land should be allowed in Palestine. He emphasized that the Zionists had no intention of setting up a Jewish government in Palestine, and that they regarded Palestine as a refuge that would serve them as a national and intellectual home. Weizmann also spoke of the progress and economic welfare that the Zionists movement would bring to Palestine, from which the Muslims and Christians would also benefit. The Syrian participants of the meeting were very satisfied with Weizmann's clarifications and even promised to send a soothing letter to the Palestinian Arabs.[36]

In early April the Zionist delegation continued to Palestine. It was received there with hostility by the local Arabs, whose suspicions concerning the Zionist intentions regarding Palestine were only aggravated by the visit. In early May the British permitted the Syria Welfare Committee to send a delegation to Palestine to calm the fears of the population about the Zionist plans. Participating in the delegation were Rafiq al-Azm, Sulayman Nasif and Mukhtar al-Sulh, and it was decided to define it as a private visit rather than an official delegation under British sponsorship, or on behalf of the Syrian committee. The delegation spent a fortnight in Palestine, during which it visited Jerusalem and Jaffa. In the two cities the delegation encountered very hostile feelings towards the Zionists, and all its efforts to convince the inhabitants that the Zionists did not intend to set up a Jewish government in Palestine, and that steps had been taken to prevent Jews from buying land in Palestine, were in vain. The local Arabs saw the delegation as an official mission that had come to handle their problems, and they began to pour out their troubles. Rafiq al-Azm promised that the delegation would do its best to assist them. When the delegation returned to Cairo it suggested to the British a number of measures, including economic means, to allay the distress among the Palestinian

Arabs. However, in its principal objective of calming the Arabs of Palestine with regard to the Zionist plans the mission proved to be a failure.[37]

From mid-1918 Arab–Jewish dialogue was reduced to the contacts between Faisal and Weizmann, which are outside the scope of this essay, and have already been studied thoroughly. It started in June 1918 with a meeting between the two north of Aqaba, and ended in January 1919, at the Paris Peace Conference, with the famous Faisal–Weizmann agreement, which, as a British officer put it several months afterwards, was 'not worth the paper it is written on'. The assessment of the British officer, Major J.N. Camp, was accurate, as Faisal was a puppet in the hands of the Syrian nationalist organizations, which were the real rulers of Syria at that time.[38]

Nevertheless, also during the existence of Faisal's short-lived state in Syria subsequent to the First World War, there was another attempt to reach an agreement between a Syrian party and the Zionist Organization. It was carried out by the Syrian National Party. As the extremist nationalist circles in post-war Syria were gaining the upper hand, a counter-reaction began among the more conservative and moderate groups – aristocrats, notables, landowners and businessmen – who stood to lose from a situation of disorder or war, which was bound to stem from the deterioration of relations between Syria and the French. These groups were less anti-French, and desired first and foremost order and tranquillity, and if possible – senior positions in Faisal's regime. When Faisal started to realize how tenuous his position in Syria was, he saw these people as natural allies, who could help him in carrying out his policy of appeasement with the French. He decided to set up a party that would support him and become a counterweight to the extremist nationalist organizations. Thus, he hoped, he would not stand alone in the political arena in his attempts to persuade the Syrian population to accept a peaceful agreement with the French. In January 1920 the establishment of the Syrian National Party was officially announced. Initiating the party was Nasib al-Bakri, Faisal's special adviser (and a brother of Fawzi), and most members of its administrative and advisory committees came from among the socio-economic groups described above. The party platform stated *inter alia* that it sought equality of civil and political rights for all of Syria's residents, regardless of creed or origin, and that it supported the principle of democratic monarchy.[39]

In March 1920 the party was involved in an attempt to reach an agreement with the Zionist movement. The initiator of the agreement on behalf of the party was Najib Sufayr, a rather dubious personality from Beirut.[40] Following preliminary talks between Sufayr, Weizmann and Moshe Shertok, a number of party members from the western region – Sufayr himself, Yusuf Mu'adhdhin, Rashid Karam, Najib Hashim and Antun Shahada – signed an agreement with Joshua Hankin, representing the Zionist Organization.

According to the agreement, the signatories acquiesced in the severance of Palestine from Syria and the establishment by the Zionist Organization of a national home (*foyer national* in the French version of the agreement, *bayit le'umi* in the Hebrew version, and *mawtin qawmi* in the Arabic one) for the Jewish people there. They also agreed to massive Jewish immigration to Palestine, and promised to prepare Arab public opinion to accept the Jews as their neighbours. All the inhabitants of Palestine, regardless of religion, were to enjoy equal civil and economic rights. The Zionist Organization, for its part, was to undertake not to encroach on the borders of Syria and Lebanon in the future, not to intervene in the affairs of the Muslim and Christian holy places in Palestine, and to assist the governments of Syria and Lebanon financially in developing their countries. The agreement bore considerable resemblance to the Faisal–Weizmann agreement, and its fate was the same: it remained an archival document without any practical consequences.[41]


CONCLUSION

During the final years of the Ottoman Empire, the Arab nationalists found themselves in confrontation with the Young Turks, the Empire's rulers. Striving for autonomy, or even independence for their provinces, they perceived the Zionist movement as a potential ally in the struggle against a common enemy. In their opinion, the shared interests of the movements prescribed such a co-operation, and they believed in the power and influence of the Zionists and especially in their financial capabilities. The Zionist activists, for their part, found it easier to negotiate with Syrian or Lebanese activists, for whom an entente of shared interests with the Zionists against the Ottoman authorities was of a higher importance than the specific interests of the Palestinian Arabs, who were the first to lose by Jewish immigration and Zionist activity. In this period, the characteristics of the Arab–Israeli conflict were not clear yet, and such negotiations could take place. However, eventually it all crumbled away owing to the distrust felt by the Arab activists towards the Zionists, suspected of collaborating with their rivals, the Turks, at Arab expense (whether this was factually true was irrelevant in this respect). During the First World War, and in its aftermath, several other attempts to reach Arab–Jewish understanding took place, but they were all to fail. The disintegration of the Ottoman Empire and the establishment of the modern Arab states did not bode well for the future of either Palestinian–Jewish relations or non-Palestinian-Arab–Jewish relations.

NOTES

1. For a thorough research of all sorts of contacts between Jews and Arabs before the First World War, see Neville J. Mandel, *The Arabs and Zionism before World War I*, Berkeley, 1976 (this is a revised version of his doctoral dissertation titled 'Turks, Arabs and Jewish immigration into Palestine 1882–1914', Oxford, 1965). Mandel also wrote two articles about this issue, the first with the same title as his dissertation, published in *St Antony's Papers*, No. 17, London, 1965, pp.77–108; the second, titled 'Attempts at an Arab–Zionist Entente 1913–1914', *Middle Eastern Studies*, Vol. I, No. 3 (1965), pp.238–67. Many of the pre-war occurrences mentioned in this essay are also described in Mandel's publications.
   For Palestinian–Jewish relations see Eliezer Be'eri, *Reshit Ha-sikhsukh Israel–Arav*, Tel Aviv, 1985, for the pre-war era; and Yehoshua Porath, *The Emergence of the Palestinian–Arab National Movement 1918–1929*, London, 1974, for the post-war period. The best analysis of the Zionist viewpoint is Yosef Gorny, *Ha-She'ela Ha-Aravit Ve-ha-Be'aya Ha-Yehudit*, Tel Aviv, 1985.
2. For the history of the Decentralization Party, see Eliezer Tauber, *The Emergence of the Arab Movements*, London, 1993, pp.121–34. While about 70 per cent of party members were Muslim, it is known that there were only two Jewish members in the party, Nisim Malul and Yosef Moyal, both in its Jaffa branch. The rest of the members were Christian.
3. *Al-Ahram*, 19 and 25 February 1913.
4. Central Zionist Archives (hereafter CZA), Z3/45: letter, Victor Jacobson (Istanbul) to Richard Lichtheim (Berlin), 10 April 1913; letter, Lichtheim to Jacobson, 13 April 1913. Later that month Da'ud Barakat approached a Zionist representative regarding the possibility of reaching an agreement between the Zionists and the party. See CZA Z3/752: letter, S. Hasamsony (Cairo) to Central Zionist Office (Berlin), 25 April 1913.
5. CZA Z3/114: 'Le mouvement arabe', by Sami Hochberg (Istanbul), 17 May 1913.
6. Two representatives of the party were to participate in the congress: Abd al-Hamid al-Zahrawi, elected the congress president, and Iskandar Ammun, the party vice-president.
7. Ibid.
8. *Ha-Herut*, 5/196, 18 May 1913; CZA Z3/114: 'Le mouvement arabe', by Hochberg, 17 May 1913. See also *Ha-Herut*, 5/216, 10 June 1913. Later on Hochberg was expected to deliver 10 liras to al-Najjar for writing an article 'wie wir es wünschen'. See CZA Z3/45: letter, Jacobson (Berlin?) to J. Neufach (Istanbul), 23 May 1913. It was not the only time that al-Najjar was expected to write articles 'suivant nos instructions'. See, for example, CZA Z3/47: letter, illegible (Berlin) to Lichtheim (Istanbul), 29 September 1913.
9. For the Reform Society of Beirut and the April events in that city, see Tauber, *Emergence*, pp.135–47. The membership of the Reform Society of Beirut divided equally between Muslims and Christians, with two Jewish members, Ibrahim Hakim and Salim Refa'el Hakim.
10. CZA Z3/114: 'Le mouvement arabe', by Hochberg, 17 May 1913; *Ha-Herut*, 5/216, 10 June 1913; *Le Jeune Turc*, 5, p.150, 1 June 1913, cited in Mandel, *Arabs*, p.158.
11. For the Paris Congress, see Tauber, *Emergence*, pp.178–97. One of the Iraqi delegates to the congress was a Jew, Sulayman Anbar. There was only one Palestinian Arab in the congress, Awni Abd al-Hadi of Nablus.
12. CZA Z3/114: letters, Hochberg (Paris) to Jacobson (Berlin), 10 and 16 June 1913.
13. Al-Lajna al-Ulya li-Hizb al-Lamarkaziyya bi-Misr [Muhibb al-Din al-Khatib], *al-Mu'tamar al-Arabi al-Awwal*, Cairo, 1913, pp.83–93; CZA Z3/114: letter, Hochberg to Jacobson, 24 June 1913; Archives du Ministère des Affaires Etrangères (Paris) (hereafter MAE), Nouvelle Série, Turquie, Vol. 122: report, Profecture de Police (Paris) 22 June 1913.
14. CZA Z3/114: letter, Hochberg to Jacobson, 24 June 1913.
15. CZA Z3/114: letters, Hochberg to Jacobson, 26 and 27 June 1913; *Ha-Herut*, 5/266, 8 August 1913.
16. For the Paris agreement and its consequences, see Tauber, *Emergence*, pp.198–212.
17. CZA Z3/753: letter, Hasamsony to Zionist Actions Committee (Berlin), 1 October 1913; letter, Jacob Caleff (Cairo) to President of the Zionist Actions Committee (Berlin), 10 January 1914.
18. *Al-Manar*, 17/4, 27 March 1914, p.320.

19. *Al-Muqattam*, 10 April 1914.

20. Ibid., 14 April 1914.

21. *Al-Ahram*, 11 April 1914; *al-Muqattam*, 23 and 24 April 1914.

22. CZA L2/94Ib: letter, Haqqi al-Azm (Cairo) to Nisim Malul, 29 April 1914.

23. CZA A18/14/6: letter, Malul (Cairo) to Nahum Sokolow and Arthur Ruppin (Jaffa), 29 May 1914; *al-Muqattam*, 27 May 1914; *Ha-Herut*, 6/232, 21 July 1914.

24. CZA A18/14/6: letter, Malul to Sokolow and Ruppin, 31 May 1914; *al-Muqattam*, 29 and 30 May, and 1 June 1914; *Ha-Herut*, 6/232, 21 July 1914.

25. CZA Z3/49: letters, Lichtheim to Jacobson, 7 June 1914, and Lichtheim to Zionist Actions Committee, 3 July 1914; As'ad Daghir, *Mudhakkirati ala Hamish al-Qadiyya al-Arabiyya*, Cairo, n.d. [1959?], p.43.

26. CZA L2/94Ib: letter, Malul to Zionist Office (Jaffa), 7 June 1914; *al-Ahram*, 3 June 1914. For another pro-Zionist article by Shibli Shumayyil, see *al-Muqattam*, 1 May 1914.

27. Letter 70, Haqqi al-Azm to Mahmud al-Mihmisani (Beirut), 20 June 1914, cited in *Le Journal de Beyrouth*, 413, 1 September 1915. A Hebrew translation of Haqqi al-Azm's article is available in CZA L2/94Ia.

28. Letter 68, Rafiq al-Azm (Cairo) to As'ad Daghir (Istanbul), 30 July 1914, cited in *Le Journal de Beyrouth*, 414, 2 September 1915.

29. CZA Z3/49: letter, Lichtheim to Zionist Actions Committee, 3 July 1914.

30. For the executions of the Arab activists, see Eliezer Tauber, *The Arab Movements in World War I*, London, 1993, pp.35–56. For the incriminating documents, see also idem, 'La Vérité sur la Question Syrienne: A Reconsideration', *Journal of Turkish Studies*, 15 (1991), pp.315–44.

31. The Public Record Office (Kew, London), Foreign Office Records (hereafter FO), 141/654/356: letter, C.A.G. Mackintosh (Cairo) to Gilbert F. Clayton (Cairo), 22 November 1917, enclosing telegram from the Syrians (Cairo) to Balfour (London) 20 November 1917; National Archives Microfilm Publications (United States) (hereafter: NA), 367/381: reports 7, 8 and 10, William Yale (Cairo) to Leland Harrison (Washington), 10, 17 and 31 December 1917; Frank E. Manuel, *The Realities of American–Palestine Relations*, Washington, 1949, p.187.

32. NA 367/381: reports 5, 8 and 10, Yale to Harrison, 26 November, and 17 and 31 December 1917; Manuel, *Realities*, pp.187–8.

33. Established ostensibly for the purpose of sending economic aid to the Syrian population, which suffered greatly during the war, the Syria Welfare Committee was in fact a feeble political framework, which disintegrated but a few months after its establishment.

34. FO 882/17: report 113/1/3744, Mackintosh to Clayton, 27 December 1917, enclosing letters, Sulayman Nasif (Cairo) to Clayton, 26 and 28 December 1917; Manuel, *Realities*, p.187.

35. FO 371/3398: letter, Nasif and others (Cairo) to Mark Sykes (London), 17 January 1918, and letter, Sykes (in name of Syrians, Armenians and Zionists), 15 February 1918.

36. NA 367/382: report 22, Yale to Harrison, 8 April 1918; CZA L4/768: letter, Kinahan Cornwallis (Cairo) to Symes, 20 April 1918, and 'The Arab Commission in Jaffa' by Isa al-Sifri (Jaffa), 22 May 1918; *Mir'at al-Gharb*, 15 August 1918, citing a letter from Nasif to *al-Kawkab*, 14 June 1918; Manuel, *Realities*, p.188.

37. CZA L4/768: 'The Arab Commission in Jaffa' by al-Sifri, 22 May 1918; NA 367/383: report 29, Yale to Harrison, 27 May 1918; *Arab Bulletin*, No. 91 (Cairo) 4 June 1918, p.182; *Mir'at al-Gharb*, 15 August 1918, citing a letter from Nasif to *al-Kawkab*, 14 June 1918; MAE, Levant 1918–29, Arabie-Hedjaz, Vol. 1: despatch 185A, Cousse (Jidda) to MAE 10 July 1918.

38. 'The Arab Movement and Zionism', by J.N. Camp (Jerusalem), 12 August 1919, cited in E.L. Woodward and Rohan Butler (eds), *Documents on British Foreign Policy 1919–1939*, London, 1952, First Series, Vol. IV, p.364. For Faisal's status in Syria during 1919–20, see Eliezer Tauber, *The Formation of Modern Syria and Iraq*, London, 1995, pp.39–48.

39. For the Syrian National Party, see Tauber, *Formation*, pp.54–5.

40. In July 1920 Najib Sufayr was involved in an attempt by the party to persuade the members of the administrative council of Mount Lebanon to co-operate with the Syrian government. Preliminary meetings to discuss the matter were held in Sufayr's house, with the participation of several members of the administrative council. However, Sufayr

regularly reported everything that had been said in these meetings to the French, then ruling over Mount Lebanon and littoral Syria. The result was that all the council members involved in the meetings were arrested by the French. See Anis al-Nusuli, *Ishtu wa-Shahadtu*, Beirut, 1951, p.49, and Bulus Mas'ad, *Lubnan wa-Suriya qabla al-Intidab wa-ba'dahu*, Cairo, 1929, p.75.

41. The agreement, in French, Hebrew and Arabic, signed by Najib Sufayr, Yusuf Mu'adhdhin, Rashid Karam, Najib Hashim, Antun Shahada, and Joshua Hankin (Jerusalem), 26 March 1920, is available in CZA S25/9907. See also: Moshe Sharett, *Yoman Medini*, Tel Aviv, 1968, Vol. I, p.65. Najib Sufayr was to continue his contacts with the Jews. In 1936 he offered Weizmann and Shertok to buy lands in either northern Syria or the Tyre-Sidon region, according to him, with French permission. His offer was declined, to his great disappointment. See ibid., pp.64–5.

# Transition from Conflict:
# The Importance of
# Pre-Negotiations in the
# Oslo Peace Process

ILAN G. GEWURZ

Since time immemorial human beings have sought to understand how conflict can be transformed into peace through non-violent conflict resolution. Particularly since the end of the Second World War, this issue has received much attention from scholars and statesmen alike. Article 33 of the United Nations Charter (1945) addresses the issue of pacific settlement of disputes saying that 'parties to any dispute ... shall first of all, seek a solution by negotiation, enquiry, mediation, conciliation, arbitration, judicial settlement, resort to regional agencies or arrangements, or other peaceful means of their own choice'.[1] While advances have been achieved in this area, there is still much to be learned regarding what brings parties in conflict to consider bilateral or multilateral solutions. Indeed, it should be remembered that 'crucial as it is, "around the table negotiation" is only a later part of a (much) larger process needed to resolve conflict by peaceful means'.[2]

There are a number of important factors which influence a state's (or a non-state actor's) decision to abandon a unilateral approach to a given conflict situation – aiming to achieve its own maximal objectives – in favour of a negotiated agreement. Changing realities within the international context, regional factors and domestic circumstances – economic, political or sociological – can all be of fundamental importance in influencing the decision. However, the process of transforming a conflictual relationship into one involving direct negotiations is not a simple one. Historical grievances, the psychological and political 'baggage' of actors and established government approaches to dealing with the conflict all pose significant challenges to the continuation, or even the commencement, of negotiations. Thus pre-negotiations were identified as an intermediary stage which is central to

Ilan G. Gewurz is writing a J.D. in Law at Stanford University.

the success of such transitions. Pre-negotiations function as a 'learning process', getting each party to understand the needs, interests and expectations of the other side. Furthermore, they enable Dovish views to be explored in a low-risk environment thereby gaining legitimacy within the mainstream of their own government's policy choices.[3]

Often parties have experienced their conflictual relationships for years if not generations and a negative portrayal of the other may be entrenched in their national ideologies. Fear and mistrust run deep and a lack of confidence in the other party's sincerity and willingness to comply with an agreement (if one were to be reached) do not lend themselves to building an environment in which negotiations can occur in good faith. Thus, 'a shift towards more accurate perceptions and images, more favorable attitudes, more open and accurate communication, increased trust and a cooperative win–win orientation would augur well for a meaningful and successful negotiation.'[4] It is in this regard that pre-negotiations are so important, as a low-risk opportunity in which the advocates of negotiations themselves can be convinced of the viability of the process as well as convince the more mainstream decision-makers of its value.

On 13 September 1993 the world witnessed the famous 'handshake' between Palestinian Liberation Organization (PLO) Chairman Yasser Arafat and Israeli Prime Minister Yitzhak Rabin on the White House lawn, and the signing of the 'Declaration of Principles' (DOP)[5] by Arafat and Israeli Foreign Minister Shimon Peres. This set in motion perhaps the most optimistic and far-reaching process in the history of the conflict. Israel at long last recognized the PLO as the sole legitimate representative of the Palestinian people. In turn, the PLO recognized the right of the state of Israel to exist, renounced the use of terrorism and all other forms of violence and committed itself to a process of peaceful resolution.

Much has been written on this 'historic breakthrough' and its subsequent agreement. The secret negotiations which took place between Israeli and Palestinian representatives – known as the Oslo process – also received substantial coverage. However, few address Oslo as a pre-negotiation which laid the foundations for the successes which followed. This paper will argue that the early stages of the Oslo talks were crucial, constituting a pre-negotiation process that allowed the official negotiating track to develop. A successful negotiation between the government of Israel and representatives of the PLO could not have taken place without first addressing various obstacles which were dealt with in the pre-negotiation process.

This paper begins by drawing attention to the nature and inherent importance of the pre-negotiation process itself. First, it expands the existing definitions of pre-negotiations in order to achieve greater clarity of both what constitutes a pre-negotiation and what role it actually serves. Second, it examines the conditions which are conducive for pre-negotiations to begin and outlines the different stages of the process itself. In doing so, it explores the functions which pre-negotiations serve and the impact they have on the subsequent official negotiation process. It suggests that pre-negotiations play a central role in helping parties reach the negotiating table and shaping the process once they are there. The process is also important for defining the parameters, in setting the agenda and selecting the participants of the official negotiations which may follow. Furthermore, it also serves to gain support among central decision-makers for the process itself.

Having analysed the literature on pre-negotiations, the paper situates this theory in the case study of Israeli–Palestinian peacemaking efforts in Oslo. It argues that what has been looked upon as one process of negotiations can be viewed as two relatively distinct stages; the first serving as a pre-negotiation which helped to shape and bring about the second. Recognizing this function of the Oslo talks and understanding the early stages of the secret channel (January to March 1993) as a pre-negotiation clarifies the way in which the negotiations evolved. This first period enabled the parties to learn more about one another, evaluate the other party's needs, interests and intentions and helped bring the process to a point where it could enter into mainstream foreign policy. It thus set the stage for the formal negotiation which developed out of these successes. The essay will conclude by drawing lessons from the experience in Oslo regarding the nature of pre-negotiations in general.

## UNDERSTANDING PRE-NEGOTIATIONS: DEFINING THE PROCESS

### Temporality

The most prominent 'working definition' of pre-negotiations was developed in 1989 and served as the basis for what has been the most comprehensive book on the topic to date. It stated that 'Pre-negotiations begin when one or more parties considers negotiations as a policy option and communicates this intention to the other parties. Pre-negotiation ends when the parties agree to a formal negotiation or when one party abandons the consideration to negotiation as a policy option'.[6] Though analytically distinct from the official negotiations, pre-negotiations are still part of the broader attempt to move parties from a situation of conflict to one of mutually agreed-upon settlement and should thus be understood as a part of the negotiation process itself. However, this temporal definition of pre-negotiations is not sufficient in and of itself. The boundaries between the pre-negotiation and the actual negotiation cannot be described as being sharp. Rather the process is dynamic and divisions are permeable. It is thus difficult to specify exactly when one stage ends and the next begins. The negotiation and the pre-negotiation often overlap, and the process may move back and forth. Furthermore, whereas this definition specifies *when* pre-negotiations occur, it does not clarify *what* the functions of this process are nor how it attempts to achieve them.

In describing the pre-negotiation process theorists have expanded on this time-based definition and have focused on the structure, the functions served and its relationship with the official negotiations which may follow. It is thus important to construct a definition of pre-negotiations which encompasses all of these aspects in order to further our understanding of the process. An exclusively time-based definition also runs into difficulties at the level of application as it can be all-inclusive and subsequently add nothing to our understanding of the transformation of conflict. For example, all secret discussions that ever occurred between Israelis and Palestinians could fit this definition and thus classify as pre-negotiations. While these may have been significant in creating an atmosphere more conducive to negotiations, they do not help to explain why the Oslo process specifically gained success.

## Psychological and Practical Functions

One of the central functions of pre-negotiations is to address the psychological barriers that impede official negotiations. This includes redefining relationships and jointly reframing the problems, addressing the parties' fears and apprehensions and creating an atmosphere of common understanding. In so doing it helps the parties to transform the conflict by generating shared understandings of the problem and encouraging definitions of the conflict which are conducive to negotiated outcomes. Thus the pre-negotiation process enables party representatives to move beyond existing obstacles and towards a mutually acceptable starting point. It provides an opportunity for the parties to become convinced that there is mutual interest in resolution and that reciprocity can be expected. This function is particularly important in cases of protracted conflict where stereotyping and vilification of the other party have become deeply embedded in perceptions and even national ideology.

## Structural Characteristics

There are also structural features which can be used to define pre-negotiations and which allow the above functions of pre-negotiations to be achieved. Pre-negotiations generally occur in informal settings, and are usually secret, taking place beyond the scrutiny of the media or domestic audiences. They typically involve discussions which do not formally commit either side to the ideas being addressed. They therefore provide an opportunity to assess the costs of commitment before undergoing a shift in official policy. They also serve to reduce the risks involved in conciliation by enabling the parties to withdraw from the process at any time without major consequences. Finally, through direct exchange of information they allow parties to identify and clarify potential risks and explore the negotiation option as a possibility for mainstream government policy.

Pre-negotiations often involve the participation of a third party, who, in performing a variety of functions, helps keep the parties and the process on track. The role of the third party varies in terms of the extent of intervention and the level of activity in the process. Pre-negotiations may include a proactive mediator who is involved in the ongoing process and actually becomes a participant to the discussions. The mediator may even apply pressure or offer incentives to achieve concessions from the parties.[7] Alternatively, pre-negotiations may involve an impartial facilitator whose role is more limited. While not an active participant in the pre-negotiation process, they may be involved in arranging the logistics, providing moral support and acting as an outside consultant.[8]

### Relationship with the Official Negotiations

Working within this secret and informal setting, pre-negotiations perform a number of tasks which lay the foundations for the official negotiations which may follow. Rothman describes these tasks by defining pre-negotiations as a preparatory stage in which parties 'jointly frame the issues of the conflict, generate various options for handling them co-operatively, and interactively structure substance and process of future negotiations'.[9] In this way pre-negotiations help parties avoid surprises at a later stage, a necessary prerequisite if formal negotiations are to avoid failure.[10]

Pre-negotiations are also important in helping to set the actual agenda of the official negotiations which follow, by eliminating 'non-negotiable' issues and bypassing those points which are likely to impede the onset of formal talks. They assist parties in avoiding non-starters, while simultaneously keeping the range of issues broad enough so as not to lock the parties into their adversarial positions.[11] As such, pre-negotiations play a central role in shaping the style and content of the official negotiations, outlining the substantive aspect and demarcating the boundaries of negotiations by delimiting the range of issues on the table.[12]

### Phases of the Process

Understanding the various roles played by the pre-negotiation process allows for a more satisfactory integrative 'working definition' to be developed. Pre-negotiations are usually secret, informal contacts between parties which provide them with the opportunity to move beyond various psychological and practical obstacles in the way of formal negotiations. They serve as a low-risk 'learning process' in which the parties can clarify misperceptions and stereotypes about one another, evaluate risks and chances for success, while jointly addressing alternatives and potential structures of the formal negotiations. They also test the viability of a negotiation approach, helping it to gain acceptance within the mainstream of government decision-making.

This definition essentially describes a step-by-step process which undergoes a number of stages fulfilling these various functions and tasks. The order of these stages is largely contextual. However, the early stages of pre-negotiations usually involve searching for mutually acceptable and creative definitions of the problem and addressing various alternatives.[13] This is generally followed by some form of commitment to enter into formal negotiations leading to a process of preparing the actual negotiations. The point at which the parties undertake the commitment to negotiate depends on the perceived risks involved. For when 'leaders consider the process of negotiation a high-risk option, with potentially large costs, the reduction of uncertainty will dominate the process and order the phases'.[14] In such cases the parties will put off any formal commitment to negotiate until they feel that the risks have been sufficiently reduced. This may result in the pre-negotiation process transforming itself into the official negotiation process.[15]

## THE CONTEXT FOR PRE-NEGOTIATIONS

### Conducive Factors Versus Ripe Moment

Distinguishing the pre-negotiation phase from official negotiations not only helps to identify the stages of the negotiation process, but also aims to understand what brings parties in conflict to the negotiating table.[16] As such it can be related to the concept of 'ripeness' which was developed in an effort to understand the transition from conflict to a search for peaceful settlement. It is important to examine the concept of ripeness in order to assess how the role of pre-negotiations fits into the broader movement from conflict to negotiations. Ripeness can be understood as particular circumstances which leave the conflict ready for the start of a negotiated process or even progress.[17] Kriesberg goes as far as to argue that no matter how skilled the negotiators may be, if the conflict situation is not 'ripe' nor ready to move towards a peaceful settlement, negotiations are unlikely to succeed.[18]

Three essential factors have been identified in producing ripeness enabling parties to explore the options of negotiation. The first two are conditions which may be helpful or may advance the transition process while the third is one that involves the absence of certain unfavourable conditions. First, a mutual perception of the potentially negative or high cost of the *status quo*, or a belief that continued stalemate will be increasingly damaging, is important. This may grow out of either a recent crisis or a desire to avoid a pending crisis, which neither side believes it can achieve unilaterally. Second, a sense of exhaustion from the costs of the ongoing conflict or disillusionment with the struggle, as well as a recognition that all other approaches which had been employed to resolve the conflict until that point had failed.

Third, ripeness requires the absence of regional and international political obstacles to peaceful conflict resolution. For example, the bipolar balance of power during the Cold War manifested itself in the Middle East conflict and made it difficult for parties to pursue peace. Leaders must be in a position to begin negotiations. This can either mean being sufficiently strong with regard to their local constituency to make concessions or sufficiently weak *vis-à-vis* external powers which have an interest in the advancement of the process, that they have no alternative but to participate.[19]

The concept of ripeness, however, has been overused and is a more limited tool for understanding conflict resolution than many scholars seem to suggest. Ripeness is not binary but rather should be thought of in terms of a continuum. Most conflict scenarios cannot be clearly defined as either entirely 'ripe' or 'unripe' though the extent of ripeness, that is, to which international, regional and domestic factors favour the parties' readiness to explore a negotiated settlement, will impact upon (though not determine) the possibility of a successful attempt at negotiations.

This makes the task of assessing what is considered 'ripe enough' very difficult. Indeed the idea is used predominantly in hindsight. It also results in the concept being used to explain events beyond its intended purpose. Ripeness is relevant in explaining why under certain circumstances, deemed 'unripe', groups would avoid the negotiating table; however it does not, nor is it meant to, explain why a peace agreement, once in place, succeeds or fails. The consequence of this overuse is the emergence of an almost tautological concept, namely when the attempt to begin negotiations fails the situation is termed unripe and when it succeeds it is defined as having been ripe enough.

Furthermore, in social conflicts leaders can help to create a reality which is more conducive to achieving a peaceful settlement, thereby bringing about 'ripeness'. Alternatively they can make decisions that perpetuate the conflict despite factors which may theoretically qualify it as ripe. As the biological metaphor suggests, ripeness seems to be a process over which we have no control; however, it can be humanly manipulated. Thus while understanding the factors which may be conducive or an impediment to beginning a pre-negotiation is important, the term 'ripeness' should be employed with caution.

GETTING TO THE OSLO NEGOTIATIONS

*Political Background to the Israeli–Palestinian Conflict*

Oslo was not the first attempt to resolve the decades-long Israeli–Palestinian conflict. There is a long list of failed plans and doctrines, many put forth by various American administrations, offering alternative approaches to settlement. The evolution of the conflict and events surrounding it, including the various attempts at settlement, all serve as background to the Oslo process. They helped to create an environment which was conducive to beginning a negotiated process and to shape the perspectives of the actors involved. In order to understand the evolution of the political backdrop to Oslo, one must begin (at least) in 1967.

In the decisive Israeli military victory in the 1967 Arab–Israeli war, Israel captured the Golan Heights from Syria, the West Bank and East Jerusalem from Jordan and the Gaza Strip and Sinai Peninsula from Egypt and was left occupying a large Arab (Palestinian) population. The war changed the focus of the conflict. Arab states now sought to regain control of the lost territory and were forced to recognize the existence of the Jewish state.[20] In contrast, the Arab–Israeli war of 1973 shook Israeli confidence in its military prowess and strengthened the Arab political bargaining position.[21] It also helped restore and strengthen a sense of Arab pride.

The official united Arab stance towards Israel began to change soon after as a result of a number of crucial events. The Camp David Accords of 1978, and the formal peace agreement between Israel and Egypt it produced, broke the unity of the Arab front for the first time. This created the possibility that other Arab states might follow Egypt's lead and pursue bilateral negotiations with Israel. The Iranian revolution of 1979 and the Iran–Iraq war which began in 1980 diverted Arab attention away from the Israeli threat. With increasing instability in the Gulf and the rise of a powerful Islamic fundamentalist state, Israel was no longer seen as the only, or even the most, dangerous threat, particularly for the Gulf states.

Israel was also facing major challenges to what had been the dominant perspective and was consequently undergoing significant changes. The Israeli invasion of Lebanon, in 1982, seen as Israel's first 'war of choice', was heavily criticized within the country. The effectiveness of a national security policy based exclusively on military strength was called into question for the first time. This debate regarding the redefinition of the sources of Israeli security was furthered by the emergence of an Israeli peace movement, which aimed to redefine the notion of security and mobilize support for its peace-oriented definitions of the problems that Israel faced.

The spontaneous eruption of the *intifada* (Palestinian uprising) in 1987 increased the level of resistance by the local Palestinian population in the West Bank and Gaza Strip. In addition to demonstrating Palestinian frustration with the occupation and bringing the Palestinian issue back into the international spotlight, the *intifada* challenged the already declining military ideology in Israel. Furthermore, it raised serious questions within Israel with regard to the costs of continued occupation particularly in terms of the infringements on the country's democracy.[22]

The Gulf War of 1991 also had implications for the Israeli position *vis-à-vis* the Arab–Israeli conflict. The Iraqi use of long-range Scud missiles against Israel reinforced the idea that with advancements in warfare technology territory was no longer the decisive factor for security.[23] Furthermore, the tacit alliance between Israel and the anti-Iraq Arab coalition (with the former restraining itself from responding to attack), demonstrated to both sides the reliability and pragmatism of their adversaries.

These events also had major consequences for the PLO leadership and the evolution of the dominant Palestinian perspectives. The Israeli invasion of Lebanon forced the PLO to move its headquarters to Tunis, distancing it further from the Israeli border and the local Palestinian population therein. The *intifada* marked a serious challenge to the Tunis-based PLO which was losing touch with the needs of the local Palestinian population living under Israeli occupation. The PLO were also threatened by the emergence of the Islamic Resistance Movement (Hamas), which was founded at the start of the uprising as the clandestine militant wing of the Palestinian branch of the Muslim Brotherhood.[24] At the 19th Palestinian National Council meeting in 1988 the PLO officially abandoned its revolutionary slogans and shifted to political pragmatism, accepting the possibility of a 'two-state solution'. When this shift reaped few tangible benefits from the Israeli Likud government, it fostered further popular disillusionment, enabling Hamas to fill the resulting ideological and doctrinal vacuum.[25]

The PLO was further threatened as a result of its decision to support Saddam Hussein in the 1991 Gulf War. The decision proved to be a catastrophe for the PLO, whose budget was virtually cut in half as payments they had been receiving from Saudi Arabia and Kuwait were ended. PLO financial support to the West Bank and Gaza Strip dropped from $120 million in 1989 to approximately $45 million in 1992, leaving funding for hospitals, universities, community centres and family payments to be either be drastically reduced or terminated.[26] Furthermore, Saudi Arabia and other Persian Gulf states began to back Hamas as an expression of their displeasure with the PLO.[27] Now able to finance both its *intifada* activities and welfare programmes, Hamas made further political headway challenging the leadership of the politically and financially isolated PLO.

The end of the Cold War, which resulted in both the collapse of the Soviet Union and the emergence of the United States as the single superpower in the world, also removed what had been a major obstacle to the pursuit of peace. First, the end of the bipolar balance of power and consequently Russia's diminished role in the Middle East region meant that the Arab–Israeli conflict no longer reflected international antagonisms.[28] Second, the new international reality served to weaken the radical Arab regimes which the Soviet Union had supported, particularly Syria and those factions of the PLO that they supported, thereby strengthening American influence in the region.[29]

It was within this regional and international context that the Bush administration, in co-operation with the government of Russia, initiated the Middle East peace conference in Madrid in October 1991. The Madrid conference achieved little in the way of actual agreements. However, the lessons of both its achievements and its failures proved significant for the establishment of the Oslo negotiations. The inclusion of representatives of so many conflicting states in the joint discussion in Madrid, was a great accomplishment and demonstrated the possibility of changing old realities. It also provided a level of interaction between the individuals in and around the process and enabled them to gain familiarity with one another.

The Palestinian delegation had decided to participate, despite Syria's decision to boycott the multilateral negotiations, thus demonstrating to Israel Palestinian readiness to search for a separate settlement and move ahead without Syrian support. Finally, the highly public nature of the talks helped legitimize the process to both populations. Even the shortcomings of the Madrid talks carried with them important lessons. It became clear that the media's constant scrutiny of every development and setback served to obstruct the process and resulted in increased rigidity by all parties. Furthermore, the inability of the Palestinian delegation[30] to make any decisions without first conferring with Arafat in Tunis demonstrated that the PLO could not be excluded from a serious negotiation process.[31]

However, the Israeli Likud government had no real intentions of ever reaching an agreement through the continuation of the Madrid talks. Prime Minister Shamir later admitted that he 'would have carried on autonomy talks for ten years' while continuing to build Jewish settlements in Judea and Samaria.[32] Thus the election of Yitzhak Rabin in the Israeli elections of 1992 was perhaps the last essential factor in creating a context which was conducive to a negotiated settlement. The Labour government was elected on a platform of peace and promised its constituency a settlement within six months to a year of getting elected. Upon being elected it entered into a coalition with the left-wing Meretz party, excluding the Likud from the government coalition for the first time since 1977.

In summary, with the united Arab front broken, the decline of the militaristic ideology in Israel, the PLO on the verge of collapse as a result of financial bankruptcy, political isolation and the rise of the more militant Hamas, the end of the Cold War, the Washington talks (the continuation of the Madrid conference) at an impasse, the Israeli election of a leadership committed to achieving peace and both sides exhausted by the consequences of the conflict, the stage was set for negotiations between Israel and the PLO.

## The Unfolding of the Oslo Talks: Participants and Setting

The origins of the Oslo talks can be traced back to 4 December 1992 and involved a high degree of coincidence and spontaneity. While multilateral talks on economics (the continuation of the Madrid conference) were being held in London, Deputy Foreign Minister Yossi Beilin, who was a member of the Israeli delegation, asked Yair Hirschfeld, a senior lecturer at Haifa University in Political Science with a specialization in economic development in the Middle East, to join him. Over the course of the preceding four years the two men had been involved in a series of unofficial secret meetings with prominent Palestinian businessman Faisal Husseini, as a way of communicating indirectly with the PLO.[33] Hanan Ashrawi, who had met the Israelis at a number of these secret meetings, had suggested that Hirschfeld meet PLO member Abu Ala who was in London at the time 'calling the shots' behind the scenes for the Palestinian delegation, to discuss economic development which was a mutual interest.[34]

Terje Larsen, the director of the Institute for Applied Social Sciences (FAFO), a Norwegian think-tank, helped arrange the actual meeting. He had strong contacts in the Middle East and was acquainted with many of the central players. Larsen was married to a senior Norwegian diplomat, and had accompanied his wife on a diplomatic appointment in Egypt where he had developed particular interest in the Israeli–Palestinian conflict.

Hirschfeld and Abu Ala first met secretly in a hotel lounge in London. Hirschfeld informed Abu Ala that he had close contacts in the government but emphasized that he was 'not authorized by anyone' and that he was 'only speaking informally'.[35] Following this initial meeting, Hirschfeld informed Beilin of his contact. Beilin urged him to pursue the opportunity although he provided no guidance or instruction.[36] Coincidentally, at the same time, Hirschfeld 'ran into' Dan Kurtzer, a US State Department official responsible for the multilateral talks and informed him of the meeting.[37] A second meeting was held the following morning, where the two men agreed to accept Larsen's invitation for them to meet again in Norway for a 'brainstorming session'. Abu Ala returned to PLO headquarters in Tunis where he met with Abu Mazen, senior member of the PLO responsible for negotiations with Israel, and informed him of the meetings in London.

The meetings in Norway began under a heavy cover of secrecy and informality. In order to preserve the secret nature of the meeting Larsen organized a small conference through the FAFO, addressing the living conditions in the Israeli-occupied territories. This provided a seemingly legitimate reason for both the Israelis and Palestinians to be there. Hirschfeld attended along with his long-time associate and former student Ron Pundak. The PLO sent Abu Ala who was accompanied by Maher al-Kurd, a Palestinian economist and Hassan Asfour, assistant to Abu Mazen. The meetings took place between 20 and 22 January 1993 at the Borregard Manor in Sarpsborg, 60 miles outside Oslo. Larsen served as host and was responsible for taking care of the logistics. Larsen's wife, Mona Juul, a senior Norwegian diplomat, represented the Norwegian Foreign Ministry, which was covering the expenses of the talks, adding an air of officialdom to the proceedings.[38]

Abu Ala set the tone by stating that the parties should avoid getting entangled in unproductive argument regarding the history of the conflict and he argued 'let us not compete on who was right and who was wrong in the past, and let us not compete about who can be more clever in the present. Let us see what we can do in the future'.[39] He also impressed the Israelis by suggesting that an Israeli withdrawal from the Gaza Strip would 'herald the beginning of co-operation with Israel'.[40] It was decided that rather than actually attempting to reach a peace agreement, the goal of the meetings would be to work towards drawing up a 'Declaration of Principles' that would outline how an agreement could be reached.

The Palestinian delegation returned to Tunis this time to brief Arafat and Abu Mazen regarding their impressions of the meeting. They were aware that there was some form of political connection and although they felt optimistic about the position expressed by the Israeli academics they were worried about the nature of the backing enjoyed by the professors. The Israelis were also concerned about the authority behind the Palestinian delegates, as Abu Ala was not well known within Israel. Nonetheless Hirschfeld expressed a degree of optimism in briefing Beilin, who in turn informed Israeli Foreign Minister Shimon Peres of the meetings for the first time. Peres presented these meetings to Prime Minister Rabin as a potential secret back-channel which could provide valuable information to the official talks in Washington.[41] For Rabin it was merely one among several secret discussions going on at the time and, though sceptical about the possible value, he allowed them to continue.[42]

The same group met a second and third time at the Borregard Manor in Sarpsborb during which time they drew up a 'Declaration of Principles'. At the second meeting (11–12 February 1993) both sides arrived with position papers laying out the vision of their respective parties and including concessions that had not been offered in the official Washington talks. Most importantly, Hirschfeld reaffirmed Israeli interest in withdrawal from the Gaza Strip and introduced the idea of a step-by-step Israeli transfer of power in the West Bank, which he termed 'gradualism'.[43] The six-page Declaration of Principles, which became known as *Sarpsborb III,* was completed in the third meeting held on 20–21 March.

In March 1993 Arafat appointed Abu Ala a member of the central committee and head of the PLO economic delegation to the multilateral negotiations, reflecting the seriousness with which the Palestinian leadership viewed the discussions.[44] The PLO simultaneously demanded some form of Israeli official commitment to the process. Arafat 'floated' to Rabin, through Egyptian President Mubarak, his acceptance of Israeli withdrawal from the Gaza Strip and the West Bank city of Jericho, a plan originally suggested by Peres and rejected by the PLO in 1992.

The Palestinian withdrawal from the official Washington negotiations in response to the Israeli deportation of 415 Hamas prisoners, in December 1992, further discouraged Rabin regarding the possibility of progress on that track. Negotiations resumed in April primarily as a result of American intervention. However, it was becoming increasingly clear that Palestinian negotiator Faisal Husseini was taking his instructions directly from Tunis, and that progress was unlikely as long as the PLO was formally excluded. Rabin was thus considering for the first time raising the Oslo talks to an official level, but wanted to guarantee that the PLO was truly ready to make concessions and that Abu Ala was in fact directly connected to Arafat.[45]

At the next round of the Oslo meetings (30 April–1 May), Hirschfeld and Pundak therefore asked the Palestinians to intervene in the official Washington track and create some goodwill in that process. The Palestinian delegation to Oslo agreed to do so and also offered concessions, including postponing the question of Jerusalem until a later date. Abu Ala was able to influence the official negotiations, which were taking place in Rome followed by a round (coincidentally) in Oslo. The former ended on an unusually optimistic note while in the latter the Palestinian delegation agreed to a number of concessions including an Israeli proposal on the issue of Palestinian refugees, which they may otherwise not have accepted.[46] This proved both Abu Ala's influence within the ranks of the PLO and Arafat's control over the official talks, strengthening the prospects for success through the Oslo track.

Reassured by the Palestinian's credentials Rabin sent the Director-General of the Israeli Foreign Ministry Uri Savir to Oslo on 13 May 1993.[47] Savir, the first Israeli official to participate in the talks, responded favourably. Thereafter, Rabin personally selected Yoel Singer to begin the official negotiation process between Israel and the PLO. On 11 June Singer, an Israeli attorney who had served under Rabin in the Israeli Defence Forces Advocate-General's department, joined Savir in order to evaluate the agreement that had been achieved.[48] Singer was highly critical of the declaration of principles that had been drawn up, but felt that there was enough common ground to reach a settlement and thus agreed to renegotiate the agreement. As Pundak later put it, 'what happened was that between May/June until July/August, we turned our pre-negotiation period ... into an official paper'.[49]

EXAMINING OSLO AS PRE-NEGOTIATION

The literature on pre-negotiations addresses how the transition from a situation of conflict to one involving a peaceful negotiation occurs. It can thus shed light upon why the initial phase of Oslo was important in achieving what it did and can improve our understanding of the relationship between the early stages and the official negotiations which followed. The early stages of the Oslo talks incorporated many of the characteristics of pre-negotiations, in terms of temporality, structure, functions and tasks. This essay will go on to examine the role that these attributes served in the evolution of the process.

*Timing of Oslo Pre-Negotiations*

Though at first glance one may think otherwise, the temporal definition of pre-negotiations is relevant to the case of Oslo. It is true that both the Israeli government and the Palestinian leadership had expressed interest in negotiations and in fact official negotiations had already begun in Madrid. Whereas, in theory, practically everything that occurred prior to the commencement of Oslo could also be considered 'pre-negotiations', the beginning of the Oslo track can be distinguished from the processes which preceded it. It was a quasi-official process that involved representatives of the PLO and thus the examination of the pre-negotiation phase can begin there. The pre-negotiations which began with the early phase of Oslo were prior to and temporally distinct from the official negotiations which followed.

*Functions of Oslo Pre-Negotiations*

The early stages of the Oslo talks were crucial in performing the functions of pre-negotiations and addressing the psychological and practical barriers with hindered the possibility of a negotiated settlement. A successful negotiation between the government of Israel and representatives of the PLO could not have taken place without first addressing these fears and various other obstacles which stood in the way. As Israeli Deputy Foreign Minister and one of the architects of the Oslo channel Yossi Beilin stated clearly, 'We didn't really know what the PLO really stood for. We knew the propaganda. We did not know the truth. Hirschfeld was the first person who checked what was more important and what was less important for them. Where their red lines were'.[50]

Hirschfeld and Pundak prepared the psychological ground and paved the way for the professionals who later joined them after the initial phase had taken place. From the Israeli perspective, the PLO had been seen as untrustworthy, riddled with internal conflicts and incapable of responding reasonably to practical proposals.[51] The Palestinians similarly feared Israeli expansionist intentions and felt that Israel's policies on the ground demonstrated their plans to consolidate control over the West Bank and the Gaza Strip rather than to make concessions for peace. Consequently, both parties needed assurances and thus a clear goal was to test both the sincerity and the reliability of the other side in the early stages of the process. Although those individuals directly involved all theoretically believed in the possibility of a negotiated settlement (many had been involved in illegal dialogue for years), the viability of the actual process had to be proved both to the individuals themselves and the leaders they represented. Without this, policies which supported negotiations could not have been accepted within the mainstream institutions of foreign policy.

Abu Ala opened the first session by expressing the PLO's interest in reaching an agreement and stressing the need to look only towards the future. Responding to his first impressions, Hirschfeld started the second round of talks by stating, 'What I have heard is extremely important We have received a message of peace from you. This message is important in affecting our political thinking'.[52] This function of creating confidence in mutual reciprocal compliance was essential as Pundak later said:

> We convinced the Palestinians that at the Israeli decision-making level there was a genuine desire to reach a peace settlement based on security, and an interest in helping the Palestinians to reach a stable, and prosperous entity of their own. In return, the Palestinian negotiators convinced us that their leadership realized that terror and armed struggle would not bring them closer to their dream, and that the only solution was reconciliation and dialogue.[53]

But more than lip service was required to satisfy the Israeli government's need for this function of testing the waters. They asked Abu Ala to influence the official negotiations and instil goodwill in the public process, as a way of testing both his influence within the ranks of the PLO and the organization's commitment to the process. The Palestinian success in this area was a major turning point in the process as the Israeli leadership began to feel more confident with regard to the capabilities and commitments of the PLO as a potential negotiating partner.

During this period the parties also had a chance to get to know one another which enabled them to build trust and helped them to overcome their fears and misperceptions. In short, they began to convince themselves that their 'dreams' of peace were attainable. Thus 'at the end of the first round it was not the points raised that had to be analysed, but rather the atmosphere of the talks and the Israeli (and Palestinian) opinions' that were important.[54] Trust and understanding were quickly being built among the parties and there soon emerged a sense that the two groups began to form one team which was working together to try to find solutions. As Pundak noted, 'Suddenly there developed this kind of a very intimate, what I call chemistry, between the negotiators, although at that time we were not still negotiators'.[55]

*Structure of the Oslo Pre-Negotiations*

The structural make-up of the early phase of the Oslo channel also corresponds to the description of a theoretical pre-negotiation process, as can be seen in the characteristics of the process. First, the setting and environment within which the process occurred was extremely important to its success. The sessions were generally set in the countryside where the negotiators could go for walks in the surrounding forests, and the meetings were often held in comfortable sitting rooms. Close attention was paid to the food and wine being served, while seating arrangements and room assignments were carefully scrutinized by the Norwegian hosts. The goal was to create a more relaxed and social environment, which became an important factor contributing to a conducive setting for confidence-building.[56]

Second, secrecy, which has also been identified as an important characteristic of pre-negotiations in general, was central to the Oslo talks. It enabled both sides to move away from what had been the official party line and make concessions which they would not have been able to make in a public negotiation. The lack of progress in the official track has often been associated with the high level of publicity surrounding it, which tends to result in rigid negotiating positions and leaves little room for concessions.[57] In secret meetings the parties were able to discuss various alternatives and jointly eliminate those which were unacceptable without having every word analysed in the media.

The secret nature of the talks also proved significant for a number of other reasons. First, the very decision to negotiate with the PLO and thereby grant it legitimacy, was seen as a concession by the Israeli government and could not have been done publicly before an agreement had been reached. The same was true for the Palestinians, who had not yet officially recognized the state of Israel's right to exist. Second, secrecy, combined with the unofficial nature of the talks (which Hirschfeld repeatedly stressed), provided deniability. This rendered a sense of security for leaders on both sides, providing them with the possibility of walking away at any point without serious cost. This created a low-risk environment in which the viability of the negotiations, which were previously unacceptable to either side, could be explored before it was undertaken as a central foreign policy objective.

Both the secret and the unofficial nature of the talks were closely tied to the fact that the Israeli representatives were academics who were not officially connected to the government. The fact that their words were not binding gave the negotiators (or pre-negotiators) a significant amount of leeway in dealing with highly sensitive issues and addressing alternative approaches to settlement. Thus secrecy was crucial to both parties. One example of how it manifested itself is seen in the fact that the entire *Sarpsborg III* document was written on FAFO stationery, in order to reinforce the idea that it was merely an academic exercise which could be denied by leaders in the event of a public leak.[58]

As is often characteristic of the structure of pre-negotiations, the role of third-party intervention was central to the process. Norway, because of its historically balanced foreign policy, was uniquely situated *vis-à-vis* the Israeli–Palestinian conflict. Thus both parties perceived it as relatively neutral, enabling its representatives to gain the trust of both sides. Furthermore, unlike the intervention of a powerful state like the United States, Norway could not be suspected of a hidden agenda nor could it be seen as imposing solutions on either side.[59] Indeed, one of the central problems with the Washington talks had been the role of the US as broker to the process. Both sides had played for better relations with the mediator and were looking to 'score political points' rather than address the issues.

In contrast, the involvement in Oslo of a non-proactive impartial facilitator forced the parties jointly to confront the underlying issues of the conflict, aiding conflict resolution rather than just political settlements. For Terje Larsen, Mona Juul and Junior Foreign Minister Jan England did not serve as proactive mediators; rather they served to facilitate the process by tending to the logistics, creating an environment that was conducive to a process of building trust. The facilitators acted as a support system, listening to both sides when they needed to 'let off some steam' and calming them down when the process met with serious obstacles. As Larsen said, 'we've never occupied the driving seat. Our job has been to create a framework that would make the peace process as successful as possible – to identify possible directions the sides could choose to take, and help them back on to the road where necessary'.[60]

## The Oslo Pre-Negotiations and the Official Negotiations

With regard to the relationship between the early stages of the process and the official negotiations, Oslo again fits the description of pre-negotiations. Non-negotiable issues were identified and jointly set aside to be dealt with at a later stage so as to keep them from preventing the beginnings of a negotiation process altogether. For example, the parties agreed to leave the question of Jerusalem, which was certainly among the most difficult issues for both sides, out of the interim self-rule phase, to be discussed only in the final status negotiations. Similarly the status of Israeli settlements in the West Bank and Gaza and questions regarding Palestinian refugees from 1948 whose right to return was seen by Israeli officials as a threat to the Jewish character of the state of Israel, were to remain off the negotiating table until after the initial self-rule phase. This process – of eliminating the most controversial questions which were considered non-negotiable – served to delimit the range of issues and created the boundaries of the official negotiations which followed.

The early stages of the Oslo process not only defined the boundaries of the subsequent official negotiations with regard to the issues being negotiated, it also established who participated in the process. Defining the parties as well as the individuals at an early stage served to create a relationship between the representatives of the respective delegations before the official negotiations began. It was in Oslo that the Israeli government had the chance to determine whether or not the PLO could truly be trusted and accepted as the Palestinian participant to the process.

On an individual level, the relationships that had been established between the pre-negotiators was an essential ingredient to the process. Abu Ala was not well known within Israel and would not have been a likely negotiator under other circumstances. Furthermore, from the Israeli perspective, 'Pundak half expected that as soon as the professionals arrived he and Hirschfeld would be eliminated, but Savir and Singer wanted to preserve the informal atmosphere and make use of their insights, and asked them to stay on'.[61] Thus while the pre-negotiation in the Oslo case did not involve the same individuals who later negotiated the settlement (at least not on the Israeli side), it did define the parties which were to participate in the process as well as dynamics between individuals which were conducive to successful negotiations.

Finally, the early stages of the Oslo talks served the pre-negotiation task of structuring the official negotiations which followed. This was a case where the pre-negotiation actually transformed itself into the official track, thereby building the official process directly upon the agreements reached in the preparatory stage. The pre-negotiations not only defined the content by delimiting the issues which were to be negotiated, it also set the tone for the official process. The style of the early stages of the process and the momentum it had achieved, which had become known as the 'Oslo spirit', carried over after the official negotiators arrived and built on the unique character of the pre-negotiations despite the difficult process which was to follow.[62]

Furthermore, the *Sarpsborb III* declaration of principles was later used as the foundation for negotiations and provided a starting point from which the official negotiators could begin to restructure the agreement and their respective positions.

## CONCLUSIONS

*Lessons from the Oslo Experience*

The experience in Oslo carries with it important lessons for the theories of pre-negotiations and for our understanding of the transition from conflict to negotiation. It sheds light on the fact that pre-negotiations not only serve to bring parties to the negotiating table, but also affect the negotiation process itself and the making of agreements. Pre-negotiations also illuminate the strengths of third-party facilitation as a form of intervention, particularly in cases of protracted conflict. Finally, it shows how pre-negotiation not only benefits the individuals involved in the process itself, but helps previously unacceptable ideas move into the mainstream and capture the political agenda and mechanisms of foreign policy.

The early stages of the Oslo process show that pre-negotiations have both positive and negative implications, carrying with them ramifications beyond intended objectives. First, in the efforts to bring parties to the table, pre-negotiations affect 'the table', shaping the evolution of the official negotiations and the final agreement. Second, the fact that the Israeli representatives to the Oslo channel were academics, who were not officially tied to the government, gave the process an unofficial and flexible nature which in many ways worked to its advantage. However, seeing as these negotiators were neither bound by nor totally knowledgeable with regard to government policy, they made concessions that ran counter to the policies of the Israeli government of the time. These posed difficult challenges for the official negotiators who had to renegotiate after the level of the talks was raised. In the initial draft of the agreement, for example, it is stated that 'the future of Jerusalem would be decided as part of the final status talks on the West Bank and Gaza after a period of Palestinian autonomy. In accepting this concept the two academics departed from Labour Party policy.'[63]

Third, while the secret nature of the talks was conducive to reaching the negotiating table it placed the process beyond evaluation by individuals from the outside. Consequently it was not assessed by legal or military experts until very late in its development. Upon entering into the negotiations in May, the legal adviser to the government of Israel, Joel Singer, noted that he 'thought the draft was (legally) catastrophic but was told to change only the really important things, since we were close to signing the DOP'.[64] Furthermore, trying to avoid leaks, Rabin had nowhere to turn for advice and thus 'lacked both military advice and an independent intelligence assessment, and ended up vetting every line of the DOP himself'.[65]

On the Palestinian side, decisions were made by a small group of individuals around Arafat who had little knowledge of legal proceedings. Furthermore, there was no consultation with other regional governments such as Lebanon, Syria or Jordan, all of whom were surprised to hear of the breakthrough.[66] Secrecy also isolated those groups which were not directly involved in the process from the agreement which had been reached. This had more serious consequences on the Palestinian side than on the Israeli, as the PLO did not enjoy democratic legitimacy. For example, poet Mahmoud Darwish accused the PLO of confusing its own political interests with that of the entire Palestinian people.[67] In so doing the PLO marginalized those groups not represented in the negotiating process, especially its Diaspora who make up more than half the total Palestinian population.[68]

Finally, by not addressing issues deemed 'non-negotiable' the Oslo channel avoided problems that threatened to obstruct the commencement of official negotiations. However, in so doing the pre-negotiation left the parties with very different perspectives with regard to what had been achieved. Key issues including the final boundaries of the Palestinian entity, the question of 1948 refugees, the future of Israeli settlements and the status of Jerusalem were postponed for later negotiation.[69] The two sides actually agreed upon so little that the accord has been called 'no more than an agreement to agree'.[70]

The peace process was consequently plagued from the very beginning by different visions of what it entailed and where it was leading. For example, following the signing of the agreement Arafat called for the liberation of Jerusalem as the future capital of a Palestinian state, whereas Rabin stated that 'Jerusalem remains under Israel's sovereignty and is Israel's unified capital'.[71] Furthermore, debates over the definition of Israeli redeployment from Jericho began almost immediately. It was unclear as to whether this referred to the town of Jericho or the entire administrative area. Thus while leaving non-negotiable issues off the agenda served to get a negotiation process started, a serious gap was left between the different visions of the peace process.

Oslo also illuminates the reluctance of officials to commit to formal negotiations in high-risk situations. The commitment to begin official negotiations in Oslo came only after most other pre-negotiation functions had already taken place, not before the parameters of the negotiations were set, as many theories would have expected.[72] In cases of protracted conflict, in which the conflict is often closely tied to ideology, parties tend to postpone any commitment to such a late stage that the pre-negotiations are likely to be transformed into the official process. This is especially true in cases where one party is a non-state and where the very granting of legitimacy is seen as a concession.

The experience in Oslo also illustrates some of the benefits of impartial third-party facilitation as opposed to highly interventionist power-mediation. Norwegian intervention helped to create an atmosphere which was conducive to the process of building trust and left the negotiators to deal with one another directly. It avoided having the parties compete for favour in the eyes of the mediator, as in the Washington talks. Facilitation forced both sides to confront both psychological and substantive issues and thus resulted in a process which was more conducive to resolution rather than a political settlement.

Finally, the experience in Oslo shows how pre-negotiations can enable ideas on the fringe of the political spectrum to be explored in a low-risk setting and gain legitimacy within mainstream political decision-making. Beilin, Hirschfeld and Abu Ala were all in favour of approaches to peacemaking that were not acceptable within the mainstream of their respective political communities. However, the low-risk exploration of these ideas through pre-negotiations reinforced their faith in the viability of this approach and paved the way for the negotiations to be acceptable within the mainstream political agenda. The negotiations involved a large risk, one Rabin for example, was reluctant to take. Facing an impasse at the Washington talks, he had preferred to pursue negotiations with Syria. Similarly, Arafat faced serious opposition within the ranks of the PLO to the idea negotiating with Israel. It was the success of the pre-negotiation that brought the Israeli–PLO talks on to the political agenda, enabled it to gain legitimacy within the mainstream and become a central foreign policy objective.

What occurred in Oslo between two Israeli academics and representatives of the PLO from January to May 1993 was a complicated interaction which cannot be understood as entirely distinct from the official negotiations which followed. It began as an informal exchange of ideas, evolved into an attempt to find ways of assisting the official negotiations, but essentially ended up serving as a pre-negotiation. Understanding the early stages of Oslo in terms of pre-negotiations helps to shed light on the evolution of that process and its relationship with the official negotiations which followed. Furthermore, the experience brought with it many lessons which are useful for our understanding of how pre-negotiations work in general.

198                                                    FROM WAR TO PEACE?

## NOTES

The author would like to thank Professor Dafna Izraeli for her constant support.

1. United Nations Charter, 'Pacific Settlement of Disputes', Chapter VI, Article 33, Section 1, 1945.
2. Harold Saunders, 'We Need a Larger Theory of Negotiation: The Importance of Pre-Negotiation Phases', *Negotiation Journal*, Vol. 1 (July 1985), p.255.
3. The low cost of information sharing allows moderate views to be expressed on both sides. See Janice Gross-Stein, 'Getting to the Table: The Triggers, Stages, Functions, and Consequences of Pre-Negotiation', *International Journal*, Vol. 44 (Spring 1989), pp.498–9.
4. Ronald J. Fisher, 'Pre-Negotiation Problem-Solving Discussions: Enhancing the Potential for Successful Negotiation', *International Journal*, Vol. 44 (Spring 1989), p.443.
5. The DOP contained a set of mutually agreed-upon principles which proposed a five-year interim period of Palestinian self-rule. Negotiations on the issue of permanent status were to begin no later than the third year, and would take effect at the end of the five-year period.
6. Janice Gross-Stein (ed.), *Getting to the Table: The Process of International Pre-Negotiations*, Baltimore, 1989.
7. Jacob Bercovitch, 'International Negotiations and Conflict Management: The Importance of Pre-Negotiations', *Jerusalem Journal of International Relations*, Vol. 13, No. 1, p.19.
8. Fisher, 'Pre-Negotiation Problem-Solving Discussions', p.445.
9. Jay Rothman, 'Negotiation as Consolidation: Pre-Negotiation in the Israeli–Palestinian Conflict', *Jerusalem Journal of International Relations*, Vol. 13, No. 1 (1991), p.26.
10. Raymond Cohen, *Negotiating Across Cultures: Communication Obstacles in International Diplomacy*, Washington DC, 1991, p.60.
11. Ibid., p.490.
12. Gross-Stein, 'Getting to the Table', p.488.
13. I. William Zartman, 'Pre-Negotiations: Phases and Functions', *International Journal*, Vol. 44 (Spring 1989), p.238.
14. Gross-Stein, 'Getting to the Table', p.487.
15. Bercovitch, 'International Negotiations and Conflict Management', p.18.
16. Zartman,'Pre-Negotiations: Phases and Functions', p.241.
17. Richard N. Haass, 'Ripeness and the Settlement of International Disputes', *Survival*, Vol. 30 (May/June, 1988), p.245–6.
18. Louis Kriesberg, *International Conflict Resolution: The U.S.–USSR and Middle East Cases*, New Haven, 1992, p.144.
19. Haass, 'Ripeness and the Settlement of International Disputes', p.245–6
20. Efraim Karsh, 'Peace Not Love: Toward a Comprehensive Arab–Israeli Settlement', *Washington Quarterly*, Vol. 17 (Spring 1994), p.143.
21. Ibid., p.146.
22. Don Peretz, 'The Impact of the Gulf War on Israeli and Palestinian Political Attitudes', *Journal of Palestine Studies*, Vol. 21, No. 1 (Autumn 1991), p.29.
23. Karsh, 'Peace Not Love', p.51.
24. Michel Jubran and Laura Drake, 'The Islamic Resistance Movement in the West Bank and Gaza Strip', *Middle East Policy*, No. 2 (Winter 1993), p.6.
25. Ziad Abu-Amr, 'Hamas: An Historic and Political Background', *Journal of Palestine Studies*, Vol. 22, No. 4 (Summer 1993), p.17.
26. An estimated 90,000 Palestinian families in the territories had been receiving payments for being relatives of 'martyrs' of the uprising. See David Makovsky, *Making Peace with the PLO: Policy and Politics in the Rabin Government*, Boulder, 1996, p.56.
27. Clyde Mark and Kenneth Katzman, 'Hamas and Palestinian Islamic Jihad: Recent Developments, Sources of Support, and Implications for U.S. Policy', *CRS Report for Congress*, December 12, 1994, p.10.
28. Jone Oliversen, 'The Facilitator', *Statoil*, Vol. 17, No. 1 (March 1995), p.30.
29. Karsh, 'Peace Not Love', p.50.
30. The Palestinians were represented by a joint Palestinian–Jordanian delegation which was not allowed to include members of the Diaspora, the PLO or residents of Jerusalem.

31. Daoud Kuttab, 'Totality of the Palestinian Problem', *Jerusalem Post*, 19 February 1992.
32. Cited in Avi Shlaim, 'Prelude to the Accord: Likud, Labor, and the Palestinians', *Journal of Palestine Studies*, Vol. 23, No. 2 (Winter 1994), p.11.
33. Husseini was a senior PLO leader and was unofficially known as such to all at the time. See Makovsky, *Making Peace with the PLO*, p.13.
34. Karin Aggestam, 'Two-Track Diplomacy: Negotiations Between Israel and the PLO Through Open and Secret Channels', *Davis Paper*, No. 53, Jerusalem, 1996, p.20.
35. Jane Corbin, *Gaza First: The Secret Norway Channel to Peace Between Israel and the PLO*, London, 1994.
36. Ron Pundak, 'Getting to the Table', minutes from conference, 'The Resolution of Intractable Conflicts: the Israeli–Palestinian and South African Experiences', Tel Aviv, March 1995, p.113.
37. The American administration later asked Rabin about the talks. By this point he was aware of their existence; however, he dismissed them as irrelevant and they were quickly forgotten by the US delegation.
38. Amos Elon, 'The Peacemakers', *New Yorker*, 20 December 1993, p.80.
39. Ibid., p.81.
40. See Abbas Muhmoud (Abu Mazen), *Through Secret Channels*, Reading, 1995, p.121. The 'Gaza First' plan was developed by Shimon Peres and was previously rejected by the Palestinians.
41. Makovsky, *Making Peace with the PLO*, p.21.
42. There were constantly secret contacts taking place, none of which (other than Oslo) achieved breakthroughs. See Ron Pundak, 'Outstanding Issues: The Time Factor', in *Prerequisites for Peace in the Middle East: An Israeli–Palestinian Dialogue*, New York, 1994, p.56.
43. Corbin, *Gaza First*, p.60–61.
44. Mohamed Heikal, *Secret Channels: The Inside Story of Arab–Israeli Peace Negotiations*, London, 1996, p.440.
45. Makovsky, *Making Peace with the PLO*, p.38.
46. Corbin, *Gaza First*, pp.72–3.
47. Savir, who was closely tied to Peres was Peres's rather than Rabin's choice.
48. Aggestam, 'Two-Track Diplomacy', p.23.
49. Pundak,'Getting to the Table', p.119.
50. Elon, 'The Peacemakers', p.82.
51. Shlaim, 'Prelude to the Accord', p.14.
52. Hirschfeld, in Abu Mazen, p.127–8.
53. Pundak, 'Towards a New Chapter in the Israeli–Palestinian Negotiations?', *Palestine–Israel Journal of Politics and Economics*, No. 5 (Winter 1995), pp.6–7.
54. Abu Mazen, p.118.
55. Pundak, 'Getting to the Table', p.116.
56. Corbin, 'Gaza First', p.49.
57. Aggestam, 'Two-Track Diplomacy', p.18.
58. Corbin, 'Gaza First', p.61.
59. Elon, 'The Peacemakers', p.84.
60. Oliversen,'The Facilitator', p.30.
61. Elon,'The Peacemakers', p.84.
62. Corbin, 'Gaza First', p.102.
63. Heikal, p.439.
64. Makovsky, *Making Peace with the PLO*, p.52.
65. Ibid., p.51.
66. Edward W. Said, *Peace and its Discontents*, London, 1995, p.3.
67. Heikal, p.462.
68. Said, *Peace and its Discontents*, p.14.
69. Avi Shlaim, 'The Oslo Accord', *Journal of Palestine Studies*, Vol. 23, No. 3 (Spring 1994), p.34.
70. Rashid Khalidi, 'A Palestinian View of the Accord with Israel', *Current History* (February 1994), p.62.
71. Heikal, p.458.
72. Brian W. Tomlin, 'The Stages of Pre-Negotiation: The Decision to Negotiate North American Free Trade', in Gross-Stein, 'Getting to the Table', pp.23–5.

# Unambiguous Ambiguity: The Opacity of the Oslo Peace Process

## NADAV MORAG

The two agreements that make up what is popularly known as the 'Oslo Accords' (including the Declaration of Principles (DOP) signed in September 1993, the Gaza and Jericho Agreement signed in May 1994, and the Interim Agreement signed in September 1995) have been hailed as a 'blueprint for peace' between Israelis and Palestinians. What is particularly striking about these agreements – as well as a number of other bilateral agreements that fall under the general rubric of the Oslo process including the Hebron Agreement of January 1997 – is that while they deal with extremely critical matters for both sides such as peace, security and the right to self-determination, the parties entered into negotiations and made significant concessions to each other without any guarantee (and indeed often without any real conception) as to the nature of the final settlement between the two parties.

The Israeli and Palestinian architects of the Oslo Accords did not provide an outline as to the nature of the final settlement between Israel and the Palestinians because, they claimed, it was impossible to do so in September 1993 since there was very little that the two sides could agree upon at that stage. Both sides felt that they were about to embark on an unprecedented journey which would change not only the Middle East but also their perceptions of each other and of themselves and hence it was impossible to carry out such profound changes within the space of a short period of time and with the signing of one agreement. Oslo was therefore envisaged as a process of change over a defined 'transitional' time-period of five years. This relatively drawn-out process was seen as necessary for two principal reasons. The first was because the positions of both sides appeared to be so far apart on the critical issues (settlements, borders, refugees, Jerusalem, Palestinian statehood, etc) that reaching an agreement on these issues appeared impossible. Thus, by developing a dynamic of gradual change and by building up a co-

Nadav Morag is Lecturer in Political Science at Tel Aviv University.

operative relationship between the Israeli government and security organs on the one hand and the Palestinian Authority governmental and security organs on the other (as envisaged by the DOP), it was thought that the mutual suspicions and ill will that seemed to preclude a comprehensive agreement would be greatly reduced. This, in turn, would enable the two sides to deal with the really difficult issues later in a more conducive atmosphere.

Second, both sides felt that, for domestic political purposes, it would be difficult enough to sell the agreements to their respective constituencies as they stood without also having determined the fate of extremely controversial issues such as Jerusalem, settlements, and the like. With the signing of the DOP, both Israelis and Palestinians were being asked to make extremely significant psychological and perceptual changes and concessions. The two populations were being asked to begin viewing each other as partners rather than continue the 100-year-old view of each other as adversaries. Israeli Jews were being asked to part with the ideal of indefinitely holding on to all of Eretz Israel (with its attendant security and religious significance), while Palestinians were being asked to finally part with the ideal of a greater Palestine encompassing all of the territory of the former British Mandate.

The Palestinian side evidenced a willingness publicly to withdraw claims to areas beyond the Green Line (the Palestine Liberation Organization (PLO) adopted the 'two-state solution' approach at the Palestine National Council (PNC) conference in Algiers in 1988 – although many Palestinians may have interpreted this as part of the PLO's 'step-by-step' strategy of the 1970s of regaining a foothold in Palestine for the purpose of eventually destroying the state of Israel). However, the Israeli side – which was being asked to withdraw physically from territory and which was faced with vociferous opposition from the centre-right and right-wing political spectrum – found it considerably more difficult to speak of a permanent break with the ideal of Eretz Israel and hence preferred to present the DOP as an interim solution and emphasize the fact that Israel, in signing the DOP, was not countersigning a Palestinian Declaration of Independence.

Hence, the opaque nature of the Oslo process, which effectively left all options open for the final settlement, served the needs of the negotiators and their political bosses by enabling the parties to achieve a breakthrough without, at the same time, relinquishing strongly held positions as to the nature of the final settlement. The PLO was able to portray the Accords as a road (from which there was no turning back), that would lead to the creation of a Palestinian state in all of the West Bank, Gaza Strip and East Jerusalem. The Rabin government was able to portray Oslo as a step towards separating Israelis and Palestinians and providing the Palestinians limited autonomy while ensuring overall

Israeli security control over the Territories for the foreseeable future. Both sides could claim victory for their positions since (despite the fact that it was clear that many people, on both sides, would be unhappy with Oslo and view the agreements as conceding far too much to the other side), its supporters could always point to the agreements as temporary and point to Article V(4) of the DOP (which was repeated in the subsequent agreements) that 'the outcome of the permanent status negotiations should not be prejudiced or pre-empted by agreements reached for the interim period'.[1]

The chief drawback – and a very big one at that – to this type of opaque approach to conflict resolution is that in absolving itself of providing any type of legal–contractual precedent with respect to the final settlement, Oslo virtually invited the parties to interpret the agreements reached in a manner that was convenient for them – even if this meant that they would be moving in opposite directions. Hence, Oslo, by its very nature, made it a logical imperative for both sides to work outside the Oslo framework in order to establish new 'facts on the ground' since whatever gains could be reached within the Oslo framework were non-binding with respect to the final settlement. This is rather like a situation in which two parties engaged in a war having signed a ceasefire agreement proceed, in the hours leading up to the predetermined hour at which all hostilities must cease, to bloody each other mercilessly in an effort to capture another hill or strong-point in order to improve their future negotiating position or the defensibility of the ceasefire line which may soon become a border. Indeed, this is precisely what has happened since the signing of the agreements: the Palestinian-initiated clashes with the Israeli army in September 1996; the continued construction of the Dahaniye Airport in the Gaza Strip; Israeli construction at Har Homa in East Jerusalem.

The Wye River Accord, which was touted by the then Prime Minister Benjamin Netanyahu and Foreign Minister Ariel Sharon as an 'improvement' on Oslo since it denied either side the right to carry out unilateral actions of this kind, has failed to deter Israel from allowing the expansion of settlements to adjacent hilltops – Sharon himself called for just such an expansion – or Yasser Arafat from publicly promising to declare Palestinian independence in May 1999 and from demanding that Jerusalem be made the capital of the new state, since Article V of the Wye River Accord calls for both sides to refrain from taking 'any step that will change the status of the West Bank and the Gaza Strip'.[2] Such analysis however, begs the question as to why the Oslo Accords in fact turned out to be so opaque. In order to determine this, we need to look at both the events leading up to the Accords and the nature of the diplomatic process that produced the agreements.

THE ROAD TO OSLO

The first precedent for Oslo was established on 17 September 1978, with the signing of the Camp David Accords in Washington. Egyptian President Anwar Sadat, aware that the Arab world viewed the signing of a separate peace with Israel as an act of treachery and feeling the sting of Egypt's growing isolation in the region, insisted on incorporating guarantees *vis-à-vis* Palestinian self-rule into what was for all intents and purposes a bilateral peace treaty. The fact that Israeli Prime Minister Menachem Begin's interpretation of the clauses that call for 'five-year transitional arrangements for the West Bank and Gaza', as well as 'Israeli military withdrawal', and 'negotiations ... to determine the final status of the West Bank and Gaza'[3] was completely different from the Egyptian interpretation, and yet did not significantly hinder the Egyptian–Israeli rapprochement, proves that these clauses were more of an Egyptian face-saving measure than a significant political demand. However, the principles with respect to Palestinian self-rule set down at Camp David would form the basis for negotiations at Oslo.

The PLO, having rejected the Egyptian–Israeli peace process as inimical to its interests, led the rejectionist camp in denouncing the treaty and condemning Egypt and it continued its execution of the 'military option' by conducting cross-border attacks against Israeli military personnel and civilians from its stronghold in southern Lebanon. The failure of Begin's subsequent attempts to foster the development of an indigenous West Bank and Gaza Palestinian leadership to offset the influence of the PLO and to negotiate with Israel on the Likud principle of 'autonomy for people, not for territory' (which was designed to perpetuate Israeli control over the territories), led him and Defence Minister Sharon to conclude that the only way to develop a more pliable local Palestinian leadership was to destroy the PLO both militarily and politically.[4] This was one of the chief reasons why Israel invaded Lebanon in June 1982 and expelled the PLO from that country.

The PLO, humiliated, militarily destroyed, and finding itself unable to operate from any of the Arab states bordering Israel, limped to Tunis and set about reconstituting itself and building the only viable option it had left: the political/diplomatic one. This apparent realization by the PLO that it could no longer depend upon the support of the Arab world or its own military option led the PLO formally to opt for the 'two-state solution' with its 1988 declaration at Algiers.[5] The outbreak of the *intifada* shortly before this (in December 1987), at once revitalized the Palestinian national movement and presented the PLO with new challenges in the form of a 'home-grown' *intifada* leadership that viewed the PLO as largely irrelevant.

Despite the difficulties involved, the PLO was largely successful in asserting control over the *intifada* and the events of the *intifada* had a profound impact on the Israeli public and leadership convincing many on the Israeli Left that Israel's only option was disengagement from the Territories by way of a political settlement. However, by the early 1990s, the PLO found itself in the midst of one of the worst political and financial crises of its history. Arafat's decision to support Saddam Hussein in the Gulf War led to the halting of financial support from the Gulf states estimated at about $120 million in annual donations. To make matters worse, the confiscation of Palestinian deposits in Gulf banks and the loss of other revenues (including those lost as the result of the expulsion of some 40,000 Palestinian expatriates living and working in the Gulf states) led to an overall loss of revenue between 1991 and 1993 of approximately $10 billion.[6]

This loss of revenue led to the closure of sizeable numbers of PLO-run institutions that provided welfare, educational and social services to the Palestinian population within the Territories as well as in the Palestinian Diaspora. This was particularly worrying for the PLO as the Islamic extremist organizations Hamas and Islamic Jihad were able to provide alternative services for the population thus enhancing their political stature and support in the Territories at the expense of the PLO. In addition, the blow to Palestinian morale as a result of the massive influx of Jews from the former Soviet Union into Israel as well as the deterioration of the *intifada* and growing Israeli military success in capturing *intifada* activists all added to the PLO's increasing weakness.[7]

Somewhat ironically, in view of Israel's previous approach towards the PLO, as well as Yitzhak Rabin's own record, the deterioration in support for Yasser Arafat in the Territories came to be viewed by the newly elected Rabin government as a sign for concern. Rabin's predecessor as Prime Minister, Yitzhak Shamir, had unenthusiastically joined the post-Gulf War American-mediated Madrid Middle East peace conference which did not allow the PLO to participate directly in the negotiations (and thus required no Israeli recognition of the PLO) and forced the Palestinians to appear as part of a joint Palestinian–Jordanian negotiating team.

Upon assuming office, Rabin continued to shun the PLO and offer the Palestinians largely the same kind of autonomy that Shamir had offered them at Madrid. Rabin preferred to work with local Palestinian leaders that he viewed as much more moderate and pragmatic and tried to marginalize the far less palatable (from the Israeli point of view) Arafat.[8] The Madrid talks, which had by now been transferred to Washington, foundered, however, primarily because they were based on the principle of moving directly towards a final settlement between Israel and the Palestinians at a time when Israel was still unwilling to envisage the creation of a Palestinian state in the Territories. In the meantime, Rabin's response to increasing Hamas terrorist attacks, including arrests and deportations of Hamas activists to Lebanon, was strengthening the Islamists at the expense of the PLO.

Rabin's Foreign Minister, Shimon Peres, and Peres' deputy, Yossi Beilin, came to the conclusion that it would be necessary formally to recognize the PLO and make every effort to strengthen it lest Israel be faced with what they felt would be a far more implacable enemy, the Islamic extremists. This was the chief reason that Beilin gave his support to the opening of back-channel negotiations between Israeli and PLO representatives in and around the Norwegian capital that began in January 1993.

OSLO, TABA, CAIRO AND WASHINGTON

The development of the Oslo back-channel proved to be extremely useful to both sides. For the PLO, the negotiations at Oslo enabled them finally to negotiate face-to-face with (initially unofficial, but later official) representatives of the state of Israel. The success of the Oslo talks would mean that Israel would be forced to recognize the PLO as the representative of the Palestinians thus enabling it to position itself in such a way that it could take the credit for Palestinian gains and Israeli withdrawals at the expense of the Hamas who could only offer the Palestinians in the Territories a continuation of the armed struggle.

Additionally, Oslo offered the PLO the chance to re-establish a presence in Palestine (and indeed control over land) for the first time since 1967. For the Israeli government, Oslo had the benefit of allowing Israel to conduct negotiations in secret with the PLO that had the advantage, in the initial stages, of deniability (Yair Hirschfeld and Ron Pundak were academics, not Israeli government functionaries).

Theorists of conflict resolution emphasize the usefulness of what they commonly refer to as 'track-two diplomacy', especially in disputes where there is a strong sense of victimhood on both sides and in which the freedom of action of political leaders is constrained by emotional attitudes among their constituencies and by a high degree of fear and loathing among the public towards the adversary.[9] Public opinion was clearly a problem for Israel in entering into open negotiations with the PLO and the secret Oslo channel, unlike the public Washington talks, allowed the building of confidence between negotiators and the kind of isolated and intensive negotiations leading to a breakthrough such as occurred at Camp David.[10]

However, at Camp David, both sides were able to agree upon not only the basic nature of their future relationship but also the details of that relationship. In fairness, it must be added that perhaps it was easier to do so at Camp David because it was a question of relations between two existing sovereign states that did not represent a structural threat to each other – as is the case when the existence of one state seems to preclude the existence of the other (something which most Israelis and Palestinians have held to be true in the past).

At Oslo, the Israeli side was unable and unwilling to commit to even the vaguest allusion as to the nature of the final settlement with the Palestinians. This was not only because of the Rabin government's fears of a public opinion backlash if it became known that Oslo was to lead to the creation of a Palestinian state, but also because the government itself was divided. One group within the government (headed by Rabin) wanted to drag out negotiations with the PLO thus ensuring Israeli control over the Territories and a *status quo* situation for as long as possible while the other (headed by Peres) felt that withdrawal from most of the Territories and the creation of a Palestinian state beside Israel was inevitable and that the five-year transitional period should be used to develop a completely new type of relationship with the Palestinians.[11]

The PLO had much to gain from Oslo (Israeli recognition and withdrawal from territory) and little to lose since, for reasons noted above, its position was deteriorating rapidly. The Israeli government, on the other hand, was taking a serious political risk in moving from the stalled Washington formula to Oslo since it entailed recognition of the PLO and, by extension, recognition of the Palestinian right to self-determination. As long as Israel shunned the PLO, it could allow itself to deny the very existence of a Palestinian people and deal with the inhabitants of the Territories on a local, case-by-case basis – perhaps recognizing certain individual rights, but not imbuing the Palestinians with collective rights as a nation. The language used by Israelis, intent on denying Palestinian nationhood, was even tailored to this with the Palestinians being referred to only as *Mekomi'im* (locals) or *Aravim* (Arabs) – the first term atomizing the national group into groups of people inhabiting a particular area and the second blending the group into an amorphous mass of people who share a particular language and some cultural characteristics – but never as *Falestinim* (Palestinians).

In recognizing the PLO, Israel would have to come face to face with the reality of a Palestinian nation whose demands for a state of their own were not unlike those of the early Zionists. In entering Oslo, Israel entered into a process of territorial partition and, in so doing, albeit in changed circumstances and with altered frontiers, returned to 1947 and the UN partition plan for Palestine that envisaged the creation of a Palestinian state alongside Israel.

The great departure that Oslo represented from previous Palestinian autonomy plans was that it envisaged a transitional autonomy period that provided the Palestinians not only with control of their day-to-day lives with respect to economic, social, educational and governmental affairs, together with other issues, but it also gave Palestinians *control over territory*. The DOP and the May 1994 Agreement on the Gaza Strip and Jericho Area are partition agreements that provide for the establishment of a different, and in many ways sovereign, political and security regime in Gaza and Jericho. This process was then continued with the Interim Agreement, to include the remaining Palestinian cities on the West Bank (except Hebron, the bulk of which was transferred to Palestinian control by the Netanyahu government in January 1997).

Those Israelis who criticized these agreements because they felt that Oslo would result in a repartitioning of the land of Israel and a setting up of the foundations of a Palestinian state were reading the situation correctly (although whether this was necessarily bad for Israel was, of course, a different question). Naturally, Rabin must have understood that once he had affixed his signature to the DOP, he had begun a process of repartitioning historic Palestine. He may have felt, however, that a Jordanian–Palestinian confederation would be the end result and thus he would not be departing radically from the legacy of his former Labour colleague, Yigal Allon. Nevertheless, Israel was entering into uncharted waters in which the PLO had far less to lose than the Rabin government.

Since Israel was the party in the strongest position when the negotiations began, Rabin could dictate the terms in such a way so as to attempt to minimize the political risks and hence the process of interim stages was viewed as attractive by the Israeli side, as Shimon Peres later remarked, 'While the proposal lacks the clarity of a map, it provides the commitment of a calendar'.[12] When the time came to determine where Israel would withdraw from first, the Gaza Strip – with its poverty, refugee camps and population density of 2,000 people per square kilometre – was the obvious choice being almost universally viewed in Israel as a burden whose continued control provided questionable security benefits, adjoining as it does a demilitarized Sinai.

When the Palestinian side demanded that they also receive some territory on the West Bank, so that Israel might not be tempted to make Arafat merely 'Sheriff of Gaza', the Israeli side agreed that the Palestinians would also be given control of Jericho. Jericho was viewed as the best candidate for transfer to Palestinian control since there were few Israeli settlements nearby and it was close to Jordan – with which Israel hoped the Palestinian Authority (PA) would be closely linked. Additionally, Israel hoped that the infant PA would set up its administrative headquarters in Jericho so that pressure could be taken off nearby Jerusalem as a potential Palestinian capital.[13] As things turned out, Arafat did not provide them with this satisfaction, choosing instead to set up his headquarters in Gaza City.

While both sides agreed to postpone dealing with the most contentious issues until the final status talks, the initial agreements also dealt with issues, and set precedents, that have very profound repercussions for the final settlement. While Israel conceded in all the agreements that the basis for a settlement with the Palestinians was UN Security Council Resolution 242, which calls for withdrawal from territories occupied in 1967, it did not renounce any Israeli claim to controlling part or all of the territories and did not undertake to promise any further withdrawals.[14]

These essentially contradictory positions allowed Israel to accede to Palestinian demands that Oslo create the conditions for the building of a Palestinian state in most of the West Bank and Gaza Strip (as well as East Jerusalem) while at the same time, keep its options open for the final settlement and not openly part with the concept of a united Eretz Israel or at least overall Israeli security control over the territories. Hence, the agreements gave Israel exclusive control over external defence and foreign relations of the PA areas as well as providing Israelis with, in most cases, 'extraterritorial' rights in PA areas.[15] In this way, the Rabin government was able to portray the Oslo Accords in terms of 'redeployment', 'interim phases', and 'Palestinian self-rule', rather than in terms of permanent Israeli withdrawals and the creation of an independent Palestinian state.

The Oslo Accords needed to be ambiguous, not only because the parties were not yet ready to deal with the most serious issues at stake, but also because the Israeli side was not prepared to concede the fact that the Oslo process would eventually lead to a Palestinian state – just as the Palestinian side was also reluctant to relinquish its ideological commitment and dream of regaining control of *all* of historic Palestine. The political price that the government and Israeli society would have to pay in terms of bitter divisiveness (and no one could have known then that this would cost the country its Prime Minister as well) was deemed too high to give the government the luxury of making a clean break with the past and making clear statements about where the process was leading to.

Ambiguity was also useful for the PLO because it could claim that its concessions to Israel were temporary, while at the same time establishing the political, military, economic and administrative infrastructure of the future Palestinian state. However, the PLO was much clearer as to what it viewed the only possible logical outcome of the process to be – the creation of an independent Palestine. While the opaque nature of the Oslo process unquestionably served very important domestic political goals on both sides, it ensured that both sides would enjoy a high degree of freedom in interpreting the agreement in different ways.

Thus, instead of Oslo providing the framework and setting the tone for future bilateral relations, it came to be pulled along by external developments to such an extent that even the seemingly most trivial events (such as a delay in Israeli air traffic control's approval for Arafat's helicopter to fly from Gaza to the West Bank) could jeopardize the peace process. However, the Accords did not deal at all with the most serious bones of contention between Israel and the Palestinians. It is to two of these that we must now turn.

## QUESTIONS LEFT UNANSWERED

The Oslo Accords are silent with respect to some of the most critical issues that divide Israelis and Palestinians. Once again, there was a conscious decision to defer these issues to the final status talks that were to commence, according to the DOP, no later than the third year of the interim period. Yet, since Oslo was establishing new 'facts on the ground' with respect to matters within its scope – nearly all of which would have an effect on final status issues – it was clear that these matters would not simply wait for resolution in the final status talks; rather, both sides would try to act to improve their negotiating position *vis-à-vis* these issues before final settlement talks were to commence. By 1998 there had not been any substantive progress towards sketching the outlines of a final settlement with respect to these problems. These issues have been dealt with in detail elsewhere so we will only briefly look at two of the most significant issues for the final settlement that have not been addressed by the Oslo agreements: demographics (and the related question of identity) and borders (and the related question of sovereignty).

### Demographics

The population within the original borders of the Palestine Mandate (Israel, Jordan and the territories) today numbers close to 12 million. Of this, some 7.5 million are Arab (mostly Palestinian) and some 4.5 million are Jews. Focusing on western Palestine (Israel and the territories), the ratio is approximately 4.5 million Jews to 3.2 million Arabs (again, mostly Palestinians). Jews and Palestinian Arabs in western Palestine live in intertwined communities – whether in 'mixed' cities such as Jerusalem, Hebron, Haifa, Acre, Nazareth, Lod and Ramle or in adjacent communities throughout the Galilee, the Wadi Ara region, the Little Triangle and parts of the West Bank and Gaza Strip.

In addition, a sizeable population of Palestinian Arabs lives in Jordan making up at least half of the Jordanian population (estimates range between 50 and 80 per cent). Hence the demographic issue is a triangular one involving Israel, the territories and Jordan (namely, all of the original Palestine Mandate). Essentially, three national groups live in this area: Jews, Palestinian Arabs and what we may term Trans-Jordanians (that is to say those citizens of Jordan of Bedouin or other stock who do not identify themselves as Palestinians but do identify with the Jordanian state in national – and not just civil – terms). While there are no Jews in Jordan and no Trans-Jordanians in Israel or the territories, there are Jews in the territories and Palestinians in Israel, the territories and Jordan.

The logic of partition-based constructs is to divide heterogeneous political units – that is, plural societies – into smaller more homogeneous ones in order to achieve self-determination, stability and legitimacy.[16] Hence, partition as a policy rests on demographic realities and perceptions of national existence. The separation of Palestinian populations in eastern and western Palestine did not reflect demographic realities, quite the contrary, but they did reflect British interests in partitioning Palestine and creating a new political entity – the Kingdom of Transjordan. The borders of the West Bank and Gaza Strip were decided largely by war and were not drawn to reflect demographic realities (unlike those of the 1937 Royal Commission under Lord Peel or the 1947 United Nations plan which at least attempted to do so with regard to western Palestine).

Hence, the existing borders of Israel, Jordan and the territories do not make allowance for demographic realities. Thus, Palestinians find themselves divided between three political units – with at least two million Palestinians living in Jordan, and some 2.5 million living in the West Bank and Gaza Strip and close to one million living in Israel – and these numbers do not to include the sizable Palestinian Diaspora in the Middle East and elsewhere. Any partition-based construct that will be based on existing borders (and Oslo is such a construct) will create a situation in which the majority of Palestinians living within the borders of the original British Mandate will not be residents of the Palestinian state (even if that state includes the *entire* West Bank and Gaza Strip as well as East Jerusalem).

This means that partition – regardless of economic and labour ties will not mean that Israel will no longer control Palestinian populations or that Israel will become more homogeneous as a virtually exclusively Jewish state. Seventeen per cent of the Israeli population (that is, close to one in five Israelis) will still be Palestinian Arabs. Much of the Palestinian population of Israel is located in areas where they form a majority or near majority. While the Sea of Galilee region and the Jezreel and Beit Shean valleys in the north; the coastal strip (stretching from Haifa to Ashkelon) and the Jerusalem corridor in the centre of the country; and the Negev and Arava in the south are mainly Jewish, much of the Galilee, Wadi Ara, Little Triangle and East Jerusalem are Arab. The Wadi Ara, Little Triangle and East Jerusalem areas are also geographically contiguous to the West Bank (a fact that is of no small significance in terms of partition).

The location of the Jewish population in Israel is also significant in the context of partition because the hills of the West Bank hold a commanding position over Israel's coastal strip to the west and the Jerusalem corridor (south of Samaria and north of Judea). The coastal strip contains 61.3 per cent of the Israeli population (overwhelmingly Jewish) and much of Israel's industry and the Jerusalem corridor (including West Jerusalem and the Jewish neighbourhoods of East Jerusalem) contains 12 per cent of the country's population. Taken together, nearly three-quarters of Israel's population live in areas geographically contiguous to the West Bank (or the Gaza Strip in the case of the southern edge of the coastal strip). This demographic reality complicates matters because it means that the bulk of Israel's population lives practically a *stone's throw* from the territories and hence is highly vulnerable to military or terrorist actions originating in the adjacent hills of the West Bank.

A further complication arises from the fact that some 140,000 Israelis have chosen to make the West Bank their home. This means that some 17 per cent of the West Bank population is Israeli (in the Gaza Strip, the Israeli population of 5,000 comprises only 0.6 per cent of the population – although this small minority controls a highly disproportionate share of the land in the Strip). Hence, partition along existing lines will also mean that these Israelis must either vacate their homes or live under Palestinian rule – neither of which is acceptable to them and to the majority of the Israeli public (at least with respect to *most* of the settlements).

The geographic distribution of the settlements also makes partition difficult since the creation of a geographically contiguous Palestinian state on the West Bank would result in some of the settlements being included in the territory of the Palestinian state. The continued existence of the settlements, from the Palestinian perspective, represents a tangible day-to-day symbol of Israel's continuing domination of their lives – the existence of the Palestinian Authority notwithstanding. For the settlers, the need to coexist with the PA and, at times, pass through PA-controlled areas, makes the tenuousness of their position painfully clear and thus creates hostility towards the PA on their part. Since the settlers came to the West Bank for either Zionist or economic motives and hence have no desire to be residents of a Palestinian state, they know that the drawing of borders will determine their fate and hence can be expected to pressure the Israeli government into insisting on drawing the borders – in the event that it appears that the creation of a Palestinian state is inevitable – in such a way that most of the settlements will be annexed to Israel.

The existence of Israeli settlements in the West Bank and the Gaza Strip represents a serious problem in terms of final status negotiations.

Just as the Jewish population in the territories represents a problem in terms of partition, so does the Palestinian Arab population in Israel. As noted above, the ceasefire lines of 1949 (namely the Green Line separating the West Bank from Israel and the Gaza Strip from Israel) created borders that were the result of war. Hence, while the greatest concentrations of Palestinians (especially as a result of the movement of refugee populations) in western Palestine were located in the West Bank and the Gaza Strip, Palestinian Arab populations also remained within the state of Israel. Eventually, through the return of some refugees to their homes in Israel and through natural increase, the Palestinian Arab population in Israel (generally referred to as Israeli Arabs) has, as noted before, come to number close to a million. Most of these individuals enjoy full Israeli citizenship (unlike their Palestinian counterparts in the territories) and formal equality before the law. However, since the state of Israel's *raison d'être* is that it is a *Jewish* state, this sizeable minority finds itself living in a state that was specifically designed for Jews rather than for all citizens of the state in a proportional manner.

It should be emphasized here that although the State of Israel has been in existence for half a century, there has been no development – or even a serious attempt to develop – an Israeli *national* identity. This is in sharp contrast with other states in the Middle East, Asia and Africa which received their independence after the Second World War or during the 1950s and 1960s and at least attempted (although in many cases unsuccessfully) to create a national identity to unite their various ethnic–tribal groups in order to ensure greater stability and the continued existence of the new-born state.

In the case of Israel, it was perceived as totally superfluous, and in fact contrary to the principles of Zionism, to attempt to create an Israeli national identity since the state was being created for an already established national group (at least in the eyes of Zionists): the Jewish people. Therefore, while not all Jews are currently Israelis, Israel's *Law of Return* ensures that they are all at least *potential* Israelis. The Palestinian Arab population in Israel, on the other hand, was granted citizenship by virtue of the fact that they *reside* within the borders of the state of Israel (meaning again, the pre-1967 borders) rather than by virtue of the fact that the state was created to express their national aspirations. Hence, their link to the state of Israel is not an *emotional* one – like their Jewish co-citizens – but rather an *operational* one (the state provides them with public goods and enables them – to varying extents – to pursue their personal interests).

One could argue that Israelis – Jews and Arabs – have over time developed elements of a common mentality which differentiates them from Jews or Palestinian Arabs outside of pre-1967 Israeli borders. However, sharing elements of a common mentality is still a long way from sharing common national bonds, especially when both groups have strong bonds with their non-Israeli compatriots. One should also remember that Palestinian Arab citizens of Israel have, especially since 1967, been undergoing a national awakening as they became increasingly exposed to Palestinian nationalism.

With what appears to be the inevitability of the creation of a Palestinian state in the not too distant future, it would be hard to imagine that Israel's Arabs would now choose to gravitate more in the direction of their fellow Jewish citizens in creating some sort of common national identity (which Israeli Jews are not interested in creating anyway) when they can find fulfilment in a Palestinian national identity, even if they themselves do not reside within the borders of the Palestinian state. While it appears that few Israeli Arabs would be interested in replacing the greater freedom and standard of living that most enjoy in Israel in favour of living under the control of the sometimes heavy-handed PA, one cannot rule out the possibility that – for whatever reasons – Israeli Arabs may someday want to live under Palestinian rule. Such aspirations could prove a serious threat to Israel's geographic contiguity and indeed its existence in the future.

All of this presents a serious dilemma for Israel and for the Palestinians. Israel cannot hope to achieve separation between Jews and Palestinians (even if this were feasible from an economic point of view) because – regardless of how one draws the partition lines (even if Israel is prepared to relinquish certain areas with a large Israeli Arab population to the Palestinian state in exchange for territorial concessions from the other side) – one cannot achieve total separation. The Jewish and Palestinian Arab populations are far too geographically intertwined to achieve a clean separation. While physical separation was touted by the Labour government as one of the chief benefits of the agreements, Oslo is emphatically incapable of achieving this (unless both parties are prepared to agree to an exchange of populations).

Clearly, the idea of physically separating Jews and Palestinian Arabs in western Palestine, although still useful as a political slogan in Israel, is a practical impossibility. Hence, Oslo, despite the Rabin government's promises, is based not so much on a *physical* and *demographic* partition as a *political* one. That is to say that both sides will theoretically be able to realize their political aspirations in the form of sovereign states (albeit with different degrees of sovereignty) but it will not result in a complete physical separation between the two populations.

Israel would like to incorporate as many of the Israeli settlers living in the territories and their settlements into the state of Israel. Nearly all Israeli partition schemes stretching back to the Allon plan of the 1970s, call for Israeli annexation of many if not most of the Israeli settlements on the West Bank. Most of the settlements are located in areas not far from the Green Line, some in areas of relatively sparse Palestinian population and others with significant pockets of Palestinian population. Any large-scale dismantling of settlements would be likely to cause civil strife within Israel as the relatively less traumatic experience of the dismantling of the Sinai settlement of Yamit suggests.

Therefore, from the Israeli point of view, a final status accord that would call for the dismantling of more than a few settlements is unimaginable. The major question for many Israelis, and certainly for the settlers themselves, is whether the settlers will be living in Israel or in Palestine. In fact, there are three conceivable possibilities in terms of the status of the settlers and the settlements. First, most of the settlements could be annexed to Israel – something which the majority of Israelis of all political stripes prefer – and then the settlers would be Israeli citizens living in Israel.

A second possibility is that the settlers retain their status as Israeli citizens but physically reside in the Palestinian state perhaps with some extraterritorial rights (such as not being subject to Palestinian law, security forces, etc) – Oslo, as noted above, already sets the precedent for this (albeit with Israel and not the Palestinians responsible for the security of the settlers). This possibility is almost universally rejected by the settler community, however, because they do not trust the Palestinian authorities and do not believe that such an arrangement could work once the Israeli army is withdrawn from the settlements. The final possibility is that the settlers become citizens of the Palestinian state and therefore become a Jewish minority in Palestine just as there is a Palestinian minority in Israel. This, of course, is totally unacceptable to the Israeli side because it represents a fundamental contradiction of the principle of Zionism as they see it – that Jews came to Zion in order to live in a Jewish state and not as a minority in an Arab state.

*Borders*

Determining the location and nature of the future borders between Israel and the Palestinian state is in many ways the catch-all of the negotiations since it will involve taking into consideration most of the factors that must be dealt with for the final settlement. As noted, the Oslo agreements are based on territorial partition. However, in keeping with Oslo's opaque and phased nature, the agreements did not undertake to determine the exact nature and location of the lines of partition, leaving this for future negotiations. The Oslo agreements created only temporary lines of partition around the Palestinian cities and much of the Gaza Strip while it was understood by both sides that these lines were strictly interim ones. Palestinian fears that the Netanyahu government – which came to power in the summer of 1996 – would change the official Israeli position and come to view these interim lines as more or less permanent (thus leaving the Palestinians with scattered enclaves under their control and no possible basis for the creation of a viable state) may have largely been responsible for the violent clashes with Israeli security forces initiated by the Palestinians in September 1996.

Those clashes and the subsequent international pressure brought to bear on Israel ultimately led to the abandonment of any hopes on the part of some members of the Netanyahu government that the interim arrangement could be transformed into a permanent one and led to the conclusion of the Hebron Accords (which include Israeli commitments to continue the redeployment – that is, partition – process).

From the Israeli point of view, three issues stand out as being crucial *vis-à-vis* the negotiations on border lines: security, resources and settlements. Suffice to say here that Israel will want to be able to annex as much strategic territory and territory with sizeable Israeli populations on the West Bank as possible so as to ensure that Israel will be able to enjoy the added strategic depth that the West Bank provides, have control over some of the land above the mountain aquifer and not have to dismantle most of the existing Israeli settlements. One other point worth mentioning is that Israel would like to retain external control over the borders of those areas in the West Bank and Gaza that will eventually come to make up the Palestinian state. Control of the Egypt–Gaza and Jordan–West Bank borders has been a high priority for Israel. This is chiefly because of the danger that extremist elements might try to enter the territories or smuggle in contraband thus increasing the threat of terrorism. To a lesser extent, economics may play a role because once goods are smuggled into the territories, it becomes more difficult to prevent them from entering Israel.

Control of one's borders, including the right to decide who or what may enter and exit them, is an important facet of sovereignty. Yet this aspect of sovereignty, like many others, will almost certainly be limited with respect to the Palestinians in the final status phase. Under the Oslo Accords, this problem was dealt with operationally without having to tackle the repercussions for sovereignty that this problems entails. Since the goal of the first two stages of the Oslo process was not the establishment of a sovereign Palestinian state, but rather an interim arrangement of autonomy for the Palestinians, this issue could be addressed without prejudice in the final settlement, according to the Israeli interpretation of the Accords, and thus enable the Palestinians to accept ultimate Israeli control over their external borders. Oslo I (the Gaza–Jericho Agreement) stipulated that all the areas under Palestinian control would be regarded as within an Israeli security 'envelope' and thus Israel would 'maintain security control and supervision over the entry of persons, vehicles and weapons at all points of entry'.[17]

Palestinian demands for some semblance of sovereignty over border crossings led to the creation of a dual-entry supervision arrangement set down in the Cairo Agreement of February 1994. This arrangement provides for border terminals with two wings: the first serves Palestinians living in the autonomous areas and visitors to these areas as well as Palestinian residents of other parts of the territories who wish to enter the autonomous areas, and the second serves Israelis and others whose destination is Israel or areas under Israel's control in the territories. Israel has overall control of the terminals and inspection rights (including the right to deny entry into the autonomous areas) with respect to those entering the Palestinian wing.[18]

While the role of Israeli security personnel with respect to those entering the Palestinian wing is supposed to be as unimposing as possible (Israelis behind tinted glass or two-way mirrors) and while the Palestinians enjoy the symbolic trappings of sovereignty such as a raised Palestinian flag at the terminal and armed uniformed Palestinian police officers, the arrangement still gives Israel overall control over entrance and exit from the territory of the PA. The solution to the problem of border crossings set down by the Cairo Agreement offers an example of creative problem-solving in which the craving for sovereignty and its symbols on the part of the Palestinians is recognized while, at the same time, Israel's need for security is addressed.

A different, but related problem, has to do with Israeli fears that the provision to the Palestinians of unlimited seaport and airport rights can also present a security threat to Israel. Under the provisions of the Oslo Accords, Israel has complete control of the airspace above the autonomous areas and control of waters off the coast of the Gaza Strip. While the Palestinian police have a naval arm, they are confined to coastal patrol duties within what is referred to in the Oslo II Accords as 'Zone L' (up to a distance of six nautical miles from the coast with the Israeli navy being responsible for overall naval security, including the areas between Egyptian territorial waters and PA territorial waters that are patrolled exclusively by the Israeli navy).[19]

The Palestinians, to date, operate two rotary-wing aircraft which must obtain clearance from Israeli aviation authorities in order to fly from PA enclave to PA enclave. In terms of security, the Israeli air force has total control of the skies above PA areas. This situation, in which Israel controls the sea and skies adjacent to or over Palestinian areas, is not likely to change under the terms of the final settlement. Air power is particularly important in terms of the Middle Eastern battlefield and it is not likely that Israel will allow the Palestinians to build an air force or restrict its own ability to fly over the territories for training, reconnaissance and defence purposes.

The Palestinians have, however, demanded the right to build sea- and airports to serve their population. The existence of such facilities is psychologically important for the Palestinians because sovereignty appears to be much more real when one can enter the territories directly by sea or air rather than via Israeli ports such as Ashdod and Israel's international airport near Tel Aviv. The creation of a port at Gaza and an airport at Dahaniye have been discussed but not resolved.

In the meantime, the Palestinians have completed their international airport which will be able to accommodate large passenger jet aircraft. Despite Israeli protests, the Palestinians have gone ahead with construction of the airport, although it is obvious that the airport will not be able to operate without clearance from Israel. The principal problem here is that Israel would want to apply the same arrangements existing at border crossings to sea- and airports. This can be problematic when one considers that, for example, if a port is completed on the Gaza City seashore, it would mean allowing Israel to return to Gaza in terms of allowing the presence of Israelis security personnel at the port. The same problem exists with respect to the airport, which is located entirely within territory under civil and security control of the PA (Area A under the Interim Agreement).

The Palestinians are understandably interested in maximizing the territorial scope of their future state and hence consider the Green Line – aside from some minor border modifications – to be their future border. The Palestinians make the point that they would require the whole of the West Bank and Gaza Strip in order to create a viable state with room to settle refugees and build industries. Any reduction in the territorial scope of their state, they argue, will diminish its viability and therefore be unacceptable to them. This is especially so in view of the fact that the Palestinians would already be severely constrained by the absence of a direct link between the West Bank and the Gaza Strip.[20]

Significantly, the Palestinians have not automatically rejected proposals such as the Beilin–Abu Mazen plan, which calls for Israeli annexation of some parts of the West Bank in exchange for Israeli transfer of lands in Israel to the future Palestinian state. Along with the importance of obtaining as much land as possible for the Palestinian state, the Palestinians want full control over their external borders as befitting a sovereign state – something which Israel is not likely to approve.

There are several options available in terms of setting the location of the border between Israel and the Palestinian state that lie within a spectrum of options in which, at one pole, represents a bare minimum of Palestinian territorial control (half or less of the West Bank with Israel controlling the Jordan Valley, Jerusalem region, western Samaria and Judean Desert), and at the other, represents a Palestinian state controlling nearly all of the territory of the West Bank and Gaza Strip.

The smaller (physically) the Palestinian state, the more advantageous for Israel, allowing it to safeguard its most important demographic, resource and security interests while a maximalist Palestinian state in the territories would be perceived by the Palestinians as the bare minimum that would be acceptable.

Both sides will most likely eventually have to compromise on this issue. The two parties can compromise either on a territorial or functional level. That is to say that Israel can retain control over some one-quarter to one-third of the territory of the West Bank with the Palestinians getting control of the rest or the Palestinians can be given control over virtually all of the West Bank with Israel obtaining extraterritorial rights for settlements and the Israeli army (so that settlements could be under Israeli authority with settlers guaranteed freedom of movement between the settlements and Israel and the army could be allowed to maintain bases and freely move in troops to the Jordan Valley in order to maintain external security).

The advantage of the second option is that it would allow Palestinians to feel that they have enough territory for a viable state and did not have to make any additional territorial concessions to Israel (since they feel that they have already made one major territorial concession – relinquishing their claim to the rest of Palestine) while at the same time it would allow Israel largely to maintain the demographic and security *status quo*. This arrangement depends on Palestinian goodwill and willingness to abide by the agreements over the long term.

Clearly then, the issues relating to demographics and borders, as well as a host of other matters such as Palestinian refugees, the status of Jerusalem, economic relations, water rights and security arrangements, will largely determine the nature of the future relationship between the two states and the stability of the peace between them. Oslo is largely silent with respect to these critical matters.

## OSLO WITH THE BENEFIT OF HINDSIGHT

Since the initial establishment of the Palestinian Authority in Gaza and Jericho, the Israeli–Palestinian peace process has proved to be far more problematic than the negotiators at Oslo imagined. The opacity of the agreements, which were viewed by some as their genius, because of the flexibility that they gave the peace process, have turned out to be their greatest shortcoming. Many of the principals, both Israeli and Palestinian, involved in working out the Accords have since modified, if not reneged on, their support for Oslo's opaque and phased structure and have, like Yossi Beilin, called for moving forward immediately to final status negotiations.

Not only has the focus of efforts on both the Israeli and Palestinian sides been on effecting changes outside the Oslo process – and often with the aim of undermining it – but Oslo did not even provide the vaguest framework as to the nature of a final settlement between the two sides. Since they did not do so, and since the changes that they did effect were still technically non-binding, the Oslo Accords were unable to force the parties to accept a mutual agenda for the future.

The chief reason for this was the hesitancy on the part of the Israeli government to effect such radical changes in a short space of time. However, in view of the severe criticism that the Rabin government had to endure from its Israeli critics as a result of the signing of the DOP and the ensuing agreements, one might think that going a few steps further (such as agreeing to the creation of a Palestinian state and gaining Palestinian concessions on borders, etc in exchange) might not have significantly changed the already high decibel level in the Knesset when the agreement was first announced.

After all, the Israeli Right immediately saw in the DOP the foundations of a Palestinian state and the Labour government expended much political capital in the negotiations with the Palestinians (in terms of making the agreements as opaque as possible) and then in attempting to win over public opinion by trying to portray the agreement as specifically not setting the foundations for such a state. Sketching the future outlines of the process would have established important – and binding – precedents that could have served to guide the process through its intermittent stages to a final settlement rather than leaving the field open to unilateral moves on the part of each side.

Finally, when looking at the 100-year-old conflict between Jews and Palestinian Arabs in Palestine, we must remember that certain things will remain unresolved, no matter how perfect the peace process itself appears to be. One such problem, as noted above, is that of the future identity of the Israeli population. The establishment of a Palestinian state sometime in the future will not result in a separation between Arab and Jew in the land between the Mediterranean and the Jordan River. The creation of a Palestinian state will not solve the identity problems of the majority of the world's Palestinians – who will find themselves outside the borders of this new state. Similarly, the creation of a Palestinian state will not, despite what the Israeli peace camp suggests, solve Israel's demographic problems in the long term because it will not guarantee that Israel will remain overwhelmingly Jewish forever. This may lead one to the conclusion that perhaps Israeli Jews and Palestinian Arabs should have tried to develop a common Israeli identity and live jointly in the same state. But of course, it is a little late in the day for this type of solution.

Hence, since Oslo has already created new physical realities, it would appear that the only realistic alternative would be to pursue Oslo to its logical conclusion in creating a Palestinian state in much of the West Bank and Gaza Strip with some type of link to East Jerusalem. However, in view of the fact that Israeli–Palestinian security co-operation has yet to prove itself and since there is currently a distinct lack of goodwill on both sides, some elements of the interim arrangements (such as Israeli security control over external borders and an Israeli military presence in the territories) must be maintained for the near future. Paradoxically, the shortcomings of Oslo – the chief one being its drawn-out nature – forces the parties to perpetuate those shortcomings because as time goes on, it becomes more difficult, rather than easier, to build a relationship of trust and co-operation between Israelis and Palestinians.

## NOTES

1. 'Declaration of Principles on Interim Self-Government Arrangements', 13 September 1993.
2. 'The Wye Memorandum', 23 October 1998.
3. 'The Camp David Accords: The Framework for Peace in the Middle East', 17 September 1978.
4. See Mark Tessler, 'The Camp David Accords and the Palestinian Problem', in Ann Mosely Lesch and Mark Tessler (eds), *Israel, Egypt, and the Palestinians: From Camp David to Intifada*, Bloomington, 1989, p.18.
5. Palestine National Council, 'Political Communiqué', Algiers, 15 November 1988.
6. Graham Usher, *Palestine in Crisis: The Struggle for Peace and Political Independence after Oslo*, London, 1995, pp.1–2.
7. Usher, *Palestine in Crisis*, pp.2–5.
8. Avi Shlaim, 'The Oslo Accord', *Journal of Palestine Studies*, Vol. XXIII, No. 3 (Spring 1994), p.28.
9. Joseph V. Montville, 'Transnationalism and the Role of Track-Two Diplomacy', in W. Scott Thompson and Kenneth M. Jensen (eds), *Approaches to Peace: An Intellectual Map*, Washington, DC, 1992, p.262.
10. Gabriel Ben-Dor and David B. Dewitt, 'Confidence Building Measures in the Middle East' in Gabriel Ben-Dor and David B. Dewitt (eds), *Confidence Building Measures in the Middle East*, Boulder, 1994, p.13.
11. Avi Shlaim, 'Israeli Politics and Middle East Peacemaking', *Journal of Palestine Studies*, Vol. XXIV, No. 4 (Summer 1995), p.25.
12. Quoted in Avi Shlaim, 'Prelude to the Accord: Likud, Labour and the Palestinians', *Journal of Palestine Studies*, Vol. XXIII, No. 4 (Winter 1994), p.14.
13. Shimon Peres, *The New Middle East*, New York, 1993, p.23.
14. 'The Oslo Agreement: Interview with Haydar Abd al-Shafi, *Journal of Palestine Studies*, Vol. XXIII, No. 1 (Autumn 1993), pp.14–15.
15. See Article V, 'Agreement on the Gaza Strip and Jericho Area', 14 May 1994.
16. Arend Liphart, *Democracy in Plural Societies: A Comparative Exploration*, New Haven, 1977, p.5.
17. 'Agreement on the Gaza Strip and Jericho Area', 14 May 1994.
18. 'The Cairo Agreement', Final Version – 9 February 1994.
19. 'Annex I: Protocol Concerning Redeployment and Security Arrangements, The Interim Agreement on Palestinian Autonomy', Article XIV.
20. See A.S. Khalidi, 'On the Drawing Board, A Blueprint of Palestine', *International Herald Tribune*, 12 February 1997.

# The Netanyahu Era:
# From Crisis to Crisis, 1996–99

## NEILL LOCHERY

The defeat of Benjamin Netanyahu by Ehud Barak in Israel's 1999 elections brought to an end one of the most interesting and complex periods of Israeli history. For three years following his surprise election victory over Shimon Peres in June 1996 Netanyahu led Israel with an administration in a state of near permanent crisis which appeared close to collapse on numerous occasions before its eventual disintegration in December 1998. During the same period Israel's youngest and least experienced Prime Minister was faced with dealing with an increasingly complex set of peace negotiations which were left over from the previous governments of Yitzhak Rabin and Shimon Peres. In effect, both Rabin and Peres had left the difficult stages of reaching agreement with the Palestinians (and the Syrians) to a second term Labour-led government.

The outcome of the 1996 elections meant that it was Netanyahu and the Likud who were charged with attempting to reach an agreement with Yasser Arafat and the Palestinian Authority (PA) over Hebron and negotiating the major transfer of lands in the West Bank to PA control. In addition, the administration was scheduled to start the final status negotiations. These negotiations include issues such as statehood, the status of Jerusalem and the question of Palestinian refugees. It is at this stage that Israel will be called upon to make a number of compromises. In reality, these negotiations were overshadowed by problems between 1996 and 1999 with the Interim Agreements which culminated in the Wye Memorandum in 1998, the event which led to collapse of the administration.

It is still too premature to detail the successes and failures of the Netanyahu era from an historical perspective. Such was the divisive nature of Netanyahu that there are two polarized academic perspectives on this period. The first concentrates on 'the wasted opportunities' between 1996 and 1999 and argues that Netanyahu nearly destroyed the peace process. The second suggests that the Netanyahu era was a

Neill Lochery is Lecturer in Modern Israeli Politics, University College London.

vital stage in laying firm foundations for peace in Israel. In effect the period saw a necessary stage of consolidating the process after the spectacular (but divisive) agreements reached by the previous administration. Proponents of the latter concentrate on the structural problems of the Oslo Accords and emphasize that any Israeli government would have encountered serious difficulties.

This essay aims to detail an aspect of the Netanyahu era, which in the highly polarized and charged atmosphere would appear to have been overlooked, namely the internal restraints that were placed on Netanyahu's actions in the arena of peacemaking. These so-called 'shackles' included the new Israeli electoral system, the numerical weakness of the Likud he led in the Knesset, intra-party and inter-cabinet conflicts and opposition to the Prime Minister (PM). In the second part of the essay the effects of the above and Netanyahu's strategy for dealing with the restraints are analysed in each of the major tracks of the peace process.

## SOURCES OF CONFLICT

Netanyahu faced both major intra-party and inter-block conflict within his government.[1] In the Likud party he led there was a sizeable group that felt that Netanyahu's 1996 election victory was achieved at the expense of the party. This group argued that the deals which Netanyahu made with Rafael Eitan's Tsomet and David Levy's Gesher Party to ensure that he was the sole candidate of the Right in the direct election for PM cost the party in terms of its own representation on the Knesset list. In essence, both Eitan and Levy, in securing places on the Likud Knesset list for their respective candidates, did so at the expense of leading figures in the Likud.[2]

The Likud–Gesher–Tsomet list won a total of only 32 seats in the 1996 Knesset elections. Out of these only 23 came from the Likud (the other places were taken by members of Gesher and Tsomet) which is a drastic reduction for a party which in the 1980s had won on average 45 seats in Knesset elections. As a result of his relative lack of strength in the Knesset, Netanyahu's powers of patronage were greatly reduced, and he was left with a large group of disgruntled Likud national figures who failed to win a seat in the Knesset. Normal patronage tools such as the appointment of new ambassadors could have helped alleviate this problem, but such appointments are normally reserved for disappointed or disillusioned national leaders who have not been included in the cabinet, and not for larger groups who failed to enter the Knesset.

At the time, Netanyahu was well aware of this problem and tried to solve it by introducing the 'Norwegian Principle' where members of the cabinet resign their Knesset seats and are replaced by the next name on the party's original electoral list. Moreover, crucially for Netanyahu the names from 32 to 40 on the Likud–Gesher–Tsomet list were mainly members of the Likud. However, opposition from cabinet members who were reluctant to resign their seats proved to be too strong for Netanyahu to force the change through the Knesset. As a result, the eight ministers (not including Netanyahu himself who would have retained his seat) from the Likud–Gesher–Tsomet list kept their seats and the candidates who occupied positions 33 to 41 in the Knesset list were not able to go to the Knesset. In the original Knesset list the Likud members occupied six of the positions between 33 and 41 and a further three between 42 and 45.

An additional problem that faced the new PM was the selection of chairpersons and members for the Knesset committees. In the past, this had traditionally been an opportunity for a leader to hand out patronage to loyal clients. Put simply, as head of the largest Knesset party and block, the Prime Minister's choice was almost certain to be confirmed in the subsequent ballot of members of the Knesset (MKs) which selects the chairpersons and composition of the parliamentary committees. However, after the 1996 Knesset election the Likud was not the largest party in the Knesset, and this fact was reflected in its number of committee chairpersons; out of 12 committees the Likud had only two chairpersons, Uzi Landau (Foreign Affairs and Defence) and Naomi Blumenthal (Immigration and Absorption). Conversely, the Labour Party, which remained the single largest party in the Knesset, was able to get five of its members elected as chairpersons. An additional problem for Netanyahu lies in that the number of Likud MKs who sit on these committees also reflects the party's relatively weak parliamentary strength, and therefore its ability to do deals with smaller parties to ensure the election of its members to the committees. Consequently, not only was Netanyahu faced with unhappy Likudniks, but also many of the Likud members who were elected to the Knesset were disgruntled because they were not occupying positions of prestige or influence within the parliament.

Netanyahu's weakness in the Likud was demonstrated not only by his lack of patronage powers, but at a more fundamental level in his lack of a clearly identifiable group of constituency support within the party. Both Menachem Begin and Yitzhak Shamir, Netanyahu's predecessors as leader, gained their respective support from the old generation of Herut supporters, many of whom they had fought with side by side in the underground during Israel's battle for independence. At the time of Shamir's departure after defeat in the 1992 election there were three major internal groupings within the Likud; the Shamir–Arens camp, the Sharon camp and the Levy camp.[3]

Of these Netanyahu was seen as being closest to the Shamir–Arens group. The surprise decision of Moshe Arens to retire from politics after the 1992 election left the leadership of this grouping wide open. However, Netanyahu was not the heir apparent of this group; many of its supporters regarded him as too young and inexperienced, others did not like his concentration on the media where he was highly visible both within Israel and in the world via CNN. In short, had the use of primaries to elect a new leader not been adopted by the party it is unlikely that Netanyahu would have been elected as its leader.[4]

In the event, during the primaries Netanyahu was able to portray himself to the 100,000 mass rank-and-file members of the party as the man most likely to return the party to power. Such an achievement should not be underestimated for, at the time of the leadership contest in 1993, the party was still in deep shock after its election defeat in 1992 at the hands of the Labour Party.[5]

Following his victory in the primaries Netanyahu moved swiftly to consolidate his power, pushing through a new party constitution which among other things limited the possibility to challenge him for the leadership from within the Likud. However, despite his victory Netanyahu clearly at no time enjoyed majority support from within the party institutions. In fact Netanyahu, almost uniquely in Western-style democracies, was unable successfully to construct his own sizeable faction within the Likud despite being its leader.

Ironically it was Netanyahu's original mentor, Moshe Arens, who challenged the PM for the leadership of the Likud in 1999. Arens came out of political retirement to fight a campaign that centred on questions of Netanyahu's leadership qualities rather than issues. The campaign was low key with the result seemingly assured. By 1999 Arens was no political match for Netanyahu in a contest that was determined by the rank-and-file membership of the Likud. Following his defeat Arens accepted the position of Minister of Defence for the final six months of the Netanyahu government. Further complications and restraints on Netanyahu arose at inter-block level, and in particular in the management of the government coalition. The tensions which became apparent in the cabinet reflected the large number of coalition partners (eight in total), and the relative electoral weakness of the Likud (never in Israel's history has a party been viewed as the major force in a government coalition which has only 32 seats).[6]

Having outlined the problems that Netanyahu faced at both intra-party and inter-block level it is important to analyse the tools that he employed to deal with them and to assess their effect on the peace process between 1996 and 1999.

NETANYAHU'S MANAGEMENT STRATEGY

Netanyahu's major strength in dealing with party, coalition (cabinet) and parliamentary sources of conflict was that owing to the new electoral system adopted for the 1996 elections he was playing by a new set of rules. Political scientists have debated the significance of the change in the electoral system and its implications for Israel's political system. Put simply, Israel no longer remained a pure example of parliamentary democracy, but nor does it fit the presidential model of government. It is not the purpose of this essay to enter the complex debate surrounding Israel's new system of government, but simply to suggest that its introduction created a high degree of ambiguity in how the government functions. In essence, the relationships between the PM, party, coalition and parliament are not as easily identifiable as in the past and are now more open to interpretation and challenge by the PM.[7] Paradoxically, this uncertainty was also Netanyahu's major weakness, because large areas of his power and spheres of influence were not as clearly defined as those of previous Prime Ministers. In addition, Netanyahu's authority was diminished by the fact that he was the first Israeli PM who did not enjoy the benefits of leading a party which is the largest force in the Knesset. In essence, Netanyahu had to mark out his areas of control and then defend them against, at times, hostile reactions from his own party, coalition and parliament.

*A New Role for the Prime Minister's Office (PMO)*
One of the first actions of Netanyahu after assuming power was to attempt to develop the PMO along presidential lines. In both pre-election statements and post-election planning Netanyahu supported the idea of creating an American-style National Security Council which would have been based in the PMO, and consequently taken large powers away from the Defence Ministry. Moreover, control of the privatization programme, which was viewed as vital to the health of the Israeli economy, was taken away from the Finance Ministry and relocated in Netanyahu's office. In addition, the PM tried, unsuccessfully, to appoint cabinet Secretary, Danny Naveh to the position of co-ordinator of the various peace talks. The overall level of concentration of power which was envisaged by Netanyahu and his Chief of Staff, Avigdor Liberman, led some Israeli journalists to state that Netanyahu's PMO was to be based not on the White House model but rather the Kremlin.[8]

Central to Netanyahu's thinking in attempting to maximize the influence of his office was his desire to control all aspects of the peace negotiations. In short, he wanted to minimize the sphere of influence of the Foreign Ministry where he had been forced to appoint his old arch rival, David Levy, as Foreign Minister. In addition, as both Rabin and Peres before him had been aware, control of the Defence Ministry was an important tool in maintaining control over the implementation of the peace process. Netanyahu was not as politically strong or experienced as

Rabin and Peres (post Rabin assassination) to be able to hold the portfolio himself in addition to his responsibilities as Prime Minister. Consequently, he aimed to strip the ministry of its key powers, and downgrade the influence of the subsequently appointed Minister of Defence, Yitzhak Mordechai.[9] In a similar fashion the decision to move control of the privatization programme to his office reflected Netanyahu's attempt again to minimize the influence of a key ministry where he had been forced by the Likud party to appoint perhaps his strongest intra-party rival, Dan Meridor.[10]

### Netanyahu and the Cabinet

Netanyahu believed that his victory provided him with the authority to alter Israel's traditional parliamentary system of cabinet government with the Prime Minister being *primus inter pares,* to a more presidential system. Here the real action was kept away from the cabinet, which was relegated to a discussion and ratification forum. This seemed a natural trend, for recent administrations, in particular the government of Rabin, saw an unprecedented move towards the presidential style where the role of the cabinet had substantially diminished. Privately, Rabin saw cabinet meetings as little more than press conferences (such was his exasperation at the posturing of ministers and number of leaks that were traced back to the meetings).

During his first years in office Netanyahu achieved some successes in the management of the cabinet, notably on ratification of the Hebron deal and subsequent troop redeployments in the West Bank. However, these achievements should not obscure the fact that he failed to alter the balance of power away from the cabinet and towards his office. On the contrary, many Israeli commentators note that Netanyahu faced stronger opposition in cabinet than Rabin did, and that ministers were far more successful in asserting influence than during the Rabin government. There are two major factors that explain this. First, there was a natural majority within the cabinet who opposed the Oslo Accords and wanted nothing to do with them. Therefore, when Netanyahu brought a deal such as the Hebron Agreement to the cabinet he started from a position of disadvantage. Second, the fact that there were seven parties in the coalition and cabinet further complicated matters. Moreover, Netanyahu's attempts to play the parties off against each other, and in particular to pit the secular parties against the religious parties, was far from successful.

### Netanyahu and the Likud

The Likud itself emerged from the 1996 elections in a state of dazed confusion; relief that Netanyahu had won a narrow victory in the election for the PM and was able to form a coalition, but despondency at the poor performance of the party in the Knesset election. Party leaders were quick to blame the new electoral system that had led to a greater fragmentation of the vote and a decline in the support for both of the two major parties in Israel. It soon became evident that Netanyahu envisaged the party along much the same lines as an American political party; a loosely organized supermarket of ideas which is pulled together at election times. In essence, the days of the party being one of the most important institutions in Israeli society were clearly numbered. The Prime Minister's attitude to the party was, to a large extent, a result of his relative intra-party weakness. Party institutions such as the Central Committee were largely controlled by Ariel Sharon and to a lesser degree the son of the ex-leader Menachem Begin, Binyamin (Benni) Ze'ev Begin.

In dealing with the party on the key issue of the peace process Netanyahu presented himself as far more hardline than his actions as PM indicated. For example, to help neutralize the hardliners in the party Netanyahu adopted a strategy of saving his more radical statements, notably on Jerusalem, for meetings of the Likud Central Committee.[11] Clearly, he was well aware of the need to play to his audiences who reflected a party where the majority of members were at best sceptical of the Oslo Accords.

The seeming incompatibility of retaining land and continuing the Oslo process was used as a key strategic tactic by Netanyahu in retaining the support of the party for his pursuit of peace. Put simply, he argued that it was possible to retain the land and still work within the framework set out in the Oslo Accords. In effect, Netanyahu attempted to postpone the moment of choice between land and peace by offering the possibility of both.

Even the meeting with Arafat, so long a demon figure in the Likud, passed with only Begin and the old guard attacking Netanyahu. Moreover, the Hebron deal, over which Begin resigned from the cabinet, did not create the uproar in the Likud that commentators thought it would, which was in no small part due to Netanyahu's careful preparation of the party during the months prior to the agreement.

### The Carrot and Stick of a National Unity Government (NUG)

During the first years of his administration the most effective tactic which Netanyahu employed against the cabinet, the wider coalition and the Likud was the threat that he would break up the government and form a NUG with the Labour Party. Netanyahu used a variety of tools to send signals that such a government was imminent including public statements by himself and controlled leaks from his office. Israeli political commentators were kept busy by constant rumour, gossip and conspiracy theories that the formation of such a government would take place. Much of the rumour originated from officials in the PMO who used the possibility of a NUG as a threat against dissenting voices during times of crisis. This tactic was employed successfully in the first years of the administration in crisis during the round of budget-cut negotiations in 1996–97 and in the ratification of the Hebron Agreement in 1997.

*Netanyahu's Third Way: Pragmatism Versus Ideology*

The period of the Netanyahu administration was dominated by a series of crises surrounding the peace process, especially the Palestinian track. In examining the progress of the various tracks of the peace process there is a need to identify where, together with why, Netanyahu felt unable to deliver concessions and where he successfully manipulated, persuaded or coerced his right-wing constituency into accepting compromises in the negotiations. Before examining the individual restraints on Netanyahu in the various tracks of the peace process it is important to locate just where Netanyahu stood himself on the peace process and specifically the Oslo Accords.

Netanyahu was a politician who in the past had prided himself on his rigid ideological beliefs of which 'Greater Israel' is the central pillar. In his book *A Place Among Nations*, which is widely viewed as the blueprint of his beliefs, Netanyahu returns time and again to the question of Israel's security and the need for it to maintain the West Bank in order to protect Israel's eastern border.[12] Taken in conjunction with his hardline views and actions while in opposition, his non-acceptance of the Oslo Accords, the building of a united national block and his leadership of militant demonstrations against the Accords, led many to presume that Netanyahu was a hardline Likud ideologue.

However, such conclusions fail to take into account a range of other factors that indicate that Netanyahu's main characteristic is his pragmatism.[13] His education in the United States and the time he subsequently spent living there helped influence his early years and provided him with a worldly view which is still absent in many of the leaders of the Likud today.[14] Netanyahu has often stressed his admiration for the American political system and, as with the majority of American politicians, Netanyahu's guiding light is power.[15] Moreover, he was well aware that in order to gain power he needed to draw support from a wide spectrum of groups. While opposition leader in Israel he clearly felt a need to unify the nationalist block (or Likud-led block) whose disunity had been one of the main reasons that the Likud lost power in the 1992 elections.[16] His robust opposition to the Oslo Accords, which was at the time certainly genuine, served an additional purpose of giving him an opportunity and rallying call to control the development of new ties, and strengthen existing links, between the Likud and the parties of the Right in Israel.

As the election campaign in 1996 started, Netanyahu and his team of advisers moved his positioning strategy to the political centre. In essence, this involved an acceptance of the Oslo Accords and a promise to continue the process of implementing the Interim Agreement. This change which was made over a period of only a few days revealed the extent of, first, Netanyahu's desire for power far above and beyond any ideological convictions; second, the new political realties in Israel where acceptance of Oslo was seen as vital to attracting the centre-ground voters.[17] In shifting his strategy Netanyahu risked alienating large parts of his party and the nationalist bloc which he had worked so hard to develop closer ties with. However, during the campaign he made it clear that he would be a reluctant participant in the process and would not make the concessions that the Labour Party would offer in final status talks.[18]

In a practical sense what this all amounts to is what can be viewed as the third way. Netanyahu's policies towards the peace process clearly rejected the ideologically dominated era of Yitzhak Shamir and the visionary new Middle East of his predecessor Shimon Peres.[19] In a keynote speech in 1997 Netanyahu summarized this vision:

> Between 'rose garden' dreams on the one hand, and paranoia and isolation on the other, there is a golden path of realism, of realpolitik. This is the path that Israel chose beginning in the Ben-Gurion era, and this must be our choice today. If we know when to compromise, when to grasp opportunities and when to display determination and decisiveness, we can bring peace with security to our country and to our people.[20]

More specifically, he set three criteria (or pillars) on which he argued that a lasting peace had to be built: security, reciprocity, and democracy and human rights.[21] However, the form that this third-way vision took in the real world remained unclear and Netanyahu's actions and restraints in each of the major tracks of the peace process need to be examined in order to attempt to provide a clearer picture of his premiership.

## THE ISRAELI–PALESTINIAN TRACK

### Ratification of the Hebron Agreement 1997

Netanyahu needed to employ all his considerable political skills to get the Hebron Agreement and subsequent troop redeployment deal (February 1997) past the cabinet and the Likud. However, the decision to procede with the Har Homa construction project in East Jerusalem, and the smaller than expected transfer of land to the PA, indicate what needs to be viewed as the pay back to the party and coalition. In addition, the extent of the difficulties that Netanyahu faced over ratification of the Hebron deal were shown with what became known as the Bar-On affair. Netanyahu, his Director of the PMO, Avigdor Liberman, and the Minister of Justice, Tzachi Ha-negbi, were all placed under investigation over an alleged plea bargain deal with the leader of the religious party Shas. The deal would have seen Shas ministers in the cabinet supporting or abstaining in the vote over ratification of the Hebron deal in exchange for a plea bargain for Aryeh Deri, the leader of Shas, who was eventually convicted of corruption charges in 1999.[22]

Central to the strategy that Netanyahu employed towards the negotiations over Hebron was the need to make any final deal over Hebron appear to be due to two factors. First, that the previous Labour-led government had already committed Israel to a withdrawal; and second, pressure from the international community, in particular the United States. An additional integral part of this strategy was to spin out the negotiations with the Palestinians over a period of time to allow the new Israeli government time to flex its muscle to its largely right-wing constituents before finally accepting a deal. However, Netanyahu failed to foresee two complications to his strategy that almost led to its failure.

The first of these complications concerned the relative lack of experience of the new Israeli negotiators appointed by Netanyahu. This was compounded by the attempt of Netanyahu to clip the wings of the Israel Defence Forces (IDF), who he felt had become too politicized under Rabin and Peres with their participation in the peace negotiations. In attempting to reduce the role of the IDF Netanyahu preferred instead to introduce his own civilian appointees to the negotiations.[23] The result of such moves was that the new inexperienced Israeli negotiators, many of whom were drawn from the Israeli Right and had not changed their view of the Palestine Liberation Organization (PLO) as a terrorist organization, conducted the negotiations in an abrasive and aggressive manner.[24] The atmosphere of the early rounds of talks was so bad there was a real chance that the negotiations would have broken down altogether if the Americans in the form of the Special Envoy to the Middle East, Dennis Ross, had not directly intervened to ensure the talks continued. Such an outcome would have damaged Netanyahu's international standing because the previous Israeli government had promised to withdraw from Hebron, which would have made Netanyahu appear the guilty party responsible for the breakdown.

After eventually signing the Hebron deal Netanyahu brought the agreement before cabinet for approval. The Labour Party had made it clear that it would act as a safety net in the subsequent Knesset vote on ratification thus giving Netanyahu a sizeable majority in parliament. Consequently, the cabinet became the sole opportunity for the opponents of the deal to secure enough support to reject it. Crucially, had the cabinet done so then Netanyahu would have been faced with bringing the deal before the Knesset without cabinet ratification, and in such circumstances it is difficult to see how the government coalition would have remained intact. However, long before the final deal had been signed Netanyahu had canvassed cabinet colleagues until he was certain that he had at least a slender majority in favour.

When the cabinet met to ratify the deal the PM adopted a strategy of letting every minister speak on the issue in the hope that ministers could let off steam for their various right-wing and religious constituencies which they represented and then reluctantly fall into line for cabinet vote. Unfortunately for Netanyahu, his strategy again revealed his inexperience, as members of cabinet, including some from his own party, were actively engaged in campaigning against the PM, such was the strength of feeling against the Hebron deal. Moreover, Netanyahu's lack of authority and a power base in the Likud was embarrassingly exposed. However, much to Netanyahu's credit the deal was ratified by the cabinet (ten to seven) due largely to the fact that the PM was able to convince enough ministers, who were keen to maintain the stability of the government, that the deal would serve the long-term interests of Israel.[25]

The events of February and March 1997 need to be seen within the framework of the internal restraints on Netanyahu which were clearly illustrated by the pay back for the deal that the PM made to his party and coalition during this period. The decision to hand over only nine per cent of West Bank and not the 25 to 30 per cent that the PA expected was aimed at pacifying the Likud and the coalition by returning the minimum amount of land possible. Again the PM intended to pursue the dual aim of continuing with the Oslo process and Interim Agreements while minimizing the land that was handed over to the PA. However, once more Netanyahu had to deal with a hostile cabinet who objected to the two per cent of land which was to be handed over from Area C (under Israeli rule and where almost all the Jewish settlements are located) to Area B (joint Israeli and Palestinian control). Key members of the cabinet, including the Likud's Ariel Sharon and Limor Livnat, objected to the agreement stating that no part of Area C should be handed over prior to the final status agreements in the year 2000. Eventually, Netanyahu won the cabinet vote on ratification (ten to six), but only as a direct result of gaining the support of some the religious ministers. This was gained only by agreeing a package with the religious parties which included the decision to build a new Jewish housing project at Har Homa in East Jerusalem.

The decision to build at Har Homa was, in part, an illustration of Netanyahu's relative intra-party and inter-block weakness. His original strategy of playing to his right-wing constituency by handing over only nine per cent of the West Bank had clearly backfired. Consequently, he turned his attention to Israel's control of Jerusalem, which is a relatively safe domestic issue for any Israeli leader. He correctly calculated that the majority of the opposition Labour Party would support his decision to build homes for 42,000 Jews in East Jerusalem and thus there would be no major domestic political confrontation which would weakened his position. After announcing the decision Netanyahu increased his rhetoric notably at meetings of the Likud Central Committee where he declared that Jerusalem is the eternal capital of Israel and that Israel has the right to build where it wants in the city. Moreover, he used the subsequent Palestinian violence in the West Bank and the suicide bombings of a Tel Aviv café and a Jerusalem market further to slow down the pace of the peace process. This allowed him further to postpone 'D-day', or more specifically the choice between returning large parts of the West Bank or causing a terminal breakdown of the peace process.

*Ratification of the Wye Memorandum 1998*

Netanyahu's conduct of the lengthy negotiations that culminated in the Wye Memorandum (23 October 1998) illustrated how acutely aware he was of the internal restraints. Prior to the negotiations at the Wye Plantation Netanyahu had been able to resist strong US pressure to agree to further West Bank troop redeployments. During this period the coalition held firm, but the peace process with the Palestinians veered towards total collapse. At the same time US–Israeli relations became increasingly strained as US officials argued that Netanyahu was putting his domestic restraints ahead of moving the process forward.

In contrast to the Hebron Agreement Netanyahu attempted to put in place the pay back before he made difficult compromises. Central to this strategy was the appointment of the veteran hawk, Ariel Sharon, as Foreign Minister. Unlike his predecessor, David Levy, Sharon played a full role in the negotiations with the Palestinians. Netanyahu believed (wrongly) that Sharon would be able to sell the deal to the cabinet, coalition and the far Right.

The ratification that led to the premature end of the Netanyahu administration illustrated the restraints that the PM operated under. It should be stressed that by October–November 1998 the Netanyahu coalition was already at an advanced stage of destruction. It survived votes of confidence in the Knesset on the grounds that the opposition could not muster the required 61 seats. Most worryingly for the PM many senior Likud MK's abstained or voted against the government in key debates. The opposition Labour Party sensed victory and despite its assurances to act as a safety net in the Knesset for Netanyahu's peace agreement moved to bring down the government.

In effect Netanyahu was forced to bring ratification of the Wye Memorandum into an already hostile political environment. At cabinet level ratification proved even more difficult than it had with respect to the Hebron Agreement, with the cabinet split and Netanyahu's exercising the casting vote. Clearly, many ministers scented the demise of the government and were positioning themselves for the expected election campaign. Other ministers simply could not bring themselves to support a deal that made difficult territorial concessions to the PA. D-day arrived for the PM at a time when he had used up any political goodwill towards him from a coalition which had become increasingly difficult to manage. In a last attempt to keep the coalition together the PM froze the implementation of the agreement, citing Palestinian non-compliance.

By late 1998 the tactical option of broadening the coalition into a NUG by adding the Labour Party was no longer viable. Secret negotiations which took place in autumn 1998 between representatives of Netanyahu and Barak produced agreed policy guidelines for a NUG but made little progress on the question of the division of cabinet portfolios. In reality, Barak had little interest in forming a NUG and had taken a strategic decision to work towards new elections. Two factors dominated Barak's thinking. First, he did not want to be number two to Netanyahu, and second, unlike his predecessor, Shimon Peres, he did not need the patronage powers of office to maintain his position as leader. On top of this it appeared probable that the coalition would collapse and Barak would be given his chance to bring elections forward. For Netanyahu the sad irony was that just when he needed to use one of his most valuable cards (NUG) against the internal restraints on him the card was taken away from him.

## THE SYRIAN–ISRAELI AND LEBANESE TRACKS

The key issue in the Syrian track lies with security and does not contain the complicated additional factor of ideology. Put simply, the Likud, other parties of the Right and the religious parties have no ideological claim over the Golan Heights, but rather believe them to be vital to the security of Israel. Consequently, in theory, if agreement can be reached with Syria that ensures Israeli security needs then there is no historical or biblical reason for maintaining control over the lands.

The closely related Lebanese track is also a question of security. In addition, it is in this track that Netanyahu enjoyed the lowest level of internal restraints, but conversely the external restraints were complicated by the control that Syria exerts over Lebanon, and to a considerable degree Hizbullah in Southern Lebanon. In short, Netanyahu faced a challenge similar to those faced by his immediate predecessors as PM; to find a way of withdrawing Israeli forces from southern Lebanon while providing northern Israel with adequate security cover against rocket and terrorist attacks from its border.

In examining, first, the Syrian track in isolation from Lebanon it is clear that Netanyahu initially adopted the hawkish position that his previous writings and speeches had suggested he would. To some degree, Netanyahu used the negotiations with Syria as an avenue to flex his hawkish credentials to his party and coalition while making difficult compromises in the Palestinian negotiations. He refused to resume negotiations with the Syrians on the basis of carrying on where the negotiations ended with the previous Labour government. He argued that Syria signed no binding international agreement with the previous government, and therefore he was not obliged to continue the policies of the previous government. Labour Party sources have confirmed that Peres was willing to hand back the vast majority of the Golan Heights in return for a full peace with Syria.

The internal restraints that did exist on the Syrian track came from both the Likud and government coalition. Security experts in the Likud rejected the formula of a total return of the Golan Heights for a total peace. In essence, they were searching for a formula different from the one employed with Egypt after the Camp David Agreement (1978) that saw all of the Sinai returned to Egypt. Suggestions from Netanyahu's close advisers included confidence-building measures such as the Syrians restraining attacks against Israel from groups based in southern Lebanon, discussions about water issues and high-level military contacts to prevent misunderstandings on the Golan Heights. However, the Likud which was having to address major ideological questions over 'Greater Israel' was not ready radically to alter its platform on opposition to a total withdrawal from the Golan Heights. Moreover, the coalition contained a party, the Third Way, which was formed by rebel Labour Party Knesset members, with the main purpose of opposing any Israeli withdrawal from the Golan Heights.

However, as it became clear that there would be no final agreement with the Palestinians before elections that were originally due in 2000, Netanyahu attempted to reach a peace agreement with Syria in late 1998. Recent papers made available from the PMO in Jerusalem (by the Barak administration) suggest that Netanyahu offered a full withdrawal from the Golan Heights to 4 June borders in return for peace.[26] Netanyahu's offer was rejected by President Asad who either felt Netanyahu's administration to be too weak, or was receiving better offers from Barak and the Labour Party or simply did not want to sign a peace agreement with Israel. Put simply, Netanyahu's apparent change of strategy on the Syrian track reflected his need to secure some positive agreement before going to the polls in Israel. The PM would have attempted to bypass the internal restraints on him from the Right by making the Israeli elections a vote of confidence on any agreement or calling for a national referendum. The shifts in Netanyahu's position on the Syria track during his period in office were substantial. These further illustrated his pragmatic approach to core issues of the peace process, and his strong desire to remain in power by holding the political centre-ground.

The question of Israel's relationship with Lebanon is very closely related with Lebanon's power-broker Syria. Netanyahu himself was keen to remove Israeli forces from Lebanon as quickly as possible; he stated publicly that he wished to leave 'yesterday'. However, he was acutely aware of the need to reach some kind of security agreement that would prevent attacks on Israel's northern towns such as Kiryat Shmona. The idea of the 'Lebanon first' was muted by Netanyahu in the early days of his term in office. In essence, this plan would have seen Israeli forces withdraw from Lebanon with Syrian agreement to exercise control over Hizbullah.

Unfortunately for Netanyahu, the Syrians rejected this proposal out of hand. Throughout Netanyahu's period of office the Syrians made it clear that they would use Lebanon as a means of increasing the pressure on the Israeli leadership to agree to a withdrawal from the Golan Heights. Consequently, Netanyahu became further entwined in Lebanon despite his strategic objective of removing Israeli forces from the area. During the 1999 election campaign Barak and Labour promised to withdraw Israeli forces from Lebanon within one year of coming into office. Netanyahu matched this offer for domestic consumption, but major external restraints remain for any Israeli PM on this issue.

## THE DOWNFALL OF NETANYAHU AND CONCLUSION

During the Netanyahu era the Israeli political system was in a period of transition, caused to a large extent by the adoption of a new electoral system in 1996 which was designed to reduce the level of political horse-trading that had characterized Israeli politics during the 1980s. In reality, the introduction of direct elections for PM reflected a shift in Israeli politics away from the central role of ideology and political parties towards a concentration on personality politics; where the personality and credibility of the leader become the most significant factor in elections. Strong evidence for this was provided by the 1999 election campaign in which the central defining issue was the personality and leadership abilities of Netanyahu.

Netanyahu found to his cost just how strong the internal restraints are on a directly elected PM, and how vulnerable the PM remains to his own party, the cabinet and the government coalition. Ehud Barak entered office in 1999 in a much stronger position than Netanyahu did in 1996. Lack of strong inter-party opposition to his leadership, a cabinet consensus (on the peace process) and acceptance of his mandate by alternative leaders would all seem to point to Barak being able to develop the strength of the executive. Consequently, the internal restraints on Barak appear less significant than those on Netanyahu. In these terms it is possible that the Netanyahu era represented a period of transition in which the full extent of the effects of the changes in the electoral system were not transferred to the political system.

The initial signs from Israel's new PM is that he intends to build a highly centralized and strong executive, staffed by professional experts who will oversee the most sensitive negotiations in the peace process. Under Barak Israel is seeing a further shift away from parliamentary democracy to a more presidential style. The Knesset remains the centre of political debate, but the key decisions are to be taken in the PMO.

## NOTES

1. 'Intra-party conflict' is defined as conflict within the Likud and 'inter-block conflict' as being within the parties of the Likud-led block which in recent years have included the parties of the Right and the religious parties.
2. Netanyahu was well aware of the need to avoid a fragmentation of the Likud-led block's vote in the 1996 election as the Likud had lost power in 1992 partly as a result of internal splits and divisions within the Likud as well as its respective block. The then Prime Minister Yitzhak Shamir cited the actions of David Levy in dividing the party in 1992 as an important factor in the party's electoral defeat and emphasized the importance of party unity at election time. Interview conducted by the author with Yitzhak Shamir, Tel Aviv, 17 August 1994.
3. For a detailed account of the internal dynamics of the Likud during this period, see Neill Lochery, *The Israeli Labour Party: In the Shadow of the Likud*, Reading, 1997.
4. As the Likud had been led by only two leaders since its formation it was natural that there was a queue of senior national leaders who were older than Netanyahu and who felt that they had more experience than the man that was regarded as a 'Likud Prince'.
5. Evidence that the main reason that Likudniks elected Netanyahu was that he offered the best chance of returning the party to power rather than any other motives was put forward by many leading figures in the Likud at the time. Interview conducted by the author with Dan Meridor, Jerusalem, 17 October 1994.
6. The problems of dealing with such a large coalition were emphasized in an interview with the author by David Bar-Illan, the Director of Communications and Head of Policy Planning in the Prime Minister's Office. Interview with David Bar-Illan, Jerusalem, 5 March 1998.
7. Netanyahu and his advisers have taken the view that it is too early to comment on the effects of the changes in the electoral system but suggest that its results have been far from perfect. Interview with Bar-Illan, Jerusalem.
8. For a detailed account of the attempt to strengthen the influence of the Prime Minister's Office, see Barry Rubin, 'No Prime Minister: A Melodrama in Three Acts', *Jerusalem Post*, 21 June 1996.
9. Mordechai was sacked by Netanyahu in January 1999 after he declared his candidacy for PM. Mordechai co-founded the Centre Party, but withdrew his candidacy on the eve of polling and begrudgingly endorsed Labour Party leader, Ehud Barak.
10. Meridor resigned in 1997 over Netanyahu's *modus operandi* and left the Likud in 1999 to co-found the Centre Party. He ran for PM but withdrew his candidacy in favour of Yitzhak Mordechai.

11. See for example, Address of Netanyahu to the Central Committee of the Likud on 3 March 1997. Netanyahu stated 'Jerusalem is ours. Whoever asks Israel to give up the unity of Israel does not understand how this chord plays on our heart. We will build everywhere we decided and no one – no one will prevent us'. Likud Party Headquarters, Tel Aviv.

12. Benjamin Netanyahu, *A Place Among Nations: Israel and the World*, New York, 1993.

13. For a highly critical account of Netanyahu's beliefs, see Colin Shindler, *Israel, Likud and the Zionist Dream*, London, 1995, pp. 284–7.

14. Many Israeli commentators argue that Netanyahu's time as Israeli ambassador to the United Nations in New York was critical in helping form his views and how his government operates. For a critical examination of this, see Yoel Marcus, 'The Robber of Dreams', *Ha-aretz*, 22 August 1997.

15. For a reference to his admiration for the United States, see Netanyahu, speech to joint session of Congress, 10 July 1996.

16. See for example, N. Lochery, *The Israeli Labour Party*.

17. It should be stressed that although the public shift in Netanyahu's position was remarkably rapid, in private as early as 1994 Netanyahu and many senior figures in the Likud were reconciled to carrying out at least parts of the Oslo process. This was made apparent in interviews conducted by the author with leaders of the Likud at the time, for example, interview with Dan Meridor, Jerusalem, 8 November 1994. However, there remained other senior figures in the party who both publicly and privately rejected all aspects of the Oslo process, notably Benny Begin. This was made clear in an interview conducted by the author with M.K. Begin, Jerusalem, 9 November 1994.

18. For an account of the attempts of the Likud to come to terms with the Oslo Accords and the deep internal divisions in the party over the issue, see, for example, Efraim Inbar, 'Netanyahu Takes Over', in David Elazar and Shmuel Sandler (eds), *Israel at the Polls 1996*, London, 1998, pp.34–6.

19. For a damming summary of Netanyahu's 'third way', see 'Now For My Next Trick', *Economist*, 25 April 1998, p.71.

20. Speech by Benjamin Netanyahu at the Graduation Ceremony of Cadets of the National Defence College, 14 August 1997.

21. For a lucid account of these pillars, see Netanyahu, speech to joint session of Congress, 10 July 1996.

22. For a detailed account of the Bar-On scandal and the reasons behind it, see Neill Lochery, 'Blocking Bibi's Bid for Power', *World Today*, 53–6, June 1996.

23. See Steve Rodan, 'Shaky Soloist', *Jerusalem Post*, 15 November 1996.

24. Many commentators have noted that the major problem between the Israel and the PA in the era of Netanyahu was the almost total lack of trust between the parties. This was in contrast to close working relationships established by the Oslo negotiators. See for example, Dan Margalit, 'Need a Giant Portion of Mutual Trust', *Ha-aretz*, 11 August 1997.

25. Interestingly, the scepticism of the cabinet did not reflect the majority view of the Israeli electorate about the Hebron Agreement, which was much more positive. This point was illustrated in a survey for the Tami Steinmetz Centre for Peace Studies at Tel Aviv University by Modi'in Ezrachi. The poll was based on a representative sample of 504 Israeli Jews (including those in the territories and kibbutzim) on 29 January 1997. The survey has a four per cent margin of error.

> 'What is your position regarding the agreement that was signed between Israel and the Palestinians over the redeployment in Hebron and the remainder of the West Bank? 22 per cent support a lot, 44.7 per cent Considerably support, 17.7 per cent so-so, 9.1 per cent considerably oppose, 9.1 per cent oppose a lot, 6.5 per cent don't know.'

26. See Nana Gilbert, 'Ramon: Netanyahu Agreed to June 4th 1967 Lines', *Jerusalem Post*, 13 January 2000.

# Jerusalem:
# Partition Plans for a Holy City

## ELISHA EFRAT

Few cities evoke such strong emotional responses from so many people as does Jerusalem. Sacred to at least three major religions, Jerusalem has long been a source and a scene of contention among adherents of these faiths and their political sponsors. During the first part of the twentieth century, each of the three religions, represented by a Christian, a Jewish and an Islamic polity, has attempted to determine the orientation of development in the city. The city's particular physical characteristics and the religious aspects of the settlement have produced a unique combination of factors that affect decisions by politicians, regardless of the controlling administration. These conditions are likely to remain influential in the future. The purpose of this essay is to describe and to analyse the main political partition plans for Jerusalem proposed both during the British Mandatory regime and after the establishment of the state of Israel as a solution to the complex situation that evolved in the city.

### SITE AND SITUATION

The status and the importance of Jerusalem throughout the course of its long history have been determined partially by its location in the Judean hills at the intersection of north–south and west–east routes. Notwithstanding the broken nature of the plateau on which Jerusalem is located, the city became a central, nodal point and a stronghold dominating a wide area. This location and the availability of local water supplies in ancient times explain both the choice of site and many aspects of the connection in recent history between Israel and Jordan.

In the twentieth century the city's centre of gravity oscillated with the changing political fortunes. At the beginning of the British Mandate the municipal boundary of Jerusalem encompassed an area of 12.7 square kilometres, 59 per cent of which was the Old City. The influx of Jewish immigration during the Mandate period forced further extension of the

Elisha Efrat is Professor of Geography at Tel Aviv University.

municipal boundaries, with the city-planning area reaching 37.5 square kilometres by 1948. After the 1948 War the city was partitioned and its settled area was reduced in size because of political uncertainties.

## AN EARLY JEWISH PARTITION PLAN FOR JERUSALEM

A plan for a political partition of Jerusalem had already existed a decade before the creation of the state of Israel, having been drawn up by none other than the Jewish Agency – the official establishment Zionist body in Palestine representing the Jewish and Zionist interests to the British authorities.[1] The Jewish Agency's plan for the partition of Jerusalem was a part of its overall reaction to the Royal Commission's plan for the partition of Palestine, which was proposed in 1937.

According to the Royal Commission's proposal the entire city of Jerusalem, both inside and outside the walls, was to be included within the borders of a British Mandate enclave. The reason for this was that Jerusalem is holy to all religions and it was necessary to guard it as a 'sacred trust of civilization'. The Jewish Agency Executive (JAE) clearly realized that there was no chance of British consent to a Zionist demand to include the Old City of Jerusalem, in which all of the places most holy to Judaism are concentrated, within the borders of the Jewish state. The JAE's position in relation to the New City of Jerusalem, in which the majority of the Jewish population and its institutions were concentrated, was entirely different. It had a few reasons to demand the inclusion of the Jewish part of the New City within the prospective Jewish state. Among these was the demographic importance of the New City's population for the future Jewish state. At that time the population of the New City comprised approximately one-fifth of the Jewish population in Palestine, or 75,000 out of 400,000. In the Old City there were only 4,700 Jews.[2] Other reasons for the inclusion of the New City in the Jewish state were the symbolism of Jerusalem and its centrality in the history of the Jewish people, apart from its being the centre of the country's political and cultural life at the time.

On this basis, the JAE assumed that its demand for the inclusion of the Jewish parts of Jerusalem outside the walls within the Jewish state would be amenable to the British government. The JAE thus drew a boundary line that divided the city into two areas: one characterized by largely Jewish concentrations of population and property, the other where the population and property were mainly non-Jewish. In its proposal the JAE gave up the Jewish holy places in the eastern part of the city, including Temple Mount, Mount Zion, the Wailing Wall and the Mount of Olives. The JAE also forwent the Jewish Quarter inside the walls of the Old City. On the other hand, Mount Scopus, where the Hebrew University complex had been built, was included in the borders of the Jewish area (Figure 1).

FIGURE 1

THE JEWISH AGENCY'S PROPOSAL FOR THE PARTITION OF JERUSALEM
(AFTER Y. KATZ)

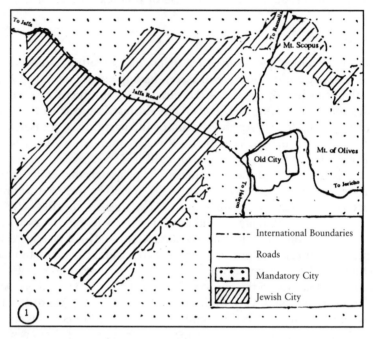

In deciding to accept the plan for partition in principle, the Zionist Organization demonstrated the political pragmatism of its leaders, who were prepared to detach the holiest sites in Judaism, the Wailing Wall, Temple Mount and the Mount of Olives, from the Jewish state to be. It is arguable that the Jewish Agency's plan for the partition of Jerusalem, while giving up the Old City, sowed the seeds of its agreement a decade later to the internationalization of Jerusalem in accordance with the UN Partition Resolution, and its subsequent acquiescence in the partition of the city following the 1948 War.

## PARTITION PLANS AFTER THE 1948 WAR

Since 1948 Jerusalem has usually been discussed in terms of a threefold division: the Old City, East Jerusalem and West Jerusalem. East Jerusalem usually refers to the parts of the city outside the walls of the Old City that were under Jordanian rule between 1948 and 1967. The population of East Jerusalem is mostly Arab. West Jerusalem has been under Israeli control since 1948 and its population is predominantly Jewish.

From 1948 to 1967 Jerusalem was politically and religiously a divided city. The armistice line in 1949 confirmed the city's partition and created a neutral zone to be administered by the United Nations between the Jordanian and the Israeli military positions. That no man's land comprised seven areas, but along most of the dividing line, hostile positions were immediately adjacent to each other. The armistice line ran through land that was open, undeveloped, or occupied by former roadways. The Jordanian army occupied the Old City and East Jerusalem, and the Israeli army controlled Mount Zion, West Jerusalem, and an important enclave on Mount Scopus (Figure 2).

FIGURE 2

THE 1949 ARMISTICE LINE IN JERUSALEM

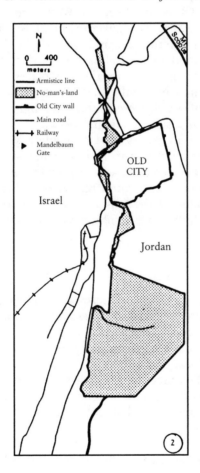

The division symbolized by the armistice line worsened during the next 19 years. Each political sector in the city underwent separate development with different orientations. Connections between eastern and western Jerusalem were effectively severed, because streets were often blocked by cement walls as a protection against snipers, and prominent buildings near the line were fortified. In the central area, the Jordanians had the advantage of occupying the massive sixteenth-century walls surrounding the Old City.

The portion of Jerusalem under Israeli control was oriented by a narrow corridor connecting it with the rest of Israel and ultimately the Mediterranean coast. Arab Jerusalem was generally focused eastwards, especially towards the Jordanian capital of Amman. The population was almost totally segregated on the basis of ethnicity: virtually no Arabs, either Muslim or Christian, lived in West Jerusalem, and no Jews inhabited East Jerusalem. The government of Israel, being concerned with the holy places in Jerusalem, and especially with the Jewish ones in the Old City, submitted a proposal in May 1950 to the UN Trusteeship Council outlining arrangements for the holy places in Jerusalem. Israel's position was that the UN should focus its attention exclusively on the holy places, most of which were at that time under Jordanian control, and should establish a special regime specifically for their control. To fulfil its task at the holy places the UN would appoint a representative body as an independent authority, and its main tasks with respect to the holy places would be: to supervise and protect them; to settle disputes between the religious communities regarding rights at holy places; to preserve existing rights at the holy places; to supervise free access and pilgrimage to the holy places, subject to the requirements of public order.[3]

## THE JEWISH–ARAB STRUGGLE FOR THE JERUSALEM ENVIRONS

A significant change in Jerusalem occurred following the 1967 Six Day War. Shortly after its conclusion, Israel's annexation of East Jerusalem and the Old City brought Jerusalem under unified political control. For security reasons, military officials and politicians made hasty decisions about the precise location of the new boundaries of the reunited city. Two goals guided those decisions: military considerations, especially the inclusion of heights to facilitate defence, and a desire to minimize the size of the Arab population. Difficulties of achieving the latter were reflected in the fact that between 60,000 and 70,000 Arabs were included in the united city that was approximately three times larger than the exclusively Jewish pre-1967 portion controlled by Israel.

The municipal boundary was drawn to include all the uninhabited no man's land and to incorporate areas of Mount Scopus on the north east

FIGURE 3

THE BOUNDARIES OF GREATER JERUSALEM

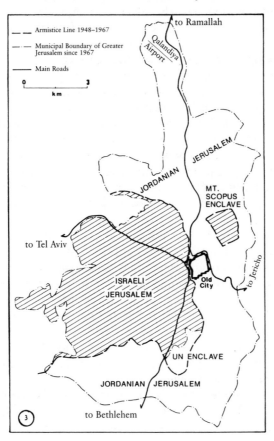

and the Mount of Evil consent and other mounts on the south, so that a defensible perimeter existed in the event of future conflict. The boundary was extended considerably to the north along the Ramallah road to encompass the airport site (Figure 3).

At the same time the demographic balance in the city had changed. The annual increase in the Jewish population was about half of the Arab and the ratio of 73.3 per cent Jews to 26.7 per cent Arabs in 1967 had shifted to 68 per cent Jews to 32 per cent Arabs by 1999. This trend has persisted since 1969, and has further accelerated with the government-assisted move of Jerusalem residents to nearby towns beyond the 'Green Line'.

An accelerated Arab construction in East Jerusalem has had spatial and political implications for the future development of Jerusalem.

These include the occupation of a considerable amount of territory by a relatively small population, control of important roads connecting Jerusalem with the environs, the placing of obstacles between sites of Jewish development, and the creation of difficulties in providing services (Figure 4).

These developments have forced the authorities to take preventive measures in the form of confiscating land. Jewish private individuals and public bodies have been acquiring hundreds of acres of land, occupying as much as possible in order to ensure the orderly future construction and development of the region. According to the settlement and development authorities, within one or two decades the settlement policy of the government will have proved to be a solution to the establishment of rural and semi-urban settlements, based on a comprehensive regional plan to the east of the Arab population.

Within this framework, many Jewish settlements were erected. The townlet of Givat-Zev, for instance, comprised in 1998 some 9,700 inhabitants. The town of Maaleh Edumim, to the east of Jerusalem, was rapidly populated to absorb by 1998 approximately 22,200 inhabitants. The Jewish expansion over the region was designed to ensure control of access to Jerusalem, there being no desire to return to the pre-1967 situation when Jerusalem was a cul-de-sac, cut off from its environs.

The Arab–Jewish struggle for the Jerusalem area had a demographic aspect as well. At the end of 1998 Jerusalem had about 633,700 inhabitants; of these 433,600 were Jews and 200,100 non-Jews. Furthermore, the city's Jewish population is ageing, while the Arab population is becoming younger.

Despite considerable efforts made by successive Israeli governments and the municipality to create new and modern city facilities, the artificial reunification of the city has not been effective. The Arabs are not impressed with what has been achieved in the city during the last three decades, and they have clearly expressed their attitude by joining the *intifada* between 1987 and 1993. During the conflict, the artificiality and basic weakness in the reunification of Jerusalem came as a great surprise to the Jewish leaders of the city. Former Mayor Teddy Kollek, often cited as a great unifying force in the face of divisions elsewhere, admitted grudgingly that the delicate peaceful coexistence between Jews and Arabs in Jerusalem had died.

Without a declared war, the artificial fabric of unity was torn asunder by demographic, geographical and political realities. Though Jerusalem has been decreed a reunified city, it has effectively returned to its earlier status as a divided city, sundering along the so-called 'Green Line'. The Israeli illusion of a Greater Jerusalem and a reunified city for the two peoples has vanished, probably for ever.

FIGURE 4

ARAB NEIGHBOURHOODS IN JERUSALEM 1997

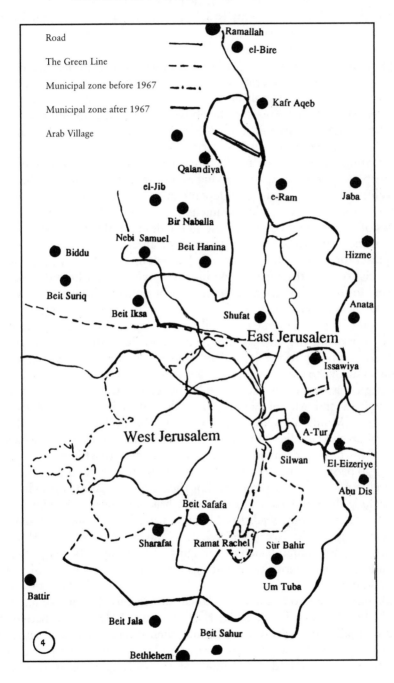

## PARTITION PLANS FOR JERUSALEM AFTER THE 1967 WAR

Following the 1967 Six Day War, demonstrating sensitivity to the holy places in the Jerusalem area, Israel proposed that they be granted the status of diplomatic missions. Christian and Muslim clerics serving at the holy places were to be granted a special status, similar to that of diplomatic representatives; Jordan would be considered the 'accrediting state' of the Muslim clerics, and the Vatican the 'accrediting state' of Christian clerics; and each holy place would constitute a separate and distinct entity with respect to the above-mentioned communities.[4]

A proposal prepared in July 1968 by Meron Benvenisti, in his capacity as adviser to the mayor on East Jerusalem affairs, was made with a view to creating a unified zone for the areas within the sphere of influence of metropolitan Jerusalem, and serving as a proper framework for the city's development; establishing independent municipal units within the framework of the extended municipal area, with due attention to the types of settlement it contained and to the desire of the minorities for self-government in East Jerusalem; and making an attempt to meet the Arabs' request for controlling part of Jerusalem while ensuring Israeli sovereignty over the territory within the city's current boundaries. The means to this end were the delimitation of municipal boundaries which would include territories under Israeli and Jordanian sovereignty; the creation of a joint umbrella-council for five boroughs: Jewish Jerusalem, Arab Jerusalem, the villages, Bethlehem and Beit Jalla; the granting of limited autonomy to the Jerusalem Arab borough and the village sector, with some of the villages placed under Jordanian sovereignty. The Jewish borough was to include the entire Jewish city as well as a strip between Sanhedriya and Mount Scopus, the Old City's Jewish and Armenian Quarters, Mount of Olives, the City of David, East Talpiyot–Ramat Rachel area, Mar Elias Monastery, Beit Safafa area and the Neve Yaacov area. This territory was to ensure development and settlement of about 100,000 people, of whom no more than 9,000 would be Arabs, and to be entirely under Israeli sovereignty. For their part, the Arab boroughs were to include the Old City's Muslim and Christian quarters, Sheikh Jarrah, the American Colony, Wadi Joz, Shuafat, urban Beit Hanina and Silwan – all currently under Israeli sovereignty – and al-Azariya and Abu Dis, which are not under Israeli sovereignty. The villages borough was to include the semi-agricultural villages around the city, some of which would be under Israeli sovereignty – Issawiya and Sur Bahir, Um Tuba – while others were to be under Jordanian sovereignty: al-Ram, Anata, Kafr Aqab, Beit Hanina, Bir Naballa, Kalandiya and Judeda. The Bethlehem and Beit Jalla boroughs were to include their municipal areas (Figure 5).

The Greater Jerusalem council had to deal with the preparation of the programme and daily running of the boroughs, as well as with

FIGURE 5

DIVISION OF JERUSALEM INTO SELF-ADMINISTRATION BOROUGHS

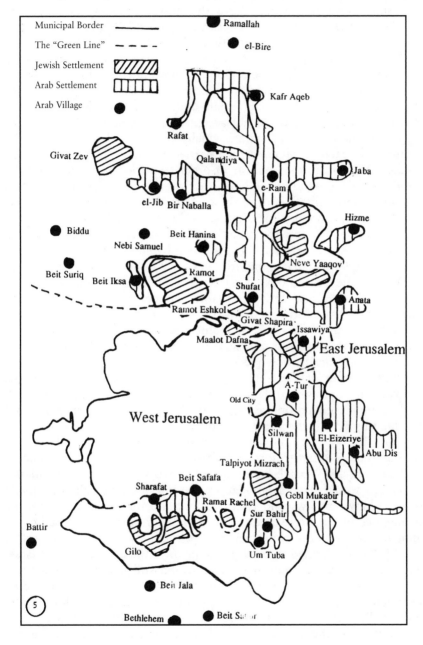

regional and rural development, economy and tourism, fire-fighting, regional sewage and water projects, and transportation and housing. The state authorities would have the power to annul any decision relating to their sovereign sphere.[5] In December 1969, at the height of the Egyptian–Israeli War of Attrition, a plan for the resolution of the Arab–Israeli conflict was put forward by William Rogers, the then US Secretary of State, only to be rejected by both Egypt and Israel. One of the reasons for Israel's negative reaction was that the plan did not stipulate that Jerusalem would remain under Israeli rule. Rather it stated that the United States could not accept unilateral actions by any party regarding the city's final status, which could only be determined by mutual agreement of all concerned parties, primarily Jordan and Israel, taking into account the interests of other countries in the area and the international community at large. According to the plan, Jerusalem should remain unified, with open access to the unified city for persons of all faiths and nationalities. The plan did not specifically refer to the holy places but did note the need to ensure free access to the city and to take into account the interests of all its inhabitants and of the Jewish, Muslim and Christian communities in the city's administration.[6]

Among the resolutions of an Arab summit conference at Fez in September 1982, a few provisions concerning Jerusalem were mentioned. These included an Israeli withdrawal from all Arab territories occupied in 1967, including Arab Jerusalem; the creation of a Palestinian state with Jerusalem as its capital; and freedom of worship for all religions in the holy places.

In the winter of 1991–92, a group of Israelis and Palestinians (C. Calbin, M. Amirav and H. Siniora) co-operating within a research project, published a proposal suggesting that Jerusalem's territory would be quadrupled by the incorporation of an almost equal amount of territory from Israel and the West Bank. The new metropolis would include Ramallah in the north, Mevasseret Zion in the west, Bethlehem in the south, and Maaleh Edumim in the east. With the new boundaries Jerusalem would have a population of some 800,000, almost equally divided between Jews and Arabs. This population balance would be maintained in the future by means of an immigration policy based on an annual increase of no more than three per cent. Metropolitan Jerusalem would then be divided into 20 municipalities; the government of Israel and the prospective Palestinian state would still handle most matters normally vested in national authorities and would maintain dual jurisdiction to adjudicate in the metropolis. The citizenship of the metropolitan city's residents would be determined by their own wishes rather than by the area in which they happened to live, and the city would be one physically open area with no checkpoints or physical barriers. The Old City would form its own municipality and be run by a city council, with decisions regarding physical planning and development approved unanimously by its residents and each faith having full administrative power over its holy sites.[7]

Two years later, in June 1994, the Israel–Palestine Centre for Research and Information (IPCRI) similarly proposed that Jerusalem be not physically divided and preserve its open character. Separate areas would be created, based on the composition of the population, in which Israeli and Palestinian authorities would respectively be vested with limited sovereignty, whereas sovereignty over the Old City would be entirely relinquished by both sides with each community maintaining its legal system in those areas where it enjoyed a demographic majority according to the boundaries between municipalities or boroughs. The holy places, as well as religious buildings and sites would not be under the national sovereignty of either Israel or Palestine. The two municipalities would establish a joint planning commission to co-ordinate between the various religious authorities.[8]

RECENT PARTITION PLANS

In October 1995 three maps, prepared by the Jerusalem Institute for Israel Studies and describing alternative plans for the final solution in Jerusalem, were passed by government officials to the Palestinian Authority. In one of these maps the recognition of Palestinian sovereignty in East Jerusalem was clearly expressed, but also the annexation to Israel of certain territories such as the Etzion Bloc, Maaleh Edumim, Givat-Zev and Betar (Figure 6).

The plan suggested five alternatives for Palestinian sovereignty in East Jerusalem, from the easy to the difficult:

1. Sovereignty over a limited area, along the fringe line of Jerusalem's municipal boundary, would be connected by a strip of land to the Palestinian territories, to be partly used as a Palestinian government compound. This fringe line might include such areas as Ras al-Ammud, Arab al-Sawahra, Um Lizan, Sur Bahir and Um Tuba at the south-east part of the city; the eastern part of the Mount of Olives, al-Shuyukh, al-Tur with the 'Continental Hotel' and Issawiya, and in the northern part – Shuafat, Beit Hanina and Kafr Aqeb. All other Arab neighbourhoods were to remain under Israeli sovereignty.

2. Sovereignty in East Jerusalem, excluding its Jewish neighbourhoods and the Jewish Quarter in the Old City. The other parts of East Jerusalem, together with the Old City, the Mount of Olives and the Town of David, which contain the most important sites for the three religions, would receive a special status of suspended sovereignty or condominium.

FIGURE 6

PROPOSAL OF EXPANDED ISRAELI AUTONOMY IN JERUSALEM 1997

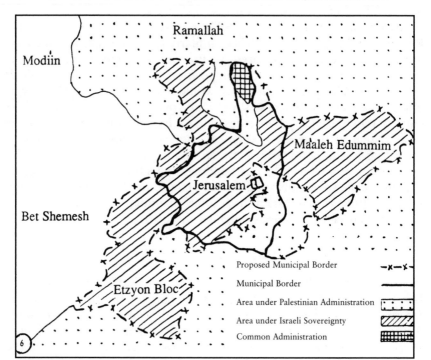

3. Sovereignty over East Jerusalem – excluding the Jewish neighbourhoods and the Old City which would remain under Israeli sovereignty.

4. Sovereignty over East Jerusalem – excluding the Jewish neighbourhoods, the Jewish cemetery on the Mount of Olives, the Town of David, the Jewish and the Armenian Quarters in the Old City, West Jerusalem, and a strip of land connecting the Etzion Bloc to Israel.

5. Sovereignty in East Jerusalem – excluding the Jewish neighbourhoods.

The advantages of these alternatives, from the Israeli point of view are as follows:

• Reconciliation with the Palestinian and the Muslim world, and a greater chance to achieve a long-term stable peace agreement.

- Preservation of Israeli sovereignty in the Jewish neighbourhoods of East Jerusalem, including the Jewish Quarter, and a substantial part of East Jerusalem.

- Palestinian recognition of Israel's sovereignty over most parts of the city, including the new neighbourhoods built after 1967 and consisting today of some 170,000 inhabitants.

- A possible territorial exchange in return for the connection of Maaleh Edumim and Givat-Zev to Jerusalem, and a connection of the Etzion Bloc to Israel after Israel's surrender of all the Arab areas in East Jerusalem.

- No need for a physical division of Jerusalem and assurance of free access to all parts of the city without disrupting the economic fabric, and without the need to rule the 170,000 Palestinians living in East Jerusalem.

- The security in the city and its foreign affairs will be kept under Israel's authority.

- The possibility of gradual long-term progression towards Palestinian sovereignty – starting with a limited government compound as an interim arrangement to a bigger part in East Jerusalem, excluding the Jewish neighbourhoods, as a final agreement.

The plan's deficiencies for Israel are as follows:

- With the functioning of two political capitals in Jerusalem, the Jewish nature of the city will be diminished and its political status as a Jewish domain might be undermined.

- Palestinian sovereignty will be established on the Temple Mount, which is a holy place for the Jews.

- The running of a mutual administration and policing is bound to be complicated and to generate conflicts between the two communities.

Another plan proposed by the same institute took for granted the existing situation in the city, created since the Six Day War, and was based on the assumption that the municipal area of Jerusalem will remain under Israeli sovereignty. Exchange of areas by mutual agreement between Israel and the Palestinians, because of pragmatic and municipal reasons, will be possible.

The advantages of this latter plan are as follows:

- Protection of Jerusalem as a Jewish entity.

- Reinforcement of the idea among Israelis and Jews that other alternatives may weaken Israeli sovereignty in Jerusalem, aggravate tension and violence between Arabs and Jews, and create breaches that cannot be healed.

- This plan may be used as a provisional step in a situation of disagreement between the two sides, enabling a return to other alternatives once the Palestinian entity has proved its stability as a political and democratic body.

The weaknesses of this plan are formidable indeed:

- It is totally unacceptable to the Palestinians.
- It may be an obstacle to the Israeli–Palestinian peace negotiations.
- It is unacceptable to the Arab states and can exacerbate the peace negotiations with them.
- It may strain American–Israeli relations.
- It may create agitation and ignite a new uprising in the Territories.

Yet another plan has been similarly based on the assumption that Israel will have exclusive sovereignty in Jerusalem in its present municipal boundaries. In the framework of a mutual agreement, the exchange of limited areas in the city with territories in Judea might be possible. A symbolic centre of sovereignty for the Palestinians in the city might be approved. The Temple Mount will be under the super-sovereignty of Israel and a Palestinian–Islamic–Jordanian administration; a similar status will be given to the Church of Sepulchre, and to the Christian Quarter in the Old City; the Armenian Quarter will get a special status, as will the space between the walls and the near surroundings of the Old City (Figure 7).

The aim of this latter plan is to administer functional autonomy under Israeli sovereignty in all quarters of East Jerusalem. Such autonomy will be supervised by the Jerusalem municipality and will include among others the following domains: collecting domestic taxes, administration of borough councils with permanent staff members, culture, education, sport, social services, gardening, health and religious services.

The idea of functional autonomy has been already accepted in principle by different institutions and organizations involved in Jerusalem's political future. The idea is to delegate some important powers to borough administrations, to develop in them domestic security with civil guard and to encourage their independence *vis-à-vis* the municipal authorities. Borough administration would be established in all parts of the city, allowing in turn the creation of a sub-municipality for the Old City with a inter-religious and international council.

In this plan it is also recommended that the existing system of borough administration would be dispersed to all city neighbourhoods. The administration in the Old City would be established on the basis of the ethnic and religious composition of the inhabitants. The boundaries

FIGURE 7

PROPOSAL FOR JEWISH AND ARAB BOROUGHS IN JERUSALEM 1997

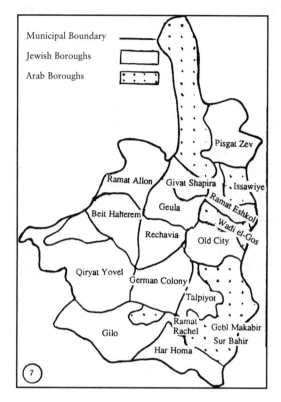

of each borough would be delineated in consultation with the residents' representatives.

Functional autonomy to the boroughs may have a good chance of being accepted. The present situation in the city is unacceptable to the Palestinians, while recognition of Palestinian sovereignty in East Jerusalem is not agreed upon by many of the Israelis. This plan, however, is flexible: it enables the proposal of different kinds of arrangements between the two communities and can be executed gradually according to future circumstances. Its main deficiency, though, is that if the rules are not strictly observed it might lead to a weakening of Israel's sovereignty in the city.

CONCLUSIONS

The above-mentioned facts indicate that Jerusalem is a site of demographic and physical competition between two populations, with the clear political purpose of holding and controlling the city and its adjacent environs. It may be assumed that without a mutually agreed comprehensive political plan and rapid systematic implementation of important aspects of it, Israel will not be able to safeguard the city as a capital. It may also be assumed that the city's reunification in 1967 did not bring an end to the division between Jews and Arabs. The animosities are deep and have survived the recent geographical shifts. None of the different partition plans of Jerusalem will ensure the city's normal functioning. It is also doubtful whether these plans will allow Jerusalem to remain a universal capital as opposed to a mere spatial political arena where two peoples find themselves embraced in hatred without any logical solution.

While in a normal city, not to speak of a capital, the boundaries usually conform to topography, building zones, homogenous neighbourhoods, efficient arteries that connect vital places to their surroundings and economic sites with optimal places – in Jerusalem the opposite situation exists. The possibility of partial sovereignty, suspended sovereignty or a common functional sovereignty for special areas will never be an optimal solution for the city.

The proposed plans demonstrate, after all, that Jerusalem has become an urban mosaic of distorted decisions unparalleled elsewhere in the world. It seems that Jerusalem has actually become a part of the territory of Judea and Samaria and may be eventually included in some of the A to C categories of the Oslo Accords for the purpose of partition.

The three-decade-long territorial conflict in Jerusalem has dismantled the city from its special urban properties to the point of making it a 'no city'. Further expansion of the city to its periphery will only exacerbate the problems. Any decision on the city's future should be based on the ethnic composition of neighbourhoods with minimal friction between Arabs and Jews, so as to ensure Jewish and Arab neighbourhoods as independent entities and to protect the Jewish nature of the city in those parts where the majority of Jews live. Should this not be achieved, one might be forced to return to the idea expressed by the late King Hussein of Jordan whereby 'Jerusalem belongs to God and not to people'.

## NOTES

1. Y. Katz, 'The Political Status of Jerusalem in Historical Context: Zionist Plans for the Partition of Jerusalem in the Years 1937–1938', *Shofar*, Vol. 11, No. 3 (Spring 1993), pp.41–53.
2. Ibid.
3. 'UN General Assembly Official Records', Fifth Session, Supp. No. 9, 1950 (A/1286), p.29.
4. U. Benziman, *Jerusalem: City without a Wall*, Jerusalem and Tel Aviv, 1973, pp.110–14 (Hebrew).

5.  M.D. Hirsch, D. Housen-Curiel and R. Lapidoth, *Whither Jerusalem? Proposals and Positions Concerning the Future of Jerusalem*, Hague, 1995.
6.  Ibid.
7.  C.H. Calbin, M. Amirav and H. Siniora, 'Jerusalem: an Undivided City as Dual Capital', Harry S. Truman Institute for the Advancement of Peace and The Arab Studies Society, Israeli–Palestinian Peace Research Project, Working Paper Series, No. 16, 1991–92.
8.  G. Baskin (ed.), *New Thinking on the Future of Jerusalem: A Model for the Future of Jerusalem – Scattered Sovereignty*, Jerusalem, 1994.

# Arab–Israeli Coexistence: The Causes, Achievements and Limitations

## EFRAIM INBAR

Many welcomed the May 1999 victory of Prime Minister Ehud Barak, in the hope that it would inject a long-awaited boost to the peace process. Indeed, the prevalent view among observers and policymakers is that the peace process is back on track after the September 1999 Sharm al-Sheikh summit and the January 2000 renewal of the Israeli–Syrian talks, although they continue to regard the Arab–Israeli peace process as fragile, with lack of progress endangering regional stability. In March 2000 the mood was again one of concern. Such a view underestimates, on the one hand, the force of the regional processes that have pushed the Arab states away from the goal of destroying the Jewish state towards attempts at solving differences primarily by diplomatic means. On the other hand, it has unrealistic expectations for further progress in the peace process and belittles the inherent regional constraints on its development.

This essay reviews first the main reasons for the entrenchment of Israel in the Middle East and for the shift towards its greater acceptance as a regular international player in regional politics. The second section argues that the peace process is quite resilient, and that it has successfully realized most of its potential. The third part clarifies the often forgotten limitations to the peace process, which the strategic and cultural realities of the Middle East impose on Arab states' relations with Israel. This article concludes by offering a few policy-relevant observations, and especially advises against impatience and diplomatic hyperactivity.

## ISRAEL'S ACCEPTANCE BY ITS REGIONAL FOES

The visit of Anwar Sadat, the President of Egypt, to Israel in October 1977 signalled a dramatic change in the pattern of Arab–Israeli

Efraim Inbar is Associate Professor in Political Studies at Bar-Ilan University and the Director of its Begin–Sadat (BESA) Center for Strategic Studies.

relations. The Arab world, in particular, was stunned by the move which recognized Israel as a *fait accompli*. The 1978 Camp David Accords and the 1979 peace treaty between Egypt and Israel were not welcomed by most of the Arab countries or by the Palestinians. Peace with Israel violated a basic tenet of Arab consensus and challenged one of the core values in Arab political culture. Therefore, Egypt was for several years ostracized by its Arab brethren. Yet, Egypt, the strongest Arab country, weathered the attempts to isolate it[1] and after the 1991 Gulf War most of the Arab world joined it in negotiating peace with Israel. Several factors led to this process.

## Futility of Attempting to Eradicate Israel by Force

The most important reason for the peace process was the growing realization by Arab political elites of the futility of attempting to eradicate Israel by force. Indeed, since 1973 we see a clear decline in the military intensity of the Arab–Israeli conflict. During the first three decades of its existence, Israel fought and won four large-scale wars, in 1948, 1956, 1967 and 1973, involving Israel's immediate neighbours, as well as expeditionary forces from 'second ring' countries, such as Iraq and Sudan, and even from more remote countries such as Morocco. Since October 1973, however, no large-scale war has been fought between Israel and an Arab country.

After 1979, when Egypt signed a peace treaty with Israel, the Arabs lost not only the strongest military force to be mobilized against Israel, but also the ability to wage a two-front assault on Israel (its worst-case scenario). Thus the destruction of Israel by a successful all-out Arab military conventional effort seemed no longer to be a practical goal, despite the fact that limited war and low-intensity conflict were (as was realized earlier), useful tools in bleeding Israel and in pressuring it into territorial concessions.[2]

Although the strategic significance of the Israeli nuclear posture in Arab eyes is not entirely clear, it probably had a sobering effect on the belligerent Arab states.[3] Israel's nuclear option, coupled with the awareness of Israel's conventional weapon superiority, certainly constitutes a contributing factor to the strategic calculus that led to the Arab realization that the price of eliminating the Jewish state by war could be extremely high.

The new links between Jerusalem and Ankara in the latter part of the 1990s reinforced the notion that Israel is militarily strong and cannot be easily removed from the map. In many Arab quarters there are considerable apprehensions about the combined might of the two, which changes dramatically the regional balance of power in favour of the non-Arab actors.[4] The burgeoning Turkish–Israeli economic and military ties have united the two strongest countries in the region, which further buttressed the position of Israel as a powerful regional actor. This relationship is resilient and likely to continue, as it is based on a shared view of the Middle East as a combative neighbourhood in which the two countries have a common list of problematic rivals – Iraq and Iran.

### Changes in Arab Countries' Foreign Policy Orientation

Parallel to the changing evaluations concerning the chances of destroying Israel, Arab countries have undergone a shift in their foreign policy orientation. They have moved since the 1970s from various degrees of allegiance to Pan-Arab ideology to a foreign policy more openly determined by national statist interests. The Pan-Arab longing for supra-state identity and political structure has always served as a legitimizing mechanism for domestic and foreign policy processes in Arab states, but has also constituted a constraint in the open pursuit of each country's own narrow statist interests. Gradually, Pan-Arabism became less appealing, and at the same time, Arab states were relatively successful in strengthening their statist structures and in crystallizing a particular Arab state identity, whether Iraqi, Jordanian or Syrian.[5] Despite the fact that only a few of the existing Arab states seem the right and natural focus of ultimate political loyalty, it is these states that have become the most important arena for political action in the Arab world.[6]

This shift in the focus of regional politics has led to a decline in the salience of the Arab–Israeli conflict and the Palestinian issue, which were central in the Pan-Arab ethos.[7] Indeed, Egypt, after the death of Nasser, the most important pan-Arab advocate, moved toward a more Egypt-centred view of regional politics.[8] Thereafter, it could concentrate on retrieving the land it lost in June 1967, without conditioning the return of the Sinai to the resolution of other disputes between Israel and its neighbours. Moreover, the success of the Palestine Liberation Organization (PLO) in establishing itself as *the* voice, *par excellence*, of Palestinian nationalism, in attracting international attention to the Palestinian issue, and in acquiring modest freedom of action in the Arab arena, allowed, paradoxically, Arab states to limit their commitment to the Palestinian cause. After the PLO reached its own agreement with Israel in September 1993 (at Oslo), the Arab states had even less of a constraint in dealing with Israel according to their own perceived interests.

### Changes in the Palestinian National Movement

An additional contributing factor to the evolution of the peace process is the changes that have taken place in the Palestinian national movement, whose main proponent was the PLO. The PLO's international status and regional influence peaked in the late 1970s.

However, in 1982, the Israeli invasion of Lebanon put an end to the PLO mini-state, resulting in the removal of the PLO leadership and thousands of its personnel to faraway Tunisia. (No other Arab state was willing to host the PLO headquarters, indicating the limits to the Arab contribution to the Palestinian cause.) The distance from Palestine made the use of force against targets within Israel a more complicated operation than ever before.

The most significant Palestinian action – the *intifada* – was not the result of a PLO initiative. Moreover, the Palestinian uprising in the Israeli-ruled territories brought a new leadership to the forefront of the Palestinian struggle – the 'insiders' – Palestinians who fought Israeli occupation inside the territories.[9] They had impeccable nationalist credentials and were less vulnerable to charges of corruption (of which a large part of the PLO leadership was suspected). Although nominally subordinate to the PLO, the 'insiders' believed that their intimate knowledge of the Israeli enemy placed them in a better position to formulate the Palestinian national strategy. The 'insiders' have infused a greater sense of realism into the Palestinian national movement, in terms of what could be achieved, as well as a certain urgency in dealing with Palestinian problems, which also moderated their demands. The influx of Israeli settlers into the territories and the building of Jewish settlements also led to a realization that time was not necessarily on the Palestinian side. In concrete terms, these Palestinians advocated accepting Israel in its 1967 lines and negotiating with it to bring about a withdrawal from the occupied territories. They were instrumental in pushing the PLO away from its maximalist position, and its refusal to recognize Israel, into adopting a two-state formula. In November 1988, the PLO finally accepted the UN 1947 Partition Plan (Resolution 181).

A major blow to the PLO was its strategic blunder of 1990. At that time it allied itself with Saddam Hussein, who chose to champion the Palestinian cause in order to evoke sympathy in the streets of the Arab world. This move angered the US and cost the PLO the diplomatic and financial support of many important Arab countries. Following the 1991 American victory over Iraq, the US convened the Madrid conference and the PLO had to be content with sending its representatives within a Jordanian delegation. Moreover, the Palestinians no longer demanded that a Palestinian state had to be on the agenda and agreed to a two-stage open-ended process following the outline of the 1978 Camp David Accords, and concentrating first on achieving an interim agreement. Again, the 'insiders' were the moving force in moderating the Palestinian demands issued in Tunis. The apprehensions that the leaders of the *intifada*, within the Israeli-ruled territories, would take over the Palestinian national movement, coupled with the deep financial crisis of the PLO, led Arafat to the September 1993 Oslo Agreement. Then the PLO recognized Israel, renounced the use of force, and promised the cancellation of the clauses in the Palestinian Covenant which called for the destruction of Israel.[10]

## Growing Significance of Other Threats to the Arab World

An important contributing factor to the peace process was the lesson learned by Arab leaders that Israel was not the biggest threat to the Arab world. Khomeini's Islamic revolution in 1979 triggered, for many, memories of another historic enemy to the Arab people – the Persians; others were frightened by the challenge the Islamic revolution posed to the legitimacy of their regimes. Indeed, most Arab states allied themselves with the aggressor of the first Gulf War (1980–88), Iraq, in order to contain the Iranian–Islamic wave. During this period, the dispute with Israel was secondary.[11] The Syrians, who sided with Iran, were allowed to face Israel on their own in 1982. Even the Palestinian uprising in 1987 did not elicit much support as most of the Arab world was busy parrying the Islamic challenge from Tehran.

An initially ostracized Egypt capitalized on the Iran–Iraq War to regain its leading status in inter-Arab affairs, without giving in to the demands that it change its policy *vis-à-vis* Israel. Its much-needed assistance to Iraq (the provision of manpower, military equipment and instruction), and its association with the US, the victor in the Cold War, brought Egypt's isolation to an end. In addition, Egypt's reintegration within the Arab system made its peace treaty with Israel more acceptable to the Arab world.

Yet, only a few years later, Arab leaders lived to see their ally make an about-turn as their fellow Arab, the megalomaniac Saddam Hussein, became intent on hegemonic pursuits and the attainment of the riches of Kuwait. His appeal to the masses in the Arab world was not lost on those in power who felt threatened by the Iraqi actions. The Americans were invited to curtail Saddam Hussein's aspirations and eventually to reverse the conquest of Kuwait. President Bush was adept at building a military coalition to free Kuwait, and Israel did its best not to spoil the coalition by absorbing 39 Iraqi missiles. Israel, at this junction, and not for the first time, was aligned *de facto* with many Arab states.

For years, the potential for an Israeli alliance was well known to the Hashemites, who shared a common enemy with the Israelis, the Palestinian national movement, and were aided more than once by Israeli military backing.[12] The events of September 1970, when Israel's military moves deterred an expansion of the Syrian effort to invade Jordan, are the best-known example of Israel's support for the Hashemites. Jordan is indeed the closest Arab country to Israel and even takes part in the Israeli–Turkish alignment. Similarly, some of the small

Gulf states see in Israel a distant power able to play a balancing role in the region, particularly against hegemonic ambitions.

*Domestic Politics*

Another development facilitating the peace process originates in domestic politics. Growing social weariness towards war has forced the political leadership in several countries in the region to redefine their national goals. Populations have grown tired of protracted conflict. This has led to moderate positions and to greater willingness to discuss the possibility of peace by all nations in the region. This was a clear factor in Egypt's disposition to sign peace treaties with Israel, and influenced the Palestinians to accept more realistic results from their national struggle. Israel likewise is war-weary and has little appetite or desire to police the areas inhabited by Palestinians. Precisely for this reason, Israel is no longer attracted to the notion of 'Greater Israel'. Hence the redefinition of collective goals in light of newly perceived realities made it possible for the two sides to move closer together.

*International Developments*

Certain features of the international system were no less important than the regional developments in fostering a greater acceptance of Israel. In the bipolar international system, Israel was aligned with the United States. The alliance with the US was an important component of Israel's deterrent power in regional politics. The October 1973 American airlift to its embattled ally remained for many years a potent indication of US commitment to the security of Israel. One important Arab strategic goal for years has been to weaken the link between Israel and its superpower ally and to deny the Jewish state international legitimacy.[13] The overall robustness of Jerusalem–Washington relations and particularly the increased strategic co-operation between the two sides since the 1980s made the Arab goal of putting a wedge between the two unrealistic. The campaign to isolate Israel in the international community also failed.

Moreover, the end of the Cold War was beneficial in strategic terms to Israel. Arab countries were further weakened by the collapse of the Soviet Union. The Arabs no longer had the backing of a superpower, thus limiting their military and diplomatic options. In contrast, Israel continued to be allied with the victor in the Cold War. The two most viciously anti-Israeli countries, Iraq and Iran, became the enemies of the US and subject to American sanctions. The fact that the US emerged as the only global superpower has made Arab countries more responsive to American preferences, including the acceptance of Israel.

The Arab world was politically further weakened by another systemic change – the emergence of a buyers' market in the world oil economy. Arab oil-producing countries, in particular, lost much political clout because of low oil prices, while the mismanagement of their economies further reduced their international standing.[14]

Indeed, in 1991, in the aftermath of the Cold War, the Americans capitalized on their victory in the Gulf War and on the trends discussed above by promoting another attempt at continuing the peace process – the October 1991 Madrid conference. This conference initiated a process of bilateral negotiations, as well as the participation of Israel and an unprecedented number of Arab countries to discuss Middle East problems.

The Americans brought the Syrians, the Palestinians and the Jordanians to the negotiating table in Madrid, primarily on Israeli terms. No preconditions previously demanded by Syria (for example, an Israeli commitment to withdraw from the Golan Heights and negotiations under the umbrella of a binding international conference) were met. Indeed, President Asad of Syria was dragged into the peace process out of weakness, following the loss of his Soviet patron and the American demonstration of military might and resolve in 1991. Participation in the peace process was a Syrian adjustment to a new international reality.[15]

However, overall, the regional processes and the fluctuating perceptions of the political leaders in the Middle East have been shown to have more clout than the global changes and superpower influence. The American efforts to bring about an Israeli–Syrian accord have thus far failed to achieve concrete results. Similarly, the American involvement in the Israeli–Palestinian track has had mixed results. And historically, the main breakthroughs in the Arab–Israeli conflict, namely Sadat's visit to Jerusalem and the Oslo Agreement, were not due to an American initiative and in fact, came to them as a surprise, albeit a pleasant one.

## THE RESILIENCE OF THE PEACE PROCESS

Several regional processes and global dynamics fuelled the Arab rapprochement with Israel. The peace process stemmed basically out of Arab weakness. As long as the trends enumerated above continue, even in the absence of progress (usually a euphemism for Israeli concessions), the likelihood of a reverse in the historic accommodation towards Israel is small. To a great extent, the Arab world has crossed the Rubicon in accepting Israel's existence, not legitimacy, as an almost irrevocable fact, and as a regular international actor in the Middle East.

In many ways, the peace process is over, and has been concluded *successfully*. Israel has had a peace treaty with Egypt since 1979. A reversal to belligerence is unlikely as long as Egypt holds on to an American orientation in its foreign policy. In 1994, Jordan formalized its good relations with Israel by signing a peace treaty. On the Palestinian track, the 1993 Oslo Agreement – in fact a repartition of Palestine – is being implemented, albeit gradually and not without difficulties. The contours of the Palestinian state, its borders and degree of sovereignty remain to be negotiated. The rationale of partition and the establishment of two entities is politically compelling.

Since 1993, the Palestinian national movement has never had so much to lose – real control over most Palestinians and exclusive rule over parts of their perceived homeland. The Palestinians have learned from their history that the lip service paid by Arab countries to their cause is rarely backed by deeds, which leaves them almost alone to face the much stronger Israelis. Thus, while low-level conflict takes place, Arafat seems to be careful so as not to provoke Israel into a large-scale conflict.

Moreover, Israel, as a whole, has moved in favour of partition of the Land of Israel. The Likud-led government (1996–99) signed agreements in which land was transferred to the Palestinian Authority (PA) – the January 1997 Hebron Agreement and the October 1998 Wye Plantation Accords. The May 1999 election results clearly show that support within Israeli society for the idea of Greater Israel is minimal (less than five per cent). Israelis have even reconciled themselves to the emergence of a Palestinian state. Nevertheless, the changes in Israeli attitudes do not make an agreement with the Palestinians inevitable, as even in the case of a Labour-led government there is still no convergence of views between the two societies, particularly on issues of borders, refugees, and Jerusalem. Indeed, the expectations that the negotiations between a Barak-led government and the PA on final status issues will be conducted smoothly and will end within a year or so are not very realistic. Barak has in the past voiced great reservations about the Oslo Agreement and several political forces within his wide coalition are unlikely to support territorial largesse toward the Palestinians.

On the Syrian track of the peace process, Asad has so far proved unwilling to move forward. He refused to accept the Golan Heights in exchange for a peace treaty, which required him to open up his closed society a little and which questioned his continuous control over Lebanon. This has been the American evaluation, and even Arab capitals recognize, unofficially, that Asad missed an historic opportunity to make a very favourable deal with Israel.[16] Indeed, Rabin offered him the Golan Heights in August 1993 and Peres repeated the offer in January 1996.[17] In all probability, even Netanyahu suggested a similar deal, but Asad did not bite the bullet.

Barak succeeded in bringing back the Syrians to the negotiating table in January 2000, but he is even more insistent than Rabin on adequate security arrangements and he has consistently been critical of Labour's negotiating formula that 'the depth of the withdrawal from the Golan Heights corresponds to the depth of peace'. His preferred equation has been 'the depth of withdrawal shall be equal to the quality of peace and the strength of the security and early warning arrangements'.[18]

It remains to be seen whether Asad's successor is ready for peace. Possibly, the talks were only a shield against stronger American and/or Israeli diplomatic and military pressures, but it is remarkable that they have been held at all. In any case, Syria has only limited potential to obstruct Israel's acceptance in the region. By now it is clear that Syria does not have a veto power in regional affairs as its opposition to Jordanian and Palestinian attempts to reach separate agreements with Israel proved futile.

Indeed, even when Arab states complained that a Netanyahu-led Israel violated the agreements with the PA and that he was not generous enough, territory-wise, towards the PA and Syria, we see very little inclination in the Arab world to heed the advice of the radical states to revert to a state of war. Since 1996, Arab summits have called upon Israel to implement its *peace* commitments and have threatened to freeze their relations with the Jewish state. Yet despite the official rhetoric, in many ways relations between Arab states and Israel are proceeding well. In October 1999, for example, Mauritania, an Arab League member, even decided to have full diplomatic relations with Israel. As such, the belligerence of the *status quo ante* is thus not a real option in the near future.

## THE LIMITATIONS ON PEACEFUL COEXISTENCE

Israel now definitely has better relations with the Arab world than it did a few decades ago. This pattern is likely to continue. Yet, there are limits to what Israel can achieve in its ties with its neighbours. Expectations that Israeli–Arab relations can emulate the type of interaction characteristic of western Europe or North America are totally unrealistic for several reasons rooted in the strategic and cultural realities of the region.

### Power Politics in the Middle East

Basically, the old patterns of regional interaction – power politics – have remained unchanged, despite the removal of the superpower competition in the area.[19] The dreams of a new Middle East are just that. President Mubarak in an interview to the Israeli press admitted that the vision Shimon Peres propagated left many Egyptians uncomfortable, reminding the Israeli audience they live in the Middle East.[20] Indeed, the dominant perception of international relations among the political leadership of the Middle East, with the exception of a few in Jerusalem, has remained power politics. This is why Cairo, Damascus and Baghdad fear the Israeli–Turkish entente.

Moreover, in the Middle East the use of force is still considered an acceptable and useful tool of foreign policy. Indeed, the region's Zeitgeist favours violence, 'where guerrillas are lauded, and peacemakers ridiculed'.[21] Even peace negotiations are accompanied by violence. For example, Syria does not desist from using the Hizbullah in bleeding Israel while it engages in peace negotiations with Israel. The PA is turning a blind eye to Hamas terrorists when it believes it suits its interests. In September 1996, the PA allowed its soldiers to shoot at the Israeli army, while Arafat often threatens Israel with a new *intifada* if his demands are not satisfied. Indeed the emerging Palestinian entity has great potential for developing into a revisionist and predatory state,[22] and Mubarak and other Arab leaders have repeatedly warned that in the absence of 'progress' there will be a violent eruption.

The best we can expect in the region is an armed peace. Egypt, despite its 20-year-old peace treaty with Israel, continues to arm itself and has developed a large and modern American-equipped army. According to some of its generals, Egypt continues to see Israel as a potential military rival.[23] Neither Egypt nor Jordan capitalized on their peace treaty with Israel to reduce defence spending. Despite the Madrid peace process, Syria used money received from Saudi Arabia (for its anti-Iraq stance in 1991), over $1 billion, to buy arms.[24] In fact, armed peace characterizes inter-Arab relations. No Arab state feels that all of its borders are safe and each harbours suspicions against its neighbours. Indeed, all of Israel's Arab neighbours have legitimate security concerns in regard to their other neighbours. Israel also, despite the reduction in threat perception, continues to arm itself and even leaders on the Israeli Left see the Israeli army as the final guarantee for peaceful relations with its neighbours.

*Border Disputes*

Generally, borders in the Middle East, which were drawn by colonialist powers, still lack legitimacy. This allows for revisionist policies. Syria never recognized Lebanon as an independent state and was successful in turning it into its satellite. Iraq still has ambitions to annex Kuwait. South Yemen disappeared as an independent state in May 1994 as it was 'united' by force with its neighbour – North Yemen. A dissatisfied Palestine could become the source for irredentist claims east and west. Indeed, Arafat's willingness 'to sacrifice even the last Palestinian child for placing the Palestinian flag on the walls of Jerusalem' and his repeated calls for Jihad indicate the potential for additional demands and tensions. As recently as the spring of 1999, the Palestinians renewed their demand that the Jewish state be confined to the borders of the 1947 Partition Plan, in accordance with UN Resolution 181.

## Non-Acceptance of Israel

The acceptance of Israel is far from being internalized by Arab societies. Notably, many Arab intellectuals and professionals refrain from supporting the peace process. In stark contrast to their Israeli counterparts (the most ardent supporters of the peace process), these groups are most critical of the reconciliation with the Jewish state and with a few exceptions boycott any contacts with Israelis. In Jordan, the peace treaty with Israel is pejoratively termed 'the King's peace'. There, as well as in Egypt, professional associations of lawyers, physicians, journalists and engineers impose sanctions on members who dare talk about normalizing relations with Israel. Public opinion in the Levant clearly indicates that the peace process is limited primarily to regimes, not societies,[25] and despite the fact that Arab states are not democracies, their political leaders are sensitive to public opinion.[26]

Though Israel is viewed in less demonic terms than in the past, fears of Israeli economic domination have replaced the fears of Israeli territorial expansion. For example, the 1994 Casablanca conference, at which dynamic Israelis displayed eagerness to enter into business ventures with the Arabs, backfired; it was misconstrued as an Israeli design to control the Middle East by economic means. Indeed, Israel's gross national product (GNP) is larger than the GNP of all of its neighbours combined. Paradoxically, Israel's efforts to integrate into the region have also triggered fears of cultural imperialism. Israel is still seen, not only by the Islamists, but by larger segments of the Arab political and intellectual elite, as an outpost of the West and its colonial legacy in the Middle East.

The litmus test of changing attitudes towards Israel in the long run is the education system, where the socialization process of a new generation takes place. Unfortunately, the school curriculum even in the Arab countries that have signed agreements with Israel remains unchanged, propagating anti-Israeli views and rabid anti-Semitic images. The Arab media (usually government-controlled) is replete with language of hate towards all Jews. In contrast, the Israeli Ministry of Education has published a unit for Peace Studies to be taught in grammar schools and searched its books in order to eliminate anti-Arab stereotypes, while new history textbooks are introduced into the state school system, which show greater empathy towards the Palestinians.[27]

## The Appeal of Radical Islam

Another politico-cultural feature of the Middle East which places limits on ties with Israel is the widespread appeal of radical Islam, particularly in Egypt, Jordan and Palestine; there, as elsewhere, radical Islamist groups oppose any reconciliation with the Jewish state. The enmity for Israel and the West is great.[28] In the Middle East, Islamic fundamentalism enjoys great support beyond Iran and Sudan – the two Islamic republics – in almost every state in the region, including secular Turkey, and its potential consequences should not be ignored. For the time being, however, the Islamic radicals have only limited ability to obstruct the peace process. Egypt and Jordan have not changed diplomatic course because of the Islamist opposition. Yet the Islamic political influence is a strong domestic constraint on openly pursuing cordial relations with Israel in many countries of the region.

## Changing Circumstances

Finally, the peace process, despite its present robustness, is not necessarily a one-way historic development. An abrupt change of direction is possible, although unlikely at this point in time. Scenarios for turmoil include an Islamic take-over in one of Israel's neighbours. If this happens in Egypt, the most important Arab country, it would be a particularly terrible blow to the peace process and to Western interests. Similarly threatening for Israel is the demise of Hashemite Jordan and its conquest by Palestine, Syria or Iraq. Jordan is a pivotal state in the quest for regional stability. Its disappearance would allow for the reorganization of the eastern front against Israel, in dangerous proximity to the strategic heartland of Israel. The return of Russian influence to the Middle East could also re-energize the radical forces in the region. The realization that change can happen suddenly in the Middle East dictates much caution, which further slows the process of rapprochement between Israel and the Arab world.

## CONCLUSIONS

The first policy-relevant observation concerns the well-intentioned policymaking community, which feels an urge to do good in the Middle East. The situation in the Arab-Israeli conflict has improved considerably, but cannot improve much further. Even if the evolving peace process were to stay its course, the attainment of the type of relations we see among democratic countries may take generations to develop in the Arab-Israeli arena. The security dilemma of all the states in the Middle East dictates that their relationship with their neighbours take the form of armed peace. While the mere nature of politics (the pursuit of national interests) makes Israeli participation in interstate interactions easier, the religious and the cultural dimensions of the Arab-Israeli conflict are less amenable to quick change. The recommendation for the diplomats, chasing after dramatic foreign policy successes, is to look elsewhere.

Second, foreigners have limited leverage, while the locals have underestimated power to block extra-regional initiatives. Almost all

American initiatives to settle the Arab–Israeli conflict have ended in failure. Breakthroughs have belonged to the regional actors and progress comes to fruition only when they are ready for it. The US can play a positive role in compensating the parties for the risks taken, but it cannot impose a Pax Americana. It can also engage in damage limitation when violence erupts. More important, America has little to gain nowadays from investing much more energy in an unattainable comprehensive settlement between Arabs and Jews. Actually, year 2000, an election year, could be a good American pretext for not doing anything dramatic and foolish in the Middle East.

The third observation revolves around the time factor. The peace process evolved over two decades, as a result of a number of regional developments, primarily the entrenchment of Israel as a strong military and economic power linked to the US, the winner of the Cold War. De-escalation in protracted disputes takes time, and there may be temporary setbacks. Much of the impatience displayed in several quarters, particularly in the West, seems to be ignorant of the pace involved in historic processes. As long as the direction of the regional and international factors that moved the Arab world into acceptance of Israel is unchanged, the peace process can be considered as viable, and even robust, despite the fact that not all issues have been satisfactorily resolved. Therefore, the widespread feeling of urgency is unwarranted.

Fourth, Israel's leverage versus the Palestinians and other Arab actors is considerable. Only recently did Arafat desist from unilaterally declaring a Palestinian state as result of Israeli threats. Indeed, Jerusalem can use carrots and sticks to achieve its foreign policy goals. Moreover, it can wait for a better offer in its negotiations with its neighbours. In retrospect, the Arabs have changed their positions more than the Israelis. So far, time has been on the Israeli side and there is little to suggest that the time vector is changing course.

Finally, we must remember that power-politics considerations led Arab political elites gradually to accept Israel as a *fait accompli*. The *realpolitik* outlook on international relations is going to persist in the Middle East. A strong Israel is, therefore, a prerequisite for the peace process. Weakening it harms the peace process.

NOTES

The author would like to thank Stuart A. Cohen, Steven David, Avi Kober, Barry Rubin and Shmuel Sandler for their useful comments on an earlier draft. He would also like to acknowledge the financial support of the Ihel Foundation at Bar-Ilan University in writing this essay.

1. For the process of Egyptian reintegration within the Arab regional system, see Ali E. Hillal

Dessouki, 'Egyptian Foreign Policy Since Camp David', in William B. Quandt (ed.), *The Middle East: Ten Years After Camp David*, Washington, 1988, pp.102–5.

2. See Shimon Shamir, 'Arab Military Lessons from the October War', in Louis Williams (ed.), *Military Aspects of the Israeli–Arab Conflict*, Tel Aviv, 1975, p.175; Bernard Lewis, 'Settling the Arab–Israeli Conflict', *Commentary*, Vol. 63 (June 1977), p.53.

3. For Arab perceptions, see Ariel E. Levite and Emily B. Landau, *Israel's Nuclear Image: Arab Perceptions of Israel's Nuclear Posture*, Tel Aviv, 1994 (Hebrew).

4. See, *inter alia*, Nadia E. El Shazli, 'Arab Anger at New Axis', *World Today*, Vol. 55, No. 1 (January 1999), pp.25–7.

5. Fouad Ajami, 'The End of Pan-Arabism', *Foreign Affairs*, Vol. 57, No. 2 (Winter 1978–79), pp.355–73; Roger Owen, *State, Power and Politics in the Making of the Modern Middle East*, London, 1992; Gabriel Ben-Dor, *State and Conflict in the Middle East*, New York, 1983.

6. R. Stephen Humphrey, *Between Memory and Desire: The Middle East in a Troubled Age*, Berkeley, 1999, p.81.

7. Avraham Sela, *The Decline of the Arab–Israeli Conflict: Middle East Politics and the Quest for Regional Order*, Albany, 1988.

8. Michael N. Barnett, *Dialogues in Arab Politics: Negotiations in Regional Order*, New York, 1998, p.198.

9. Helena Cobban, 'The PLO and the Intifada', in Robert O. Freedman (ed.), *The Intifada*, Miami, 1991, pp.70–106.

10. For the PLO's long road to Oslo, see Barry Rubin, *Revolution Until Victory: The Politics and History of the PLO*, Cambridge, 1994.

11. Paul C. Noble, 'The Arab System: Pressures, Constraints, and Opportunities', in Bahgat Korani and Ali E. Hillal Dessouki (eds), *The Foreign Policies of Arab States: The Challenge of Change*, Boulder, 1991, pp.81–2.

12. The most comprehensive work on Israeli–Jordanian relations is Moshe Zak, *Hussein Makes Peace*, Ramat-Gan, 1996 (Hebrew).

13. Efraim Inbar, *Outcast Countries in the World Community*, Denver, 1985.

14. For a review of the demographic and economic conditions in the Arab world after 1991, see Eliyahu Kanovsky, *The Economic Consequences of the Persian Gulf War: Accelerating OPEC's Demise*, Policy Papers No. 30 , Washington Institute for Near East Policy, Washington DC, 1992; and Muhammad Faour, *The Arab World After Desert Storm*, Washington DC, 1993, pp.15–32.

15. Raymond A. Hinnebusch, 'Asad's Syria and the New World Order: The Struggle For Regime Survival', *Middle East Policy*, Vol. 2, No. 1 (1993), pp.1–14.

16. Interviews with Egyptian and Jordanian high officials. See also Daniel Pipes, 'Asad Isn't Interested', *Jerusalem Post*, 29 August 1999, p.6.

17. For a review of the Israeli–Syrian talks, see Itamar Rabinovich, *The Brink of Peace: Israel and Syria, 1992–1996*, Tel Aviv, 1998 (Hebrew).

18. Foreign Minister Ehud Barak's speech in the Knesset, 25 December 1995 (Israel Information Service Gopher). This is the formula he has used ever since.

19. For the persistence of the old rules of the game in the Middle East, see Max Singer and Aaron Wildavsky, *The Real World Order: Zone of Peace/Zones of Turmoil*, Chatham, 1993; L. Carl Brown, 'The Middle East After the Cold War: Systemic Change or More of the Same?', in George Downs (ed.), *Collective Security Beyond the Cold War*, Ann Arbor, 1994, pp.197–216; Efraim Karsh, 'Cold War, Post-Cold War: Does It Make A Difference for the Middle East?', in Efraim Inbar and Gabriel Sheffer (eds), *The National Security of Small States in a Changing World*, London, 1997, pp.77–106.

20. *Maariv*, Shabat Supplement, 1 September 1995, p.3.

21. Daniel C. Byman and Jerrold D. Green, 'The Enigma of Political Stability in the Persian Gulf Monarchies', *MERIA*, Vol. 3, No. 3, September 1999.

22. Efraim Inbar and Shmuel Sandler, 'The Risks of Palestinian Statehood', *Survival*, Vol. 37, No. 2 (Summer 1997), pp.23–41.

23. For the tensions between the two countries, see Fawaz A. Gerges, 'Egyptian–Israeli Relations Turn Sour', *Foreign Affairs*, Vol. 74, No. 3 (May–June 1995), pp.69–78.

24. For an analysis of the military capabilities in the region, see Anthony H. Cordesman, *Perilous Prospects: The Peace Process and the Arab–Military Balance*, Boulder, 1996.

25. See Hilal Khashan, 'Polling Arab Views on the Conflict with Israel', *Middle East Quarterly*, Vol. 2, No. 2 (June 1995), pp.3–13.
26. Barnett, *Dialogues in Arab Politics*, pp.44–5.
27. See Ethan Bronner, 'Israel's History Textbooks Replace Myths with Facts', *New York Times*, 14 August 1999, pp.A1, 5.
28. See, *inter alia*, Emmanuel Sivan, *Radical Islam: Medieval Theology and Modern Politics*, New Haven, 1985; Graham E. Fuller and Ian O. Lesser, *A Sense of Siege: The Geopolitics of Islam and the West*, Boulder, 1995.

# Abstracts

## The Forgotten War: Jewish–Palestinian Strife in Mandatory Palestine, December 1947–May 1948
*David Tal*

This essay examines the Jewish–Palestinian struggle that preceded the 1948 War. In doing so it analyses the key developments that ultimately led to conflict between the opposing parties. It argues that the defining event was the Jewish acceptance of the United Nations Partition Resolution of 1947, as this determined the strategy that was adopted by the Jewish forces in the initial stages of the conflict. It then argues that, though determined to prevent the creation of a Jewish state, the Palestine Arabs, divided as they were by internal conflicts and disagreements within the governments of the surrounding Arab states, were neither prepared nor equipped for the task they undertook.

## Shall We Go to War? And If We Do, When? The Genesis of the Internal Debate in Israel on the Road to the Sinai War
*Motti Golani*

This essay attempts to analyse the process that ultimately led to Israel's entry into a joint offensive with Britain and France against Egypt in 1956. In doing so it assesses the centrality of various senior figures in the decision to go to war, focusing in particular on the roles of three individuals: Moshe Dayan, David Ben-Gurion and Moshe Sharett. It shows the antagonism between Prime Minister Sharett on the one hand and Defence Minister Ben-Gurion and Chief-of-Staff Dayan on the other, in the years preceding the Sinai War, and argues that it was the latter two who guided Israel's security policy in the face of opposition from within the political establishment and the government.

## The 1956 Sinai Campaign: David Ben-Gurion's Policy on Gaza, the Armistice Agreement and French Mediation
*Mordechai Gazit*

This essay seeks to highlight several ignored aspects of David Ben-Gurion's policies during the 1956 Sinai Campaign. Thus, for example, it demonstrates that, contrary to the received wisdom, Ben-Gurion did not rule out Israeli control of the Gaza Strip. While in 1949 he expressed his willingness to incorporate the Strip into Israel and to integrate its entire Arab population, after the capture of this territory in 1956 he opted for maintaining a hold over the Strip without its annexation. The essay also highlights the role played by the 1949 Armistice Agreement in the 'Understanding' of 1 March 1957 ending the crisis caused by the Suez Campaign. By way of doing so it details the political manoeuvres of US Secretary of State Dulles, including the orchestration of French mediation as a means of bringing about an Israeli withdrawal from the Sinai Peninsula.

## The 'Tranquil Decade' Re-examined: Arab–Israeli Relations During the Years 1957–67
*Menachem Klein*

This essay takes issue with the claim that the period between the 1956 Suez War and the 1967 Six Day War was the 'tranquil decade' in regard to the Arab–Israeli military conflict. In doing so the author looks both at the relationship within the Israeli political–security elite throughout these years, and at the military and political interaction between Israel and several Arab states. Its conclusion is that the notion of the 'tranquil decade' was a conscious attempt to hide Israel's failure to achieve its long-term political objectives in the 1956 War.

## Israel's Nuclear Programme, the Six Day War and Its Ramifications
*Shlomo Aronson*

The main thesis of this essay is that Israel's initial effort to acquire the ultimate deterrent, aimed at driving the Arabs to accept the Jewish state within its 1949 boundaries, was accompanied by a strategy of conventional pre-emption which was eventually implemented during the May 1967 crisis. The essay then proceeds to argue that following the Israeli conventional pre-emptive operations in June 1967, the Arabs adopted conventional war aims leading to the 1973 Yom Kippur War. Combined with Israel's nuclear option, which survived the 1967 crisis unscathed, the peace negotiations between Israel and its neighbours following the 1973 War, the active regional role played by the United States, and changes in the Arab world and in the former Soviet Union, may explain the current peace process.

## Towards a Paradigm Shift in Israel's National Security Conception
*Uri Bar-Joseph*

This essay examines the shift in Israel's national security conception in the face of new internal and external factors. The author argues that various developments such as the end of the Cold War and the collapse of the Soviet Union, the Arab–Israeli peace process and the new attitudes of Israelis to their society and state as they enter a 'post-Zionist' era are making the old preconceptions regarding national security obsolete.

## Patterns of War Initiation in the Arab–Israeli Conflict: A Note on the Military Dimension
*David Rodman*

Six Arab–Israeli wars have been fought over the past 50 years. Each side has initiated three of these wars. The Arabs began those of 1948–49, 1969–70 and 1973, while the Israelis began those of 1956, 1967 and 1982. This essay argues that each side's decisions to initiate these wars rested in part on its perceptions about its chosen military strategy. Specifically, the Arabs initiated the 1948–49, 1969–70 and 1973 wars in part because they perceived that their chosen strategy of attrition was favoured at these times. Likewise, the Israelis initiated the 1956, 1967 and 1982 wars in part because they perceived that their chosen strategy of manoeuvre was favoured at these times. This relationship between war initiation and military strategy, however, has not been consciously explored in the literature about the Arab–Israeli wars. Hence this essay is a first attempt to fill a lacuna in that literature.

## Israel's Nuclear History
*Edwin S. Cochran*

Beginning with the earliest years of the state, this essay provides a detailed, historical account of the development of Israel's nuclear-weapon capability. Dividing the development of Israel's nuclear programme into five distinct chronological phases, the author investigates both the debates within the state's political, military and scientific elite in each stage and the actual efforts to build up the human and scientific resources needed to pursue the nuclear path.

## Jewish–Non-Palestinian-Arab Negotiations: The First Phase
*Eliezer Tauber*

Negotiations between Zionists and non-Palestinian Arabs from the beginning of the Young Turk rule until the start of the Mandatory era are the subject of this essay. It assesses the various organizations that looked to negotiate with the Zionist Movement and shows the complex, and at times contradictory, motivations behind Arab sympathy and hostility towards the Zionist project. It also looks at various (fruitless) efforts to foster possible Arab–Zionist negotiations in the final years of the Ottoman Empire.

## Transition from Conflict: The Importance of Pre-Negotiations in the Oslo Peace Process
*Ilan G. Gewurz*

This case study of Israeli–Palestinian peacemaking efforts in Oslo concentrates on the role and inherent importance of the pre-negotiation process (especially in the early stages of the secret channel between January and March 1993) in determining the way that negotiations evolved. It argues that this first period enabled the parties to learn more about one another, evaluate the other party's needs, interests and intentions and helped bring the process to a point where it could enter into mainstream foreign policy. The essay concludes by drawing lessons from the experience in Oslo regarding the nature of pre-negotiations in general.

## Unambiguous Ambiguity: The Opacity of the Oslo Peace Process
*Nadav Morag*

This essay analyses the Oslo peace process. In doing so it concentrates on the ambiguous nature of the agreements at the heart of Oslo. While explaining why the Oslo process needed to be of an open-ended, non-committal nature, the author argues that it is this ambiguity, nowhere better seen than in Oslo's avoidance of specific issues vital to a final settlement between parties, that is the most damaging aspect of the agreement. Issues such as demography and borders are analysed in the context of the Oslo process to highlight the extent to which the process has ignored, or is unsuited to dealing with, some of the most critical issues at the heart of the Israeli–Palestinian conflict.

## The Netanyahu Era: From Crisis to Crisis, 1996–99
*Neill Lochery*

During the Netanyahu era the Israeli political system was in a period of transition, caused to a large extent by the adoption of a new electoral system in 1996 which was designed to reduce the level of political horse-trading that had characterized Israeli politics during the 1980s. In reality, as Netanyahu was to find to his cost, the new system severely constrained the Prime Minister's room for manoeuvre, making him ever more vulnerable to his own party, the cabinet and the government coalition. This, in turn, had an adverse impact on the Arab–Israeli peace process, as Netanyahu vainly sought to navigate between Likud's ideological precepts and his own pragmatic disposition.

## Jerusalem: Partition Plans for a Holy City
*Elisha Efrat*

Because of strategic location and religious importance, Jerusalem presents formidable challenges to politicians. Israelis and Palestinians each have different perspectives on the city, but neither has so far been entirely successful in prescribing a solution that would benefit the two peoples. Different partition plans and spatial alternatives have been proposed for Jerusalem during the past half-century, based on the city's geographical and demographic position. None of these plans has thus far been approved or accepted by both sides to the conflict; meanwhile Jerusalem has been losing its urban fabric as a planned and rational capital.

## Arab–Israeli Coexistence: The Causes, Achievements and Limitations
*Efraim Inbar*

This essay analyses the military, political and domestic reasons that have resulted in the increased Arab acceptance of Israel. Having shown that Israel's relationship with the Arab world has improved greatly in the last few decades, the author attempts to place this new state of affairs in its proper context and cautions against unrealistic optimism or expectations given the possible barriers to further relations. He argues that the Arab–Israeli peace process cannot be expected to achieve more than the limitations of the regional situation allow.

# Index

# Other Titles in the Series

## Israeli Politics and Society since 1948

c.288 pages  2001
0 7146 4961 9 cloth
0 7146 8022 2 paper
*A special issue of the journal Israel Affairs*
*Israel: The First Hundred Years, Volume 3*
*Israeli History, Politics and Society Series*

## Israel in the International Arena

c.288 pages  2001
0 7146 4960 0 cloth
0 7146 8021 4 paper
*A special issue of the journal Israel Affairs*
*Israel: The First Hundred Years, Volume 4*
*Israeli History, Politics and Society Series*

## Israel in the Next Century

c.288 pages  2001
0 7146 4959 7 cloth
0 7146 8020 6 paper
*A special issue of the journal Israel Affairs*
*Israel: The First Hundred Years, Volume 5*
*Israeli History, Politics and Society Series*

 **FRANK CASS PUBLISHERS**
Newbury House, 900 Eastern Avenue, Ilford, Essex, IG2 7HH
Tel: +44 (0)20 8599 8866  Fax: +44 (0)20 8599 0984  E-mail: info@frankcass.com
**NORTH AMERICA**
5804 NE Hassalo Street, Portland, OR 97213 3644, USA
Tel: 800 944 6190  Fax: 503 280 8832  E-mail: cass@isbs.com
**Website:** www.frankcass.com